WOMEN IN NEW WORLDS

VOLUME II

Historical Perspectives on
the Wesleyan Tradition

WOMEN
IN NEW
WORLDS

VOLUME II

Editors
ROSEMARY SKINNER KELLER
LOUISE L. QUEEN
HILAH F. THOMAS

ABINGDON

NASHVILLE

Women's History Project
General Commission on Archives and History
The United Methodist Church

Women in New Worlds:
Historical Perspectives on the Wesleyan Tradition

Volume Two

Copyright © 1982 by Abingdon

Library of Congress Cataloging in Publication Data (Revised)

Main entry under title:
WOMEN IN NEW WORLDS.
  Selected papers presented at the Women in New Worlds Conference
held in Cincinnati, Ohio, Feb. 1-3, 1980.
  Vol. 2. also edited by Louise L. Queen.
  Includes bibliographical references and index.
  1. Women in church work—Methodist Church—Congresses.
  2. Methodists—United States—Congresses.
  I. Thomas, Hilah F. (Hilah Frances), 1941–
  II. Keller, Rosemary Skinner. III. Queen, Louise L.
  IV. Women in New Worlds Conference (1980: Cincinnati, Ohio)
BX8207.W48   287'.088042   81-7984   AACR2

ISBN 0-687-45968-0 (v. 1)
ISBN 0-687-45969-9 (v. 2)

MANUFACTURED BY THE PARTHENON PRESS AT
NASHVILLE, TENNESSEE, UNITED STATES OF AMERICA

CONTENTS

INTRODUCTION

The United Methodist Church celebrates two major anniversaries in this decade of the 1980s. Methodism in America was organized as a denomination two hundred years ago at the Christmas Conference of 1784, in Baltimore, Maryland. On a single day, the committed layman Francis Asbury was ordained deacon, elder, and superintendent of the Methodist Episcopal Church in America. Assisting in those ordinations was Asbury's good friend Philip Otterbein, who became co-founder of the United Brethren Church. Even before the political structure of the United States was formed, Methodism was a part of our nation's heritage.

One hundred years ago, the major women's movements in each original denomination of the present United Methodist Church were inaugurated. Home and foreign missionary societies were founded, the deaconess movement was begun, the first unmarried women missionaries were sent to other countries, and women launched their initial drives for ordination and lay voting rights.

From the grass roots to the general structures of the church, United Methodists are seeking appropriate ways to commemorate the 100th and 200th anniversaries of the ministries of men and women, lay and clergy. Some insights for a fitting celebration are contained in a letter from John Adams, in which he visualized the way American independence from Great Britain should be celebrated. In July 1776, he wrote from the Continental Congress to his wife, Abigail, who was at home tending the family and farm:

I am apt to believe that it will be celebrated, by succeeding Generations, as the great anniversary Festival. It ought to be commemorated as the Day of Deliverance by solemn Acts of Devotion to God Almighty. It ought to be solemnized with Pomp and Parade, with Shews, Games, Sports, Guns, Bells, Bonfires and Illuminations from one End of this Continent to the other from this Time forward forever more.[1]

Adams' exuberant prophecy, which has been fulfilled in every Fourth-of-July celebration for more than two centuries, suggests some important guidelines for commemoration of the United Methodist anniversaries. First, these observances are meant to be "solemn Acts of Devotion to God Almighty," not opportunities for self-glorification. Yet United Methodists can be rightfully proud of their heritage of organization, evange-lism, and service, and also of women's devoted ministries through the church. And we should celebrate with festivity and flair, having a good time through it all!

But can United Methodists go farther? Can their celebration also include a critical evaluation of the past? May they seek, in faithfulness and honesty, to reap all the guidance their heritage can offer for ministry in the century ahead?

The editors and contributors of *Women in New Worlds: Historical Perspectives on the Wesleyan Tradition* submit volumes 1 and 2 to the general public, the church, and the historical profession, to probe, preserve, and justly celebrate with thanksgiving the ministries to and by women in this denominational background. Further, we seek to stimulate the church and the larger society to examine more fully the dual heritage of the inclusion and exclusion of women, as individuals and through institutional movements, in the service of the church. A spirit of critical self-examination springs both from the canons of scholarly integrity and from the belief that only as committed Christians openly evaluate themselves, can they grow in service, stature, and authenticity.

The publication of this second volume of *Women in New Worlds,* as a companion to volume 1, issued in November 1981 by Abingdon, is itself a notable event in the recovery of the true and lively history of the Wesleyan tradition on the one hand, and of women in British, German, and American religious life on the other. All but three of the forty essays included in the two volumes were chosen from the almost sixty papers delivered at the Women in New Worlds Conference in Cincinnati, Ohio, February 1–3, 1980. The conference was noteworthy as the first to recover the heritage of women in a major American denomination and the first to be sponsored by a historical agency of a mainline Protestant church, the General Commission on Archives and History of The United Methodist Church.

While the essays in these volumes focus on the history of women in the Wesleyan and related traditions, and on movements which directly influenced them, the wider significance of these collections for church history, women's history, and the social history of the United States is immediately discernible. Alert to the racial and ethnic inclusiveness of Methodism and related movements in America, the essays consider the place of women in Indian, Hispanic, Asian, and black cultures. Further, this story of churchwomen helps to recover the contribution and condition of females in the major streams of evangelism, social reform, mission, and preaching in American church history. Moreover, to understand women's place in and contribution to American history, one must discover the relationship of women to religious institutions. The ideologies underlying both the constriction and liberation of females in society are inherent in the messages conveyed to women through the church. Finally, the church has influenced more directly the lives of women in America than has any other form of voluntary organization. More women have participated in religious institutions than in all other social-reform movements combined.

The essays in this volume are grouped in two major parts: Prescriptions and Practice. This allows readers to compare attitudes toward the place of women in Wesleyan and related traditions with the ways women and men actually have related as laity and clergy in the ministries of the church.

The four articles comprising Part One, Prescriptions: Attitudes and Ideology Underlying Woman's Role in the Church, affirm belief in the essential equality of women and men, and in the liberation of females to exercise their spiritual gifts in mutual service with males. Equally clear, however, are attitudes which consign women to a sphere separate from men, often through the rationalization that woman's domestic world is of greater spiritual worth than the public world of men.

Alan Hayes provides a refreshing and enlightening perspective on the Father of Methodism in the opening article, "John Wesley and Sophy Hopkey: A Case Study in Wesley's Attitude Toward Women." On one level, Hayes recovers an early flirtatious relationship of the then unmarried Wesley with seventeen-year-old Sophy Hopkey in Georgia. As a youthful and awkward preacher, Wesley made bungling overtures of affection and marriage, interpreted by some as inappropriate conduct for a young pastor. On another level, the author helps us demythologize Wesley and encounter him as pioneering a tradition of enlightened relationships between men and women that was firmly grounded in his personal integration of the Christian faith. Wesley related to Hopkey, not as if she were a possession of her uncle before marriage, or of her husband, William Williamson, in the years following, but as an individual responsible for her own salvation, with a right to spiritual and intellectual independence. Yet the Sophy Hopkey episode may have left Wesley with a tension between his liberated ideas on relationships between men and women, and the reality—that society provided little freedom for friendships between males and females outside pastoral, pedagogical, or marital relationships.

Hayes contends that Wesley's affirmation of women's spiritual independence and capacity for religious leadership was more advanced than succeeding Methodist tradition. This position is borne out by other essays which analyze prescriptions of female roles in nineteenth-century society as the church became increasingly institutionalized.

"'The Sun in Their Domestic System': The Mother in Early Nineteenth-Century Methodist Sunday School Lore," by Joanna Gillespie, focuses on Methodist church school literature that was intended to instill in children moral values of piety, patriotism, and purposefulness in a society rapidly shifting from an agricultural to an industrial order. The paradoxical nature of the mother's role as modest, passive and subordinate to men, and on the other hand, as the powerful molder of husband, sons, and daughters through moral and religious influence, has been well documented in recent literature of women's history. Gillespie demonstrates the power of Methodism in shaping

INTRODUCTION

woman's role as a conservative force of social control in a turbulent, mobile society. She establishes the significance of Methodism within the evangelical movement in promoting the belief that women were morally superior to men, endowed with the religious and cultural task of redeeming a fallen, disreputable social order.

The underlying question of James Leloudis' essay follows upon Gillespie's study. How does woman's role expand in a society and church steeped in traditional ideas of men's and women's exclusive spheres? In "Subversion of the Feminine Ideal: The *Southern Lady's Companion* and White Male Morality in the Antebellum South, 1847–1854," Leloudis examines a short-lived but distinctive periodical which, for eight years, voiced woman's discontent in southern society. The journal appeared to endorse the South's unquestioned patriarchal structure, in which the ideal of submission of women was a cornerstone of the slave system and the entire southern way of life. In fact, however, the *Companion* sought to redefine subordination as significantly different from the predominant cultural model. The subordination of a married woman was interpreted as one-half of a paired set of duties, with the husband's reciprocal responsibility to demonstrate kindness and respect to his wife, in a society where man's brashness and immorality toward women was an accepted but unacknowledged reality of private life. Few men actually read the journal regularly, but it was a medium through which women could ventilate their anger and envision a less oppressive concept of woman's role. In this way, prior to the Civil War, the *Southern Lady's Companion* pioneered in raising the consciousness of women to seek greater respect and justice for themselves and a voice in their church and society.

In contrast to the brief tenure of the *Southern Lady's Companion, The Christian Advocate* is sustained today as the oldest important publication within the United Methodist tradition. James M. Buckley, controversial editor of *The Christian Advocate* for thirty-two years, was prominent and articulate in molding opinion on the "woman question" and other issues confronting Methodist readers. Saranne O'Donnell's article, "Distress from the Press: Antifeminism in the Editorials of James Monroe Buckley, 1880–1912," reviews those arguments of editor Buckley that had a formative influence on the church in the late nineteenth century.

Buckley questioned whether Methodism should harmonize with "the spirit of the age," or should maintain a just independence and even an uncompromising opposition to popular positions on social issues. Though he spoke out against stereotyping woman's role and favored higher education and equal pay for women who did the same work as men, Buckley was an uncompromising opponent of female suffrage, ordination, and laity rights. His first priority was the constitutional integrity of the Methodist Episcopal Church, and contemporary disciplinary provisions allowed no options for the lay or clergy rights of women. Buckley's views contrast notably with John Wesley's more expansive ideas on the equality of women in the church one hundred fifty years earlier, as Wesley stood over against the social conventions of female subordination in his own day.

Part Two, Practice: The Life Experience of Women in the Wesleyan Tradition, examines the ways these "prescriptions" were carried out in the daily experiences of women in the church. A broad panorama of conditions and issues are introduced, from our sixteenth-century predecessors of English background to women of the 1980s. The experiences of women as clergy wives, in national and global ministries, in social reform, and in professions in the church enable women and men to identify readily with the persons and movements that emerge through these pages.

Section One, Clergy Wives, deals with one of the most easily identifiable groups of women in church life. While the stereotypical picture of the clergy wife as the pastor's assistant in the church and parsonage contains truth, the historical studies contained in these chapters reveal a more complex legacy.

The British precedent contains both the seeds of this stereotype and the wider options that pastors' wives have opened for themselves, as illustrated in articles by Anne Barstow and Frank Baker. Barstow's essay, "An Ambiguous Legacy: Anglican Clergy Wives After the Reformation," examines the first two generations of post-Reformation wives in the sixteenth century. Marriage of clergy in England had been legally prohibited for the four centuries between 1139 and 1549, and now hostility was heaped upon new clergy families by a society that continued to uphold priestly celibacy as the ideal. Maintenance of a married clergy in the face of such adverse social reaction meant that ministers' wives were restricted to the most conventional female relationships of subjection and obedience to husbands. As acknowledged conservators of socially approved images of women, early Anglican clergy wives did not provide adequate models for the challenges Methodist women in America would face, Barstow concludes.

In contrast, Frank Baker portrays "Susanna Wesley: Puritan, Parent, Pastor, Protagonist, Pattern," as the pioneer model both for her son's advanced ideas on the worth of women and for Methodist women who would seek their identities beyond stereotypical images. An Anglican clergy wife of immense spiritual and intellectual stature, Susanna herself, for a period of time, conducted large public religious gatherings in the rectory during her husband's absences at Convocation in London. Wesley accorded women higher status than did society in general and incorporated them widely as class leaders and preachers in Methodist societies, due in significant measure to his mother's example. Susanna Wesley also provides a model of the clergy wife who is superior at every task—she read and wrote theology; was disciplined in prayer and meditation; juggled marital, family, and her own evangelistic responsibilities in a seemingly flawless manner—in short, she fulfilled the Superwoman image that haunts many women today. Indeed, a more negative effect of Susanna's influence on John Wesley may have been that her astonishingly competent example lessened his own possibilities of attaining marital happiness.

Two further articles on clergy wives relate to the legacy left to the later American scene by those early women. Emora Brannan develops the story of an engaging minister and wife in his essay "A Partnership of Equality: The Marriage and Ministry of John and Mary Goucher." By all discernible public standards, John Goucher was the head of their household. In fact, however, their marriage was a mutual career, with the energies and resources of both partners vigorously committed to the work of the church. While Mary and John Goucher established their identities as individuals through their contributions to the church, their work resulted in a notable complementarity in their public and private relationships.

Protestant Christianity was characterized by its burgeoning world mission program at the end of the nineteenth century, often made possible by the generous contributions of philanthropists such as the Gouchers. Equally significant was the development of institutions of higher education for women during this period. The primary story that unfolds in Brannan's essay surrounds the beginning of the Woman's College of Baltimore (later renamed Goucher College), which functioned as a principal training ground for female missionary and educational enterprises in the Methodist Episcopal Church. Through the story run threads of the spirited and independent Mary Fisher Goucher and the Women's Educational Association of the Baltimore Conference, vital contributors to the vision of the equality of women and men in the church.

Moving from the ministry of a notable pastor and wife on the east coast, Section One closes with a survey of the evolving role of clergy wives on the opposite shore of the United States. "The Pacific Northwest: Changing Role of the Pastor's Wife Since 1840," by Rosa Motes, traces the evolution of prescriptions and practices in one of the youngest conferences in the United Methodist tradition. The broad outlines of Motes' study have wide applicability, however, and bring together the themes of this section.

Motes defines three eras in the changing roles of pastors' wives in the one hundred forty years of Methodist experience in the far Northwest. In the first period, wives of clergy were pioneers, picking up any personal or professional functions that needed to be performed. As the church became more institutionalized and the region more settled in the late nineteenth and early twentieth centuries, the flexibility of the role of the early pastor's wife passed away. The "ideal" clergy spouse became characterized by stereotypes drawn from conservative interpretations of the Epistles ascribed to Paul: the pastor's assistant, parsonage hostess, and backbone of the Ladies' Aid. Characterizing the contemporary period as an Age of Liberation for ministers' wives, Motes refers to the pioneer

16

roles women are forging today. She points out the potential hazards that must be faced in juggling multifaceted functions and the reality of rapidly increasing divorce in clergy families, also a part of the larger picture as pastors' wives gain their own needed identities today.

In Section Two, National Missions and Social Reform, we see that strands of continuity between their British predecessors and American Methodist women are also found in the movement of women into home missions and social reform work. Just as Hayes and Baker contribute to the demythologizing of John and Susanna Wesley, Mollie Davis provides new insights into another foremother, Selina Hastings, in her article, "The Countess of Huntingdon: A Leader in Missions for Social and Religious Reform."

Davis interprets the countess, whose life spanned most of the eighteenth century, as a pioneer in developing new religious roles in the Church of England for women of the upper class. After her husband's death, the countess, at age thirty-nine, forged a new and significant identity for herself. She successfully managed what, in the late nineteenth century, would have been termed her mid-life crisis. More than a mere patroness of early Methodist preachers and a financier of worthy church projects, she waged an assault on her own class to convert the elite and channel their resources into assistance for the poor, evangelization of the Indians, and church development. The countess extended her mission to the colonies through support of ministerial training and aid to the indigent and the Indians in America. Her religious commitment enabled her to gain remarkable independence and authority for an eighteenth-century woman and to empower other females through missionary groups and informal networks of prayer.

Whether or not conscious of the legacy, many females who began mission work among the Indians in North America followed the pioneering role of the Countess of Huntingdon. Initial work on the interaction between Methodist and American Indian women has been done in Frederick Norwood's essay, "American Indian Women: The Rise of Methodist Women's Work, 1850–1939." Early secretaries of the Indian Bureau such as Harriet McCabe and Lydia Daggett were women of middle-class background who took the

Countess of Huntingdon's example one step farther and carried the mission of the church directly to the Indians, particularly the women. The available sources indicate that Native American women recognized the degradation of their position as females within Indian culture through the Christian teaching of ideal equality of men and women in the faith. Missionaries were able to educate many Indians to give women more humane treatment, a goal similar to that of the *Southern Lady's Companion.*

Essays by Anastatia Sims and Arnold Shankman trace the founding and development of strong institutions for home missions and social reform by white Methodist women in southern society. Sims' article, "Sisterhoods of Service: Women's Clubs and Methodist Women's Missionary Societies in North Carolina, 1890–1930," compares the work of the Woman's Home Missionary Society with that of the Federation of Women's Clubs, in one of the most advanced southern states during the Progressive era. Both groups gained an unprecedented role in making public policy for women. Recognizing the obstacles confronting them because of their lack of suffrage, women successfully campaigned for membership on school boards and for laity rights at their denomination's General Conference. Their arguments for expansion of women's power, however, grew out of the conservative ideology predominant in American culture: Women could make a unique contribution in cleaning up church and society because of their domestic experience and their moral superiority to men. This ideology played a large part in finally gaining national voting rights for females. Women had moved into decision-making positions in public life to a greater extent than ever before, but their power was gained through an ideology that feminists would one day brand the "feminine mystique."

In "Civil Rights, 1920–1970: Three Southern Methodist Women," Arnold Shankman compares the efforts of Methodist leaders Carrie Johnson, Jessie Ames, and Dorothy Tilly in race relations in the South. The women organized and led secular organizations dedicated to fighting racial injustice, gaining racial harmony, and confronting white society with the evils of white racism. Shankman develops the increasingly militant concerns and tactics of each woman. He portrays them as realists in doing what they believed possible to advance conditions for blacks in southern society, but also as bold politicians for their times. The religious basis of their work is woven throughout the biographical sketches.

Section Three, Foreign Missions and Cultural Imperialism, first presents a fitting model which foreshadowed the evolution of female involvement in world missions—found not in the Church of England, as in preceding sections, but in an earlier enterprise issuing from American Protestantism. Joan Brumberg analyzes the zeal and message of the "premier model of American female mission work" in her essay "The Case of Ann Hasseltine Judson: Missionary Hagiography and Female Popular Culture, 1815–1850." Adoniram Judson and his first wife, Ann, the first American couple to attempt evangelization in foreign lands, were commissioned first by Congregationalists and then, in Burma, by Baptists.

Ann Judson's work was the earliest expression in world missions of what Brumberg describes as "religious feminism"—concern for the moral uplift and education of native women, as well as their conversion to Christianity. Ann Judson's articulation of religious feminism foreshadowed the basic approach of women's foreign missionary involvement in every Protestant denomination. In the United States, Judson's approach reinforced the "cult of true womanhood" by encouraging churchwomen to believe that they were morally superior to men and that it was their duty to uplift women abroad. While the conservative ideology provided an effective fund-raising appeal for missionary crusades, it diverted religious women's motivation and energy from the drive for political equality in the United States.

In his essay "Doing More than They Intended: Southern Methodist Women in China, 1878–1898," Adrian Bennett demonstrates the way Methodist female missionaries in Asia further developed the Judson ideology. The women of the Methodist Episcopal Church, South, were basically unsuccessful in converting the women of China to Christianity. Their greatest influence was as cultural imperialists through the introduction of new values, ideas, and institutions that they deemed superior to those of the Chinese population. A primary goal was to develop strong Christian wives and mothers who would be the center of influence within the family. Female missionaries impressed upon Chinese women that God had ordained them to this sphere. On the other hand, unmarried women missionaries who were young, capable, and independent provided significant role models of professional women—as Bible instructors, teachers, doctors, and nurses. Bennett's thesis is that the nineteenth-century western female missionary effort was an important influence in laying foundations of revolutionary social, political, and economic consequence on women's role in Chinese society. Yet the process of cultural imperialism through which these gains were made, and the ideology of female superiority that underlay social advances, must be questioned.

Sylvia Jacobs and Carol Page study black women's missionary work in Africa. Through case studies of "Three Afro-American Women: Missionaries in Africa, 1882–1904," Jacobs explores the special mission which black Americans placed upon themselves at the turn of the century, to Christianize and civilize Africa. Many acknowledged and embraced the reality of their African heritage while also sharing the western image of Africa as the "dark" continent. Amanda Berry Smith, Sarah Gorham, and Fanny Jackson Coppin were African Methodist Episcopal missionaries who worked actively to improve the lives of women and children and adhered to the need for a "civilizing mission" on the African continent.

Jacobs interprets these three missionaries as sensitive to the evils of cultural imperialism, each being concerned to preserve African culture by structuring religious training around patterns already existing in the society. Coppin openly questioned British imperialism as an attempt to crush the hopes of black South Africans to secure equality. She believed herself constantly under surveillance by British rulers who feared that education and religious training would lead black Africans to demand justice and equal status and to revolt against white rule.

The complexities of the Afro-American mission to South Africa are further developed by Carol Page in "Charlotte Manye Maxeke: Missionary and Educator in South Africa, 1901–1930." In the later twentieth century, as churches recognize the need for governance by indigenous leadership rather than by western missionaries, Charlotte Maxeke's story carries important lessons. Maxeke was a South African, trained at Wilberforce University in Ohio and supported by the Woman's Parent Mite Missionary Society of the African Methodist Episcopal Church in the United States. Committed to advancing the Afro-American connection, she returned to South Africa to work in the church's education program. Maxeke was the first African woman to earn a university degree and one of the few college-educated natives of her country, at the time the Union of South Africa was founded. Through her leadership of women's groups in the church and in politics, she realized the deleterious effects on African family life of capitalist development under British imperialism. Yet her solutions to the family dislocation, low income, malnutrition, and landlessness of the peasantry were marred by her inability to separate her Christian faith from white, western rule. Maxeke's Christian training and the entire mission enterprise had not enabled her to look critically at the social and political evils against which the church should take a stand.

Professions in the church began to open for women one hundred years ago, as females sought ordination and formed deaconess orders. This occurred during the same period that women's voluntary missionary societies were founded. Elements leading to the success or failure of women who entered church-related occupations varied greatly. Articles in this fourth and final section, Professions in the Church: Individual and Corporate Responsibility, point to the significance of female organizational movements and support groups in opening church professions to women and other minorities and, once opened, in providing realistic prospects for achievement.

Essays by James Will and Janet Everhart provide differing but complementary perspectives concerning the gaining of clergy status by females. Will's essay, "Ordination of Women: The Issue in the Church of the United Brethren in Christ," surveys the ordination of women in that denomination, beginning with the earliest efforts of women, in the 1840s, to gain licenses to preach. Between 1889 and 1901, ninety-seven United Brethren women were ordained, according to the denominational directory. Merger with the Evangelical Church to form the Evangelical United Brethren, in 1946, however, resulted in abandonment of further ordination for women. Will invites further inquiry as to the reason the clash of heritages in the uniting denominations resulted in attenuation of clergy rights for women, after a fifty-seven-year tradition in the United Brethren Church. One may well question whether a base of support or advocacy for female clergy actually existed in the United Brethren Church by 1946, as well as why the sentiment to exclude women from ordination was so strong in the Evangelical Church.

In "Maggie Newton Van Cott: The Methodist Episcopal Church Considers the Question of Women Clergy," Janet Everhart develops a case study of the first woman to be granted a license to preach in the Methodist Episcopal Church. Van Cott was never ordained, the logical step after her licensing in 1869. Rather, the right of women even to be licensed to preach was withdrawn by the General Conference of the church in 1880. Everhart questions the attitude toward female ordination from the perspective of three concerned parties: Van Cott, who did not see ordination as necessary to authenticate her ministry within the Holiness movement; ministers who worked against her licensing, doubtlessly fearing female invasion of a male preserve; and pastors who supported Van Cott's license to preach. At a time when evangelists such as Van Cott had popular followings, Everhart queries whether pastors favorable to her believed that she would be more controllable and her ministry more contained through official recognition. Or was their support a genuine effort to recognize Van Cott's outstanding contribution to the church and give her equal status with male clergy? If answers cannot finally be given, the questions at least call women entering the ministry today, and the officials admitting them, to examine their own motivations more searchingly.

As individual women became candidates for ordination in antecedent denominations in the 1800s, deaconess orders were founded. The survival and success of these organized movements for professional service differed in various Protestant churches. Catherine Prelinger and Rosemary Keller examine a major cause for endurance and growth in their article, "The Function of Female Bonding: The Restored Diaconessate of the Nineteenth Century."

INTRODUCTION

Two of the earliest deaconess movements in the United States were the Lutheran order, formed in Pittsburgh in 1849 by William Passavant, and the Chicago Training School of the Methodist Episcopal Church, founded by Lucy Rider Meyer in 1887. Though both were modeled after the German order developed by Theodor Fliedner from New Testament precedents at Kaiserswerth, the Methodist movement flourished, while the Lutheran order was abandoned. The authors posit that the differentiating factor in the success of the two American institutions was the ability of Lucy Rider Meyer to develop a strong female support system, binding deaconesses to one another and to women in local churches. While this bonding was present in the Kaiserswerth institution, Passavant incorporated only its outward trappings of impressive buildings and administration; he was unable to convey the imagery of women's experience and the reality of female community.

"The Legacy of Georgia Harkness" by Joan Engelsman provides the final article on women in church professions. Harkness, whose life spanned a twenty-two-year teaching career at Garrett Biblical Institute and the Pacific School of Religion, was the first female professor of theology in a Methodist seminary. As part of her legacy, she created an opening wedge for females on seminary faculties, though the percentage of women teaching in such institutions is low even today. Her legacy to women and men of the church was much larger, however. Though not ordained herself, Harkness was an early advocate of the ordination of women and maintained her support until they were granted full clergy rights by The Methodist Church in 1956. Harkness' strong commitment to the ministry of the laity was most clearly demonstrated through her prolific writings directed toward empowerment of lay people, both in the private life of prayer and in social activism. She pioneered in calling the church to advocacy of racial justice, ecumenism, world peace, and nuclear disarmament. Finally, Georgia Harkness was actively engaged in the everyday life of the church, from participation at local levels to seats at national and international conferences of Methodism and on interdenominational church councils.

Georgia Harkness, as much as any one woman in the United Methodist heritage, competently entered a host of new worlds for women in church and society—a fitting legacy on which to close these two volumes on women in the Wesleyan tradition.

Each account in the two volumes forms a provocative episode in the emerging story of women in the Wesleyan tradition. Taken together, they do more: They point toward significant alterations in previous understandings of the history of the church and of women. In concluding, five primary points of analysis are offered on the writings as a whole.

First, the experience of women in the United Methodist and African Methodist Episcopal heritages has not been a one-dimensional story of subordination and constricted participation in patriarchally governed churches, though this reality is part of the full story. As the essays document, the struggle for clergy rights for women was long and reached its culmination in Methodism only in 1956, while these rights were renewed for women in the United Brethren tradition and established for those in the Evangelical, in 1968. Further, while deaconesses gave fundamental service, enabling the church to sustain a national mission program, the order of deaconesses was always accorded a status second to the clergy, and their work was often performed in the role of pastor's assistant.

Yet significant examples of leadership by women, and supportive relationships among men and women in the background of United Methodism, challenge commonly held stereotypes of women's place in the church. Though constricted to a separate sphere of national and global mission service, women created powerful autonomous missionary societies that were essential to the churches' outreach, and they became the training ground for wider female leadership in the church, even into the present day. The essays also demonstrate that the traditional image of the minister's wife has been too narrowly defined and that notable models of service and personal realization by clergy wives exist in United Methodist history.

Second, the essays provide insights into the increased rigidity and narrowness with which women's functions were defined as the church became more highly structured. John Wesley's belief in the equality of women and men before God, and his efforts to allow women leadership in loosely organized class meetings, gave way to an ideology of subordination and exclusion of women from mainline structures. In Part Two of the second volume, readers may find that pattern duplicated in each section. Essays throughout the books also demonstrate the need for women's personal support of one another, as in expanding their roles as clergy wives, and for their corporate support through missionary-society work and entrance into church professions. As a seminary professor, Georgia Harkness could make her mark as one woman in a profession dominated by men. This would not be true, however, of female clergy, deaconesses, or those who contributed to missionary society development.

Feminist theology is a third important area of study to which *Women in New Worlds* contributes. A theology of the inclusion of women in the full life of the church, growing out of a belief in the equality of all persons before God, is fundamental to the whole Wesleyan heritage. Running counter to this affirmation, however, is a theology of exclusion, which has been rationalized through a "separate but equal" sphere of women's activity and by an ideology of the moral superiority of women. As historical studies, these volumes give primary emphasis to actual experience and to historical tradition in the development of theology. Scripture and reason obviously are of equal importance in formulating a theological base, however, and their interaction with personal experience and tradition pervades the volumes.

Fourth, subtle and unacknowledged differences often exist between perceptions of women's role and actual practice in the life of the church and in society. Many women have professed a belief in the subordination of females, while they acted boldly to promote programs and carve out a sphere where they could work with independence and power. This paradoxical reality pervades every facet of female experience in these volumes. One also might compare the ways in which the church has perceived women's roles with the opportunities it has opened for them. Since the Civil War, the church has never failed to recognize the necessity of women's organizations in maintaining financial stability, in contributing major material support for missions, and in providing womanpower in national and global mission programs. It often has acknowledged the effectiveness of women in the pulpit, particularly when conversion and saving of souls have been the primary emphases. Too often in the tradition, however, the church has delegated responsibility to females while withholding or only begrudgingly granting them parallel power and authority.

Finally, many chapters in *Women in New Worlds* effectively probe the relationship of women to other minority groups in the Wesleyan tradition. Females have shared with ethnic and racial minorities a marginalized position of authority in the church—a position generally incongruent with the services they have rendered. As these volumes demonstrate, the major work of the church in national and global missions and social reform could not have been accomplished without the contributions of untold numbers of women. Yet the conversion, education, and social advancement of ethnic minority and foreign groups have sometimes been accomplished through the negation of values of the indigenous cultures and the imposition of mainline American ideals and practice. Too, women often have worked at cross purposes with other minority groups, rather than recognizing the need for mutual support to achieve common ends.

Women in New Worlds helps us to understand that changing relationships between men and women and new opportunities for the ministry of women in the church did not originate with the present generation, but are rooted in the events of one and two centuries ago—events that are celebrated in the current anniversaries of United Methodism. These volumes enable both men and women to celebrate the past with integrity, acknowledging its shortcomings and failures, and praising its breakthroughs. They contain models to cast aside and models to affirm, as women and men seek shared ministries and ideologies of equality in the century ahead.

—Rosemary Skinner Keller
Evanston, Illinois

I

PRESCRIPTIONS: ATTITUDES AND IDEOLOGY UNDERLYING WOMAN'S ROLE IN THE CHURCH

1

JOHN WESLEY
AND SOPHY HOPKEY

Alan L. Hayes

John Wesley's ministry affirmed the spiritual independence of women and their capacity for religious leadership far more vigorously than did the Methodist tradition that survived him, and his relatively liberated attitude toward women in the church was far more a factor in the opposition to his work in that day than generally has been recognized. These two conclusions emerge from an investigation of Wesley's brief ministry in Savannah, Georgia, during 1736 and 1737, providing a conveniently focused case study of conflicts with his opponents over issues of sexism.

Wesley had left his teaching position at Oxford in 1735 to be a missionary in the colony of Georgia, which had been established only three years earlier. At the end of 1737 he returned to England under a cloud, feeling defeated and dejected. During the next year and a half, he experienced "a long series of spiritual upheavals and frustration,"[1] including the Aldersgate experience of May 24, 1738, when, as Wesley put it, "I felt my heart strangely warmed." He began regaining his self-confidence in March 1739, when his Oxford friend George Whitefield, another Anglican priest, invited him to join in a preaching crusade in Bristol. Although reluctant at first, Wesley found his ministry there attended by conversions and emotional displays so dramatic that he was convinced that God was at work. Accordingly, he remained there to preach and to set up societies of followers. This early Methodist movement, however, disturbed many townspeople who regarded it as a society of fanatical working men, hysterical women, and possibly rebels, and they sought means to suppress it. Significantly, a favorite strategy of the Bristol anti-Methodists

29

was to attack Wesley's credibility as a religious leader by circulating stories from Georgia about his unconventional attitude toward women.

During 1740 the Bristol anti-Methodists were distributing copies of an affidavit by a merchant captain named Robert Williams, who had served on a Savannah grand jury in 1737, stating that Wesley "had been guilty of using too great familiarities" with a pretty seventeen-year-old girl named Sophy Hopkey.[2] Even after she had married, the affidavit reported, Wesley had urged her to meet him at various times and places, sometimes in the middle of the night and sometimes even in his own house, notwithstanding the fact that her husband, William Williamson, had "applied" to Wesley "to desist from such proceedings" and notwithstanding that Wesley had promised to do so. The grand jury, on the evidence of letters and at least ten witnesses, had presented him accordingly. But Wesley, rather than face trial, had surreptitiously left Savannah in the middle of the night. As far as we know, Williams' affidavit contained the first charges to be made public in England against Wesley's behavior in Georgia, although similar charges contained in an affidavit by Hopkey herself had already been published in America.[3] The anti-Methodists apparently found Captain Williams' affidavit effective, since they distributed it again in 1741 and yet again during 1742. Significantly, the affidavit did not touch on Wesley's unconventional religious views: It attacked an even more sensitive nerve, implying that with Wesley, no woman was safe.

To drive the point home, anti-Methodists reprinted the affidavit in 1743 as an appendix to doggerel exploiting male (and female) anxieties that popular preachers like Wesley could easily lead the simpler sex astray. Referring to Wesley's crowd-gathering sermons:

> Three-fourth parts, of what attend 'em,
> Are Female Sex, and John's to mend 'em,
> For Women are most prone to fall,
> Like Eve, their Mother, first of all.

The writer then satirized Wesley's alleged spiritual tyranny over women's consciences, the sexually integrated early-morning watch nights, and the kiss of peace between men and women at the love feasts. Eighteenth-century folk with a strong view that women should be confined to quiet roles in the background of ecclesiastical affairs might well have been shocked at the high profile of women in early Methodism.

The theme of Wesley's exploitation of naïve women was treated also by a group of Georgia malcontents, who in 1741 published a history of their grievances against the English clique that controlled the colony. They, too, rehearsed the Sophy Hopkey episode and, like the versifier, charged that "those who had given themselves up to [Wesley's] spiritual guidance (more especially women) were obliged to [disclose] to him their most secret actions, nay even their thoughts and the subject of their dreams."[4] Thus four years after returning from Georgia, Wesley was notorious for relating to women much too directly and for defying contemporary social conventions.

Wesley's biographers seldom have dealt very seriously with suggestions that he deviated from the usual standards for relationships between men and women, preferring, perhaps, not to believe them. Specifically, most have agreed that the grand jury's presentment of Wesley for improprieties with Sophy Hopkey was "an artifice of Mr. Causton's," the chief magistrate, who was Hopkey's uncle. But the charges of the anti-Methodists are important evidence indeed for understanding Wesley's attitude toward women, as well as the popular reaction to it. If their charges are phrased unflatteringly, it is because they are loaded with outrage against Wesley's affirmation that women are, in things of God, independent of men and equal to them. As to the essential facts—that Wesley was close to Hopkey, that he was unwilling to let her husband control her Christian life, and that he encouraged women in general to attend to matters of the Spirit on the same basis as men—the anti-Methodists were correct. It was not on the facts of the case that Wesley and his opponents disagreed, but on their evaluation.

John Wesley himself did not specifically deny the anti-Methodists' version. It is true that in 1740 he began to publish his *Journal,* in order, as he explained in the preface, to answer Captain Williams' affidavit; but in it, although he artfully portrayed the charges as malicious and distorted—and of course they were—he did not actually refute them, nor even deny them. For example, the *Journal* is significantly quiet on the issue of Wesley's "familiarities" with Hopkey before her marriage. He acknowledges communicating with her after her marriage in the line of pastoral duty. He does not deny reaching an understanding with her husband. He acknowledges the grand jury indictment and his departure from Savannah while awaiting trial, although he retells the story in a different light: He was exercising appropriate pastoral discipline over Hopkey, but her uncle, Thomas Causton, unjustly attempted to avenge her honor by manipulating the colony's judicial machinery against him. He left town as the only way to escape the injustice of frontier tyranny. To be sure, Captain Williams' coterie later accused Wesley of writing "willful falsehoods" in his *Journal*.[5] But if we consider that Wesley was couching the story in language flattering to himself, while his opponents put the most merciless construction possible on everything, we find relatively little substantial disagreement on the course of events.

What then is the truth of Wesley's relationship with Hopkey? And what part of it offended his opponents? Wesley's version of these events appears in two important extended narratives, in addition to the *Journal* account, but only portions of these narratives have ever been printed. To judge from several such expressions as, "I desire that document may be read in Court," one was a brief, written in Georgia in response to charges made in Hopkey's affidavit and in the grand jury presentment. The other appears to have been written outside a controversial context; it is, as Wesley titled it, a "personal account of Miss Sophy."[6]

These manuscripts show that Wesley had both a pastoral relationship with Hopkey and an intimate personal one and that the dynamic between the two produced dangerous confusion. As Williams attested, Wesley did indeed "use familiarities" with Hopkey before her marriage and, after her marriage, did indeed urge her to meet with him, ostensibly for the good of her growth in Christ, but in circumstances likely to contribute to misunderstanding. A detailed look at Wesley's dealings with Hopkey both before and after her marriage is necessary to form a judgment about the meaning of the whole episode.

As to the "familiarities" before the marriage, Hopkey

asserted in her affidavit that although about August 1736 the Caustons, as her guardians, had committed her to Wesley's care, within a few months he was urging her to leave them and cohabit with him for the good of her "progress to salvation," that he made several "overtures of marriage" without informing them, and that he offered, if she would have him, to change his personal religious practices and settle as minister of Savannah, notwithstanding his previous resolve to evangelize the Indians. In apparent contrast, Wesley contended that it was precisely the Caustons who had encouraged his relationship with Hopkey, and that it was precisely his sense of Christian vocation that had prevented their marriage. Are these two versions ultimately inconsistent? Not, it turns out, when each side has made its necessary modifications.

In his personal account Wesley stated that at first he "had a particular dislike to [Hopkey's] person, and a still greater to her common behaviour, which was reserved, as I thought, even to affectation." He had begun speaking to her soon after his arrival in Georgia, but only, he maintained, because she faithfully attended his weekday dawn services. Soon, he stated in his trial brief, Martha Causton (Sophy's aunt) was hinting at marriage ("There goes a husband for my Phiky" [her nickname for Hopkey]) and asking him to counsel Sophy in regard to a distressing love affair with one Tom Mellichamp ("Sophy minds no one but you"). Thereafter he spoke with her every two or three days. On one of these occasions, he kissed her, "and from this time I fear there was a mixture in my intention." General Oglethorpe, who was virtually the governor of Georgia, reported to Wesley in mid-August Hopkey's desire for instruction "in the duties of a Christian life." After suffering from a fever, during which Hopkey nursed him back to health, Wesley was telling her that he felt a special responsibility for her; perhaps, as Hopkey's affidavit asserted, she now had been "committed to Mr. John Wesley's care . . . by her relations." Wesley, indeed, records Causton's remark, "I give her up to you. . . . Take her into your own hands," although Wesley implies, misleadingly, that this was an invitation to marriage.[7] On Wesley's evidence, the Caustons clearly approved of his interest in Hopkey, but they had no reason to be aware of its romantic dimension. He did not tell them. At that time, he himself was inclined to think that marriage was incompatible with his present Christian vocation, and he never planned to court Hopkey.

Did Wesley urge Hopkey to cohabit with him? Apparently so, but not in the way Wesley's opponents were insinuating. When she returned to Savannah in October 1736 (in Wesley's boat) after several weeks in Frederica, she was reluctant to return to the Caustons' house, where, not unlike other seventeen-year-olds, she found little privacy, excessive nagging, certain "shocks," and harsh treatment. Wesley therefore suggested that she take "a room in my house, or (which I think better), you may live at the Germans." The argument that Hopkey's "progress to salvation" would be improved by her removal from the Caustons' was emphasized by Wesley's assistant, Charles Delamotte, who judged that "she would not be so good a Christian in that family as out of it."[8] In the end, however, Wesley negotiated with the Caustons the conditions of her remaining with them.

Did Wesley actually make "overtures of marriage" to Hopkey? By February 1737 she certainly had enough reason to think so. We know that Wesley was increasingly assailed by doubts about his commitment to celibacy as he struggled with his strong personal affection for Hopkey, and although Methodist historiography often has held that Hopkey grew so impatient with Wesley's indecisiveness that in desperation, she married William Williamson, her uncle's clerk,[9] Wesley's own manuscript accounts suggest that he was far more romantically interested in her than she in him. The following passage is characteristic:

While I was teaching her French, when being obliged (as having but one book) to sit close to her, unless I prayed without ceasing, I could not avoid using some familiarity or other which was not needful. Sometimes I put my arm around her waist, sometimes took her by the hand and sometimes kissed her.[10]

Between November and February, he resolved several times not to touch her, but yielded to temptation each time. Once he blurted out, "Miss Sophy, I should think myself happy if I was to spend my life with you!" On February 3, he "hinted at a desire to marry her, but made no direct proposal"; Hopkey replied that she thought clergymen should not marry, nor should she. But that did not end matters for Wesley. Two days later he went on a personal retreat to weigh the issue further, and after a week, he made what seems to be the accommodation Hopkey's affidavit refers to: He would not remain celibate indefinitely in America, but only until he had evangelized the Indians. Hopkey might well have considered Wesley's physical "familiarities" and his "hints" and discussions of marriage to amount to "overtures."

At this point Hopkey decided that she and Wesley should no longer see each other alone, because, she said, people were gossiping about them. Wesley reasoned wishfully that her decision was a defensive one, in disappointed recognition that they could not marry; he felt confirmed in this reasoning by her statement to him after her marriage, "I could not have denied you, had you pressed me to marriage at any time when my temper was ruffled."[11] But that does not sound like an overwhelming enthusiasm. And on April 10, Wesley would hear from one of Causton's servants that Hopkey had been romantically interested in Williamson long since. He had begun courting her soon after arriving in Savannah the previous summer and had resumed the courtship in November after her return from Frederica. "In December," the servant continued, "she began to seek [Williamson's] company, sitting near him and talking familiarly with him. . . . After a while, she would not eat without him. . . . They commonly sat up together, after the family was in bed, one or two nights a week."

In late February she already had decided to marry Williamson, but "I won't let Mr. Wesley know anything of it, for I know he will be against it." No wonder she told Wesley on February 15 that she would no longer see him alone! Of course Hopkey was fond of Wesley—fond enough to accept his caresses and to say reassuring things; fond enough to consider him a friend unlike the others—but Wesley, like most of his biographers, misunderstood her fondness.

Wesley's relationship with Hopkey after her marriage is also significant. Wesley began to "force his private discourse to her," her affidavit said, and he suggested to her "the danger her soul would be in if she did not continue to spend her time" with him. The grand jury found that Wesley "did . . . several [times] privately force his conversation to" and "write and privately convey papers to" Hopkey, contrary to her husband's command and Wesley's own promises, occasioning "much uneasiness" between husband and wife.[12] Many Georgians found it irregular for Wesley to speak to Hopkey privately, since he was known to be unhappy about her marriage: He disapproved of the match as unsuitable; he saw Hopkey as a devout Christian with much promise of spiritual growth, while Williamson, he wrote, was "a person not remarkable for handsomeness, neither for gentleness, nor for wit or knowledge or sense, and least of all for religion."[13] Moreover, he looked on the wedding itself as irregular. It took place three days after the engagement, without banns, in a border town in South Carolina on March 12, 1737. Finally, it was understood that Wesley himself had wanted to marry Hopkey. When he learned that her marriage to Williamson was planned, he reportedly was "inconsolable" and in tears, finally revealing to the Caustons what he apparently assumed they had intuited, that he was in love with her.[14]

After the marriage, Wesley talked to Hopkey six times, by his count, always from what he persuaded himself was a sense of pastoral responsibility. But he apparently was not aware how much his emotional involvement with Hopkey complicated that pastoral relationship. He was tactless and his reports of the conversations lack insight into their emotional dynamics. Wesley had two points to make with her. First, he "taxed her with insincerity before and ingratitude since her marriage."[15] For by now, he had heard gossip of Williamson's long secret courtship, and he had heard, too, that she still felt affection for Tom Mellichamp, the young man in her past. Wesley also criticized her dwindling church attendance. He expected her to continue coming to the dawn worship services every morning and to the intimate religious discussion groups he held afterwards; he wanted her to continue the fastings he had taught her to practice. True, most Savannah residents neither observed fasts nor attended dawn services and intimate discussion groups, but, reasoned Wesley, since she still acknowledged her obligation to both practices, there was "a wide difference between her neglect and that of others."[16] How uncomfortable Hopkey felt about Wesley's bid to continue directing her spiritual life, we cannot know with certainty, but her husband forbade it. On April 8 she excused herself from Wesley's criticisms with the argument that her husband disapproved and that "a wife ought to have no will of her own"; but Wesley rejoined with a principle of extreme significance: "In things of an indifferent nature you cannot be too obedient to your husband, but if his will should be contrary to the will of God, you are to obey God rather than man." Hopkey probably was sincere in saying that she understood Wesley to be suggesting that her soul was in danger.

The most bizarre incident of the relationship was soon to follow. In June, Wesley was giving great thought to whether he should withhold Communion from Hopkey, for now she was even neglecting attendance at these services. True, she had missed only one Sunday and three saints' days, at a time when few Anglicans received Communion more than four times a year; but Wesley entertained the unusual principle of Communion every Sunday and every saint's day. Seeing her "insincerity" and her neglect of church services, Wesley prepared himself to repel Hopkey from Communion until she "owned her fault, and acknowledged her repentance of it."

The rubrics of the Prayer Book extended this authority to a minister, provided he "give an account of the same to the Ordinary fourteen days after at the farthest." Since there was no bishop in Georgia, Wesley, claiming "all the ecclesiastical authority which was entrusted to any within the Province," apparently assumed himself to be "the Ordinary."[17] This self-promotion was to figure among the charges of the Savannah grand jury.

Before excommunicating Hopkey, Wesley intercepted her after church on July 3 and accused her of "insincerity and other faults." She became increasingly distraught, denied the charges, and finally turned away. On July 5, he wrote her, again accusing her of dishonesty. On July 11, Hopkey miscarried. Wesley took the trouble to assure himself in his own mind that his own assaults had not been to blame, and then resumed his preparations for the weightier duties of disciplining her for her sins. On August 7, he repelled her from Communion. In the wake of this incident, came a lawsuit from William Williamson, the grand jury presentment, affidavits galore, and a host of appearances in court. One might well wonder what reaction Wesley himself anticipated when he took that step.

If one were to use Wesley's ministry to Hopkey as an example of pastoral practice, it would be difficult to see what more he could have done wrong. He allowed himself to be manipulated into taking Hopkey's side against the Caustons; he confused his emotional needs with his pastoral responsibilities and thus mistakenly interpreted his own need to forgive as Hopkey's need for forgiveness; he was blind to the limitation of his hierarchical model of ministry, which led him to see the priest as acting for Christ in judgment and in the dispensing of grace; he turned a pastoral issue into a political one, and as a result, divided the community.

But the purpose of this study is not to judge Wesley the pastor, but to explore the way Wesley's relationship with this young woman of Savannah reflects his ideological differences from his opponents in respect to the role of women in the church. As already suggested, Wesley and his accusers agreed reasonably well, in the last analysis, on the facts of the case. He did show his affection for Hopkey and discuss marriage; he did urge her to leave the Caustons; he did move toward accommodating marriage within his sense of Christian vocation; and in trying to maintain a spiritual directorship in Hopkey's life after her marriage, he did urge her to meet him at his dawn services and at other odd times, for the good of her soul.

But if Wesley broadly agreed on the facts, he totally differed in interpretation, for he rejected his opponents' sexist assumption that Hopkey was her uncle's possession before her marriage and her husband's afterward, with no need for spiritual growth independent of those men. On the contrary, from the beginning, Wesley considered Hopkey as a separate person in need of pastoral care and spiritual nurture. He invited her into his religious discussion groups—the "little society," which foreshadowed the class, and the "smaller number," which foreshadowed the band. Although religious societies at the parish level had emerged in England in the late seventeenth century, they at first had been comprised only of men and seem to have remained cautious about admitting women. To invite young single women into a small intimate group was an innovation which, as we have seen, inspired comment among Georgia malcontents as well as among Bristol anti-Methodists.[18] Furthermore, Wesley apparently allowed women to exercise leadership in those groups; perhaps these were the "deaconesses" he is reported to have appointed.[19] Similarly, Wesley taught Hopkey French and Christian divinity, a distinctly progressive undertaking, by eighteenth-century standards. This was a period when, as Dr. Johnson remarked with pardonable exaggeration, "A woman who could spell a common letter was regarded as all accomplished," and when, as Lady Mary Wortley Montagu remarked, most men regarded such an education for women as being "as great a profanation as the clergy would do if the laity should presume to exercise the functions of the priesthood."[20] If journals like the *Spectator,* which Wesley read at Oxford, promoted the cause of women's education at all, they generally stressed the value of "useful" instruction in such areas as domestic crafts, handwriting, and the personal graces.

But, as we have seen, Wesley insisted on the principle that a woman has the right to seek spiritual and intellectual growth as a person in her own right. Even after her marriage, he required Hopkey to acknowledge her own responsibility for her personal situation, in spite of her inclination to conform to the convenient social convention of deferring to her husband's judgment. In all these things, Wesley offended against eighteenth-century social standards that put well-born women on pedestals and protected them paternalistically. Wesley's trial brief suggests the sharp public reaction to his view that a woman must obey God rather than man: This advice had been "much controverted" and, he implies, unfairly represented. Nevertheless, he says defiantly, "I will avow [it] before all the world."[21]

Wesley's *Journal* did not deny Captain Williams' charges; instead, by implication, it reinterpreted them and challenged their presuppositions. By the same stroke, it sought to legitimate much of Wesley's Bristol ministry, which followed the Savannah pattern in its acknowledgment of the full personhood of women in Christ and its encouragement of their participation in education and spiritual exercises. Soon Wesley would introduce women to widespread leadership in classes and bands, and even in preaching.

Where did Wesley derive his advanced opinions? From church tradition, from his theological background and reflection, and from his experience of spiritual realities. The religious significance of Wesley's Georgia ministry in this respect, as in others, lies in his use of it to test contemporary church values and practices against these three touchstones.

In studying the tradition of the early church, Wesley had discovered that Christians nearer the time of Christ had appreciated the spirituality of women more keenly than did the contemporary Church of England. For example, the *Apostolic Constitutions,* which is now assigned to the fourth century, but which Wesley dated earlier, acknowledges that women were ordained deaconesses and includes a prayer which somewhat defensively justifies their ordination by reminding God of the women in Scripture whom he filled with his Spirit.[22] Wesley also had read *Primitive Christianity* by William Cave, a patristic scholar who had lived a quarter of a century earlier. This work devotes a page to deaconesses, whose origin was "of equal standing with the infancy of the Church." Cave specifically identifies Phoebe (Rom. 16:1) and three later deaconesses and discusses their ecclesiastical duties.[23] The eighteenth-century Church of England did not recognize deaconesses, and it is highly significant, therefore, that Wesley is supposed to have taken it upon himself to appoint women to that position in Savannah.[24]

Wesley's theological background also was significant. The main current of eighteenth-century Anglicanism stressed the extent to which God could be known through what he had created in the world; since the submission of women seemed to be part of the order of nature, most Anglicans believed it to be the incontrovertible will of God. But Wesley had not been raised in mainstream Anglicanism. His parents belonged to the "high church," which emphasized, on one hand, the wide difference between natural and human orders, and on the other, the revelation of God's will. The social inequality of women was no proof of God's will, for on biblical and pastoral grounds, women and men appeared spiritually equal. For example, William Law, the high-churchman whom Charles

Wesley called "our John the Baptist," insisted that women should not "trifle away their time" in the fashionable ways that satisfied most divines but, equally with men, must "consider themselves as persons . . . devoted to holiness." Similarly, the high-church tradition, in principle, affirmed the education of girls as well as boys, and since the turn of the century, through the Society for Promoting Christian Knowledge, it had provided dozens of charity schools for girls.[25]

Finally, Wesley's own faith had been greatly influenced by strong Christian women. His mother, a spiritual leader in her community, is the best example. She had given him the foundations of divinity and continued to counsel him until her death. His friend Sally Kirkham may have been his "spiritual guide" for several years.[26] His understanding of women's capabilities no doubt also was formed by the progressive practices of his mother's household, where his sisters, for example, when they reached age five, learned to read better "than the most of women can do as long as they live."[27] Thus Wesley's own experience demonstrated that women were persons in Christ equally with men. His experience with Hopkey must have confirmed his view. Compared to a Susanna Wesley or a Sally Kirkham, Hopkey was a very ordinary young woman, but Wesley saw spiritual gifts in her beyond those he found in any men of Savannah. Her "insincerity" and her submissiveness to an un-Christian man disappointed Wesley the pastor, as well as Wesley the lover. His discipline of Hopkey at the Communion table may be seen as a distorted testimony to the esteem in which he held her, and not merely as an act of revenge.

Primitive example, high-church theology, and his own experience of spiritual realities, unfortunately, could not help Wesley deal fruitfully with the powerful attraction he felt toward Sophy Hopkey. Primitive tradition afforded few illustrations of friendships between men and women that were not also pastoral, pedagogical, or marital. The high-church views of sexuality that had formed Wesley were principally those of Jeremy Taylor, the seventeenth-century Anglican divine, for whom virginity was better than married life—"not that it is more holy, but that it is a freedom from cares, an opportunity to spend more time in spiritual employments."[28]

One of Wesley's earliest reactions against high-church teaching was precisely the struggle which Hopkey provoked in him concerning his theology of marriage. And as for his personal experience, his mother stood as a model of feminine Christianity to which no other woman could ever have measured up. In any event, Wesley had imbibed deeply of the sentimental attitude toward women that had emerged in the early eighteenth century with the "reformation of manners," the efforts at moral clean-up in society.[29] The precious, artificial style of his university letters to his women friends, with whom he sought honesty, but whom he feared to shock, testify to his highly idealized view of unspoiled womanhood—hence Wesley's bitter disappointment over the ill-starred friendship with Hopkey. As he struggled between cultural stereotypes and high-church ideologies, he continually either idealized Hopkey's femininity—"her soul appeared to be wholly made up of mildness, gentleness, longsuffering"—or questioned her Christian commitment, as when he discussed with his colleagues whether they had "sufficient proof of her sincerity and religion."[30]

Wesley's background prepared him to affirm Hopkey's right and duty of spiritual growth, but it prevented him from seeing her as she was. The failure of their friendship is indicated by the fact that even when Wesley was agonizing during every waking hour, Hopkey herself played no active part in the struggle, other than to cut it short by marrying Williamson. For her part, the combination of Wesley's heartfelt affection and earnest support, together with his poverty of insight into her character and needs, must have given her a painful sense of isolation. His relationship with Hopkey remained significant for Wesley long after the fact: in his theology, in his emotional life, and in his ideology of women.

Theologically, in choosing between marriage and vocation, Wesley was choosing between a God who forgives shortcomings and uses earthen vessels, and a God who requires exclusive obedience and personal holiness as the price of his favor. It seems never to have occurred to Wesley that marriage might perfect vocation, just as God's forgiveness is the perfection of his sovereignty. By choosing a jealous God and a strict vocation, Wesley was decisively establishing the masculine theological dynamic described in the very word *Methodism,* qualified though it might be in his writings.

In addition, the relationship with Hopkey reinforced Wesley's tendency to distance himself from others emotionally. Never, except perhaps with his mother, did he succeed in committing himself entirely to another: At the worst of times, he acted against all charity with those he loved, whether father, brother, Whitefield, or fellow-Methodist; but even at the best of times, he was tentative in revealing his inner self to others. "Paradoxically," as V. H. H. Green writes of him in another context, "because of the way in which he tried to spread the love of God abroad among his fellowmen, the real intimacy of love . . . passed him by."[31] With Hopkey, he hovered on the brink of a commitment to intimacy but finally withdrew, suffered rejection, reacted in anger and self-justification, and in the denouement, suppressed even the most common fellow-feeling toward her. Interestingly, the almost identical pattern recurred a decade later when Wesley fell in love with a woman named Grace Murray.[32] Like Hopkey, she nursed him back to health when he was ill; he then indecisively meditated marriage, lost her to another man, and thereafter, as far as he could, banished her from his sight forevermore. When he finally married, it was to a woman with whom he was not prepared to talk seriously.[33] Had Wesley succeeded in deciding for Hopkey, and for an accepting God, he might have found personal contentment, community support, and historical obscurity as pastor of Savannah. Instead, he left Georgia with a deep sense of frustration with himself;[34] he fell into a lifelong compulsion for work, an unhappy marriage, a tendency to view the human relationship with God in isolation from its social context, and fame.

Finally, disappointments notwithstanding, Wesley's relationship with Hopkey crystallized his conviction that women enjoy the right of spiritual independence from men and that they deserve to be trained in Christian divinity. He maintained this conviction, even though it was one of the major complaints of the people of Savannah against his ministry, and the first of their criticisms to be publicized in England by his opponents. It laid the theological foundation for early Methodism's use of women as class leaders, teachers, administrators, worship leaders, and preachers. One of Wesley's most important experiences in the spiritual equality of women, and certainly his most painful, was provided by Sophy Hopkey.

2

"THE SUN
IN THEIR DOMESTIC SYSTEM"

Joanna Bowen Gillespie

Early nineteenth-century family life, as pictured in Methodist Sunday school books, presented the mother as the dominant figure.[1] The mother, not the father, was the spiritual authority—the model of progressive, intelligent citizenship and of leadership in her world. Although society and her religion adjured her to be modest, passive, and "passionless," the mother of Sunday school books emerged as a powerful figure who did not appear to feel deprived because she did not participate in the important man's world outside the home.[2] In fact, this woman saw herself at the very center of her sphere and indeed of society itself, through the home's influence on the family. As one anonymous Sunday school author said of these mothers, they were "a kind of sun in their domestic system, dispensing an inexhaustible fund of smiling beams and fertilizing influences."[3]

American Methodist Sunday school literature published before 1855 presented an idealized prescription for life which contrasted dramatically with the turbulence of the times. As those morality tales and memoirs were first being read around pioneer firesides in the Jacksonian era, major societal changes were underway. Cities were overflowing, reform and other voluntary associations were being formed, technological inventions were expanding industry and contracting geography. In that era of the Common Man, churches, schools, and political movements were increasingly being influenced by ordinary people rather than by an exclusive elite. The public mood was exuberant. There was a dark side to rapid social change, however; anxiety and a sense of dislocation were also prevalent. "Everything is possible, nothing certain, and life short."[4]

The Jacksonian era was "modern" in that large numbers of young adults were moving from farm to city or to frontier settlement, apparently free from traditional family or institutional control.[5] "Self-elevation as the grand American Principle" had its price; this new American mobility was exhilarating but disruptive.[6] A resulting anxiety is reflected in the emphasis on self-control and duty in early Methodist Sunday school literature. Before young readers could experience the heady freedom offered by the Jacksonian world, ministers, evangelists, and mothers were cautioned to establish firmly within them a "resistless authority" that would shape their attitudes and safeguard their lifelong behavior.[7] The authors sought to provide an updated version of communal and religious duty in order to hold their youth fast in the face of secular temptation.

The literature's other emphasis—in dynamic opposition to its message of social control—also leaps from the pages: the empowering of the individual. American and British evangelicalism appears to have been the logical religious counterpart of Jacksonian economic and political optimism.[8] As the new religious form of revival meetings spread, most extensively in the United States, ordinary people found that they could make dramatic public commitments to a new sense of identity and direction for their lives. Such momentous decisions were entirely personal, motivated by the Holy Spirit's special action in each individual. The intense focus on the *self* involved in self-examination and conversion naturally enlarged people's concept of their own efficacy, their ability to manage their own lives—within a fellowship of like-minded citizens. Methodism, one of the most rapidly expanding denominations of the period, was also the most overtly revivalistic.[9] Its Sunday school books illustrated a complete rejection of fatalism: Limitless possibilities were open to any person who tried hard enough.[10]

Certain paradoxes of the Methodist belief-system in this era become emotionally intelligible when we see the useful ethos provided by Methodism in the midst of Jacksonian anxieties. "Free grace," humble people's gift from God and John Wesley, brought freedom from anxiety about who was or was not one of the heavenly elect and was combined with a step-by-step formula for spiritual perfection—that is, a careful plan of "good works." The Puritan's "divine uncertainty" about being saved was channeled into work habits that were highly rewarded in an industrializing nation.[11] The Puritan's "spiritual account book" mentality was recycled into behavioral prescriptions for the use of time and the significance of appearances. A winning combination of Puritan methodicalness and Wesleyan assuredness helped large numbers of people confront and cope creatively with the early nineteenth century.

The Sunday school mother knew this combination, accepted the transmission of it as her God-given task, and wove it into her curriculum. This study focuses on how she viewed the world and how she prepared her children for moving into that world, as depicted prescriptively in early Methodist Sunday school library books.

Sunday Schools, Citizenship, and Mothers

British Sunday schools were originated by rich evangelicals in the late 1700s and early 1800s as literacy classes for the poor, but their potential for "Christianizing America in the bud" was quickly appreciated.[12] School as an organizational form became popular in America with the decline of the apprenticeship system. Sunday schools were useful because they "provided gratuitous instruction," took no "important time away from worldly business," and "provided a library which supplied reading for an almost indefinite period not only to a school but to a neighborhood, and of a kind equally fitted for adults and children."[13]

In the intense denominational self-consciousness of the early nineteenth century, Methodist Sunday schools maintained a separate and, it was felt, a distinctive voice. When the interdenominational American Sunday School Union was formed in 1817, Methodists refused to join. They thought their "methods" would be despised by other denominations; "If we had not our own [publications], our young would grow up in complete alienation from Methodism; for our faith, usages, and system are so diverse from all others . . . that our church lives in an atmosphere of polemic hostility."[14]

It is impossible to calculate precisely the effects of this staunch sectarian stance since there is as yet no adequate way to

47

claim causal relationships between reading particular Sunday school literature and specific changes in individual self-perceptions or in the larger society. One can assert at best that Methodist Sunday school libraries were both an evidence of change and a help in bringing it about, because thousands of Americans taught and read these materials as circuit riders distributed them across the continent.[15] At a mid-century convention, when the nation had expanded beyond the Mississippi to incorporate Louisiana, Arkansas, Iowa, and Texas, the Methodist Sunday School Union could boast "a truly imposing army of children and youth" who had been exposed to their books—"6,758 sabbath schools, 70,264 officers and teachers, and 357,032 scholars."[16]

Sunday school library books were written to tell readers how to live, what kinds of questions to ask themselves and others, what kinds of dreams and hopes to have, and how to realize them. Though the two purposes of entertainment and improvement were less separate then, these books were intended for improvement. The hunger for "thinking something new," for print itself, was a kind of entertainment. Nineteenth-century language was as filled with moral precepts as the eighteenth-century Puritan had been laden with spiritual metaphors. Earnest delight in reading as an activity was constantly reiterated.[17] The medium itself was a crucial part of the message of the stories. In a print-devouring era, these little four- by six-inch books were emblems of civilization on the frontier, of middle-class respectability in the cities.[18] They symbolized an educational and religious culture, perceived at the time as setting the upwardly mobile and pious family apart from others. They offered new standards for achievement, channels for ambition, and patterns of taste.

Concern about children's attitudes toward authority and duty had been expressed by the Puritan fathers.[19] After the War of Independence, Enlightenment ideals, evangelical Protestantism, and the chauvinism of new nationhood combined to exalt "the moral mother" who would build the citizens of millennial America.[20] In fact, she was the true patriot, the "mother of the Republic."[21] Advice on raising children ceased to be addressed to the father and now was directed to the mother.[22] A new appreciation of the mother's special qualities for nurturing and instructing and character building was expressed: "Love of children in a man is a virtue, in woman, nature."[23] Women were "made for God's purposes, and not for man's."[24] Recognized as closer to their emotions, they were idealized in both religious and secular culture as being more virtuous than men; they were "the moral conservators in the home and for the nation."[25]

No power other than mother power ever built a great nation; no instrument will throw deep roots into a country unless it reach children through the mother and men through women. The mother of a family is a moral power, ripening thought at the same time that she opens hearts to love, and souls to character.[26]

The educated consensus on motherhood's national importance thus was that if only one sex could be educated, it should be the female.[27]

In this cultural context, it is hardly surprising that the Methodist Sunday school idealization of the mother should be one of calm authority and purposefulness.

Sunday School Literary Patterns

The Methodist Sunday school library books in the Drew University collection can be grouped by author nationality and by literary form. For this paper, thirty-seven family narratives published before 1855 were analyzed. The first British Sunday school stories are distinctive in that they frequently were written by evangelical women rather than by clergymen, and they focus on the lives of the working-class people who so enthusiastically first embraced the Methodist reform movement.

Although these British prototypes are in the form of the morality tale, their style reveals a novelistic sensibility.[28] The characters move within an almost tangible imagery: pots of geraniums set out in the rain to be refreshed, shiny pewter on the cottage mantelpiece, a cat curled in a rocker, a little girl's tangled hair being combed—even a peek under the lid of a pot of stew. The stories illuminate for us the magnified sense of personal power and control over one's own destiny with which Methodism endowed the humble English worker.[29]

In the second quarter of the nineteenth century, the British tales evolved into a dialogue form, or masked catechisms, between a mother and her son. Though the characters had names, few details about them were presented; there was no plot or action. The dialogue was central and its conversational balance uneven. Little Alexander (a favorite name for the child) had all the questions and mamma had all the answers. In this genre, authors put very complex natural history or scientific information into the mouth of the mother-instructor. The mothers and sons were definitely middle class, though imbued with the same boundless optimism and religious pragmatism as their working-class prototypes.

The American books imitated the British models, although frequently taking a more hortatory and less imaginative tone. The American stories were largely biographies—memoirs of eminently pious children, family chronicles, or small-town "beautiful death" stories. Like the British books, they carried a prefatory sentence attesting to their factualness: The reader was to understand that real people actually lived these experiences. "No fiction" was the editorial position for Methodist Sunday school books. Both British and American books were humorless by modern standards, but the American were more strongly didactic.

Stylistically, the major difference between the British and American stories lay in the portrayal of patriotism. British mothers wore their citizenship and the burdens of Empire comfortably, but not smugly;[30] American mothers, on the other hand, glowed with the emerging virtues of ideal American womanhood:

No mock fastidiousness . . . no vain, supercilious airs, no sickly squeamishness . . . [She] moved erect, with conscious dignity, carrying a heart pure and untainted . . . to which [her] open, frank countenance was the sure and unerring index . . . the beau ideal of Connecticut ladies of [her] class ninety years ago.[31]

In stories of both types, the average nonministerial male received a bad press. The father was generally absent. In the

British stories, he was either dead or in India; in the American, either dead or working hard in business. One American story involved the father in the children's instruction up to the point of setting the topic, after which he excused himself—"I have some important business which claims my time."[32] The mother was left to make the connection between the lesson and daily life.

Ministers were shown at deathbeds or reported upon in terms of their sermons. Husbands, when present, were to be prayed for and converted from their unsaved ways. If by some chance the parents were united in their spiritual and earthly goals for their children, they could not fail; but if the father, who *should* be head of the family, was "pursuing the course which leads to death," the mother, "*yes the mother alone* may guide the children to realms of bliss" (emphasis in original).[33]

The Mother's Curriculum

In both British and American family narratives, the mother was both apotheosized and subjected to strenuous prescription regarding her task. She often was forced to undo the evils of the father's influence and help the children save the father, "who would have led them down to perdition, but for the counteracting and more powerful influence of their mother's instruction, example and prayers."[34] However, "if the fires upon our altars shall ever go out, it will be because the mothers of our land have forgotten their duty."[35] The agent of salvation also had fearsome responsibilities.

All but two stories in the sample were set in the home, that "first nursery of religion," where the mother's influence could be "imperceptibly diffused in the everyday intercourse of the family."[36] However, the actual regime of actions and duties required of the mother was much more systematic than that flowery phrase implies. One mother's advisor spelled out the following schedule for her spiritual work, similar to those presented in the Sunday school stories: "Give one hour every morning, undivided, alone to the children; ere they retire, secure another portion of equal length; review what has been learned through the day, its deeds, its fault, its sorrow, its blessings."[37]

A surprisingly sophisticated understanding of child development is visible in these stories. Mothers understood that their children could not help imitating behavior around them, learning "lessons" whether intended or not. Therefore they employed themselves actively in shaping the lessons their children received: instructing, questioning, assigning meaning, interpreting actions, building within the children the necessary strengths to control both thought and action. The continual admonitions and metaphors were organized primarily around two major concepts: the value of time and the importance of appearances.

Time was the mother's major currency. In these stories she supervised every waking moment of her child's early life. Children never were allowed very far away from her, even to attend school. The American stories never showed the mother in any activity other than instructing; the English sometimes included visiting the sick, or sewing. The mother's major verbal task was to implant a sacramental view of time. She established within each child an "internal master" that would guard him or her against wasting or misusing time. She inculcated the precept that time belonged to God—a belief producing the inner compulsion to discipline and work that was central to the Protestant ethic.[38] If time was sacred and the use of one's time a subject for God's favor or disapproval as mediated by the mother, then anything frivolous—a glance, a lesson shabbily copied, an unnecessary detour on the way home—must be corrected.

The externally visible counterpart of this sacramental view of time was concern over appearance. Use of their own time and concern for the way they appeared to others were the only matters over which poor people had any real control. For example, only through refusing to compromise his control over his time and guarding the impression his neighbors received, could a newly converted English shepherd demonstrate the new meaning in his otherwise wretched life: "Being poor, I never get a chance to do anything great; so I am judged by the little round of daily customs I allow myself."[39] By setting his own standard as to what he would or would not let his neighbors see him and his family do, he could make an external statement about his inner life; *he* was in charge of his own appearance.

Material goods were part of that appearance; but they, as well as time, belonged first to God, so one's appearance must reflect a heavenly rather than a worldly interest. An extra ribbon or curl was evidence that too much time and attention were focused on nonserious concerns; appearances must be read as proof of inner commitment and discipline.

The mothers in these stories were "method-ists" in their systematic intervention in the children's thoughts and actions. The ideal prescription for mothering involved making a list of virtues to be inculcated sequentially, plus another list of faults in character, thought, or behavior to be rooted out. When one fault was eradicated, the next was attacked. The approach of the "story mother" was an amalgam of Methodist evangelicalism, Jacksonian optimism, and Puritanical disciplined self-evaluation. Nothing in a child was to be viewed as a *given;* everything could be improved, even that which was already virtuous. All character traits could and should, somehow, be perfected.

A mixture of evangelical imperative and very American aspiration for their children's secular "self-elevation" motivated American story mothers.[40] Many stories revealed that the mother's ambitions encompassed occupational as well as spiritual improvement—for example, "Two or three times you wanted to go to a trade, and your father was willing, but I knew the Lord had other work [a profession, such as the ministry] for you."[41] Although they relied on verbal intervention, these mothers gave their children far more powerful unconscious persuasion through their own dreams and goals as they taught them the definition of success, failure, joy, and sorrow.

The mother used herself and the emotional bond with her children as the instruments of their shaping. Daughter Ella of the Wilmot family said earnestly, "Yes, Mamma, I see all the praise is due to you and none to us. When we are naughty we ought to be blamed for doing what we have been told so often not to do; and when we are good, it is you who deserve the praise for teaching us right."[42] Poor mortally ill Thomas Rogerson, weeping because he did not want to be put in a grave and eaten by worms as his little brother had been, begged to go to heaven in a chariot of fire like Elijah. He was gently reproved for this grievous error by his mother, who said, "You surprise me, my love. You are very ambitious. Your father and I shall be put into the earth when we are dead; and we are content. Surely Thomas does not desire greater honor than his parents?"[43]

The mid-century Methodist mother's pedagogical philosophy was clearly expressed in the preface to a British story:

Intelligent children are so curious that an astonishing variety of information can be imparted to them merely by answering their questions; . . . a judicious teacher [can] *avoid the evils of desultory conversation* . . . while habits thus formed . . . prepare children to deduce instruction from the trivial and unconnected incidents which make up the sum of everyday life.[44]

Instruction time was all-embracing; even conversation was to be viewed sacramentally. Every action, as well as every fleeting thought, possessed a significance far beyond itself. There was no end to the process of self-examination, itself an external sign of salvation.

The Methodist story mother, expressing her religious zeal and her aspirations for social improvement through her children, was directing her energies into the space and sphere allotted her. She was supposed to embody, as well as to instill, the *goal of perfectibility*. Each child could and must do better each day, in every way. Though her work was confined to the home, it was *her* job, *her* duty, *her* calling.[45] She was pictured as heroic. The language in these Sunday school stories celebrated a version of womanly heroism that would produce the millennium. There was simply nothing mothers could not accomplish by planning, prayer, methodical instruction, and discipline.

A British mid-century mother reflected this mind-set when she said, "A little more knowledge will soon banish the words 'lucky' and 'unlucky,' my son."[46] An American child reading those words on the Illinois frontier of the 1850s would have understood the message instantly; he would have agreed that the future was in his own hands, not controlled by dark mysterious forces. He would know that he could succeed at anything, with God's blessing, if he tried hard enough. Methodist energy, paired with Jacksonian optimism, was able to dispel any residual feelings of inadequacy an early-nineteenth-century American might harbor.

"THE SUN IN THEIR DOMESTIC SYSTEM"
Prototypical Methodist Mothers

The virtues of method—the application of "scientific" or rationally analytic principles of organization to one's life and religious practice—were most explicitly stated in a three-volume British story titled *The Week, or The Practical Duties of the Fourth Commandment.* The three-hundred-page novella, re-published in New York in 1829, contrasted a good mother, Mary, her working-class husband, and her children, all faithful Methodists, with her neighbor Nanny. The key difference between them—between misery and serenity, fault and virtue— was *method.* Method was most obvious in the sacramental use of time.

The first volume, subtitled *The Last Day of the Week,* has as its thesis that in order to use Saturday properly and thus be prepared to honor the Sabbath, one must organize the entire week around it: baking on Friday, mending on Thursday, and so on, back to washing on Monday. Nanny, for instructive contrast the embodiment of the negative, was introduced as she tracked dirt into Mary's neat cottage to borrow a broom. Uncomplaining, Mary wiped up after her, quietly observing the importance of keeping one's work "done up" on the last day of the week. Nanny bemoaned her own inadequacy, saying, "Whenever you say 'God says' in that way it always gives me a pain in the heart, as if I'd heard bad news."[47]

The narrator rejoiced in the decency and order in Mary's cottage, from the rosy baby sleeping in a cradle by the hearth to the basket of neatly mended stockings. It was obvious that Mary's mind was endued with a principle of action that provided a method and plan for everything she did.[48] The story implied that if all humble folk managed their family lives as systematically, their spiritual lives would be exemplary, their work lives prosperous, and the world a much better place.

By comparison, Nanny's slovenly cottage demonstrated that *lack* of method spelled spiritual and environmental disaster. Mary shared the narrator's perspective: "Poor Nanny has lots of misery, *all from her bad method,* for I can't make her think as I do, that it is best and happiest to seek first the kingdom of God by diligence and order. She is always behindhand."[49] Not only was Nanny unkempt, her children pre-delinquent, and her life out of control, but her husband arrived home from work drunk and abusive, knocking to the floor the wet laundry hanging near the fire.

Meanwhile, across the unpaved alley, Mary's house was wreathed in domestic and spiritual harmony. The family was doing its last-day-of-the-week tasks: reckoning and paying the accounts, including the tithe for Sabbath school classes; studying Sunday's Scriptures. Later it would be time for Saturday-night baths and hair washing. The narrator, wanting Nanny [and the reader] to share in this earthly felicity, asked Mary for her "method" for finishing all her work by Saturday. Then followed pages of instruction about Mary's household management, emphasizing the values of organization: "getting well forward with the work each day"; making sequential plans, so that on Saturday night, one could "lie down with a quiet mind, waiting for the blessings of the Sabbath."[50]

This recipe for method in her everyday life helped Nanny enormously; she and her family were economically and spiritually saved. For the reader, the story dramatized the tremendous mental and emotional advantage that an English working-class family could gain from a planned, meticulous attitude toward time. It would prepare them for living in the emerging industrial world of factory whistles and middle-class predictability. The methodical use of time became a sacrament, and as its priestess, the mother became the agent of salvation for her whole family.

A typical American Methodist story heroine was Mrs. Alison, struggling against poverty with ten living children and a gloomy husband, a veteran of the War of 1812. In fits of depression, or "malignant dyspepsia," the father became suicidal. In this desperately real scene, Mrs. Alison was the emotional anchor for the family, holding them together as economic disaster forced them to move from their rented Massachusetts farm to find work in a mill town—a town where the children were subjected to every kind of worldly temptation.

Edward, the oldest, converted during a Methodist revival, wanted to become a minister. The father objected, needing his sons's earnings. But Mrs. Alison had "long since given her firstborn to God, as the ancient covenant people were wont to yield the first fruits to the service of God."[51] She convinced the father that having a minister in the family might help them "out of debt into competence." Then as now, a professional son bolstered the dream of upward mobility.

Persevering lovingly in spite of her husband's debility and her children's trials, Mrs. Alison inspired this book "written by a minister" (probably Edward). The author's deep admiration for his Methodist mother was phrased in terms that reflected his perception of her task and mirrored the language of his times:

She knew her sphere. It was a humble one, indeed, for a person of her capacities, but God had placed her in it, and she felt it her duty to faithfully discharge [it]. She affected no superiority over her husband; his abilities shone not so brightly as her own; but she never reproached him or spoke arrogantly. She loved to manage affairs so as to anticipate his wants and render him happy. . . . The children were taught to revere and love their father no matter his weaknesses; but for their mother there was a different kind of attachment. She was a kind of sun in their domestic system, dispensing an inexhaustible fund of smiling beams and fertilizing influences.[52]

The thrust of 1840s modernity is reflected in the use of commercial terms: *manage, affairs, system, fund.* Mrs. Alison's life was "entirely *organized*" around the salvation of her large family, along with knitting, spinning, cooking, and nursing. "The family circle is a glorious and most propitious field of religious labor," the author extolled. "Mrs. Alison gave her whole soul to it, and prospered. Toil on, then, Christian parents. . . . Hope in God, ye anxious mothers."[53]

The only really bad American mother portrayed, Mrs. Jacobs, was not unsystematic as much as frivolous—the kind who would go to a revival meeting as an excuse to wear her new frock, and then worry about whether the rough bench would snag it. She came to a sad end, serving the author as a negative ideal of preoccupation with external appearances. Unlike this foolish mother, her already-converted daughter Eliza had no trouble deciding what to wear to the camp meeting.

She had but one clean dress which she wore wherever she went . . . a neat calico one, kept very clean, and she was contented with it. She thought it very kind in the good Lord to give her clothes that enabled her to go to meeting, and not have to think anything about her dress. If she had not a neat one to wear; if she had been obliged to go in a soiled or torn one, she would have felt mortified; she would have been suspicious that persons were making remarks about her. As it was, she thought nothing about it, and was thus able to give her whole attention to the acts of worship.[54]

Being easily distracted as well as fashion conscious, Mrs. Jacobs allowed a friend to call her away from the mourner's bench where her soul might have been reached. Three days later, she fell into a raging fever and died, unsaved. The messages of this literature are plain.

Conclusion

Rediscovering the early nineteenth-century Methodist Sunday school mother allows us to examine prescriptions and techniques for raising children during a significant period in our national history. This literature's "method" appears in the story mother's unflagging, passionate attention to the smallest details in a child's life: She measured them against a standard, used them as the basis of approval or disapproval, related them to a higher meaning. Described in evangelistic terminology, her ultimate objective was to endow each child with an unassailable character for coping with the Jacksonian world and its temptations.

Strong initiative by mothers was enhanced and celebrated by this "mass media" of their times. Whatever the actuality of influence in the home may have been throughout western history, the father's role in shaping a child's life had been discussed as primary. But by the early nineteenth century, in evangelical circles, the mother's historical moment had arrived. The feminine ideal of modest appearance and downcast eyes masked her power. For modern readers, the prescription for modesty need not obscure ways in which the mothers in this Sunday school lore circumvented the external restrictions in their world.

While eloquently praising "passive" mother images, Sunday school writers were delivering implicit tribute to the powerful impact felt by the domestic circle into which the evangelical mother poured all her energy and drive. Obviously shaped by her impact, the authors reflect her understanding that her authority was based on a moral superiority that underlay and was confirmed by an external appearance of "passionlessness."[55] Historians now believe that the evangelical religious movement was a major mechanism, through which a conception of women's moral superiority expanded into a widely shared cultural view that women would redeem a troubled and unseemly world. If so, the mothers in Methodist Sunday school literature were surely among the print models for this ideology, and these Sunday school library books were among the tools through which it was transmitted.

3

SUBVERSION OF
THE FEMININE IDEAL

James L. Leloudis, II

Whites in the antebellum South divided their society by sex as well as by race. Authors of secular and religious advice literature prescribed distinct realms of activity and patterns of behavior for men and for women. They taught that God and nature had ordained man to occupy the worldly arena of business and politics where he exhibited the harsh virtues of necessity: greed, competitiveness, and lust for power. By contrast, woman was weak and timid and therefore was restricted to the calmer setting of the domestic sphere. Within the home, woman assumed responsibility for the moral complexion of society by preserving the nobler virtues of love, sympathy, benevolence, and piety. She served her husband and children as teacher and guardian, counseling them in religious matters and diverting them from the paths of sin and self-destruction. Southern moralists proclaimed woman's refining influence as essential to the maintenance of social order, warning that in its absence, man would be left to worship "the God of this world in the hot beds of intemperance, debauchery, sacrilege, and every other crime."[1]

This conception of womanhood was linked closely to southern dependence upon a slave economy. The idolization of woman characterized antebellum American culture in general, but it achieved special prominence in the South as a cornerstone in the ideological defense of slavery.[2] Southern men incorporated notions of female piety in a romantic portrayal of southern domestic relations which they contrasted with the supposed chaos of family life in the North. They argued that slavery fostered extended patriarchal families that carried woman's moral influence to the lowest levels of society and thereby sustained civilization, whereas the northern system of free labor bred anarchy by fracturing familial bonds and denying the laboring classes access to feminine virtue.[3] This glorification of the southern home and its female custodian severely circumscribed women's lives, defining the ideal woman as a selfless creature capable of fulfillment only through her family. Yet the sentimentalization of domestic life was not entirely oppressive, for it also had the capacity to legitimate women's claims to social authority. White Methodist women and their male allies in the ministry discovered the paradoxical implications of the proslavery argument in the 1840s and 1850s as they lashed out against the coarseness of male behavior. In attempting to discipline men, these laywomen and ministers subtly redefined the southern model of woman and took the first step in establishing a more promising role for women in southern society.

Antebellum southern men considered worldly indulgences and arrogant displays of authority essential to their masculinity. This view of manhood, like the southern feminine ideal, was the product of a slave society. The maintenance of slavery rested largely upon force or threat of force. Thus fathers trained their sons to believe that they were "born to command" and encouraged them to adopt the "habit of ruling without resistance." This education bred an "irascible temper and ungovernable self-will" in the young southern gentleman, "all with a view of enabling him to . . . exercise a greater sway over those around him."[4] The advisors of youth also counseled them to seek "a large acquaintance and intercourse with the world." According to William J. Grayson, that experience customarily included the enjoyment of "gambling, drinking, and libertinism." He and others dismissed the questionable morality of such practices by noting that it was "the order of nature . . . that the male should be much of his time removed from his mate and offspring . . . roving in the pursuit of pleasure and neglect of the pledges of his love." These vices were considered collective rituals through which southern men reaffirmed the "bold daring" that defined their manhood.[5]

Male brashness and immorality were a constant source of disillusionment for white southern women. As young girls, they dreamed of chivalrous suitors and gentle, loving husbands.

Upon marrying, however, they discovered that gentlemanly manners often amounted to little more than clever affectations intended only for public consumption. "'Tis when we go out into the world," lamented Mary Bailey, "and find that the ideal picture we had drawn for ourselves is blotted and defaced . . . that where we would have looked for purity, there is deceit and double dealing—'Tis then that the heart recoils and sickens." Similar expressions of despair pervade the diaries and private correspondence of other women, revealing the suffering of wives who were denied the kindness and devotion they expected from their spouses.[6]

Southern women also voiced their discontent in domestic periodicals. Foremost among those magazines in the antebellum period was the *Southern Lady's Companion.* The *Companion* commenced publication in 1847 under the auspices of the Nashville *Christian Advocate,* a journal of the Methodist Episcopal Church, South. It was initially an experiment pursued in the leisure of the *Advocate*'s editors, the Reverend Moses M. Henkle and the Reverend John B. McFerrin. Henkle and McFerrin at first appear as unlikely associates. Little is known of Henkle's early life, except that he was born in Virginia in 1798 and entered the ministry at an early age. He moved to Tennessee sometime in the early nineteenth century and distinguished himself as a theologian and polemicist. His major works include tracts on church government and an eloquent exposition of the southern church's position on slavery.[7] McFerrin was born in Rutherford County, Tennessee, in 1807 and entered the ministry at age eighteen. Unlike Henkle, he preferred administrative duties to intellectual speculation. Between 1840 and his death in 1887, McFerrin served the church as a presiding elder, a secretary of the Board of Domestic Missions, and a book agent.[8] These two men seem to have grounded their friendship in a common desire to establish an independent publishing house for the southern church, a goal they achieved in 1854.[9]

Henkle and McFerrin published the *Companion* as a substitute for the *Ladies' Repository,* a magazine sponsored by the Methodist Episcopal Church prior to the schism of 1844 and maintained thereafter by the northern church. They felt that with the loss of southern influence over the *Repository*'s content, a monthly journal designed specifically for southern women was "strongly demanded."[10] The editors promoted their new journal by asking ministers to solicit subscribers from among their congregations and by awarding prizes to subscribers who persuaded friends to take the *Companion* into their homes.[11] These tactics proved remarkably successful, for within five years the *Companion* had attained a peak paid circulation of 9,000 and a readership of approximately 25,000.[12] Middle-class women—the wives and daughters of small planters, merchants, artisans, and rural doctors and lawyers—comprised the bulk of the magazine's patrons. These women preferred the *Companion*'s religious devotion and practical simplicity to what they considered the secularism and social pretentiousness of less successful elite periodicals such as the *Southern Ladies' Magazine*.[13] Their enthusiasm for the *Companion* so impressed church leaders that in 1850 the General Conference adopted the magazine as an official church publication and named Henkle as its full-time editor.[14]

Ironically, the *Companion* began to experience grave difficulties soon after this advance in its career. Like most southern periodicals, it relied upon subscribers and unpaid authors for most of its copy.[15] Nineteenth-century literary conventions prevented most contributors from signing their compositions, but it seems that women and ministers provided articles in roughly equal proportions. These writers originally supplied more material than Henkle could publish, but by 1853 they had become so remiss in submitting articles and letters that the *Companion* almost collapsed. The magazine also suffered from its subscribers' failure to pay. A review of the journal's records in 1851 revealed that the accounts of some persons were as much as three years in arrears.[16] These problems plagued all antebellum southern periodicals, but in the *Companion*'s case they seem to have been exacerbated by rising male intolerance to criticism. By the 1850s, the growth of abolitionism had so frightened southern men that they began to use the courts and vigilante violence to suppress all internal attacks upon slavery, or upon any other aspect of their society.[17] Women and ministers must surely have found it difficult to continue to challenge male behavior within such an increasingly repressive environment. Official church records contain no mention of this problem, but evidence suggests that members of the General Conference considered it when they decided in 1854 to replace the *Companion* with a new publication, the *Home Circle*. Complaints against men are notably absent from the *Circle*'s pages.[18]

Although it survived only eight years, the *Companion* was outstanding for both its longevity and its sensitivity to women's needs. Its existence appears brief by modern standards, but in comparison with other women's magazines published in the antebellum South, whose life-span seldom exceeded two or three years, the *Companion* was surprisingly long-lived.[19] Its relative success derived in large measure from Henkle's editorial policies. While its competitors published only occasional items concerning male behavior, the *Companion* offered a sustained discussion of the topic.

The status of clergymen in southern society perhaps best accounts for Henkle's willingness to consider women's complaints, and for other ministers' readiness to join women in censuring male brashness. By the 1840s, religion had become defined as a predominantly female concern because of women's identification with morality and virtue, and consequently, ministers lost much of their social prestige as men began to consign them to the domestic sphere and to scoff at their remarks concerning the affairs of the practical world. As the French journalist Harriet Martineau noted while traveling in America, ministers were "deprived . . . of the highest kind of influence which is the prerogative of manhood." Such disrespectful treatment made ministers the natural allies of women.[20] The *Companion* thrived because it provided a forum in which members of both groups could share their common frustrations and seek a means of disciplining southern men.

The most frequent complaint of the *Companion*'s contributors concerned men's disregard for the burden of women's domestic duties. There were few ladies of leisure in the Old South, for the wives of all but the wealthiest planters led very demanding lives. A plantation mistress served her family as cook, seamstress, maid, gardener, and washwoman. Frequent pregnancies and the enduring threat of illness among both the slaves and her own family meant that she also spent considerable time in the nursery and in the sickroom. The work of women who lived in towns was no less trying. The wife of a Vicksburg railway official, for example, tended a garden and was constantly involved in cooking, washing, housecleaning, and the raising of children. She was in fact so encumbered with work that she felt guilty if she relaxed in her parlor without some sewing in her hands. As Frederick Law Olmsted observed in 1854, the women of the South worked as hard as the men did.[21]

Many women appear to have received little or no recognition for their labors, and this was a persistent cause of irritation and anger. In May 1862, Catherine Edmonston wrote in her diary, "What a drag it is sometimes on a woman to 'lug about' the ladder upon which man plants his foot and ascends to the intellectual heaven of peace, in ignorance of the machinery which feeds his daily life." A female contributor to the *Companion,* after enumerating "only *half*" of a typical woman's labors, vehemently pronounced her disgust with the male judgment of those labors as "*light, trivial* annoyances."[22]

To make matters worse, when men did take heed of their wives' work, it was often to command them to some neglected task or to criticize what they had accomplished. One contributor to the *Companion* exemplified such callous behavior with the story of a young wife who greeted her husband with joy at the end of the day, only to have him throw himself into her favorite chair and command coolly, "Bring me my slippers, my love, and do help me off with these confounded boots." "What a pity," exclaimed the author, that some of men's exaggerated public politeness "could not be *saved up* for home consumption." Another lady added that it also seemed "to be the heart-felt wish of all men, that their 'better halves' should be perfect. . . . If fault-finding on their part could have accomplished this," she quipped, "we would long ere this have issued from the fiery furnace pure and refined." The second writer also hinted throughout her article that when men were not issuing orders or grumbling, they were usually away from home, amusing themselves with alcohol and games of chance.[23]

The plantation legend depicts drinking as one of the pleasant social graces of the Old South; in reality, it was a serious social problem. A writer for the *Western Carolinian* reported in July

1820 that no holiday was considered properly celebrated unless everyone succeeded in "getting a little corned."[24] Holidays, however, were not the only occasions for overindulgence. Saturday night "frolics" were common among young men of all classes, many of whom became so intoxicated that their friends had to carry them home and put them to bed.[25] In the homes of the well-to-do, the consumption of large quantities of wine and liquor was a regular form of evening entertainment. Henry Barnard, a Connecticut traveler in the South, noted that after the ladies had retired for the evening, "the gentlemen begin to circulate the bottle pretty briskly."[26] Heavy drinking was a "noticeable recreation" also on county court days and even at funerals.[27]

Thoughts of drunken husbands raised fears of impoverishment and physical abuse in women's minds. The *Companion* articulated those apprehensions through charges that intemperate men crushed female hearts, destroyed homes, and brought great suffering to children. To illustrate its claims, the magazine published accounts of the destitute state of the families of inebriates. Those unfortunate souls lived in little huts with fallen chimneys and leaking roofs, furnished with the "coarsest and simplest furniture." Often they had no food and were warmed by only a few smoldering embers.[28] The *Companion* usually only hinted at the physical abuse inflicted upon wives by drunken husbands, but in one article, it related the grisly tale of a young woman's murder by her intoxicated spouse. The husband, after spending his day in a nearby tavern, returned home and ordered his wife to dress in her bridal gown. When she had done so, he slit her throat and stabbed her repeatedly.[29] The *Companion* considered a drunken husband to be much more than a simple nuisance.

Gambling equaled drinking as a favorite male pastime in the antebellum South. Card games were the regular fare at country taverns in North Carolina.[30] In Kentucky, William Reynolds found men so absorbed in gambling on horse races and cards that it was difficult to engage anyone in conversation without hearing the phrase "I'll bet you."[31] Betting often became extravagant; it was not unusual for slaves and vast tracts of land to change hands during a single night of gaming.[32] Thus women worried that gambling, also, might reduce them to poverty. In the *Companion,* this concern took the shape of articles recounting the lives of young men who had squandered their wealth at the card table. These gamblers always managed to hide their evil habit until they had descended to a level of utter disgrace and desperation. Their wives then learned their secret too late to save themselves and their children from indigence.[33]

From women's perspective, however, worse than either drinking or gambling was male involvement in miscegenation. Illicit sexual contacts between white men and black women were frequent occurrences in southern society. In *Country Life in Georgia,* Rebecca Latimer Felton spoke of male "violations of the moral law that made mulattoes as common as blackberries."[34] A Virginian queried in 1833, "How many have fallen to this temptation?" and answered, "So many that it has almost ceased to be a temptation to fall!"[35] The census of 1860 confirmed these observations, recording that 12 percent of the South's black population—more than a half-million persons—was mulatto.[36]

The diaries of southern women are replete with expressions of outrage over men's promiscuity. Laura Beecher Comer, whose husband was a habitual offender, wrote:

O, what mortal tongue could tell or heart conceive of what barbarities I have suffered within the last twelve years of my life? It almost makes me writhe to think how my situation has misrepresented me and of what I have endured! And God only knows how much more I am still to endure from that man and his negroes![37]

Another lady expressed similar indignation, exclaiming that the "boundless licentiousness" of slavery made the plantation mistress "the chief slave of the harem." She identified, as did countless others, with the victims of her husband's lust, considering herself equally degraded by unrestrained male passion.[38]

The *Companion* was rather quiet on the subject of miscegenation, since an open discussion of the matter could have given support to abolitionists' claims that the South was "one great brothel, where half a million of women are flogged to prostitution."[39] Such treason would have drawn the wrath of southern men and probably would have ended the magazine's career prematurely. On the one occasion when the *Companion* did comment on miscegenation, however, it attacked one of the most popular defenses of the practice—that the availability of black women enabled southern men to satisfy their physical urges without violating the virtue of white women.[40] A writer in the *Southern Literary Journal* in 1838, for example, supported this argument and added that the use of female slaves by white males also prevented the social problems associated with white prostitution. An illegitimate white child was a burden on society, but the mulatto child of a slave woman was a welcome "acquisition to her owner." Moreover, a slave did not lower her station in society or impair her means of support by illicit sexual activity, as did the free white prostitute.[41] The *Companion,* being as bold as it dared, indirectly countered such assertions with an article titled "Thoughts on English Women." The female author of that piece angrily ridiculed Englishmen for contending that prostitution was required in their society if their desires were to be fulfilled and the purity of English-women simultaneously preserved.[42] Despite its foreign target, the article was a clear expression of the *Companion*'s contempt for white men who visited the slave quarters with less-than-pure intentions.

Severely limited in their means of protest and reform, the *Companion*'s contributors sought to redress their grievances through manipulation of the culturally prescribed image of the southern woman. They developed this tactic in response to the ambiguity of that ideal. Male social commentators in the Old South agreed that woman was inherently pious and therefore responsible for preserving Christian values and steering society along a proper moral course. Possession of that responsibility, however, did not entitle her to chastise her spouse. The perfect woman was submissive, as well as virtuous, and lived only to honor and obey her husband. This notion of correct female deportment limited woman's moral influence over men to a mysterious persuasive power, or "magic spell," which she created by means of her beauty and charm. The southern lady was "at once the ruler and the governed," observed the *Companion,* "whose duty it is to obey and to yield, and whose privilege it is to command and sway, even by obeying and in yielding." The magazine endorsed these concepts of woman-hood in their broadest terms, but refused to accept the constraints they imposed upon woman's moral authority. Its readers attempted to escape those restrictions by redefining their domestic duties in a manner that would enable them to employ the submissive ideal itself as a disciplinary tool.[43]

The submissiveness demanded of women was absolute. Slavery required a rigorous enforcement of authority and led white men to regard their plantations and homes as "domestic monarchies" which they governed without restraint.[44] Christopher C. G. Memminger explained this view to a group of young men in 1851: "Each planter is in fact a Patriarch—his position compels him to be a ruler in his household. From early youth, his children and servants look up to him as head, and obedience and subordination become important elements of [their] education."[45]

It was imperative that women, as well as children and slaves, remain obedient to the head of the household, for to challenge male sovereignty was to threaten the structure of authority upon which slavery rested. Thus in 1834, Adam P. Empie, then president of William and Mary College, advised his newly married daughter never to oppose her husband or show displeasure with him, regardless of his actions. "A difference with your husband," he warned, "ought to be considered the greatest calamity."[46] The social isolation and economic insecurity of spinsterhood were the penalties for assertiveness. As Caroline Gilman explained in 1839, a wife's "first study must be self-control, almost to hypocrisy. A good wife must smile amid a thousand perplexities, and clear her voice to tones of cheerfulness . . . or else languish alone."[47]

In several of its articles, the *Companion* appeared to consent to the male ideal of female submissiveness. It instructed wives to maintain the home as an "earthly paradise." The best way for a woman to accomplish this was always to meet her husband with a smile and to be forever yielding and obedient to his opinions and desires.[48] Beneath its surface agreement, however, the *Companion*'s view of female submissiveness was significantly different from that held by male proponents of the general cultural model of woman. This was evidenced by other articles, which indicated that submissiveness was half of a paired set of duties of husbands and wives, rather than an exclusive imperative for women. The correlate duty of the husband was to respect his wife and her labors within the home. He was never to speak to her harshly; if she needed reproof, he should deliver it in soft, affectionate terms. Similarly, if he expected to be greeted at the end of each day with a smile, he was to meet his wife in such a manner "as to draw forth the smile—natural and involuntary." He also was never to indulge in fault-finding, but let his love show forth in all his actions.[49] In reiteration of this rule, the *Companion* rebuked husbands who taunted and teased their wives or were in any other way unkind. "Base indeed," wrote one contributor, "is the man that will be unkind or indifferent to a wife, when he knows that she does her duty."[50]

In addition to being kind, men were to demonstrate their love and respect for their wives by providing them with companionship. One woman writer explained to husbands, "If [your wife] spins and weaves, makes and mends all the clothes for her household, never lets you put on a buttonless shirt, or a stocking with holes, she will not have much of anybody else's company but yours." She then asked that they plan to spend some time with their wives and that they make that time enjoyable. They might, she suggested, consider staying home at night and reading to their spouses from the great works of religion and literature, rather than going out to drink and gamble.[51]

As paired duties, submissiveness and respect were reciprocal prerequisites; neither was required in the absence of the other. Obedience, declared the *Companion,* could be reasonably required from wives only if they were respected by their husbands.[52] A wife could justly cease yielding to her husband's will if he were unkind or indifferent toward her or if he participated in drinking, gambling, or miscegenation.

The disciplinary potential of the *Companion*'s stance on submissiveness derived from the fact that it offered a grave threat to the concept of the home with which southern men defended slavery. During the years between 1830 and 1861, northern abolitionists condemned slave labor as an immoral institution and clamored for emancipation. Southern men countered the reformers' rhetoric by creating a romantic vision of domestic life, which they presented as proof of slavery's moral worth. The *Companion* joined in this extolling of the home, although it was more interested in improving woman's condition than in preserving the slave system.

Praise of the home was common throughout mid-nineteenth-century America, but in the South it rose to the level of idolization. Joseph Jones, a young professor of chemistry at Georgia Medical College, in 1859, wrote his fiancee of his longing for "a Dear home, the *sweetest,* and *purest,* and *dearest spot* on earth."[53] The *Companion* shared Jones' sentiments, for it published numerous articles glorifying home life and recounting personal memories of its pleasures. In one such article, the author observed that after "all the eulogies that can be passed upon society in its various forms, after all the pleasures that can be realized in its flowing paths, there is no place so sweetly romantic, and so intimately connected with the best and most treasured feelings of the heart, as *home.*" The home, she concluded, was the focus of southern society and the source of its vitality.[54]

The home also came to be seen as a temple of virtue, a veritable heaven on earth. In 1857, George Barnsley, a student at Oglethorpe University, described the family as "a holy circle" of sentiments, affections, and virtues. Expanding this idea, William Gilmore Simms noted that the sensibilities found within the home were "the moral property of society."[55] Naturally, then, the home replaced the church as the center of training in piety and virtue. Within the confines of the domestic circle, woman exercised her innate piety to train her children in the teachings of Christ and to replace their inherent selfishness and bad temper with love, humility, and sympathy.[56] Her deeds made the home into the true source of all the human "charms which are spread through the universe."[57]

White men supposed that their slaves shared the benefits of the domestic sphere equally with their own children. Many southerners actually regarded black servants as members of the white family. Familial references to slaves abound in southern literature and in the letters and diaries of slaveholders. R. F. W. Allston of Charleston, for instance, spoke of blood relatives and slaves in the same sentence, closing a letter to his aunt by requesting that she tell "Mamma and all the niggers howdye for me."[58] Virginia Cary pointed out in her *Letters on Female Character,* published in 1830, that slaves were "peculiarities of the domestic establishments . . . [that] surround our homes, and constitute a portion of every family."[59] Bishop Stephen Elliot of Georgia considered the association to be even more intimate, declaring that slaves were "a race who form a part of our household and stand with us next to our children."[60] The *Companion* concurred with these views, stating that the relationship between master and slave was next to and sometimes equaled the family relationships of father, mother, sister, and brother.[61]

This imaginative inclusion of slaves within the plantation family completed the foundation for a response to northern abolitionists. Southerners could refute their opponents' charges that slavery was immoral by noting that slaves, as members of the white families who owned them, received the love, security, and moral training that only the family could supply. As James Chesnut explained, this arrangement was superior to the northern system of free labor, under which the extended family declined and servants were excluded from the domestic circle. The southern slave partook of the family's "discipline, its tone, its comforts, its joys and its affections, and thus [was] bound by the cohesion, protected by the feeling, and secured in well-being by the steadfastness of society." The northern hireling, on the other hand, was "isolated from respect by loneliness, embittered by the imparted sense of servility, and stimulated to wrong by the temptation to his aspirations and cupidity." Chesnut concluded from these observations that the virtue of southern slaveholders was impeccable, for unlike northern capitalists, they were willing to train and care for their servants as they did their children.[62]

The *Companion* endorsed this proslavery argument but warned that its validity depended upon woman's agreement to remain in her subservient role. Contributors to the journal explained that an insubordinate woman could undermine the tranquility of domestic life. She could fill her home with strife by refusing to assume a cheerful spirit, by becoming unamiable, fretful, and fault-finding. Such conduct would drive her husband, children, and slaves away from the family circle, forcing them to seek comfort in debauchery.[63] The assertive woman also could impair the home's ability to transmit approved moral values. Upon contrasting her unaffable behavior and supposed piety, her son would conclude, "If this is religion, the less I have of it the better."[64] If a woman's biological child would respond in this way, then surely her other "children," the slaves, would react no differently. These observations affirmed woman's power to determine the success or failure of the proslavery appeal.

This lesson on domestic relations used the *Companion's* reinterpretation of female submissiveness to predicate that maintenance of the romantic defense of slavery depended upon male behavior. Through such instruction, the magazine offered white southern men a simple choice. They could abide by their wives' standards of morality and thereby preserve their defense of slavery; or they could persist in ignoring those precepts and risk collapse of that defense through a loss of women's cooperation. These options were intended to force males to comply with a code of marital conduct partly determined by women, for in the *Companion's* view, southern men had no alternative for ensuring the continued legitimacy of their society.[65]

The *Southern Lady's Companion* probably failed to alter male behavior in any meaningful way, since few men, if any, read it with regularity.[66] The extent of the journal's disciplinary power, however, is not a proper measure of its significance. Far more important were the new attitudes its female patrons developed toward themselves and their place in society. White southern women complained of male immorality long before the *Companion's* publication, although they continued to assent to a male definition of womanhood.[67] The *Companion* provided a medium through which their anger could be focused and translated into a less oppressive conception of woman's role. In reinterpreting the submissive ideal, the *Companion's* subscribers rejected the notion that they could bring their moral authority to bear upon the world only through the passive channel of "female influence" and charm. They chose instead to make their piety an active force in shaping and improving society, using its leverage initially in an attempt to change the domestic behavior of male slaveowners.

As they worked to redefine submissiveness, the *Companion's* subscribers also developed a new sense of feminine solidarity. These women freed their disgust for male behavior from the confines of diaries and private letters to share it in public discussions that bound them together through common suffering, anger, and protest. The *Companion* provided its readers with a public network of emotional support and friendship that greatly lessened their isolation. One woman advised her fellow subscribers quite appropriately, "It is the best . . . and most agreeable Companion you will ever meet."[68]

These new perceptions of self affected more than a few scattered rebels, for with its large readership, the *Companion* spoke to and in behalf of a broad sector of white southern womanhood. The magazine's precise impact upon women's lives is difficult to assess without the ability to study individual subscribers, but other evidence suggests that the new assertiveness and collective self-confidence it generated among its readers was profoundly transforming. Slavery's oppressive presence prevented antebellum southern women from acting upon the *Companion*'s concept of womanhood. After the Civil War, however, the journal's view of submissiveness became a basis for their movement out of the home into the realm of public affairs through such new organizations as the Methodist Woman's Home Missionary Society, the Woman's Foreign Missionary Society, and the Woman's Christian Temperance Union. Members of these associations belonged to the same middle-class groups that had so avidly supported the *Companion;* perhaps they often were daughters of the magazine's subscribers. These reformers focused their attention on women's issues, choosing Woman's Work for Women and Home Protection as mottoes for their work. The missionary societies labored accordingly to deliver social services to destitute women and children whom they considered victims of male neglect and abuse. The WCTU displayed a similar sense of sisterhood, striving not only for prohibition, but also to lower the infant mortality rate, eradicate the double standard, and redeem juvenile delinquents. Underlying these programs was a conviction that women should use their refined moral sensibilities to uplift the world around them. The activities of the Methodist missionary societies and the WCTU comprised a campaign to convert a patriarchal social order to feminine standards of virtue and propriety.[69]

The women in each of these organizations elaborated upon the ideological position established by the *Companion* during the antebellum era. They modified the cultural image of the southern woman so that piety and reciprocal responsibility in marriage took precedence over submissiveness. That reorientation enabled women to expand the boundaries of the feminine sphere and engage in public activities their mothers never had known. These women, however, were not feminists. Like the *Companion*'s readers, they worked within the context of traditional notions of womanhood and based their projects upon the idea that women and men are fundamentally different in temperament and therefore should occupy separate domains. Yet the *Companion* and its successors did create a spirit of solidarity and purpose that motivated women to rebel against the cult of southern womanhood when men later used it in an attempt to constrain their increasing social involvement: That spirit animated members of the Methodist Woman's Missionary Council in 1910 when they defied their male detractors by adopting the motto Grow We Must, Even If We Outgrow All That We Love.[70]

4

DISTRESS FROM THE PRESS

Saranne Price O'Donnell

In 1882, an editorial in *The Christian Advocate* asserted:

It is the duty of the Church of the living God to stand like a rock in the way of all evil tendencies. It is its prerogative to guide no less than to stimulate. A Church that floats on the stream of worldliness is not worthy its name or place in the world, and becomes a social club with officers and forms, rather than an organized moral force. . . . The spirit of the age and Methodism, in some respects, should harmonize; but in others, Methodism should be its uncompromising opponent. Whether it can maintain a just independence of it, is the problem of the time and of every Methodist.[1]

In his stance against the "spirit of the age," James Monroe Buckley, editor of *The Christian Advocate* (New York) from 1880 to 1912, might well be described as the embodiment of his ideal of the duty of the church. For this man stood like a rock in the way of every wind of doctrine that he saw beating at the integrity, the sensibility, the faith of the Methodist Episcopal Church. And as editor, he made use of the primary organ of that church, *The Christian Advocate,* to perform what he saw as the church's duty.

The woman question, as it was called, was one of those "evil tendencies" to be blocked—or, if not evil, then at least questionable in the eyes of Dr. Buckley. In an age when women had few legal rights, excluding the right to vote, the right to be lawmakers in the church, and the right to be ordained preachers of the gospel, the question of equal rights for women was powerfully debated.

Although Buckley's stance on those rights remained basically unchanged during his editorship, yet one may see a development in his arguments over a period of years. Before analyzing

Buckley's expressions concerning the woman question, however, some background about the man himself may be useful in
understanding his points of view as they developed.

Background

James Buckley's mother exercised a guiding moral and
spiritual influence during his developing years, for before
James was six years old his father, a Methodist Episcopal
preacher, had died, leaving James' mother to care for him and
his three-year-old brother, Henry. In order to support herself
and her children, Abby Lonsdale Monroe Buckley established
a private school and was subsequently appointed preceptress of
a public school, where she remained for the next twenty years.[2]
From his childhood experience, Buckley was moved to write of
his mother,

Our ideas upon the sphere of women in the Church were derived
largely from her example and precepts. . . . While she has doubtless
had reason to think that her training has not brought forth all the fruits
that she hoped, we tremble to think what would have been our fate had
she been turned aside by a 'mission' to rival man on the rostrum or in
the halls of legislation.[3]

Here Buckley seemed not to oppose women in the government
of the church because of their unworthiness, but because of
their supreme worth in other arenas. Buckley placed his ideal
woman on a pedestal, and from this flowed his strong conviction
that women's purity ought not to be tainted by a "man's world."
This is correlated with his disgust at the phenomenon of the
morally depraved woman. "No human being is more pure and
noble than a true woman," he wrote. "No creature known to
the human race is worse than a depraved, abandoned woman."[4]
Buckley served pastorates from 1859 until 1880. When he
moved into his position as editor, he carried with him the
philosophy that *The Christian Advocate,* too, could function in
a pastoral way: "If *The Christian Advocate* be what its name
implies, and what the Church designed it to be, it is a
modification of the pastoral work, as we shall have the
opportunity of instructing, edifying, and comforting those who

receive our 'epistles.'"[5] And so the paper became an extension of Buckley's intellect and personality and faith—his deadly seriousness, as well as his almost impish wit.

The religious press in the nineteenth and first part of the twentieth centuries was a vital means of communication. In a time when neither radio nor television existed to provide on-the-spot news and instant commentaries, the religious press was a significant purveyor of news of the world. And as a house organ, it served to bind together people of the same denomination. Unquestionably, it had a powerful influence upon its readers.

An indication of the *Advocate*'s strength is found in an excerpt from a speech by the Reverend Anna Howard Shaw, given at the National American Women's Suffrage Association Convention of 1892. Said Shaw of the Reverend Anna Oliver: "She was attacked by that influential Methodist paper, the *Christian Advocate,* edited by the Rev. James M. Buckley, who declared that he would destroy her influence in the church, and so with that great organ behind him he attacked her."[6]

Through his keen, analytical mind, Buckley commanded wide respect. Rather than being a creative thinker, he was a responder, critically approaching new ideas from every possible angle. Precisely because of this legal mind, he was a brilliant parliamentarian and a deadly foe of the woman's movement.

As Buckley's mind was brilliant, his ego was just as magnificent. In all his careful descriptions of the qualifications and characteristics for lawmakers, he seemed to be describing himself and appeared to imply that if a person did not have those kinds of gifts, then lawmaking was not the place for him, and especially for her.

Was Buckley married? George Preston Mains notes in his biography, "He was three times married. In each case he married into a family of high social standing and influence."[7] Buckley's first wife died in 1866, his second in 1883, and his third in 1910.

An Overview

The sweep of Buckley's expressed opinions and attitudes about women from 1880 to 1912 shows that as time passed, his attitudes did not shift; rather, his emphases changed. He followed certain sociological and ecclesiastical trends, analyzed them to one degree or another and, of course, expressed his opinions.

Prior to 1888 and the great debate on the admission of women to the Methodist Episcopal General Conference, Buckley did not find much ecclesiastical grist for his mill, but focused on secular events and on attitudes concerning women. Here his ideal image of woman was the basis for his opinions. Then during the years of debate, when the woman question touched the nerve of the Methodist Episcopal Church, Buckley editorialized frequently on women in the church, using the constitution of the church, the Bible, and his own image of woman as bases for his arguments. After 1896, when the issue was more or less settled, and all that was going to be said had been said, Buckley turned again to conditions and situations in the secular world for the content of his editorials, once more relying on his concept of the ideal woman for his critique and analysis.

It is interesting to note that when dealing with secular phenomena, Buckley seemed to be more realistic about his "prophecies" and was generally milder and wittier in his criticism of women's rights than when he entered the ecclesiastical realm. Since the Methodist Episcopal Church was his bailiwick, it may be that he felt the threat of an invasion of women there much more keenly than when he confronted the prospect of general woman suffrage.

Buckley's chief virtue was that he heard and scrutinized the many sides of an issue. Now, almost a century later, he bears listening to because he himself listened and because he considered several sides of the woman question. In his critical analyses, he brought out issues that had not been addressed. His challenges served to temper, to refine, to sharpen, and generally to strengthen the argument and sympathy of those who advocated women's rights. And so ironically, in his own way, Dr. Buckley served to further the movement of women into the higher governing bodies of the church; for after examining their aims and goals and principles, it was necessary for all advocates of women to answer him.

And answer they did. In August 1892, a "great debate" took place between the Reverend Anna Howard Shaw and Dr.

James Monroe Buckley at the New York Chautauqua Assembly, where apparently "the evident sympathy of the immense audience [was] with the side of the question presented by the former."[8] And in June 1897, Buckley himself admitted that Catherine Spence, Australian social and political reformer, "impressed us as a woman of remarkable penetration and large mental activity. We had some protracted conversations with her upon all the phases of the so-called woman question. She undoubtedly has far more ability and education than the average man."[9]

The Early Years, 1880–1888

In his initial years as editor, Buckley set about establishing his own positions on diverse issues, setting them forth in his writings in such a way that his readers were always clear as to just where he stood. With regard to women in the secular world, his concept of "good women" and "bad women" was clear. "Bad women" were sinners whose shamelessness sprang from their passion. These he called "abandoned women."[10] Women murderers and swindlers were also "bad." Of women swindlers, he wrote, "Bad as a confidence man is, a confidence woman is a great deal more dangerous. 'The horse-leech hath two daughters, crying Give, give.' The New Version gives in the margin for horse-leech 'vampire.' We suggest that all confidence women be known hereafter as *vampires*."[11] A notorious example of a "bad woman" was Sarah Bernhardt: "'She has had several children without having any husband,' and has never seemed ashamed of it."[12]

A "good woman," for Buckley, was one who forgives—for example, the woman who took in a young woman needing help who previously had been turned away by "benevolent institutions."[13] Buckley added a sidelight to the story: "A woman's insight often finds a truth, while man's plodding reason fails to reach it. . . . If Pilate had listened to his wife, who said: 'Have thou nothing to do with that just man,' he might have been spared the infamy of ordering the crucifixion of the Lord of life and glory."[14]

Buckley felt that the normal activity of woman should center around orphan asylums, the education of youth, missions, temperance, the care of the aged, and the Christian church. However, "The Spirit of some . . . women seems to be such that they would thrust man aside, and do his work, whether their own be done or not. . . . This should be satirized."[15]

In those early years, Buckley began to show his ambivalence toward the widening sphere of woman. He wrote in 1881, "Strange as it may appear, we, who do not believe in admitting women to the regular ministry, nor in forcing political responsibilities upon them, have always favored their admission to the medical profession." In 1885 he listed those occupations a woman cannot do: "street scavengers and cleaners of out-houses . . . butchers . . . sailors . . . attendants in the male departments of lunatic asylums . . . keepers of prisons," firemen, policemen, and soldiers. And in 1887 he advised farmers' wives and daughters to "take a hint from this. We see no objection to a woman's farming. If you try it and succeed, give *The Christian Advocate* the credit. If you don't succeed, say nothing about it."[16]

In a limited way, Buckley was a champion of equal rights for women. On equal pay for equal work, he asked, "What possible reason can be given for the practice in Philadelphia of paying the female teachers only once in three months, while the male teachers are paid once a month?"[17]

In regard to woman suffrage, Buckley was neither ambivalent nor humorous, however. He felt the issue was "artificially stimulated," that it was not generally desired by women, and that it would give power to Catholic priests, since "women . . . are more easily led by their religious guides."[18] As a religious guide himself, however, he used sentimental appeals to women concerning the impropriety of "electioneering"—appeals that may have proved transparent to the advocates of woman suffrage.[19]

In the ecclesiastical realm, Buckley's opinions with regard to women in the church began to be manifested late in the proceedings of the 1880 General Conference. On the fourteenth day of that conference, a petition was presented "to abolish all distinctions of sex in the Discipline." Also, "an extended debate occurred to allow Miss [Frances] Willard to speak ten minutes—which was awarded her." Buckley

81

"strenuously opposed" granting Willard permission, because "she did not represent an ecclesiastical body."[20] On the twenty-third day of General Conference, two judiciary reports were adopted. The first, "referring to the case of Miss [Anna] Oliver," ruled that "the Discipline did not authorize the ordination of women"; the second, referring to the "case of the license of Sister [Katharine] Lent," ruled "that the Discipline did not authorize the licensing of women."[21]

The petition for the removal of distinctions of sex in the *Discipline* resulted in an amendment stating, "The pronouns, *he, his,* and *him,* when used in the Discipline with reference to stewards, class leaders, and Sunday-school superintendents, shall not be so construed as to exclude women from such office."[22] A statement was made in two church papers: "It would seem . . . that there was some intention to include the office of trustee in this amendment; but it does not so stand."[23] Buckley immediately responded that the amendment *did* include the office of trustee: "By the action of the last General Conference women are, by the Discipline, eligible to vote for trustees, and to be voted for as trustees, on the same terms as men." Buckley's own rationale for this action was that "the church might then be made and kept neat, and some interest might be taken in its surroundings."[24]

It is not unusual to find Buckley concocting a strange mixture of disciplinary and practical reasons for following a proposed plan of action. One also finds him less legalistic in his earlier years as editor, especially in his attitude toward women in the church, as can be seen from his interpretation of church law (see above, the pronouns), of traditions, and of Scripture (see below). "Methodism," he noted, "has always given encouragement to the work of women. When other Churches prohibited women's speaking in meeting . . . Methodism brought her forward."[25] He justified the fact that the Methodist Church allowed women to speak in church:

Now, as the apostle [Paul] certainly did not mean to contradict himself, he must in this passage [I Cor. 11:4, 5] mean that when a woman prays and prophesies in a promiscuous assembly (for if she were alone or with other women only, it would make no difference whether her head was covered or not), provided she conforms to the proprieties of her sex, it is right. The meaning of the apostle in the other passage [I Cor.

14:34] is easily to be inferred from the usage of the primitive Church. In some places the passages refer to wrangling and in others to the assumption of formal, authoritative ruling and ministerial functions in the Church of God.[26]

In his specific references to women as pastors in the earlier years of his editorship, it is worth noting that Buckley never raised scriptural arguments, but only disciplinary reasons against their functioning as ordained Methodist Episcopal pastors. Of Anna Oliver, he said in 1882:

Miss Oliver was professedly licensed as a local preacher by a Church down East. The General Conference decided all such licenses invalid. She is an energetic person, and there can be no objection to her trying any experiment on her own responsibility she pleases, but she has no right to call her society a Methodist Episcopal Church.[27]

As time passed, however, Buckley developed his thinking along scriptural and even organizational lines, rather than adhering to his original opinions based on the *Discipline*.

The Fight Begins, 1888–1892

The quadrennium from 1888 to 1892 was important to Buckley and to the woman question, for it opened up new ways of thinking as the ideological threat that women would enter General Conference actually became flesh. In 1888, five women were duly elected by lay electoral conferences as principal delegates to General Conference. These election results were to dominate Buckley's thoughts and words about women for the next eight years as few other circumstances did. During that period he wrote no long editorials on women that did not relate to the election of delegates to General Conference. His attention to women in the secular realm was overshadowed by his primary focus on women in the church.

He was not without humor in the situation, however. One of his editorials concerned the editor of the *Western Christian Advocate,* who had graphically described the chapel of the New York Book Concern: "The walls [of the chapel] are being transformed by the oil portraits of founders and leaders into a hall of Methodist historic art. It was gratifying to see Barbara Heck's firm and benign face highest of all over the pulpit—even New York rendering this noble tribute to woman's place in the Church."[28]

To this, Buckley responded, "The portrait . . . which Dr. Moore [has seen] transfigured into a woman [is] that of Thomas Coke!" And then in a comment full of sensitivity to gender hierarchy, Buckley posed the possibility that some day when Dr. Moore himself rose to thrill General Conference with "words that breathe and thoughts that burn," the presiding officer "will assign the floor to Miss ——— or Mrs. ———!" Buckley urged, however, that "without superseding, lowering, destroying, or transforming Coke—there should be a portrait of Susanna Wesley, and another of Barbara Heck," and so began a drive to collect money to pay for such portraits.[29]

Buckley championed biblical and theological training for women, legal training for women, women's physiological and psychological fitness for work in the church, and women's higher education. At the dedication of the John Crouse Memorial College for Women at Syracuse University, Buckley gave a lengthy address and printed the text of it in *The Christian Advocate*. He asserted that "the influence of woman is, or may be, equal to that of man," that "[the wife] can share the larger number of [her husband's] thoughts or converse intelligently with him," that she can provide "knowledge in the family," "set the standards for the sermons of the minister," and "defend her faith." He believed, however, that a woman's training should be different from that of a man. That is, her "head and the heart must be trained at the same time."[30] We are left to suppose that it would suffice for men's heads alone to be trained.

Although championing some women's causes, Buckley still continued to oppose woman suffrage and to satirize women when they proposed to act as men did. His strongest and most frequent argument concerning woman suffrage was that women themselves did not wish it. His second argument was that women had their own realm, and men theirs, and that women could help civilization most by keeping to their *own* duties, which did not include the franchise.

The General Conference of 1888, after an extended debate on the admission of the five women who had been elected as lay delegates, adopted a report stating that the women were *not* eligible. But the report contained an amendment requiring the question to be sent around to annual conferences to discover the sentiment of the grass roots. While the voting was taking place in the annual conferences, articles came to *The Christian Advocate* fast and furiously. Swamped with contributions, Buckley edited several supplements titled *Woman and the Church,* which included articles both for and against the admission of women, written by men and women alike.

During this time Buckley's own pen never ceased. No sooner had he pronounced "Finis" to one aspect of the question than he began to deal with another. While the arguments necessarily overlap, Buckley's editorials relating to the admission of women to the highest governing body of the church can be grouped into four general categories: (1) those that presented arguments from as many angles as possible; (2) those that attempted to prevent the church from making hasty decisions that might later prove to be detrimental to the order of the institution; (3) those that pointed to the despicable practice by secular movements—especially the woman suffrage movement—of "using" the church controversy to further their own purposes; and (4) those that reflected Buckley's personal conviction that woman's presence and activity were not intended to be made manifest in any lawmaking assembly.

Buckley's creed concerning the function of an editor of a church paper was that he "shall give all sides of every debatable question . . . a fair hearing." And this Buckley did, publishing "more than sixty columns of contributions" in favor of admitting women to General Conference, "ten more contributions in favor of it than against."[31]

Buckley's second concern was to avoid changes, in order to preserve what was working satisfactorily in the present system. He pleaded more than once for the church to use caution and deliberation in its actions, lest the whole institution come crumbling down. To Buckley, admitting women to governing bodies was out of the natural order established by God, and he feared the worst if there was an attempt to undermine God's will.

In a personal letter to his "Dear Christian Sisters," with an overdose of saccharine rhetoric, Buckley appealed to that natural order, which rested "upon the family, that human trinity . . . of father, mother, and child," urging women to vote against the proposal to admit women to General Conference. To vote no would preserve the true influence of woman, "the queenly crown of pearls, the talisman of faith, hope, and love," so that the "iron crown of authority . . . [would be] fitted to the head and shoulders of man."[32]

Just as Buckley seemed plagued by fears of ruining appropriate church order, he also feared, not without justification, that other groups—especially the suffrage movement and the movement for women's ordination—were using the laity rights controversy in the Methodist Episcopal Church as a means to their own ends. In a lengthy editorial, he described nine arguments against the admission of women: that the church would be "used"; that there might be errors in judgment; that it would weaken the moral power of women; that women were "not adapted to participation in such a body as the General Conference"; that it would weaken the relationship between the Methodist Episcopal Church and the Methodist Episcopal Church, South; that the German work would receive a "fearful blow"; that women would be brought into the ministry; that admission would be a new "bar to organic unity"; and that the General Conference, with the presence of women, would become a "more social, less deliberative" body.[33]

Ironically, Buckley placed himself in the position of *encouraging* women to vote so that they might register their sentiment *against* the admission of women. On one hand, he attempted to persuade them that it was awkward and even indelicate to go to a voting place, march up to the ballot box, and deposit a vote.[34] Yet he could not help making that "iron crown of authority" seem rather appealing as he described the "well-considered scheme" of the advocates of women "to induce [women] to vote, to give them a taste of that kind of power with the certainty that having once sipped the nectar they would be anxious for its full enjoyment."[35]

The fact is, Buckley was convinced that women ought not to be admitted to any lawmaking body "because they are *women* and not men. . . . Because they are preoccupied with work of equal importance to that of legislation, and when they do that work properly and confine themselves to it they exert greater influence for good, even over legislation and its results, than they could if [they were] members of legislative bodies." He called this "a noble sort of disfranchisement."[36]

Even beyond the "noble disfranchisement" argument, Buckley went so far as to say that it was *unnatural* for woman to be put into the same position as men in church and state and that "the more brain a woman has, the more harm may be done."[37]

A month after Buckley made the statement concerning the differing characteristics of men and women, he contradicted himself, asserting that man, too, had woman's "intuition." In the same editorial, he then proceeded to dismiss that statement as he listed the characteristics of the ideal delegate to General Conference: "hard-headed, deliberative, mature . . . accustomed to weigh, to decide slowly, and firm enough in texture and made steady enough by the struggles of life not to be blinded by oratory or tears or laughter or sentiment, or embarrassed by gallantry, persuaded by a smile, or captured by a compliment."[38] Not surprisingly, these ideal delegates were created in the image of Dr. Buckley himself!

During this quadrennium (1888–1892) Buckley's scriptural arguments concerning women as church legislators began to take shape. Moving from a basic feeling that something was amiss in the natural order, Buckley eventually gave his scriptural argument precedence over all others in his opposition to the woman's movement. He developed his argument in two ways. First, he vehemently attacked those who would "take the Scriptures lightly." "Discredit Paul, you discredit Christ," he said.[39] A year later, he became agitated in his editorials: "We confess both grief and alarm at the treatment of the Bible in this crisis. It is not only the proposition to make women rulers, but the ruthless tearing in pieces of the Scriptures."[40]

Second, Buckley carefully developed a position concerning the aspects of Scripture that could not possibly be "transient"—that is, that which could be held true for all time and had not been true simply at the time of their writing. In January 1891, he introduced the term *antiscriptural*.[41] Stronger than *unscriptural*, "antiscriptural" illustrated that "God's Word

87

explicitly forbids the investing of women with such functions." This he supported "by the almost unanimous opinion of Christian scholarship."[42]

In arguing this position, Buckley found himself refuting many scriptural arguments put forward by the women's advocates. To this he devoted at least two long editorials, "Errors Refuted" in October 1890 and "Has the Scriptural Objection Been Met?" in August 1891.[43]

Why did Buckley wait so long to express his scriptural objections so strongly? He would say only that "those who believed it contrary to the Word of God expected, when it [the question of the eligibility of women to General Conference] was submitted [to a vote of the church], to give their reasons for that belief."[44] Oddly enough, when writing about women as pastors, Buckley did not use his antiscriptural argument, but dealt with the reality of differences and tastes and beliefs of individual congregations concerning women pastors.[45]

The Next Quadrennium, 1892–1896

Buckley's editorial attention to women in the secular world continued to wane as his ecclesiastical concerns dominated the editorial pages of *The Christian Advocate*. In the secular realm, concerning changes of language, Buckley took a dim view of the term *lady* used in place of *woman*. He said that the correlative of *saleslady* was *salesgentleman* and that *woman* was correct and "will command the approval of most persons of sense."[46]

More seriously, an outraged Buckley struck a blow *for* women's rights when deaconesses were being "auctioned off" to raise funds for their home. That type of insensitivity to women moved him to say that if something like that should ever take place again, "for the sake of the Church . . . for the honor of the sex to which they belong," and "for their own self-respect" they should protest.[47] It was a strong sign that other values of importance were at stake, if Buckley urged any woman to be so bold as to protest in public.

The General Conference of 1892 was largely passive concerning the issue of women in church polity. As none were elected delegates, "the issue of eligibility did not naturally come before the Conference."[48] On the last day, however, J. W. Hamilton proposed an amendment which provided basically that, first, a proposition be sent to annual conferences stipulating that members of General Conferences must be male; and that second, if the proposition did not receive a vote of three-fourths of the annual conferences and two-thirds of the General Conference, the existing rule should be interpreted to mean that both men and women were eligible to seats in General Conferences.[49]

From June until September 1892, Buckley's editorials were directed against this "trick" to have women admitted to General Conference. In the meantime, a woman was elected to the British Conference, and Buckley busied himself with attempts to show that there was no comparison between the British Conference and his own General Conference. Other than a few editorials on women and the General Conference, Buckley said little about the eligibility question for the remainder of the quadrennium.

He did, however, write about women as pastors. In July 1894, he was concerned with a group of women who were speculating as to whether John Wesley would approve of women ministers. Buckley disapproved such speculation: "Neither woman's intuition nor man's ratiocination would enable any uninspired being to say [what Wesley would approve]."[50] In the same editorial, he had some rather perceptive insights into the phenomena of women preachers:

So long as it remained a curiosity, no doubt women preachers, if under the sanction of any of the great denominations, would attract hearers from all quarters; probably a considerable proportion of men. Afterward, as now in most of the few communities where women are settled in the ministry, no remarkable change would be seen, though an inferior man might be unable to compete with a superior woman.[51]

Enlightened as Buckley may have seemed, he was still bound to the *Discipline* when it came to women pastors: "A presiding elder's signature to the license of the woman as a local preacher is worth no more than any man's check on a bank in which he never had an account."[52]

The Subsequent Years, 1896–1912

As Buckley grew older, a new Methodist Episcopal Church constitution was being written—in response to inadequacies that had been brought out during argument on the woman question, among others; the format of *The Christian Advocate* became more streamlined; and industrialization caused dramatic changes in society. And the length, number, and temper of Buckley's editorials about women in the church appeared to wane.

Buckley's attitude toward women's entrance into "the world," as reflected in his editorials, was a grim one, however. Month after month, the readers were confronted with editorials about women and divorce, women and kleptomania, women and strong drink, women and strikes, women and tobacco, and women in prisons. Never resigned to the fact that women were gaining equal rights, Buckley was determined to show the worst that equal rights could contribute to the world. "Woman debased is more thoroughly ruined than man. The higher sinks the lower."[53] He saw women becoming a nuisance as they promoted reform.[54] One article even took a disgruntled view of attractive schoolteachers who quit their jobs to marry.[55] All this was written to substantiate Buckley's claim that woman's natural place was in the home.

Still, there was a positive and perhaps even liberal side to Buckley, which manifested itself as he once again spoke out in favor of equal employment rights in two editorials, "Oppressive Discrimination" and "Shall Adult Women Be Forbidden to Work in Factories at Night?"[56] He also spoke out against stereotyping and advocated higher education for women. And he never stopped acknowledging the great women active in church and society. But when "women misleaders" urged women to "'withdraw from active work' in the Church until [they] were admitted as delegates to the General Conference," and when women brought "disgrace upon their cause," Buckley became incensed at the whole suffrage issue.[57]

In the realm of the church, the General Conference of 1896 finally produced an apparently congenial conclusion to the woman question. Four women had been elected as delegates to this conference. Three withdrew "in graceful terms."[58] The fourth, when she arrived, also withdrew, finding that if she did sit, it would be under a title in dispute. This conference finally agreed that if three-fourths of the members of annual conferences voted for the change in the constitution, the election of women to General Conference would be legal.[59]

In the aftermath of the conference, Buckley continued to urge his readers to act with caution, emphasizing his antiscriptural argument. Oddly enough, he also wrote an editorial in 1897 which defended the rights of ministers' wives, implying that they would be fair representatives of the laity to General Conference.[60]

Buckley noted that during the 1900 General Conference, "the woman question . . . lighted upon the third article of the . . . new constitution then under consideration."[61] Ultimately, "an amendment to the third article, substituting in the requirement for membership of the General Conference 'lay members' instead of 'laymen' was adopted." He repeated his belief that "woman by nature and by the Scriptures is intended to occupy a relation in the Church, the State, and the Family in which she exerts an influence equal to that of man, but exercises it by a different mode, moving in the sphere of persuasion rather than in that of authority."[62]

From 1900 until his retirement in 1912, Buckley's references to women were infrequent, but consistent with his attitudes and opinions of previous years.

The Value of Distress from the Press

Frustrating as James Buckley was, he proved to be of some value to the woman's movement. Exasperating as he was, it cannot be disputed that the man was devoted to his church. In fact, Buckley's first priority *was* the church—specifically, the integrity of the Methodist Episcopal Church. He also possessed his *own* integrity as a representative of that church. He believed the church to be a scriptural body. Thus when women's proponents appeared to be taking the sacred Word lightly, Buckley became the defender of the faith. He believed the church to be bound by its constitution, and when advocates of women seemed to trifle with that constitution, he defended it.

He believed that to maintain church unity, church doctrine should be uniform, so he valued the practices and tradition of the church. When women's or any other movement ignored or dismissed that tradition, he reacted negatively.

Buckley's method and perspective were conservative. Even as he was an analytical rather than a creative thinker, he sought with every fiber of his being to maintain what he felt was good and right. And so the champion of conservatives sought to preserve the church unblemished. He truly embodied what he asserted. Personal integrity was his hallmark, and he lived up to his own standards.

With all his strengths, James Monroe Buckley was not without his flaws. Without the "enlightened" tools of sociology and psychology, then only in the process of development, Buckley was fearful of shift in social structures, as society rapidly changed during his lifetime. Moreover, he did not, and temperamentally could not realize that all men were not like himself, and could not be; nor was he an ideal "man's man." Although his strong ego contributed to his personal integrity, it also somewhat blinded him as to the way other men, not to mention women, functioned. Buckley often seemed baffled by those who operated apart from his own norm. He also did not foresee that different types of people moving into different spheres could add richness and diversity to life. He saw only chaos resulting. Correllatively, his view of the natural order was far too simple for the complex world around him and for the complex beings that humans are, and so it proved an inadequate pattern for the establishment of the society he wished to see realized.

But Buckley felt he had a purpose, and although he could not stop the inevitable, he derived some satisfaction in slowing it down.

While to the woman's advocates of the late nineteenth and early twentieth centuries James Monroe Buckley and *The Christian Advocate* may have seemed The Devil's Advocate, and while the periodical was indeed a powerful and influential organ of the Methodist Episcopal Church, ultimately the religious press was not the whole church, and it did not hold the final word concerning the status of women in the church.

Buckley and *The Christian Advocate,* however, did prove

useful, even in slowing down the progress of women's entrance into the church's highest governing body. By preventing the church from making hasty decisions based upon the emotion of the moment, Buckley may have helped to preserve the integrity of the institution. In a negative way, moreover, he helped the women of the church prove the integrity of their own movement. While one never could accuse the Methodist Episcopal Church of making a slapdash decision, by virtue of the struggle, one could well acknowledge the women's strong substantial arguments, their tenacity, their ability, and their faith in God's will as they experienced it: that women are an integral part of the Body of Christ and rightfully could be members of the Methodist Episcopal governing body and pastors of its churches.

II

PRACTICE:
THE LIFE EXPERIENCE
OF WOMEN
IN THE WESLEYAN
TRADITION

AN AMBIGUOUS LEGACY

Anne Llewellyn Barstow

For four hundred years, from 1139 to 1549, marriage for the English clergy had not been legally possible—indeed it was forbidden all clergy in the West. What is often forgotten is that before the twelfth century, many women had been the respected wives of parish clergy. After the Roman legislation of 1139, however, a woman who lived with a priest could be seen only as a mistress, a concubine.[1] Then in the 1530s, led by none other than Archbishop Cranmer himself, English priests who followed the new Protestant ways began again to take *wives*. This striking change has been largely ignored as a significant fact by church historians; however, secular social historians have begun to press considerations of the nature and results of clerical marriage into our consciousness.

Here we will investigate the effect of those four centuries of compulsory celibacy on the church's view of women. Those women's lives concern us, furthermore, because they were the forerunners, at least, of those who would be models for the first Methodist ministers' wives. Susanna Wesley and her daughters-in-law were, after all, the wives of Anglican priests, as Susanna's own mother was wife to a Dissenting minister.

We will concentrate on the first two generations of post-Reformation clergy wives in the sixteenth century, drawing occasionally on the seventeenth. Who were these women? How did their church and society react to them? What did they contribute to the reform of the English church? And how did they feel about their roles? Unfortunately, because no diaries and virtually no letters have been preserved from

English clergy wives of the sixteenth century, a scholar cannot uncover the women's own feelings. Answers to the first three questions imply, however, that those forerunners left an important and disturbing legacy for later Methodist clergy wives.

The Social Identity of
Post-Reformation Clergy Wives

It has been assumed, rather than proved, that all the women who married priests during and after Cranmer's time were from the servant class. Why this assumption? The medieval scorn of priests' "women" had been very strong. Suspecting that this opprobrium carried over into Reformation times, and reflecting on the medieval practice whereby many priests used their housekeepers as their mistresses, scholars postulated that the Anglican clergy, once they were permitted to marry, would or could choose wives only from the servant class and that not until the eighteenth century would respectable Englishwomen marry into the clergy.[2] (Susanna Annesley, marrying Samuel Wesley in 1688, would fall into the late seventeenth-century category. Her family was well placed socially—her father was a graduate of Oxford and second cousin to the Earl of Anglesey, and her maternal grandfather, John White, also an Oxford graduate and a noted lawyer, was elected to Parliament for Southwark. White was also a member of the Westminster Assembly of Divines.)[3]

There is little question that the Anglican Church approached the issue of priestly marriage with ambivalence, as it approached many other controversies between Romanists and Protestants, and that in Lutheran and Calvinist lands clerical marriage attained acceptability more quickly.[4] There is evidence that this ambivalence hindered English clerics' marriage plans for many years and that some of the objections centered around the issue of the women's class. As late as the 1660s, when a young chaplain of good family fell in love with "a serving wench" and announced his intention to marry her, he was reprimanded by the Archbishop of Canterbury himself: "How criminous to your hopes of future preferment [this is] that I would advise you well to consider before you engage your life further."[5] The outcome of this particular romantic conflict is unknown, but the record shows that as late as the 1730s, Lady Mary Wortley Montagu *complained* that girls of good family were marrying curates and that, far worse to report, the daughter of the Earl of Huntingdon had "disposed of herself to a poor wandering Methodist."[6] Indeed, as exploration goes forward into the conditions under which clerical marriage was resumed in England, many reasons appear for the refusal of women to consider priestly suitors and take up lives that were not only looked down upon, but were dangerous as well.

And yet careful study of the sources does not bear out historians' former assumptions. Instead, what emerges is that the Anglican clergy, who at the time of the Reformation were themselves drawn from all classes, married women *from their own class*. Men from the peasant class married servant women; sons of the lower middle class, who made up the bulk of the parish clergy, married daughters of shopowners and craftsmen; and the first generation of reformed bishops found their wives in the families of prominent lay reformers, wealthy merchants, and gentry. And as soon as this first generation of clerical families had produced offspring, bishops and future bishops began to marry the daughters of bishops.[7] Bishop Barlow of Chichester provides the classic example: Each of the bishop's five daughters married a man destined to become a bishop.[8] Englishwomen of all classes were, in fact, willing partners in the new and far-from-accepted experiment of clerical marriage.

How Did Church and Society React to These Marriages?

In the first heady days of the English Reformation, so many time-honored customs were abrogated that a priest and his woman might well have assumed—or at least have hoped—that compulsory celibacy would quickly go the way of papal supremacy, the annates tax, and the king's marriage to Katharine of Aragon. Archbishop Cranmer himself married the niece of the German reformer Osiander, but King Henry's disapproval forced Margaret Cranmer into severe seclusion. Rumor had it that Cranmer carried her around in a chest.[9] Other priests followed the archbishop into marriage, but their optimism was, alas, not confirmed. The majority of bishops in Convocation and, more important, King Henry himself, stated that priests who took wives were "carnally evil" and adamantly declared that the practice should cease.[10] The statute known as the Six Articles, passed by Parliament in 1539 and annotated in the king's own hand, spelled out the grim realities: Priests were to repudiate the women and children living with them, and any who persisted in cohabiting were to be *executed as felons*.[11] Since the couple's property was to be confiscated, their children were, presumably, to be thrown on the mercy of neighbors. Many priests sent their wives away. Margaret Cranmer and the two Cranmer children fled back to Germany. In England the break with Rome did not yet mean the affirmation of clerical marriage.

Although these harsh punishments gradually were repealed, it was not possible to legislate legal marriage for the clergy until after King Henry's death in 1547. Both the Convocation and the House of Commons then immediately agreed that all laws against the marriages of priests must be abolished, but opposition in the more conservative House of Lords delayed the passage of the statute until early 1549. The language of the following section is most revealing of the still conflicting beliefs:

Although it was not only better for the estimation of priests and other ministers in the Church of God, to live chaste, sole, and separate from the company of women and the bond of marriage, but also thereby they might the better intend to the administration of the gospel, and be less intricated and troubled with the charge of household, being free and unburdened from the care and cost of . . . wife and children, and that it were most to be wished that they would willingly and of their selves endeavor to a perpetual chastity and abstinence from the use of women.[12]

In sum, English bishops continued to think of celibacy as the ideal, and of vicarage families chiefly as a burden and distraction to men in the ministry. But they were now grudgingly willing to admit that priestly marriage was the lesser of two evils, and so the statute continued:

Yet forasmuch as . . . such uncleanness of living, and other great inconveniences, not meet to be rehearsed, have followed of compelled chastity . . . it were better and rather to be suffered in the commonwealth, that those which could not contain, should . . . live in holy marriage, than feignedly abuse with worse enormity outward chastity or single life.[13]

The bishops knew well that the abuses of four hundred years of "compelled chastity" had contributed heavily to the climate of anticlericalism and thus to support for the break with Rome. Although any "use of women" by priests was repugnant to the Anglican leadership, they were forced to admit cohabiting couples into parsonages, though they would not welcome them. This attitude toward the holy sacrament of marriage was hardly enthusiastic.[14]

Perhaps the bishops also feared rebellion in the ranks of the priesthood, for immediately after the statute was enacted, many priests availed themselves of the privilege—so many, in fact, that one supposes many of these unions to have been long de facto. Exactly how many married? We can patch together a few estimates: In the strongly Protestant southern and eastern counties, in the four years before clerical marriage was again abolished, the following percentages of clergy married: Essex, 27; Norwich, 25; Lincoln, at least 11; London, 33; Cambridge, 20; and in the more conservative north, York, 10.[15] Reasons varied, and not all priests can be said to have married for love. When the 68-year-old Archbishop of York married 22-year-old Barbara Wentworth, he defended his action by saying that he feared he would be called a papist if he remained celibate! Not all who married held Protestant views, either, which is a surprise.

Because those marriages took place in a brief four years—1549–1553—during which clerical unions were legal, they indicate a strong trend away from the centuries-old celibacy. Apparently many priests were willing to be "intricated and troubled with the charge of the household." And yet the numbers are hardly overwhelming.

Given the lukewarm quality of the official endorsement, it is not surprising that the English society that witnessed the first generations of priestly marriage largely rejected it. Although criticism of the celibate priesthood had been rampant in English literature since the fourteenth century, it did not follow that the laity was ready overnight, as it were, to accept a woman who lived with a priest as his lawful wife. Prejudices lingered: There remained "a widespread popular taboo," "a genuine popular antipathy" to the innovation of priestly marriage, which would take many decades to run its course.[16]

Just what sort of hostility might a clerical couple face? When Robert Horne took his wife, Margery, to live with him when he was dean of the chapter at Durham, he was accused of "polluting the cathedral precincts."[17] Old women in Yorkshire called the vicarage children "priests' calves" and midwives refused to deliver the babies.[18] As late as 1552, a parliamentary bill complained that many "spoke slanderously of such marriages, and accounted the children begotten in them to be bastards." When the conservative reaction to the Protestant reforms of the church triggered an armed revolt in Devon and Cornwall, the rebels demanded that celibacy again be enforced on the priesthood.[19]

Thus even in the favorable days of Edward's reign, from 1547 to 1553, the position of married couples in parsonages was not easy. But those were the best of times compared to what lay ahead—the attack on clerical marriage launched by Mary Tudor when she reestablished Roman Catholicism in England. In fact, the main thrust of Mary's attack on the clergy fell precisely—not on denial of transubstantiation or of papal supremacy, not on any of the so-called major theological issues, but—on clerical marriage. Her bishops passed bills through Parliament that forbade the marriage of priests; declared their children illegitimate; removed all married priests from office; confiscated their revenues; and declared with special punitive intent that priests, even after being deprived, could no longer live with women. Priests who attempted to resign from their vows would receive special punishment.[20] No relief whatever was granted to the women and children thus deprived of their homes and their heads of household.

Immediately all over England, the newly appointed Marian bishops called their married clergy into court, forced them to separate from their wives, and stripped them of their livelihood. And to show their final contempt for the institution of clerical marriage, the women were granted the right to marry others, as if they never had been married to their clerical spouses. The priests' beliefs were not questioned; indeed, many of those deprived of office were impeccably Romanist in their theology. It was the issue of celibacy, their having offended against the ideal of a sexually pure priesthood, that most offended the Marians. Perhaps the words of the Marian bishop of Bath and Wells, Gilbert Bourne, sum it up: He would deprive "all in holy orders keeping in adulterous embraces women, upon show of feigned and pretensed matrimony" and would "separate and divorce from their women or their wives, or rather concubines, and enjoin penances, as well to the clerks as to the women for such crimes."[21] The penance required was a public confession of sexual sins before their congregations. Bolstered by these actions of the new regime, public hostility now increased. Clerical couples were mocked by the populace, who pointed fingers and shouted after the women: "concubines, whores, harlots."[22]

Faced with this massive attack, what did the clerical couples do? Some went underground. Matthew Parker, future Archbishop of Canterbury, his wife Margaret, and their growing family all lived in hiding, in great danger. At one point, Parker, forced to flee for his life, was badly injured by a fall from his horse. Nonetheless, during this period he dared to publish his *Defense of Priests' Marriages.*[23] Economic hardships were severe; one priest, Thomas Godwin, supported his family by practicing medicine, but many couples piled up debts.[24]

Some couples went into exile, fleeing to Protestant centers on the continent, Zurich, Strasbourg, Basel, or Frankfurt, depending on their foreign hosts to support them. Edmund Allen's wife bore him eight children while in exile—children who were illegitimate under Mary's rule.[25] At least one priest's wife and child died of the plague, and doubtless many others suffered physical and mental hardship as refugees.[26]

Other priests, unable to face inquisitional examination by their bishops, gave in, renounced their wives and children, did penance, and accepted reappointment in parishes far from those they had served as married men. Although priests who risked imprisonment by remaining married excoriated those who renounced their wives—Thomas Becon called them "filthy dogs"—many did choose the humiliation of renunciation, promising not to see their former wives except in public, and providing witnesses to the fact that they now slept alone, all in order to remain in the church's employ.[27]

As to the anguish of the women caught in those degrading proceedings, the record is silent. One couple, Bishop Scory of Chichester and his wife, Elizabeth, separated and accepted the annulment of their marriage. Scory, however, did not accept reappointment, but fled the country. He returned after Queen Mary's death, and Elizabeth is known to have survived him *as his wife*. What would we give to know of the understandings, misunderstandings, and final reconciliation of this pair![28] The postmortem fate of one clergy wife, Katherine Vermigli, widow of the noted reformer Peter Martyr, is recorded. Katherine died at Oxford during King Edward's reign and was buried in the cemetery at Corpus Christi College. When Queen Mary placed Cardinal Pole in charge of the English church, he worried that the pollution Mrs. Vermigli had incurred as the wife of a priest would render her remains too contaminated to lie close to the relics of St. Frideswide. Her bones, accordingly, were dug up, and, sufficient proof of heresy lacking to burn them, they were thrown on a dunghill.[29]

A final glimpse of Marian England's opinion of priests' wives gives a slightly different slant: When a certain woman was being examined for bringing Protestant books into the country, her accuser remarked, "You know so much about Scripture you must be a priest's woman or wife."[30] Perhaps women who had married priests were beginning to be recognized, after all, for traits other than being "carnally evil."

England's return to Anglicanism in 1559 did surprisingly little, at first, to relieve clergy couples of their sufferings. Queen Elizabeth, also, disapproved of clerical marriage. She was rude to the wives and tried to prevent them and their children from living in cathedral precincts. Making marriage as difficult as possible, she ruled that a clergyman must obtain permission from his bishop and two justices of the peace before he could take a wife; that the woman, no matter what her age, must have the sanction of her parents or, lacking family, of her master and mistress; and that clergy not complying with these humiliating restrictions could be forbidden to hold any ecclesiastical office. When Elizabeth reproached her married bishops in coarse, violent language, Archbishop Parker, himself married, reported that he "was in an horror to hear such words come from her mild nature."[31] Thus both Tudor queens mirrored their much-married father's contempt for clerical marriage, and clerical spouses learned that female sovereigns brought them not clemency, but ire.

So conservatives continued to hound married priests. At Worcester in the 1560s, Bishop Sandys was accused of not being a gentleman, since he kept his wife with him. The dean and chapter were charged with breaking up the church's organ to melt it down into dishes and bedsteads for the wives of the prebendaries. And the wives were said to place themselves above the other women of the town by their behavior in church and by their luxurious dress. Hostile laity attempted to ruin Bishop Sandys again—this time by planting a married woman in his bedroom and surprising the two of them there. But Sandys took the scandal to the royal council and was exonerated.[32]

And yet despite the persecutions, clerical families not only survived, but prospered. They prospered in the literal sense, since clerical incomes rose with the agricultural boom of the late sixteenth century; parsonages were expanded and a few luxury features were added. Once the legality of clerical marriage was settled in 1559, many clergymen appear to have gotten ahead by marrying upward. But the clergy's upward mobility came about even more markedly because of the life-patterns of their children: Their daughters' hands were sought by the gentry, and their sons went to university in increasing numbers, sat in Parliament, and secured or even inherited parish livings. In a recent work, the historian John Pruett observes, "With the Reformation came clerical marriages and, shortly thereafter, clerical sons—new competitors for parish livings." He adds that, whereas during the Reformation most priests were from the middle or lower ranks of society, by 1700, because many came from the now-established clerical families, they were seen as gentry. And by the end of Queen Anne's reign, the *majority* of clergy were sons of parsons or of gentry, the clergy having acquired a more exclusive, genteel social image.[33]

In the earlier days, of course, some families still struggled with insufficient incomes. One wife supplemented the meager earnings by washing the church's linen, and widows of clergy, especially those with large families, seldom were sufficiently provided for. But by and large, marriage increased the standing of Anglican clergy in general, both financially and socially, Pruett argues.[34] Clearly, the wives had contributed to that happy condition.

The contributions for which they were praised, however, are those for which women stereotypically are praised—prolific families of six, eight, ten, or more children and abilities that enabled them to be "prudent and provident managers" and "gracious hostesses." Impressive as these accomplishments are in the private sphere, for our task in women's history, it is necessary to ask, What did the wives themselves contribute to the new religious movement? When research reveals almost no trace of their public participation, a further question arises— Why not? Some clues lie in the church's general views of marriage and of womanhood.

What Did Clergy Wives Contribute to the New Church?

As one result of the continuous pressures against married clerics during the reigns of Mary and Elizabeth, Anglican clergymen were inspired to write defenses of marriage in general, and of clerical marriage in particular. No longer did they compose devotional literature praising virginity and celibacy, but instead—and here is the clue to the remainder of this essay—they published many tracts defending the godliness of marriage.[35]

By *marriage,* however, what did they mean? A prime source for their views can be found in the *Book of Homilies* as republished early in Elizabeth's reign. This important collection of sermons, designated to be read from every pulpit in England, and when completed, to be read through again, had been published first in 1547 as a compilation of twelve homilies—none, it is important to note, on marriage. The original edition came no closer to the topic than the homily "Against Whoredom and Uncleanness," which expressed a strongly negative attitude toward sexuality, failed even to

106

mention marriage until the last part of the sermon, and required the preacher to perorate:

Finally, all such as feel in themselves a sufficiency and ability, through the working of God's spirit, to lead a sole and continent life, let them praise God for his gift, and seek all means possible to maintain the same; as by reading of holy scriptures, by godly meditations, by continual prayers, and such other virtuous exercises. If we all on this wise will endeavour ourselves to eschew fornication . . . glorifying [God] in our bodies by . . . leading an innocent . . . life, we may be sure to be [among the] Blessed . . . the pure in heart.[36]

Written for all Christians, this sermon is of a piece with the ideology expressed in the same year in the statute on clerical marriage: Marry if you must, to avoid fornication, but celibacy is the better way.

When the *Book of Homilies* was reissued fifteen years later, the Anglican magisterium was of a somewhat different mind. Praise of "a sole and continent life" had vanished and been replaced by a warm advocacy of "the friendly fellowship" of marriage. The extent to which experience with fifteen years of priestly marriage was responsible for that change is a subject worth researching elsewhere. Indisputable is the fact that a sermon titled "An Homily of the State of Matrimony" was newly added. There both spouses are urged to pray with and for each other, to forbear each other's faults, to avoid the snares of wrath and jealousy laid by the devil. In noticeable contrast to medieval instruction, husbands are even urged not to beat their wives and, in an early antimacho argument, are assured that such forebearance is not "womanish."[37] When the sermon gives its reasons, however, its deeper presuppositions emerge. Men should not beat their wives, because, after all, wives are like a merchant's property, and they should be well-handled. Women are to be honored: "[Give] honour to the wife, as unto the weaker vessel, and as unto them that are heirs also of the grace of life, that your prayers be not hindered (I Peter 3:7)." Because of the wife's weakness, the husband must be the leader and author of love, using moderation, not tyranny. Having established the man as the head of the family, the sermon then fully describes woman as a weak creature, not endowed with like strength and constancy of mind; therefore they be the sooner disquieted, and they be the more prone to all weak affections and dispositions of mind, more than men be . . . and more vain in their phantasies and opinions.[38]

Husbands must "teach them, weed out the uncomely manners from their minds."

Wives are admonished to maintain the hierarchy of authority—that is, to obey their husbands, but to command their children and their servants. The good wife pleases her man, does not offend him, acknowledges his authority, and above all, seeks her true adornment in suffering, in "the griefs, pains, and perils of matrimony," in "relinquishing the liberty of [her] own rule, in pain of [her] travail and of bringing up children." And women could cooperate with the royal government's plan, as expressed a year or two later in the famous Statute of Laborers, to provide sufficient workers at every level of the English economy: If a husband holds only a minor job, the wife is not to complain or in any way put pressure upon him to "better himself."[39] Here is a godly admonition that is pure Tudor co-optation of the working class!

In sum, the "Homily of the State of Matrimony" of 1562 documents the early Anglican view of women as obedient and mindless partners in a strongly male-centered family ideal. Continuing this thesis, in earnest tracts such as Thomas Becon's popular *Book of Matrimony* and the Puritan Robert Cleaver's *Godly Form of Householde Government,* Anglican writers put forward an entirely androcentric, Pauline view of gender relations: Woman is inferior, must submit in all things to her husband, and must remain silent in all public matters. When the theologians finally declared acceptance of clerical marriage to be an article of faith in the Thirty-Nine Articles, and again in 1567, it was this patriarchal form of marriage they had in mind.[40]

An even more condescending attitude toward womanhood was expressed by the Nonconformist minister Richard Baxter, normally known for his moderation, who wrote in 1673:

Few [women] are patient and manlike. . . . It is no small patience which the natural imbecility of the female sex requireth [husbands] to prepare. . . . Women are commonly . . . of weak understandings, and unable to reform themselves. They are betwixt a man and a child.[41]

Writing at about the time young Susanna Annesley was growing up in a Nonconformist home, Baxter, that great Puritan divine, concluded his thoughts on the subject of wives: "Live in a voluntary subjection and obedience to your husbands."[42] Other Puritan authors laid great stress on the duty of breast-feeding one's children and of meeting—indeed, anticipating—every need of one's husband. Their comments reflected the common opinion that women were inferior to men and, even worse, possessed no power of reasoning at all.

It followed from this that women could take no public leadership in the church. Having abolished convents, the Church of England retained only one vestigial role for women's public participation—the right of midwives, in an emergency, to baptize the newborn. Although some of the sects—for instance, the Quakers—introduced new roles for women, including the offices of missionary and deaconess, and permitted women to preach, in shocking contradiction to the mores of English society as a whole, the Anglican church held firm to its view that since women could not be ordained, there was no point at all in assigning them ecclesiastical roles.[43]

Given this lack of encouragement, or even of permission, to function as thinking adults, it is not surprising that the record gives no sixteenth-century evidence of "leadership" among English clergy wives, of ideas generated, of projects launched. The Puritan upheavals in the seventeenth century, by contrast, will bring out the self-hood of clergy wives, but during most of the sixteenth century, they remained in the traditional arena of the home.[44] There, it must be acknowledged, in circumstances that would have tried the saints, those women made their contribution to clerical marriage and to later clergy wives simply by surviving massive sexual/social ambivalence. Given the official and popular hatred unleashed in the 1540s and 1550s, the first clerical wives did well to remain alive, to remain married, and to found families. Even after the legal restrictions against them were lifted, they faced several generations of suspicion and hostility from many sides. That, within a century, clerical families will have emerged from the onus of a centuries-old taboo to become part of the English establishment, and that the wives will have risen from being members of a despised group to positions of acceptance, is surely to be credited greatly to those women.[45]

And yet we must ask if clergy wives, then or now—Anglican or other—ever have won a place of full respect. Very few critical studies of ministers' wives have been made by any denomination in any period, but several recent reports indicate that spouses of ordained persons often are taken for granted, used, or even resented by congregations and ecclesiastical hierarchies, despite the fact that many spouses have religious callings and religious training of their own. Perhaps, now that male spouses of female clergy have begun to appear, the role of "minister's wife" will be reevaluated.[46]

We will conclude with some reflections on an ordinary clerical couple of the mid-seventeenth century, Jane and Ralph Josselin. Their life during and after the Puritan Revolution is known from Ralph's copious diary.[47] Although his beliefs were Nonconformist, he managed to trim his sails sufficiently after the Anglican Restoration of 1660 to retain his East Anglian village parish.

Jane Constable and Ralph Josselin appear to have fallen in love at first sight. They married when she was nineteen and he twenty, and lived out what must be called a happy marriage for forty-three years. They appear to have chosen each other and never to have regretted it, except perhaps for a period late in life after their children had left home. Ten children were born live to them, five surviving the parents, and in addition, Jane suffered five miscarriages.[48]

Ralph took deep pleasure in their parenthood, carefully recording Jane's announcements of pregnancy; taking part in the births; registering great concern for her pain in labor, her difficulties in recovery, her ability to nurse; and, in fact, declaring that he valued children "above gold and jewels." Ralph and Jane shared many decisions about child-raising and pretended to themselves that they chose their children's mates (when in fact the children did their own choosing). They also shared much of the endless work of the yeoman farmer, even working together to pull down trees.

The marriage bond seems to have been the most important experience in this East Anglian clergyman's life—and indeed, in his wife's, if we may infer such a private sentiment on her part from her husband's diary. The Reverend Mr. Josselin even referred publicly to his love for Jane, in a sermon at a parishioner's funeral:

> You can consider, here I was wont to see my dear Wife; here to enjoy her delightful imbraces; her counsel, spiritual Discourses, furthermore, encouragement in the wayes of God, I was wont to finde her an help to ease me of the burthen and trouble of house-hold-affairs, whose countenance welcomed me home with joy.[49]

Yet even this exemplary relationship was vulnerable to the conviction of male superiority—the sexist prejudices built into the Josselins' society and religion. In summing up the problem this ingrained mentality caused, he reflected on the text from First Peter—the same text that had been embedded in the 1562 Elizabethan sermon on marriage:

> I find my heart apt to unquietnes in my relation [i.e. wife] and it troubles mee, and yett it returneth on mee, I thinke I have cause, but I am sure I should bee more patient, and counsellable than I am, oh that I could looke at my wife not as under weakness but as an heire of the same grace of life and live with her as such.[50]

Oh, indeed, that woman might have been looked upon as heir of the same grace of life—and not as under weakness! This was the teaching, not so different from the medieval belief that women do not have souls, which kept all women—clergy wives included—from that full participation in their world which we long to hear about. The Reformation may have revalued all marriage, both lay and clerical, but the full benefits to women that might have accrued from that revaluation could scarcely be explored in so rigidly patriarchal a world, and indeed were sacrificed in the name of preserving the time-honored superiority of the male. The image of the post-Reformation Anglican clergy wife which emerges from close study of the sources therefore is restricted to the most conventional female roles. It certainly did not provide an adequate model for the challenges that early Methodist women faced.

6

SUSANNA WESLEY

Frank Baker

Methodism loves her saints, and the average Methodist is tempted not to inquire too closely into the fleshly reality behind the plaster images. Methodism canonized one woman many generations ago, chiefly because she was the mother of the Wesleys, and all except a few suspicious scholars have done her reverence ever since. Yet in a time of advances in the history of women, it is surely necessary to probe the blend of myth and mystique that surrounds this woman who bore, nurtured, educated, encouraged, and prayed for the founders of a major movement of modern Christianity—to discover if Susanna Wesley's halo truly fits. Because many facts unknown to her canonizers must be uncovered, close examination of Susanna is difficult and challenging. Like her son Saint John, however, Saint Susanna bears minute scrutiny well; she makes perhaps an even greater impact upon the mind armed with facts than upon the uncritical imagination.[1]

The main facts of her life may be quickly summarized. She was born Susanna Annesley on January 20, 1669 (Old Style), in a tall gloomy brick house that still stands in Spital Square, off Bishopsgate in London. On November 12, 1688, she married Samuel Wesley, a newly ordained deacon of the Church of England. She was then nineteen to his twenty-six.[2] They had many children, almost half of whom died in infancy. She was widowed at age sixty-six and died in 1742, at seventy-three.

Behind this humdrum outline, however, what were her childhood dreams? How did she get along with her husband? What kind of mother was she? What were her frustrations as a woman in a man's world; what were her principles, her enthusiasms, her triumphs, her lasting influence? This study seeks to answer such questions, if far too briefly for full satisfaction, by tracing the unfolding of her life as a Puritan, a parent, a pastor, a protagonist, and finally, to discover how she became a pattern.

Puritan

Susanna Annesley was born into Puritanism, the daughter of the Reverend Dr. Samuel Annesley (c. 1620–1699), who was called the St. Paul of the Nonconformists and praised even by the sceptical Daniel Defoe for "the zeal, the candor, the sincerity of his mind, the largeness of his charity, the greatness of his soul, the sweetness of his temper, and the vastness of his designs to propagate the kingdom and interest of his Master."[3] Susanna was the last of twenty-five children.[4] The Annesley household was in fact a family church, where were laid, in Susanna's words, "the foundations of solid piety . . . in sound principles and virtuous dispositions."[5] Puritanism certainly meant "solid piety" to her, but it did not imply either joylessness or tyranny.[6] Indeed, from her youth Susanna was what now might be called a liberated woman—because her father was a liberated man. In an era of arranged marriages, Annesley told John Dunton, suitor to his daughter Elizabeth, that a father's consent was not enough—Dunton must win the girl's love. The same was surely true when Samuel Wesley came a-courting young Susanna, whom he apparently had met at Elizabeth's wedding, when Susanna was twelve and Samuel was a young student training for the Dissenting ministry.[7]

Even at twelve, however, Susanna Annesley exercised a thoughtful independence and deliberately turned away from her father's presbyterianism to embrace the episcopal Church of England, drawing up a document carefully recounting her reasons for such a step. Her understanding parent generously accepted her allegiance to the church that had thrown him out of his living before her birth, and they remained warmly attached to each other to the end of his days, when he bequeathed to her his manuscripts.[8] She also inherited much of Dr. Annesley's own acumen, his gentle disposition, and his independent spirit and was the only one of his children to make

113

a major contribution to Christian history. Meanwhile, her future husband was following a similar theological path. Shortly after young Susanna had done so, Samuel Wesley also renounced the Nonconformists, to continue his education at Exeter College, Oxford.[9] Both seem to have been prompted by mixed motives. The greater sense of Christian continuity in the Church of England weighed heavily, as did a desire to shed the religious controversies that had embittered the middle years of their century. Remembering their greater sufferings for the sake of conscience, the Nonconformists remained more militant concerning those controversies. After their marriage, Samuel and Susanna seem not to have discussed those adversities with their children; it was not until his middle years that John Wesley discovered the Nonconformist martyrs in his family heritage.[10] Nevertheless, much Puritan independence and piety did enter Methodism through John, derived from his parents, and especially from his mother.

Parent

Political and ecclesiastical turmoil were ushers at the wedding of Susanna Annesley and Samuel Wesley. Some months before, seven Anglican bishops had protested against the Roman Catholic pressures of King James II. On June 8, 1688, they were committed to the Tower of London and on June 29, tried for seditious libel. Their acquittal and release on June 30 was very popular, and on that same day William of Orange was invited to replace James as king of England, to begin a new era in British history. On June 19, Samuel Wesley had graduated from Oxford, and he returned to London on July 1 to the peal of church bells all along the road, saluting the released bishops. On August 7, Samuel was ordained deacon and accepted a temporary appointment as curate of St. Botolph, Aldersgate, London. This gave him the welcome opportunity to marry Susanna on November 12 in the parish church of St. Marylebone—where later their son Charles was buried.[11]

Within a short time, however, the couple realized that their "most passionate love" had led them into an improvident union: A temporary appointment was not a good base from which to support a young wife and a prospective family. Fortunately, Susanna escaped pregnancy for several months, though Samuel was anxious. Needing money, he accepted a naval chaplaincy (which paid twice as much as a shore-based curacy), and Susanna conceived their first child shortly before he left for his ship. In his absence she returned to her parents' home in Spitalfields, where they both seem to have been staying. After a ghastly voyage, Samuel returned in November 1689, just in time for their first wedding anniversary and picked up a little more money as a hack writer and printer's reader. Their first baby was born at the Annesleys' on February 10, 1690, to be christened Samuel, like his father and grandfather. Shortly afterward, Samuel Wesley was offered a curacy at Newington Butts, in Surrey, and took a house there for his new family. In the summer of 1691 he at last secured a permanent church living as rector of South Ormsby in Lincolnshire. In 1695 he was instituted to the "living" at Epworth, vacant through the consecration of Dr. James Gardiner as Bishop of Lincoln, though for a couple of years Samuel continued to serve as a paid curate at South Ormsby. Only in 1697 did he take up permanent residence in Epworth, in the isolated low-lying Isle of Axholme, drained in the previous century.[12]

The marriage of Susanna and Samuel was prolific, though the number of their offspring fell short of her own parents' total. Susanna was just past twenty-one when she gave birth to her first child, and either forty or forty-one when she had her last. During those twenty years she bore a minimum of seventeen to a maximum of nineteen children. The solid documentation of nine births has led to the correction of several errors in family tradition, passed on by John Wesley himself, including the belief that he had been christened John Benjamin. Much remains obscure, however. The children were almost evenly divided in sex, with nine girls and eight boys documented, and two possible children of unknown sex. The boys were subject to greater mortality, only three of the eight surviving, while seven of the nine girls reached maturity.[13] The highest mortality was among the two, or probably three sets of twins. Of these only one child survived—Anne, the twin of the real John Benjamin, whose daughter would marry John Jarvis, a founder of John

Street Methodist Church in New York.[14] Although during this arduous twenty years never a year passed that Susanna Wesley did not either begin or end a pregnancy, her tendency toward twinning and the frequent deaths brought her the occasional luxury of a few months' vacation from child-bearing. Her longest respite from pregnancy preceded the birth of John. Here a contemporary source enables us to clothe a legend with flesh.

The coming of William and Mary to the throne of England in 1688 caused much searching of conscience among loyal clergy, who found it impossible to swear allegiance to a king who was not of their own divinely appointed royal line and thus break their previous oaths to James II. Nine bishops and about four hundred priests, as nonjurors, were thereupon deprived of their church livings. For Samuel Wesley, this raised no problem, especially as William's elected status was legitimized by the fact that his wife Mary was the daughter of James II. Susanna's sympathies were with the nonjurors; she was distressed, but maintained a discreet silence. Nor did the death of Mary in 1694 cause any family eruption. With the death of the exiled James II, however, on September 6, 1701, the way was paved for marital conflict. One evening early in 1702, Samuel Wesley called Susanna to his study after family prayers, to ask why she had not said "Amen" after the prayer for King William. As she recounted the incident to Lady Yarborough, Susanna could not recollect the words of her reply, but continued: "Too, too well I remember what followed. He immediately kneeled down and imprecated the divine vengeance upon himself and all his posterity if ever he touched me more or came into a bed with me before I had begged God's pardon and his for not saying Amen to the prayer for the King."[15] Following John Wesley's account, Adam Clarke recorded Samuel's words more epigrammatically: "If we have two kings, we must have two beds."[16]

Nor did Samuel relent after March 8, 1702, when King William died and was providentially succeeded by Queen Anne, another daughter of James II. He threatened to go to sea again as a naval chaplain, though he did not leave Epworth until after Easter—and then to take his seat in London in the lower house of Convocation, the ecclesiastical body parallel to the houses of Parliament. After a two-day visit to Epworth in July, Samuel claimed that he was leaving his wife forever, though a fellow clergyman persuaded him to return at least for a time. The almost complete burning down of the parsonage on July 31, 1702, finally brought him to his senses. Again he began to sleep with Susanna, and the first fruit of their reconciliation was John.

That remarkable child, born a little more than two years after his mother's previous child, might serve students of family planning as a notable example of the benefits of "spacing." Susanna's claims in her letters during this period—that a husband "has no power over the conscience of his wife," and that "I value neither reputation, friends, or anything, in comparison of the single satisfaction of preserving a conscience void of offence towards God and man"—are powerful statements of the applicability of Christian liberty to women, and they resonate for students of church history with other great "protestant" statements.[17] At the same time, students of women's history may marvel that a woman of thirty-three, having already given birth to twelve or thirteen babies and surrounded by six children ranging in age from twelve years to nine months, could complain so bitterly about the absence of a man she insisted on calling "my master" and his denial of her conjugal rights.

In an era when most women read poorly or not at all, Susanna Wesley was well-read, independent, and thoughtful. She developed her own ideas of child-raising—largely from the influential contemporary philosopher John Locke. One principle which she took from Locke, and which has been attacked most vehemently by modern educationists, was that the first essential in training children is "to conquer their will."[18] Harassed mothers of today may marvel that by using this principle, Susanna was successful in teaching all her children, by the time they were a year old, "to fear the rod, and to cry softly," so that "that most odious noise of the crying of children was rarely heard in the house, but the family usually lived in as much quietness as if there had not been a child among them." Susanna's practice, however, was no expedient of desperation, but a deeply held spiritual policy. "This is the only foundation for a religious education," she wrote. "When this is thoroughly done, then a child is capable of being governed by the reason of its parent, till its own understanding comes to maturity. . . . Let none persuade you it is cruelty to do this; it is cruelty not to do it."[19]

Because it was practiced with both patience and love, her principle, however theoretically arguable, proved successful. While their father was a somewhat aloof figure to be respected and sometimes feared, Susanna became the focus of the children's deep affection. This was especially true as she conscientiously sought to develop their early obedience into mature understanding. Although primitive educational facilities were available in Epworth, Susanna taught her children at her own knee, from the ABCs to the deeper problems of ethics and theology. Young Samuel was even more slow to speak than most boys. John Wesley told Adam Clarke about his first words:

My brother Samuel did not attempt to speak till he was between four and five years old. . . . There was a cat in the house [at South Ormsby] which was a great favourite with him; he would frequently carry it about, and retire with it into private places. One day he disappeared. The family sought up and down for him to no purpose. My mother got alarmed for his safety, and went through the house, loudly calling his name. At last she heard a voice from under a table, saying, "Here I am, mother!" Looking down, she to her surprise saw Sammy and his cat.

Clarke added: "From this time he spoke regularly, and without any kind of hesitation." Following Locke, Mrs. Wesley took the development of speech as the signal to begin formal education of a child.[20] On February 11, 1695, the day after Samuel's fifth birthday, she arranged her household chores so that she could devote a few hours to teaching him the alphabet; she went on to teach him to read from the first chapter of Genesis, spelling out each verse in turn—reading it over and over "till he could read it off-hand without any hesitation"— and then moving on to the next. Two years later, the same process was begun with Emilia, and it was continued in the same way to the last child, little Kezia—except that in her case Susanna was persuaded to begin earlier than the fifth birthday—though in fact Kezia took much longer.[21] By this time Mrs. Wesley had regular school sessions, from 9:00 to

12:00 and from 2:00 until 4:00, in a room set apart for that purpose.[22]

She refused to teach any so-called practical skill until her children, especially the girls, could read well, claiming: "The putting children to learn sewing before they can read perfectly is the very reason why so few women can read fit to be heard, and never to be well understood."[23]

Pastor

By a combination of events, Susanna Wesley's motherly devotion to basic education was gradually transformed into a self-conscious pastoral ministry to her family, and from that into a ministry that extended to the parish in general. John Wesley clearly recognized this, testifying that his mother, "as well as her father and grandfather, her husband, and her three sons, had been, in her measure and degree, a preacher of righteousness."[24]

When she was about thirty (with apparently only five young children at home) Susanna began to follow her father's pattern of setting aside an hour morning and evening—and occasionally even a period at noon—for reading and private devotions, including self-examination and meditation. In conjunction with this practice, she compiled a journal which furnished her with material for letters on moral and religious themes.[25]

Later, menopause brought a deepening of her spirituality. She seems to have undergone a strengthened urge to commune with her journal. At least much more of it remains from this period. As her child-bearing years ended and the pattern of grounding all her children solidly in their elementary education was established, her emphases in child-rearing almost inevitably moved from concerns of the material and mental to those of the moral and spiritual. To all these she rededicated herself in her journal:

It is, perhaps, one of the most difficult things in the world to preserve a devout and serious temper of mind in the midst of much worldly business. . . . But where a numerous family and a narrow fortune oblige to it, it is not to be declined, lest we break the order of providence . . . We must work so much harder, we must be careful to redeem time from sleep, eating, dressing, unnecessary visits, and trifling conversation.[26]

The fire that destroyed the parsonage during the night of February 9, 1709, constituted a terrible emotional shock for Susanna Wesley, in the last month of what was probably her last pregnancy. Unable to climb to safety through a window and forced back from the door three times by the fury of the flames, she wrote, "I besought our blessed Saviour's help, and then waded through the fire, naked as I was."[27] The ordeal was worsened by fear for five-year-old Jackie, trapped by himself in an upper bedroom. The trying months of the aftermath were almost as traumatic. For nearly a year, while the new rectory was being built, their devout, carefully ordered life was disrupted. The children were scattered over the country, in homes perhaps as loving, but not so lovingly regimented. When finally they were reunited, Susanna was in great distress because some of them had learned "a clownish accent and many rude ways."[28]

During this period Susanna struggled to continue the devotional education of her older children by correspondence, as she had been doing for some years with Samuel at Westminster School.[29] To her namesake Susanna, now fourteen or fifteen, staying with Mehetabel at their Uncle Matthew's in London, she wrote: "Dear Suky, Since our misfortunes have separated us from each other, and we can no longer enjoy the opportunities we once had of conversing together, I can no other way discharge the duty of a parent, or comply with my inclination of doing you all the good I can, but by writing." This introduced a detailed and lengthy exposition of the Apostles' Creed, and a few weeks later Susanna sent a copy to Samuel.[30] Similar original treatises followed, even after most of the children had returned home. Some of these have been preserved in whole or in part, including a noteworthy dialogue on the being and attributes of God, together with the principles of natural and revealed religion.[31]

The return of her scattered family to the rebuilt rectory reinforced Susanna's pastoral vocation as she sought to reform their bad habits. She instituted "the custom of singing psalms at beginning and leaving school, morning and evening." She enrolled the older children in leading the younger ones in Bible study, followed by private prayers, both before breakfast and in the early evening.[32] In her own private devotions she continually turned her mind to devising more that she could do for her children. Her journal for May 17, 1711, five days after young John had been nominated for Charterhouse School, recorded a new vow: "I would, if I durst, humbly offer thee myself and all that thou hast given me. . . . I do intend to be more particularly careful of the soul of this child that thou hast so mercifully provided for, than ever I have been, that I may do my endeavour to instil into his mind the principles of thy true religion and virtue." A week later she admonished herself: "'Tis necessary to observe some method in instructing and writing for your children. Go through your brief exposition on the Ten Commandments, which are a summary of the moral law. Then briefly explain the principles of revealed religion. . . . Subjoin by way of essay a short discourse on the being and attributes of God."[33] Within a few months her call to the care of souls was to find its method, and to find also a new depth and strength, through the reading of a book.

From December 11, 1711, the rector of Epworth had been in London attending the sessions of Convocation. His wife wrote to him on February 6, 1712:

Soon after you went to London Emily found in your study the account of the Danish missionaries, which, having never seen, I ordered her to read to me. I was never, I think, more affected with anything than with the relation of their travels. . . . Their labours refreshed my soul beyond measure. . . . For several days I could think or speak of little else.

Then came a kind of revelation:

At last it came into my mind, Though I am not a man, nor a minister of the gospel, and so cannot be engaged in such a worthy employment as they were, yet . . . I might do somewhat more than I do. . . . I might pray more for *the people,* and speak with more warmth to those with whom I have an opportunity of conversing. However, I resolved to begin with my own children.[34]

She went on to describe to her husband her new family regimen. She set aside an hour or so every evening to discuss their "principal concerns" with each of the two sons and six daughters then at home, from four-year-old Charles to the two oldest girls—with whom she met on Sunday evenings. Little Kezia was still too young for schooling, let alone for pastoral counseling. John Wesley experienced only two years of this guidance, but twenty years later, they remained a golden memory. Seeking his mother's spiritual advice, he wrote from Oxford: "If you can spare me only that little part of Thursday evening which you formerly bestowed upon me in another manner, I doubt not but it would be as useful now for correcting my heart as it was then for the forming my judgment."[35]

Like the basic education that she was still furnishing all her children, this deepened pastoral concern was important for her three boys, but much more so for her seven daughters, to whom few schools and no colleges or universities were open. Susanna Wesley changed from schoolteacher to a kind of Mother Superior, helping her girls prepare to face an unsympathetic man's world by endowing them with good habits, firm principles, and a deep religious faith, and she maintained this role by correspondence long after they left home. The handful of her daughters' letters which survive reveal their warm response to her care, though none would make her mark in history as did Susanna, or reflect her character as fully as did John. Sadly, even Susanna's loving care, stiffened by Spartan discipline, was not able to forestall the problems to which their relatively sheltered life in an extremely isolated part of the country made her daughters an easy prey: for Emly (Emilia), a thwarted love affair, a cold, late marriage, and a long widowhood; for Suky (Susanna), a brutish husband from whom she fled with her four children; for crippled Molly (Mary), what her mother termed an "unequal marriage," from which she was released by death in childbirth;[36] for Hetty (Mehetabel), an illicit pregnancy, followed by a shotgun marriage to a boor, and the death of all her children in infancy; for Nancy (Anne), desertion by her husband for at least some years;[37] for Kezzy (Kezia), a brokenhearted death because her promised husband threw her over for her older sister Patty (Martha)—who, in the end, had the worst of the bargain, since the soft-spoken Oxford charmer turned out to be a seducer and a polygamist. Yet with the limited options open at the time, even to gentlewomen, it is doubtful whether any of these misfortunes could fairly be laid at their mother's door—and only a few at their father's.

Susanna's pastoral vision began, but did not end with her children; even before the *Account,* she had added a new dimension to her vocation. When away at Convocation, Samuel Wesley paid a succession of curates to perform his parish duties. These were usually young men and formed a natural source of titillation for the teenage daughters, who were starved for educated male companionship on the inland Isle of Axholme. In reconstructing the stages by which Susanna gradually was led to conduct public religious gatherings in the rectory, which in time outnumbered the regular congregation in the parish church, it is important to remember the ecclesiastical background. Of the 627 parishes in Lincolnshire, Boston was the only one that held three services on Sunday, and that only during the summer. Very few held any public worship other than morning prayer on Sunday.[38] Epworth was one of these exceptions, for when at home, Samuel Wesley also conducted evening prayer—sometimes termed the afternoon service. To fill the spiritual vacuum during his lengthy winter absences, Susanna would gather her total household—all the children and the two or three servants—to sing psalms and listen to printed sermons, apparently with some discussion of the spiritual problems thus introduced.[39] After this she would read the Order for Evening Prayer from the Book of Common Prayer. During the winter of 1710–1711, some neighbors began to join in these exercises, until time for the reading of evening prayer. This was "purely accidental," as she defensively informed her husband a year later, not wanting him to think that she had deliberately invaded his rightful territory: "Our lad told his parents; they first desired to be admitted. Then others who heard of it begged leave also. So our company increased to about thirty, and seldom exceeded forty last winter."[40]

In the winter of 1711–1712, however, two new factors were introduced—Susanna Wesley's heightened sense of pastoral vocation, from reading the *Account,* and the coming of the Reverend Godfrey Inman as temporary curate. He was a man over forty who was finding it difficult to secure priest's orders and a living, though he was more self-assured, if more inept, than most of his predecessors.[41]

Susanna's resolve to "speak with more warmth" to those who attended the Sunday evening society at the rectory quickly bore fruit. On February 6, 1712, she responded to her husband's mild remonstrance by giving him fuller details:

With those few neighbours who then came to me I discoursed more freely and affectionately *than before;* I chose the best and most awakening sermons we had, and I spent more time with them in such exercises. Since this our company has increased every night; for I dare deny none who ask admittance. Last Sunday I believe we had above two hundred, and yet many went away for want of room.[42]

And another problem had arisen. On the previous Sunday, February 3, after the meeting of "our society," the people wanted to stay on for her reading of the Order for Evening Prayer with the family. About this she was very uneasy, not sure that it was "proper for *me* to present the prayers of the people to God." She explained: "Last Sunday I would fain have dismissed them before prayers; but they begged so earnestly to stay, I durst not deny them." Now she was offering her neighbors a complete Anglican service, writing about "evening service" and "public worship," when it seems clear she is referring to this unorthodox rectory gathering.[43]

The curate Inman, angry at his failure and her success, wrote to the rector complaining that Mrs. Wesley was holding an illegal conventicle. Samuel again wrote to her, more sharply this time. Susanna did not answer until February 25, informing her husband that it seemed wiser "for both of us to take some time to consider before you determine in a matter of such great importance." The "you" was deliberate, for she left the actual decision to the one whom she had promised to obey. She carefully pointed out, however, that at the regular evening service they had usually had an attendance of no more than twenty or twenty-five, whereas now at the rectory there were between two and three hundred. The people in general were more friendly, their behavior reformed; "some families who seldom went to church now go constantly; and one person who has not been there for seven years is now prevailed upon to go with the rest."[44] Because of Inman's public objections, however, she doubted whether she would be able to persuade such as these to continue to attend church if the rector forbade the Sunday evening exercises. She suggested that it would be far wiser to let the meetings continue, at least until Samuel returned from London, which, she said, "now will not be long" (actually, Convocation in 1712 was not adjourned until July 8).[45] Susanna ended:

If you do, after all, think fit to dissolve this assembly, do not tell me that you desire me to do it, for that will not satisfy my conscience: but send me your *positive command,* in such full and express terms as may absolve me from all guilt and punishment for neglecting this opportunity of doing good when you and I shall appear before the great and awful tribunal of our Lord Jesus Christ.[46]

Wisely, the rector allowed the parsonage society to continue—with young Jackie Wesley a thoughtful member, making mental notes about an unusual but highly successful method of deepening the religious life of a community.

Protagonist

Susanna's husband died in 1735, just before her sons John and Charles set sail for Georgia; their elder brother died in 1739, shortly after their return. Thus neither of the senior male members of the family lived to see the Methodist revival, though the younger Samuel died somewhat unhappy about his brothers' experimentation with extempore prayer and their emphasis upon a personal experience of salvation. Several of the Wesley sisters, however, lived to be associated with Methodism—notably, Emly, Hetty, and Patty. Their mother lived until 1742—just long enough to see the revival well under way, with some of its emotional extremes softened and its tightly knit organization in smooth running order, ready to bring reform to a reluctant church.

On June 8, 1738, very soon after his heartwarming experience at Aldersgate, John Wesley visited his mother in Salisbury, where she was staying with Martha, and read her his spiritual autobiography, later incorporated into his *Journal.* Her own devout spirit resonated to his self-analysis. Only a year earlier she had written to a friend in words that fitted John's initial approach to religion exactly: "I verily think one great reason why Christians are so often subject to despond is that they look more to themselves than to their Saviour: they would establish a righteousness of their own to rest on, without adverting enough to the sacrifice of Christ, by which alone we are justified before God."[47] In August 1739, however, during Holy Communion, Susanna experienced a personal assurance of God's forgiveness of her sins—an element in Methodist teaching about which she had held strong reservations, probably voiced to John when he read her his now-celebrated entry for May 24, 1738: "I felt my heart strangely warmed. I felt I did trust in Christ, Christ alone for salvation; and an assurance was given me that he had taken away *my* sins, even *mine,* and saved *me* from the law of sin and death." Now, a year later, Susanna Wesley echoed those emphatic personal pronouns: "While my son Hall [Martha's husband] was pronouncing those words, in delivering the cup to me, 'The blood of our Lord Jesus Christ, which was given for thee,' the words struck through my heart, and I knew God for Christ's sake had forgiven *me* all *my* sins."[48] Not only had Susanna's Puritan piety set the stage for Methodism; but in her old age she had reached a new stage of vigorous spiritual life through a typically Methodist "heart-warming." She became even more en rapport with her sons.

It was his Methodist mother, almost certainly in 1741, who restrained John Wesley from hastily destroying Methodism's greatest instrument for spreading the revival nationwide and worldwide—the lay preacher. "Take care what you do with respect to that young man, for he is as surely called of God to preach as you are," she said, with which Wesley eventually agreed: "It is the Lord: let him do what seemeth him good."[49]

As the revival gained momentum, Susanna Wesley even entered the literary lists as one of Methodism's earliest protagonists in print. When George Whitefield, now converted to predestinarianism, in *A Letter to the Reverend Mr. John Wesley* (1741) attacked his former tutor's sermon *Free Grace,* Wesley's mother, age seventy-one, sprang to the defense with a reply: *Some Remarks on a Letter from the Reverend Mr. Whitefield to the Reverend Mr. Wesley, in a Letter from a Gentlewoman to her Friend.*[50] She refuted the extremes of Calvinism: "If, as Calvin says, 'God speaketh by his ministers to reprobates that they may be deafer, he gives light to them that they may be the blinder,' what good man would not rather choose to be a hangman than a minister of the gospel?" Shrewdly she asserted that the greatest stumbling block in the Wesleys' teaching was their proclamation of the possibility of Christian perfection rather than universal redemption, and that "if they would let the former alone," many predestinarians "would forgive them the latter."[51]

The "friend" to whom this pamphlet was addressed was almost certainly Whitefield's patron, the Countess of Huntingdon, to whom Susanna wrote from the Foundery in London:

I do indeed rejoice in my sons, and am much pleased that they have in any measure been serviceable to your ladyship. You'll pardon the fondness of a mother if I exceed in commending them, but I've known few (if any) that have laboured more diligently and unweariedly in the service of our dear Lord. And blessed be his great name, he hath set his seal to their ministry, and hath made them instrumental in bringing many souls to God. And though in the eye of the world they appear despicable, men of no estate or figure, and daily suffer contempt, reproach, and shame among men, yet to me they appear more honorable than they would do if the one were Archbishop of Canterbury and the other of York, for I esteem the reproach of Christ greater riches than all the treasures in England.[52]

Methodists, like Puritans, "died well." Susanna Wesley, at the end, left physical weakness behind; her last moments were described by her son John: "Her look was calm and serene, and her eyes fixed upward, while we commended her soul to God. . . . And then, without any struggle or sigh or groan, the soul was set at liberty. We stood round the bed, and fulfilled her last request, uttered a little before she lost her speech: 'Children, as soon as I am released, sing a psalm of praise to God.'"[53]

Pattern

That John Wesley was a remarkable man and that his mother was a remarkable woman is widely accepted. Too often, however, we have failed to see that they were remarkable in many of the same ways and that this was largely because of her example and advice. Seeking a contemporary model to place alongside the great example of Jesus, Wesley patterned himself after his mother, just as she had patterned herself after her father. Later Methodists frequently have patterned themselves after John Wesley. For Methodist women, especially, the pattern has sometimes been Susanna, rather than John. Yet in effect, the patterns are one and the same: What Susanna as a woman did more or less in private, John did in the public eye.

The preparation and presentation of John Wesley's correspondence with his mother for volume 25 of the Oxford Edition of *Wesley's Works* has revealed anew to this writer the immense spiritual and intellectual stature of a woman who had received no formal higher education and who was surrounded by large families throughout her life. Editing those letters has also brought fresh awareness of the many-sided nature of her influence upon her son. It becomes clear that John Wesley constantly turned to Susanna for advice, not simply because she was his mother, but because she was exceptionally well-read and extremely wise in the ways of both God and man. As a critic she successfully challenged the pertinence and logic of his thoughts about humility, set him right on an appropriate definition of faith, and claimed that "the doctrine of predestination, as maintained by the rigid Calvinists, is very shocking . . . because it directly charges the most h[oly] God with being the author of sin." She was fully prepared to discuss philosophical points, and added a warning:

Dear J[acky], suffer now a word of advice. However curious you may be in searching into the natures or distinguishing the properties of the passions or virtues, for your own private satisfaction, be very cautious of giving definitions in public assemblies, for it does not answer the true end of preaching, which is to mend men's lives, not to fill their heads with unprofitable speculations.[54]

As a matter of course she remained his informant and mentor on family matters, telling him how she had visited Hetty in a frustrated attempt to reconcile the daughter with her angry father, and chiding, "Charles is greatly to blame in not writing to Sam." With something of a mother-in-law's jealousy— though in this instance with far more justification than is usual—she warned John about his brother Samuel's wife, who treated him (though not his brother Charles) with remarkable civility: "Never put it in the power of that w[oman] to hurt you; stand upon your guard, and converse with caution." She warned him also that it was not wise to continue to correspond with his "dear Varanese" after her marriage to the Reverend John Chapone. In this instance her counsel was fruitless; although Wesley sought and carefully considered his mother's advice, he did not always take it.[55]

By nature, John Wesley had been a very thoughtful child. His eventual style of life was largely the result of his mother's example and training, to which he was highly sensitive. She herself accomplished so much under the most trying circumstances because she had a daily timetable and a set of household rules, as well as a disciplined mind. She was a "methodist" long before her son was—indeed, long before the critical term was coined. Perhaps he was a Methodist *because* she was. In answer to his repeated requests, she "collected the principal rules [she] observed in educating [her] family" and set them down in a famous letter. She began: "The children were always put into a regular method of living, in such things as they were capable of, from their birth; as in dressing and undressing, changing their linen, etc." Here is surely the seed of Wesley's passion for rules—rules for "band" leaders, rules for sick-visitors, rules for preachers, the *General Rules* for Methodist societies, and a host of others. His rules for Kingswood School were closely patterned upon those of the Epworth household, as were many of Charles Wesley's hymns for parents and children.[56]

Individual features of John Wesley's spiritual discipline, such as self-examination, the need for regularity in devotions, the value of meditation, and the redeeming of time were dependent upon his mother's practices.[57] These Susanna had gained chiefly from her own Puritan father, who had urged his congregation to "perseverance in godliness": "You may live by faith, while you walk by rule; you may walk believingly and cheerfully, while you walk regularly." Even the strong influence of Roman Catholic mystics was evident first in Susanna Wesley, for whom *Spiritual Combat* (then attributed to Juan de Castaniza), with its emphasis upon the pursuit of Christian perfection and a readiness to suffer in that quest, became a favorite work.[58] It was a favorite for John also, used with his Oxford colleagues in 1732, though he probably knew it earlier.[59] His mother's reading ranged far and wide, and she encouraged him in similar eclectic tastes. The extant correspondence for his Oxford years touches on Seneca, Thomas à Kempis, Tasso, Juan de Castaniza, Bishop Jeremy Taylor, Richard Baxter, Bishop John Pearson, Gaston de Renty, Bishop Thomas Sprat, William Sherlock, Henry Scougal, John Norris, "heretic" Samuel Clarke, Bishop George Berkeley, Richard Fiddes, George Cheyney, and Alexander Pope.[60] John Wesley later published abridgments of several of the books Susanna had recommended.[61] Even his strong eucharistic emphasis seems to have sprung from the high Puritan tradition represented by his mother.[62]

Susanna's piety, however, was combined with a strong rational element, which also seems markedly to have affected John, who was never ready to let his emotions run away with his reason. Yet again she anticipated him in stressing that while God did not expect human beings to cast aside their powers of thought, some essential ingredients in the full Christian life are beyond the comprehension of the human mind; the essence of religion is revealed and conveyed by God alone and can be perceived and accepted only through faith.[63] In sum, she was able to crystallize his theological thought and assist him in his pastoral functions as an Oxford tutor and Methodist leader.[64] Although his mother's approach was at first somewhat legalistic, as was his, the seeds of Wesley's later teaching on the way of salvation were present in her letters even during his Oxford days, and they would be more fully articulated after her own experience of Christian assurance.[65]

At the time Susanna led the large enthused society meetings in the Epworth rectory, her son John was a thoughtful young boy on the verge of being confirmed by Bishop William Wake.[66] No remaining documents detail the impact upon his budding churchmanship of her independent proclamation of the gospel to needy people in unorthodox surroundings (in spite of legalistic complaints), but there can be little doubt that the rise of the Methodist societies owed much, not only to the latent Nonconformity in Wesley's genes, but to his mother's prophetic example in the rectory fore-kitchen. Family worship at Epworth also accustomed him to sing psalms as an expression of warm Christian fellowship, apart from public worship in a church—later a trademark of Methodism. In their early correspondence he and his mother discussed the theme of Christian liberty—the freedom to obey a God-guided conscience, whatever man might say or do. Undoubtedly those letters helped John to his final position on ecclesiastical priorities: "I dare not in conscience spend my time and strength on externals"—including his response to the Church of England as an establishment—"I neither set it up nor pull it down. But let you and I build up the City of God."[67] Such thinking gradually broadened into a truly ecumenical approach, summed up admirably in his 1755 sermon, *Catholic Spirit.*[68]

Nor can there be any question that Wesley's mother affected his approach to women in general, giving them a higher status in his eyes and a higher function in his societies than they otherwise would have had. His admiration for her nurtured similar qualities in his own character, some of which might be termed feminine traits: neatness, uncomplaining acceptance of hardship and suffering, meekness and patience in teaching others, serenity in the midst of a whirl of activities, chaste precision of speech and writing.[69] Perhaps this very admiration, which almost amounted to reverence, also lessened Wesley's chances of deep marital happiness, for it was almost impossible to find another such woman. Nevertheless, his mother's example did prepare him to incorporate women widely as workers and officers in the Methodist societies, not only as sick-visitors and band and class leaders, but even for a few, who were specially gifted and called, as preachers.

As Susanna Wesley provided a pattern for her famous son, so she has for his spiritual sons, and especially for his spiritual daughters, through the centuries and across the oceans. As thinkers and seekers; as daughters, mothers, wives; as Christian preachers, leaders, social workers; as educators, writers, historians, Methodist women—and their sisters in other traditions—will continue to find challenge and inspiration in Susanna Wesley, not simply as a figure for joint veneration with the male founder of Methodism; not simply as the mother of the Wesleys, but in many respects as the devotional, theological, and ecclesiastical mother of the Methodist revival.

A PARTNERSHIP OF EQUALITY

Emora T. Brannan

In 1877, the enterprising young pastor John Franklin Goucher sought the hand of Mary Cecelia Fisher in marriage. Mary's father, Dr. John Fisher, was a wise, prudent, respected member of the Methodist Episcopal Church and the first president of the lay electoral college of the Baltimore Conference. Fisher was impressed with the zeal and industry of his daughter's suitor, who already had served a charge of eight churches on the Baltimore circuit. His abilities recognized and rewarded by church officials, Goucher was now pastoring a single charge in Baltimore City.

Yet the wealthy Dr. Fisher had reason to be dubious about Goucher's intentions. Fisher openly questioned whether the young preacher, realizing that Mary possessed a large personal fortune and would inherit an even larger one, might be desiring this marriage for the money involved. Undaunted, the Reverend John Goucher replied, "I want her for her own sake, but I think I could do a great deal of good with the money too."[1]

This unabashed reply so delighted Dr. Fisher that he gave his immediate positive response. A wedding was planned for early 1878, but three days before Christmas 1877, John Fisher died. In a quiet private ceremony, the marriage of Mary Fisher and John Goucher was solemnized on December 24, 1877.

Together, John Franklin and Mary Fisher Goucher embarked on a marriage that is well characterized as a unique career in ministry. Here we will seek to recover the vision toward which their three major philanthropic efforts were directed in the Methodist Episcopal Church: world missions and the education of blacks and of women.

Mary Cecelia Fisher, five years younger than her future

husband, was born on March 22, 1850, in Cecil County, Maryland. Her Methodist heritage was impeccable. Her great-grandfather had been a class leader in the Lovely Lane Society at the time of the organization of American Methodism in 1784. As a leader of the laity in one of the major conferences of Methodism, the spiritual and material commitments of her father, John Fisher, had been channeled directly into the institutional church. At age eighteen, when Mary met John Goucher, she had only recently joined the Methodist Episcopal Church through a personal decision of faith. Private piety and social activity, which would characterize the partnership of Mary and John, had been ingrained in her from childhood. A collection of her favorite hymns, included years later among her surviving papers, illustrates this dual emphasis. Foremost among those favorites is Martin Luther's testimony to personal trust in God, "A Mighty Fortress." The second is Wesley's call to holiness and service, "A Charge to Keep I Have."[2]

The Fisher family possessed great wealth, accumulated over six generations of successful Maryland residence. John Fisher, who had been a prominent physician, retired to pursue agricultural activities; when Mary was three years old, the family moved to Alto Dale, a large farm northwest of Baltimore. Not only did John Fisher himself own much property, but his bachelor brother, a leading Baltimore merchant, left his large fortune to his two surviving brothers and their children. Since her younger sister had died at an early age, Mary, at twenty-seven, was a wealthy woman when she entered marriage.

Mary Fisher received the best education available to a female child at that time. In her early years, her father secured the services of a governess in the home. She later attended two of the better schools for girls and graduated in 1867. She was adept in languages, being reputedly as proficient in French as in English. History and English literature were also among her special interests. She was described as a woman who continued to study "long after her school days were over." Probably her awareness of both her ability and her lack of opportunity was a source of Mary Fisher's zeal for the educational endeavors that she and her husband would so substantially support during their marriage. A person who had known her well stated, "Mrs.

Goucher in her later life, like many of her sisters, often expressed sorrow that she had not enjoyed privileges similar to those which she did so much to secure for the young women of Baltimore at the end of the nineteenth century."[3]

Mary met John Goucher shortly after he joined the Baltimore Conference in 1869. He was lodging with a family named Turner, whose farm was near the town of Pikesville. When eighteen-year-old Mary came to supper at the Turner home, the two began a friendship which culminated in marriage after a "suitable" courtship of eight years!

John Franklin Goucher, too, had grown up in a home of ardent Methodists, and his father, like Mary's, was a physician who maintained a highly successful practice. Born in Waynesburg, Pennsylvania on June 7, 1845, John spent most of his youth in Pittsburgh. Physical weakness as a child kept him home much of the time; in later years he recognized the strong influence of his mother and sister, pointing to the nearly "perfect life which his mother lived in Christ Jesus."[4]

Goucher's long Christian nurture, also like that of his future wife, was accompanied by a personal commitment during the teen years. During a revival meeting which he attended with his parents and a young female friend, he did not at first respond to the invitation from the preacher. On the second evening, however, deeply moved, he turned to his friend and, with his characteristic courtesy, murmured, "Excuse me, Miss, I'll go to the altar." What occurred then was no mere courteous convention, but a decision that shaped the course of his life. As he recounted the events to a friend in later years, his prayer that night was simple: "If you will forgive my sins, whatever you ask, I'll do with the greatest pleasure"; and he experienced an almost immediate conviction to enter the ministry.[5]

John Goucher still held that clear determination when he entered Dickinson College. There he encountered a severe intellectual struggle with doubts regarding revelation, but that struggle merely strengthened his personal faith. He was able to overcome his religious doubts through practical implementation of his beliefs—in Carlisle, he initiated a Sunday school that later would grow into a church.

After graduation in 1868, Goucher made good his decision to enter the ministry by joining the Baltimore Conference of the

Methodist Episcopal Church. His departure for the conference session reveals both the depth of his conviction to his call and the commitment of his family to education. After sending him through college, Goucher's father asked John to enter the medical practice with him, promising to send his son both to medical school and to Europe to study surgery. When John declined and made his reasons clear, the physician overcame his disappointment and offered to send the youth to theological school for more training. When this too was declined, for cogent reasons, the exasperated father agreed. He told John to send him the bill for "your horse, harness, and buggy."[6]

Goucher began his pastorates in the Baltimore vicinity in 1869. Until 1871, he traveled the Baltimore circuit, some eight churches scattered in the rolling countryside north and west of the city. In 1782, he moved to Catonsville, and by 1875, he had begun his work in Baltimore City, with successive assignments to the Huntingdon Avenue, Gilmore Street, and Strawbridge churches. He led in the erection of new church buildings at the last two locations. In 1883, John Goucher was assigned to First Church: Baltimore City Station, the lineal descendant of the Lovely Lane Society, host to the organizing conference in 1784. Here, with remarkable force, he directed the congregation as they relocated and erected a unique church building. This present structure of the Lovely Lane United Methodist Church was designed in 1884 by the aspiring young architect Stanford White, as a monument to the Christmas Conference which marked the denominational beginning of American Methodism one hundred years earlier.[7]

During their twenty-five years of married life John and Mary Goucher had five children, three of whom—Janet, Eleanor, and Elizabeth—survived to adulthood. Their home was a center of seemingly boundless hospitality. Both were short in stature and modest in dress, and each soon became the center of any social gathering. By all discernible public standards, John was in charge of the household: "Where he sat was the head of the table." But the qualities Mary brought to the relationship begin to point to the deeper reality of mutuality in their union. James M. Buckley, editor of the *Christian Advocate* and a sharp judge of character, recalled that she combined grace, vivacity, brightness of intellect, and refinement with "a conviction, conscientiousness, and firmness such as tradition attributes to the Puritans of New England."[8]

Their marriage may be described as a unique career of vigorous commitment of energies and resources to the work of the church. Less than a year before his death in 1922, John Goucher reflected on the scope and direction of his active life:

I have had six definite and distinct calls. First to be a Christian. Second, almost immediately to be a minister. Then, third, as clear and definite, to minister to young people. Fourth, for missionary work. Fifth, for Christian Education in all lands. Sixth, a clear call to work for the Unification of Methodism.[9]

Mary Goucher's involvement in institutional church work and social reform reflects the same broad diversity of causes. Beyond assuming the myriad of expected tasks as a pastor's wife, she was one of the organizers of the Baltimore branch of the Woman's Foreign Missionary Society, the first branch south of Philadelphia, and was one of its vice-presidents. She was also president of the Auxiliary to the Women's Foreign Missionary Society of the First Methodist Episcopal Church of Baltimore. Reflecting a long-standing interest of the Fisher family, Mary Goucher served on the Board of Visitors of the Maryland Asylum for the Feeble-minded, and on the board of the Home for the Aged of the Methodist Episcopal Church. In addition to these activities, she was vice-president of the Association for the Extension of University Education for Women and was also active in two women's literary associations.[10]

Most notably, however, the joint work of Mary and John Goucher was a venture in philanthropy for the church, made possible by their common vision and the financial resources of the Fisher family. In reference to Goucher's listing of his six calls, it must be said that both John and Mary were committed Christians and committed to the ministry, he as a clergyman and she as a laywoman. In at least three expressions of Christian ministry—mission work, Christian education, and ministry to youth—the Gouchers worked as a team. James Buckley described this harmony, particularly as it was reflected in their outreach for missions:

Coming into the possession of a very large property, her relations to her husband in the disposition of it were ideal. Their literary and artistic tastes were similar; what was more important their religious ideals were the same; both believed in the possibility of the evangelization of the world; both felt that the age was ripe for great and rapid development; yet their interest in and their personal responsibility for the promotion of this result were independently evolved.[11]

Shortly after their marriage, letters from the Baltimore couple began to arrive at the desks of missionary secretaries of the Methodist Episcopal Church in its New York office, pointing out needs and opportunities and offering to finance projects if the Board of Missions would staff them. In this manner, the Gouchers opened and financed the field inspections of the church in Korea and in west China and were among the prime movers in the opening of mission work in East Africa.[12]

Their characteristic mode of operation is exemplified in the Korean work. In 1883, President Chester Arthur sent a United States ambassador to the Hermit Kingdom. In response, the Korean government commissioned a delegation, including the nephew of their queen, to the United States. Coincidentally, John Goucher traveled on the Union Pacific train with them and became acquainted with them. The entire delegation was then invited to Baltimore, where Mary Goucher learned of the Korean need for mission aid. By the end of 1883, the "General Missionary Items" in *The Christian Advocate* included "$1,000 appropriated to open work in Corea, based upon a special gift of $2,000 from the Rev. J. F. Goucher. It is confidently expected that other special contributions will be made for this purpose."[13]

The Gouchers projected the Anglo-Japanese Methodist College Aoyama Gakuin, donated the money to buy the land, and erected the central building. They also gave initial impetus to the founding of the West China Union University, and John Goucher became chairman of the board of directors. His proposal, along with land and cash, led to the organization of the International University at Chengtu, China. These projects were among numerous other educational institutions the Gouchers supported in the Far East and Southwest Asia.[14]

Among the most remarkable of those ventures was the founding of an entire network of vernacular schools in northern India. The system included more than 120 schools and was personally established and supported by the Gouchers. Parallel institutions for girls and boys were developed. The brightest primary students were sent to secondary schools, and the most qualified graduates went on to college. John Goucher received individual reports on the students and gave direct financial aid to the one hundred best scholars. After twenty years of operation, the experiment was abandoned due to administrative reasons, but by that time, an entire generation of Christian leadership had been trained.[15] So important were these schools to the population of India that one young missionary serving in 1885 was convinced that *Goucher* was the Hindustani word for *primary school*.[16]

John Goucher served on the Mission Board of the Methodist Episcopal Church from 1884 until 1922. At his own expense he visited mission stations and schools, and attended numerous conferences on behalf of the church. He crossed the Atlantic twenty-five times, the Pacific eight times, traversed the Suez Canal three times, and crossed Asia via the Trans-Siberian Railroad twice.[17] Mary Goucher enjoyed travel and made many of those journeys with him. Besides several trips to Europe, she visited Egypt, Algiers, Mexico, Alaska, Cuba, and almost every part of the United States.[18] She loved art, and both Alto Dale and their impressive townhouse in Baltimore City became veritable museums. They contained a variety of relics, both beautiful and curious—including two Egyptian mummies.

A glimpse of Mary Fisher Goucher, traveler and woman-in-her-own-right, is caught in a story told by John Goucher upon their return from a trip to Egypt in 1896.

Bravely she entered the tombs of the Old Egyptian kings. She was alone and the scene was a gloomy one; but in answer to the "you 'fraid?" of her Arabian guide she shook her small head scornfully.

While she was enjoying with an experienced traveler's eye these monuments of Egyptian glory, the Sheik drew near, sat down at her feet, and began in a most offensive manner to chew tobacco. This little woman, accustomed to the respect of all men, could not and did not look kindly on this deed, even though the great Sheik was the offender. She requested the guide to ask him to leave. But that dark-faced one shook his head, and showing all his white teeth, said: "No, no; he Sheik." For a few minutes longer she ignored the presence of the noble neighbor; then, drawing up her small height haughtily, she made to the high and mighty Sheik a gesture that he could not mistake. "Go away," she demanded—and sullenly but surely he went. She turned to her guide just in time to hear him say in an awed tone to his companions: "She Sheik herself."[19]

The Gouchers' international vision did not make them insensitive to needs at home. The education of black youth was one of their special concerns. In 1879 they donated the land and building to house the Centenary Biblical Institute of Baltimore. For more than forty-two years, John Goucher was president of the school's board of trustees. He guided it into coeducation, teacher training, and full collegiate status in 1890, as Morgan College, and in 1917 enabled it to acquire a new campus, still in use today. In addition, the Gouchers personally founded the Princess Anne Training School in Somerset County, Maryland. Now a branch of the University of Maryland, before integration, it was the only institution for higher education of blacks on the eastern shore of Maryland.[20]

The mutuality of commitment brought by Mary and John Goucher to their marriage is strikingly dramatized in their concern for the higher education of women. The Gouchers were principally responsible for the founding of the Woman's College of Baltimore City, which opened in 1888 and later was renamed Goucher College. The college was the ninth institution for female higher education in the United States and the only college for the exclusive training of women in the Methodist Episcopal Church that granted full degrees. For two generations, it was a principal source for the training and equipping of women for the missionary and educational endeavors of the denomination. The story of The Woman's College of Baltimore City is a significant chapter both in the formation of institutions of higher education in the church and in the role of women's organizations for making them possible. Further, it strikingly conveys "the partnership of equality" of John and Mary Goucher.

The origin of the college is traced to the General Conference of 1880, in which the Board of Bishops directed attention to the denomination's coming centennial. The bishops recalled that,

139

since the Christmas Conference of 1784 had founded a college, it would be most appropriate if the centennial offering were directed toward the cause of education.[21] The national press of the church took up the theme and amplified the call. In January of 1884, the centennial year, James M. Buckley's editorial in *The Christian Advocate* declared:

We have passed from the era of exclusive evangelism to the era of education. The schoolhouse has the place as a symbol of Methodism which the saddle-bags had a hundred years ago. We are evangelists still; we are pastors more than was possible then, but we have girded ourselves for a mighty work as educators. Today we must preach and *teach* wherever we go. . . . What better can we do than give to education, as the plan of the Church advises, freely, lavishly, as our thank-offering for all that has come to us since 1784? The evangelizing energy of Methodism may in the coming century be equalled by its energy in the promotion of Christian culture.[22]

The call of the Board of Bishops left each annual conference at liberty to carry out the centennial education emphasis as it might choose. The Baltimore Conference revived a long-cherished desire to found a Methodist-controlled school within the conference bounds. In 1881 a committee was appointed to consider a "conference seminary." By the time this committee reported in 1883, a collateral centennial committee had suggested three educational projects to the conference: establishment of a conference seminary, an endowment for Dickinson College, a college for men at Carlisle, Pennsylvania, and an endowment for Centenary Biblical Institute of Baltimore, a school for blacks founded in 1867.[23]

The Committee on a Conference Seminary reported that the centennial of the Methodist Episcopal Church would be an excellent time to found a school, and it requested the appointment of yet another committee to carry on the work. Nine leading ministers and prominent laymen were selected, and the new committee set about its task with enthusiasm under the vigorous leadership of the Reverend John B. Van Meter, editor of the conference newspaper, *The Baltimore Methodist.*[24]

The turning point in the committee's deliberations came at a meeting held on December 27, 1883. Earlier, on December 2, the pastor of the First M. E. Church (now Lovely Lane) of

Baltimore, John Franklin Goucher, had sent a letter which Van Meter shared with the full committee.

> Appreciating in a measure the urgent demand for some adequate provision whereby the daughters of Christian parents may have an opportunity to secure higher Education in an Institution positively Christian in its influence and thoroughly first class in all its appointments . . .
>
> I desire to tender to you and through you to the Baltimore Annual Conference of the Methodist Episcopal Church a tract of ground situated on the West Side of St. Paul Street extended, between the piece recently purchased by the First M. E. Church of Baltimore upon which to erect their new church buildings, and 4th Street . . . which I will grade, pave, and deed in fee to a Board of Control when incorporated under the direction of the Baltimore Annual Conference for the use of such an Institution.[25]

The letter went on to state some qualifications: First, the Baltimore Conference must accept the gift at its next session for the purpose proposed by the donor; second, the conference must secure $100,000 "in cash or bona fide subscriptions during the Conference year 1884-'85 . . . to be used in buildings and as the nucleus of an endowment."[26] Further, the school was to be for women.

Present at the meeting, John Goucher stated that he would give either the land for the college or its value of $25,000 in cash. Suddenly the whole enterprise had been given a new and unique focus. The committee decided to accept the proposal and take the offer of land.

A new momentum was produced among the churches and throughout the larger community upon the Gouchers' intervention in the painful and slow process of founding a new school. The Gouchers were able and willing to give toward a school specifically designed for women. John B. Van Meter, who presided over the committee that accepted the offer, was in a pivotal position, as editor of *The Baltimore Methodist,* to persuade others to support the venture. Advocates of women's education began almost instantly to mobilize the press and public opinion in order to gain support. An effective lobby on behalf of women had been created.

By mid-January 1884, the Goucher proposal was reported to the general membership of the Methodist Episcopal Church in the national *Christian Advocate*. The reporter from Baltimore, however, made no mention of the fact that the gift was designed specifically to aid the education of women.[27]

The women of the Methodist Episcopal congregations in Baltimore City immediately took up the challenge represented by the Goucher proposal. Less than two weeks after the announcement of the gift, a small group of women met to consider forming an association to assist the project. The small meeting resulted in the calling of a larger gathering.

Significantly the second meeting, which convened on Tuesday morning, January 22, 1884, and numbered more than one thousand people, met in the old building of the First M. E. Church (which was used through November 1885) where John Goucher was pastor. The women had imported some powerful friends whom they hoped to make allies. Goucher gave a short address, and bishops Matthew Simpson and Edward Andrews both gave speeches favoring the Goucher initiative. The assembly adopted a resolution commending the gift of land and pledged to cooperate by securing an average of $5 per female member in 1884.[28]

Out of this meeting also came a decision to organize The Women's Educational Association of the Baltimore Conference, The Methodist Episcopal Church (WEA). The organization was composed exclusively of women and committed entirely to the objective of bringing the Goucher initiative to fruition. The WEA proposed to accomplish the goal by inspiring women through a series of mass meetings to see the vision of a possible school for women. It was also hoped that these meetings would overcome opposition among those who were hostile to progressive education in general, or to the education of women in particular.

The Women's Educational Association held regular meetings. Usually it worked closely and harmoniously with J. B. Van Meter and John F. Goucher. The women collected money from the churches and, further, drew up a petition to the Baltimore Conference urging favorable action on the gift and the decision to found a women's school.[29]

In the meantime, the forces in favor of a women's college organized to capture the body of opinion being generated on behalf of education in general. When a rally for the latter purpose was held in Washington, D.C., the friends of the women's school announced that there would be a second meeting the following day. This gathering was held in Foundry Church, January 30, 1884, and was addressed first by John Goucher and then by Matthew Simpson. At the close of the meeting, an older, humbly dressed woman approached the altar and said to Isabelle Hart, the secretary of the Women's Education Association, "For years I have been hoping and praying for some such movement as this." She then gave Miss Hart a $5 gold piece as her offering for the school, the first recorded gift toward the enterprise. A similar meeting was held in Cumberland, Maryland, for the western portion of the conference.[30]

As the Baltimore Conference session of 1884 drew near, the Women's Education Association sought to broaden its appeal. In an editorial in the February 8, 1884, issue of *The Baltimore Methodist,* J. B. Van Meter announced his intention to utilize the paper, through publication of supplements, to aid the association in advocacy of the women's college. On February 11, the women sent a circular to all pastors in the Baltimore Conference asking for the names of persons in their congregations who would benefit from complimentary copies of the conference newspaper.[31] On the eve of the conference session, a special supplement to *The Baltimore Methodist* was issued, paid for and written entirely by the Women's Education Association. The supplement dealt with the general cause of education and even praised Dickinson College, but it was relentless in its call for a college for women. Its clarion summons was clear in words printed entirely in capitals:

ONE HUNDRED AND FIFTY THOUSAND DOLLARS HELD BY THE EDUCATION BOARD OF THE BALTIMORE CONFERENCE FOR THE BENEFIT OF ITS SONS AND NOT ONE CENT FOR ITS DAUGHTERS. IS THAT FAIR? IS THAT WISE? NOT THAT WE LOVE OUR SONS LESS OR OUR DAUGHTERS MORE, BUT LET US GIVE THEM EQUAL ADVANTAGES IN THE BUSINESS OF LIFE.[32]

The 100th Annual Session of the Baltimore Conference marked the decisive event in the movement toward a women's college. The meeting was held in Washington, to give geographic isolation from the site of the proposed new institution. Opposition was swift when J. B. Van Meter submitted the report of the Seminary Committee, calling for a "Female College" as the "*single* object" of the centennial effort. Debate lasted most of three days, with some objections coming from opponents of women's education. Other persons objected to the exclusive nature of the project, it being directed solely to women. The advocates of the Goucher proposal conceded nothing on the first point, but they compromised on the second. The conference unanimously approved a motion to "make the foundation and endowment of a FEMALE COLLEGE the *special* object of its effort."[33] The education of women was not to be the *only* interest of the Baltimore Conference, but it was to be a goal of high priority. This nuance was sufficient to secure passage.

The conference then went on to direct the bishop to appoint a new committee of twelve preachers and twelve laymen to take all steps necessary to make the new school a reality. This committee was given liberty to add the resident bishop to its number as chairman and to incorporate as trustees. The twenty-four persons, together with the bishop, later became known as the Corporators.[34]

With the first decisive victory won, and with a clear mandate for its work from the entire conference, the Women's Education Association became increasingly active. Another circular was sent to pastors in the Baltimore Conference on March 20, 1884. It reminded the preachers that the Children's Day offering was to be given to this great educational effort and that a centennial medal was available for each child who made a donation. It also urged pastors to plan "a general Centennial meeting in your Charge," and the association volunteered its services to obtain speakers for such gatherings.[35]

Another circular was sent on March 20—to all corresponding secretaries of the Women's Education Association in local churches, requesting that they serve as the secretaries for their congregations. These persons were to relay information to fellow members and to central officers. The letter closed with a plea: "Do not decline to serve. You have been named as a suitable person for this work and *we need your help*. This is a

WOMEN'S INTEREST and we trust that like a woman you will spring to the work."[36]

The association planned a mass meeting for May 12, 1884. This "grand demonstration" was held in the largest hall in Baltimore at the time, The Academy of Music. The building was filled and more than one thousand people were turned away. This vast throng was addressed by no less than three guest speakers. Bishop Henry W. Warren stressed the need for education. As a layman, General Clinton B. Fisk inspired listeners with his assessment of the practical possibilities of the new school. It was Charles C. McCabe, however, who focused on raising the money that was needed to meet the Gouchers' challenge. Before the night was over, $32,000 in additional funds had been subscribed—this included another $5,000 from the Gouchers themselves.[37]

The Corporators also laid plans for a series of meetings to generate support for the new school that was to celebrate the centennial of American Methodism. October 1884 was designated as the month to receive the Centennial Thank Offerings.[38] The rallies were held in October and November of 1884, to complete the effort.

By January 1885, the Corporators had received nearly $140,000 in subscriptions. Accordingly, they decided to incorporate. A charter was prepared, Bishop Edward G. Andrews became a member, and twelve trustees were selected in accordance with Maryland law. On January 26, the charter was officially obtained and The Woman's College of Baltimore City came into existence. The original charter stated that the corporation was formed for the single purpose of "creating and maintaining a College for the higher Education of Woman."[39]

But the Gouchers' challenge had not yet been met. The final subscription of funds must be completed in order to secure title to the land for the new school. As the Baltimore Conference assembled on March 5, 1885, the Corporators held a final rally in the old Eutaw Street Church. Bishop Randolph S. Foster presided. The keynote speaker was James M. Buckley, editor of *The Christian Advocate*. John Goucher then announced that subscriptions amounted to $140,000 and that he and his wife had increased their original gift to $50,000. Others raised their gifts proportionately. Goucher next raised their gift to $70,000.

Various churches and pastors reported their donations and other donors increased their subscriptions. It was finally announced that $200,000 had been raised. The local newspapers reported that "the doxology was sung with a will."[40]

John Goucher always traced the date of the founding of the college to this final mass meeting. Here the Gouchers' challenge was met and the conditions of the gift were fulfilled. One week later, the Baltimore Conference dismissed the Corporators and the school was under the exclusive direction of its own trustees. In June 1885, the Women's Education Association, which had raised half of the $200,000 subscription, called for the recognition of "the eligibility of women as Trustees." It was promptly approved by the trustees and executed. Except for a brief revival to secure funds to furnish the first building of the college, the Women's Education Association had now merged its work directly with that of The Woman's College of Baltimore.[41]

The efforts of Mary and John Goucher on behalf of The Woman's College of Baltimore City, which opened in 1888, were only beginning. When the trustees could not complete construction of the first building, the indefatigable couple underwrote the cost. It was their largest single gift.[42] Additionally, the Gouchers regularly made up operational deficits of the school in its early years. In 1890, after the resignation of the first president, John Goucher was unanimously invited to assume direct leadership of the institution.[43] With some reluctance, he accepted the invitation and remained at the post until 1908. When the school's name was officially changed to Goucher College in 1910, it not only honored its retired president but was also a conscious tribute to its great "Exemplar and Friend," Mary Fisher Goucher.

When Mary Fisher Goucher died on December 19, 1902, John Goucher did not abandon the work they had undertaken. He was faithful to their mutual goals. Their good friend, Bishop Earl Cranston, wrote of this fidelity: "For the husband it was, beyond all the agony of their parting, God's call to double responsibility in caring for all they had planned and planted together."[44] Twenty years later, when John F. Goucher died on July 19, 1922, he was buried next to his wife in Druid Ridge cemetery, created from the Turner farm where Mary Cecelia

Fisher and John Franklin Goucher had first met, fifty-three years earlier. As a friend had written: "Surely so perfect a complement each of the other with such responsibilities could not have had its roots in chance or causeless coincidence. What seems romance in human relations is sometimes God making history and destiny."[45]

THE PACIFIC NORTHWEST

Rosa Peffly Motes

Introduction

Encompassing Washington state and the Idaho panhandle, the Pacific Northwest Annual Conference of The United Methodist Church remains relatively close, mentally, to its beginnings.[1] There were few white settlers in the region before 1850, and much of the area was developed after 1880.[2] A great many people living today remember pioneers who survived well into the twentieth century, and they regard the tales they told more as current events than as history. The perspective given by time, so essential to a proper evaluation of past relationships and actions, is often lacking here. However, old documents recently accessioned in the conference archives add depth to the historical analysis of a group of women sorely neglected until recently by church historians: the wives of Pacific Northwest Methodist clergymen.[3]

The record shows that clergy wives have participated actively in the drama of Methodist growth and development in the Pacific Northwest, from the earliest in 1840 to their present-day counterparts. The roles of these "unsung heroines of the church" have not, however, been as ever-expanding as one might suppose in a burgeoning community on one of the last American frontiers.[4] Rather than a linear progression from domestic to wider-world responsibilities, research reveals that the expectations of Methodist clergy wives in the Pacific Northwest, and the scope of their contributions, have varied with the era. There have been "tides" in these women's affairs. Three separate eras emerge from the sources: The first, an age of competent pioneers, roughly spans the period 1840–1920; the second, an epoch of Pauline stereotyping, extends from 1885 to about 1960; and the third, an era of liberation from well-defined role expectations, begins about 1955 and continues to the present. These eras have overlapped, with a long rather amorphous transition between the first and second, and a shorter more clearly defined passage between the second and third. While the third period—that of freedom to experiment with new roles and responsibilities—is worthy of study and can be partially documented from written sources, its course is still unfolding and its assessment involves living people. Here we note it chiefly as a field for future attention and focus instead on the first two periods, which alone encompass a full century of the lives of clergy wives and their contributions to the church, their communities, and their clerical husbands.

The First Era: The Pioneers

The first Methodist attempt in the Pacific Northwest was the Indian mission at Nisqually on Puget Sound, later judged to have been "foredoomed."[5] It was established as an outpost of the Oregon Mission in 1840 and abandoned in 1842. America Richmond, wife of the leader of the Nisqually Mission, was not, properly speaking, a pioneer wife, but a missionary in a foreign land occupied jointly by the United States and Great Britain.[6] The first Methodist clergy wife to reside within the boundaries of the present conference, she became an indelible part of Washington state history in 1841, when, at a Fourth of July celebration in disputed territory, she and other Americans (including members of the Wilkes Expedition) gave American Lake its name.[7]

During 1851 and 1852, a few services of worship were held in western Washington, but the major thrust of Methodist work among white settlers began in 1853.[8] The prospects for women in the new Washington Territory were neatly summed up in 1854 by Catherine Blaine, wife of Seattle's first resident minister: "A woman who cannot endure almost as much as a horse has no business here."[9] The first wife of John DeVore,

149

who organized and built the first Methodist church in Washington at Steilacoom in 1853, died after only "a few years of toil," leaving two small daughters. Her sister Evelyn, also a charter member of the Steilacoom church, became the pastor's second wife and raised the children.[10] At least one early circuit was so large and undeveloped that for twelve years it was supplied only by single men who lived chiefly in canoes.[11] Some married couples, like Ellen and L. N. B. Anderson, lived apart for years so that their children might attend school.[12]

Progress was slow in the early decades in the Washington Territory. Thirty-two years after the Blaines arrived at Seattle, and the DeVores at Steilacoom, an incredulous Puget Sound pioneer, Charles McDermoth, when his appointment was read at annual conference in 1885, asked, "Where is Aberdeen?" His wife, Cora, remembering this charge in later years, called it a "newborn child on Grays Harbor," where dugout canoe, shank's mare, and rowboat were the only transport. She described herself at the time as "tall, very thin, overworked, and hungry for meat." The pastor had no time to harvest for his own table the abundant game and the seafood that was within easy rowing distance of his front door. He was building a church and a parsonage, in that order, while his family camped in an abandoned hotel.[13]

As late as 1890, just after statehood, land companies recruiting settlers for southwestern Washington advertised for "strong, earnest men without families," pointing out that the state already had too many "salvation armies, and other ornamental gentry."[14] In sum, before 1900, ministerial appointments in the Pacific Northwest were hardship posts, in the parlance of government service, and with a concomitant effect on clergy marriages.

Religious fervor brought Methodist ministers to the harsh frontier. But what motivated their wives? Many unquestionably felt a call to Christian service akin to their husbands' call to the ministry—women like Wealthy Maria Warren Hopkins, who said, "God has called us to this work and we must be true to Him."[15] On the flood tide of God's call, such wives did much work outside their own homes and immeasurably improved the quality of life in fledgling communities. Decades before 1907, when Mrs. J. A. Sutton called the Pacific Northwest "a place greatly in need of high ideals," full of great opportunities for "true Christian women," pioneer clergy wives were saving souls, healing the afflicted, teaching school, and battling Demon Rum.[16] Given the near-primitive circumstances of daily life, the time expended by those women in activities outside the home is remarkable.[17]

It is worth remembering that Pacific Northwest pioneer wives in the nineteenth century were the contemporaries of celebrated woman's rights activists. Before her marriage, Catherine Blaine at age nineteen might have attended the 1848 Seneca Falls Convention spearheaded by Elizabeth Cady Stanton, since it occurred in her home town. Writing to her betrothed of their contemplated move to the West Coast, young Catherine asked, "If we go, shall you wish to have me exchange my present convenient dress for the long skirts? . . . In that new country we can hardly suppose that the same degree of odium attaches to it there as here, and I think it will commend itself to the inhabitants."[18] This was wishful thinking. On occasion, pioneer women in the Pacific Northwest were "prairie-pantsed," but most photographs of the day show them with skirts trailing in the mud.[19] In matters other than dress, however, Mrs. Blaine was a liberated woman of affairs who did pastoral work with her husband David, had well-matured opinions, a keen business ability, and a lifelong interest in public affairs.[20]

Almost without exception, Methodist wives who found time for leadership in one cause were also leaders in others. Their multifaceted roles were possible, in part, because their formal education was superior to that of most pioneer women. While a college degree was not a requisite for the Methodist ministry in pioneer days, a great many clergymen were university graduates, as were the women they married. Most college-trained wives were school teachers, but some of them were adept in other fields. Lucretia Ann Wilbur—her husband's able and unpaid assistant in a long mission to the Yakima Indians—served as secretary, accountant, and teacher.[21] Both Isabel Whitfield and her husband were practicing physicians before he was called to preach. They "worked their way west" on a succession of frontiers before reaching the Pacific Northwest. Mrs. Whitfield was also a leader in WCTU circles and missionary societies.[22]

Of the clergy wives involved in education, some taught in elementary schools for pennies—for example, Catherine Blaine, Seattle's first teacher.[23] Some were involved at the university level and on the Chautauqua Circuit, as was Mary J. Pomeroy.[24] There were organizers—Luella Kimball, with her husband, founded the Kimball School of Theology.[25] Maggie Brown and many other wives taught without pay in mission schools operated in conjunction with their husbands' pastoral appointments.[26]

From the point of view of pioneer clergymen, the worth of a schoolteacher wife could not be overestimated. Often in the Pacific Northwest a one-room log cabin served as the only school in a large county where roads were nonexistent, waterways were treacherous, and most pupils boarded near the school for a short term of two or three months each year.[27] To clergymen farsighted enough to marry teachers, these conditions were no problem— the literacy of their children was assured.

It is hard to determine whether the formal education of children or Demon Rum was of greater importance to clergy families in boom towns where every other building was a saloon-*cum*-bordello. In any event, clergy wives were as deeply involved in the temperance movement as in the educational system. The first president of the Woman's Christian Temperance Union in the Washington Territory was a Methodist clergy wife, Margaret A. LeSourd.[28] Some became temperance workers after meeting the great WCTU leader Frances E. Willard. Susan D. Overton Barrett did so after attending a meeting in Chicago at which Miss Willard presided.[29] Mary Elizabeth Stubbs, after meeting Willard, became Washington's WCTU evangelist, representing the west at national and international conventions, a post she held for many years.[30] Nellie Clulow, a noted Pacific Northwest evangelist, used her rhetorical talent in the campaigns that transformed Washington into a dry state.[31] Many local chapters of the WCTU were organized by Methodist clergy wives who were powers in the temperance movement in the Pacific Northwest throughout both eras discussed here.

The Second Era:
The Pauline Stereotype and Its Limits

The transition from the first to the second era began around 1885 and ended in the early 1920s. The region was becoming a settled society, based on logging, lumbering, and prosperous agriculture. Relieved of the dawn-to-midnight labors of pioneer days, women of this period became housewives, with time for cultural pursuits and worthy causes, and it became unfashionable for married women to work outside the home. Later, schoolboards would refuse to hire married women, and a profession once open to clergy wives would be closed. For a generation, when either these women or their secular sisters worked, they were considered "unfortunate" rather than "privileged."[32]

Survivors of the second period themselves, when interviewed for this study, perceived it as an age of "Pauline stereotyping" of clergy wives. Retired clergy and those nearing retirement age spoke of an unwritten law in the first half of this century, which defined the role of the clergy wife as precisely as it did that of her pastor husband—the wife, of course, being "assistant to" her husband. Wives recalled dress codes and "living within the system." Laymen observed, and this was corroborated by clergy, that the "unwritten law" often was explained in detail to each new pastor by leaders of local congregations. A portrait of the ideal clergy wife was emerging. That one-dimensional, conservative, unpainted, modestly dressed lady was expected to be the pastor's helpmate, parsonage hostess, Sunday school teacher, choir director, angel of mercy, backbone of the Ladies' Aid, mother, and indispensable participant in the Parent-Teacher Association.

Written records show that this simplistic appraisal, however suggestive, by no means told the whole story. Within the system, and in spite of "dress codes," women of the second era were more versatile than they are given credit for being, and in their own way, as "involved," adaptable, and competent as were the pioneers. As an organized group, these wives successfully campaigned for the adoption of parsonage standards by the annual conference.[33] As individuals, they were

153

organizers and officials of local and conference missionary societies, leaders of Sunday school classes, young people's societies, and the WCTU. Some of them also earned money by giving private lessons in music and art. Edith Covington was the first police matron and traveler's aid worker in Bellingham, Washington.[34] Mary Selleck became a published author in 1975, at age 107.[35] Letitia Bergstresser, the oldest surviving clergy wife in the conference today, and a local deacon who preached in her husband's absence early in this century, has augmented her retirement income in recent years by piecing quilts of heirloom quality. Her life story was published in 1981.[36] The singing evangelist Augusta Willman is one of many wives who were involved in the campaign for full clergy status for Methodist women.[37]

The progression toward ordination of women in the Pacific Northwest followed the similar pattern elsewhere: Pioneer wives filled pulpits in their husbands' absence; later women were licensed as local preachers; and in 1956, after decades of struggle, full ministerial rights were granted.[38] One facet of that chronicle is particularly germane to this study: the concept of the dual service of pastor and wife. The constant refrain in obituaries since the 1880s—"He was appointed; They served"—captures this concept well. Rachel A. Sickafoose, for example, was a soul-winner for thirty years, always "at her husband's side . . . ready to go into the battle for the Master." Elizabeth Ann Jones "and her husband entered the ministry in 1890. . . . They served until he died in 1918."[39] As recently as 1978, all but one of fifteen memoirs for recently deceased clergy wives contained such phrases as "they served" and "she served with her husband," though the wives were not ordained. The words state a fact, for the occupation of pastor's wife was a full-time if unpaid vocation. It was so regarded by church officials until recently, as evidenced in a district superintendent's 1975 report that refers to a married couple who began "*their* new ministry," although the wife was not a minister.[40]

The Ministers' Wives Association

The pioneer women who conceived of a clergy wives' association were hardly a submissive lot. However, in that 1897 climate of "two for the price of one," whether by happenstance or by design, through this association, wives of the first era who had been educators, temperance leaders, and preachers in fact, if not in name, restyled themselves and schooled their younger counterparts for roles less enterprising and visible than those they themselves had enjoyed in pioneer days. Perhaps they were bowing gracefully to cultural pressures beyond their control in a rapidly changing society. In any case, the Pauline stereotype they helped to fashion would be considered the norm for half a century.

In a 1902 historical sketch, Cora McDermoth, one of the pioneer women referred to above and the first president of the wives' association, explained how the organization came into being: "During the session of the Annual Conference held in the Old Opera House at Everett in 1897, the brethren, for the sake of some private discussion, banished all without the bar to the outer regions without the door," and "some bantering talk occurred as to our being excluded." Irrevocably committed to a shared ministry in which *he* was appointed and *they* served, the wives, it seems, bridled a bit at this reminder that they were not in fact full partners. A suggestion that "we ought to have a conference of our own" was seconded by Mrs. McDermoth, for the idea "had long laid *(sic)* close to her heart." Inadequate transportation would have precluded an earlier organization of this much-needed support group. "It was left with the writer," said Mrs. McDermoth, "to arrange some plan by which the suggestion to organize could be carried out. This was done by taking things for granted and announcing through the host of the coming conference that place and opportunity was desired for such a meeting." In September of 1898 the Pastors' Wives Association of the Puget Sound Conference was formally organized.[41]

A quick glance at Cora McDermoth's own life puts this turn-of-the-century development into perspective. She came to Washington Territory in the 1860s and died unexpectedly in 1944, a few hours after entertaining the Ladies' Aid in her new retirement cottage.[42] She was by no means the only clergy wife who lived through most of the first two eras and glimpsed the innovations that the third might bring. Such women who had lived with change could be expected to make further adaptations with equanimity, and they were well fitted to help younger wives adjust to the inevitable. Through the 1920s, the association minutes outline programs designed to implement a purpose set forth in the bylaws of 1898: "The object . . . is to encourage mutual acquaintance, and by suggestions and varied experience endeavor to make ourselves more fit helpmates in the Master's service."[43]

To make themselves true ribs of Adam in the "help meet" role accorded women in Genesis 2:18 (KJV), wives of the pioneer generation exhorted *each other* as much as the younger wives: Be peacemakers, be tithers of time as well as money, be attentive to children, lend an ear to the aspiring young, be a willing participant in women's societies in the church—but "don't be president" of the Ladies' Aid, a veteran cautioned. Obviously the association leaders considered themselves more than helpmates as they spoke of "*my* experience on *my* first circuit" and heard annual reports given by each woman "concerning *her* work" (italics added). Incorporated in the programs they presented is the concept of the minister's wife as the power behind the throne—one who could make a king by encouragement, inspiration, and dedicated participation in his ministry, or could break him by gossip, complaint, neglect of *her* duties, or the failure to measure up to congregational or community expectations. So important to church officials was the relationship of the pastor's wife to the community that Bishop Richard Cooke addressed the matter at the wives' 1913 annual meeting in the governor's mansion at Olympia, Washington. As a participant in a symposium focused on the duties of pastors' wives, the bishop discussed what was expected of those women by the community in general, noting that their mission was helpfulness to others.[44]

The matter of keeping up appearances was of perennial concern to clergy wives, but on the subject of clothing, the pioneers were adamant: "Dress neatly, not extravagantly, watch carefully the husband's wardrobe. . . . Always dress so as not to attract attention."[45] So they said. And yet, in portraits at the turn of the century, some of the pioneer women are elegantly attired.

In 1907, Mrs. J. A. Sutton spoke of the "unjust burdens" thrust upon the pastor's wife by virtue of her husband's position which made her, perforce, a leader in the community. Noting that in the Pacific Northwest, even ministers' wives were in danger of "falling below the standards we held . . . in places where the moral and social basis of society was more settled and stable," Mrs. Sutton advised the wives that they should neither isolate themselves from their environment nor try to be all things to all people. Isolation, she said, would cause them to miss opportunities for service; total availability, on the other hand, would create an inability to distinguish between the worthwhile and the worthless. Remarking that Robert Browning did more to establish her own faith in God and people than "any source outside the Bible," she recommended his poetry.[46] This was landmark advice for Pacific Northwest wives, who five years earlier had agreed that only the Bible and Methodist publications were suitable reading material for clergy wives.[47]

For two decades the association programs emphasized duty to God, to church, to husband, to congregation, to community. The year 1921, however, is the last in which there is a reference to "duty" in the minutes of the organization. In the late 1920s, programs focused instead on problems incident to the "business of being a preacher's wife," an interesting change of idiom.[48] There was a subtle difference also in the purpose of the wives' association as set forth in the 1898 and in the 1930 bylaws. In 1898, the women were to make themselves "more fit helpmates" in God's work. In 1930, they joined under less traditional phrasing, to study "common problems of the work of the members."[49] This shift in language represented a change in the women's perception of their roles that becomes increasingly evident as years go by.

In the decade of the 1930s, a light handling of serious matters, one of several survival techniques of the depression years, pervades the clergy wives' minutes. The association ushered in the decade with a tongue-in-cheek debate: "RESOLVED, that a minister's wife with long hair is more efficient than a minister's wife with bobbed hair," which was decided in the negative.[50] By that time, most of the wives had followed popular entertainer Irene Castle's lead and bobbed their hair, but a few congregations still may have considered the new style "sinful." This debate and other programs like it may have been an expression of the wives' contention with the petty constraints they felt in ultraconservative communities.

In the 1940s and 1950s the association explored topics of interest to all women of the day, giving these a slant that made them peculiarly relevant: the *Christian* woman's role in world peace and international crisis; the wife's appropriate involvement in a husband's career—that is, the *responsibilities* of the *pastor's* wife and her *unique* role in Christ's work.[51] Between the association's duty-bound "helpmates" of 1900, and the wives of the 1950s, who considered themselves as having "a vocation with responsibilities," the line of demarcation is fine, but the self-definition of the later women is closer to the phrases used by men in referring to their professions, while the earlier is gender-differentiated in a very traditional way and conveys less sense of choice.

The Homemakers

Although we have focused on wives' public activities, there have been clergy wives through all the eras who defined their primary role as that of homemaker, and they have received too little praise. While memoirs in conference journals are lavish in their encomiums for wives active in church and community affairs, most obituaries for those perhaps shyer wives who were principally homemakers simply list vital statistics, with brief comments about the deceased having been a good Christian, a faithful wife, and a loving mother. By contrast, the eloquent 1978 tribute of the then Pacific Northwest Bishop Wilbur W. Y. Choy to his deceased wife, Grace, honors in full the role of homemaker. She, the bishop said, was "not one to take leadership roles in the church," but "she encouraged her husband to enter the ministry and was supportive of him throughout his career." At age twelve, Grace Choy had assumed care of her four younger brothers following their mother's death. "Such a traumatic experience might have caused a life-long negative response to the role of homemaker," the bishop noted, but instead, she had "gloried in that responsibility and, with a profound sense of God's call, found marriage, motherhood, and home-making the avenues for self-expression." Bishop Choy concluded his moving tribute by borrowing the words of an old spiritual: "She was convinced that she was precious in the sight of God for she was a child of God. . . . She was my amazing Grace."[52]

The Third Era: An Age of Liberation

In the years from about 1960 to the present, Pacific Northwest clergy wives experienced rapid and shifting pressures, as have their secular sisters. Few wives today fit the Pauline mold. More often than not, present conference wives are career women with vocations that are not church-related, but they are at the same time homemakers. Some are as active in church work as their predecessors; some are not.

Wives interviewed for this study pinpointed the mid-1950s as concluding the Pauline era. Indeed, a researcher finds that almost overnight, in minute books, in programs, and in yearbooks, wives began to use their Christian names, identifying themselves as individuals in their own right, rather than seeing themselves as adjuncts of their husbands by the use of "Mrs. John" and "Mrs. Robert." Interviewees who had lived with dress codes and recreational restrictions expressed pleasure at the new freedom to dress and use cosmetics as other women did, to style their hair becomingly, read modern novels, and attend movies. Younger clergy wives find it hard to realize how recently those activities were taboo.

More crucial innovations in the third era, however, have been the acceptance of full-time paid employment by large numbers of clergy wives, the advent of female clergy and clergy couples (in which both spouses are ordained), and the appearance of divorce in the clergy family. The sources used for this study are inadequate for analysis of these matters. Independent study is needed, with information obtained from the women themselves in such a way that confidentiality is assured. To date, there have been very few such studies nationwide.[53] Generally, conference journals and organization minute books do not mention changes until new patterns have been adopted widely enough to make an impact on the church, the clergy family, and the community. While admittedly scanty, however, some information is available and reliable.

The first mention of working clergy wives was the revelation in a 1965 newsletter that roughly one-third of the conference pastors' wives were then, or had been, employed. Among their occupations were nurse, teacher, secretary, director of Christian education, police judge, and justice of the peace.[54] Thirteen years later, the matter was brought to the attention of the annual conference itself by a district superintendent: "Whether through economic pressures or pursuit of careers of their own, the majority of ministers' wives work."[55]

Recognized as a "knotty problem," divorce in the parsonage is addressed by the Pacific Northwest Annual Conference through the Pastor-Parish Relations Committee. Matters of separation and divorce are treated confidentially, and clergy families are advised that counseling is available if needed.[56] There is nothing in the wives' minutes, to this date, to suggest that as a group, their association is grappling with the question.

In 1978 a Pacific Northwest district superintendent stated that, in relation to the church, the most important impact of the Women's Liberation Movement had been the growing number of women clergy and clergy couples. The annual conference is giving serious attention to the problems presented by clergy couples in this region where only a handful of communities can support two United Methodist pastors.[57] The wives' response has been straightforward and pragmatic. In 1978 their organization became the Ministers' Spouses Association. Its minutes refer to workshops on perceptions of the role of the clergy *spouse* and affirm that meetings "together served a much needed function . . . for spouses to gather, greet one another, and share common joys, concerns, and support."[58] These last words are a suitable expression of purpose for the organization, which functions informally, without constitution or bylaws.[59] The minutes reveal that husbands of ministers participate in the association's annual workshops and luncheon programs.[60]

It is too soon to determine definitely, but it is possible that ultimately, 1960 to 1980 will be considered a period of transition rather than as a separate era.

Conclusion

This essay has focused on a highly visible, structurally permanent, and important but little studied group of women who are a vital part of United Methodism. Sources are not lacking, but church historians until recently have seen these women primarily as adjuncts to their husbands.[61] In fact, the wives of clergymen have earned and rightly deserve equal consideration as actors in the history of the church as a community of faith and witness. Studies of these women add information also to wider explorations in United States history concerning the ambiguities in the status of women who are married to professional men. The point that stands in clearest profile is the remarkable adaptability of the wives of Methodist clergy to the changing needs of church and community, as a wilderness in the Pacific Northwest has rapidly become an industrial society.

Section Two
National Missions and Social Reform

9

THE COUNTESS OF HUNTINGDON

Mollie C. Davis

Sadly neglected by historians, the Countess of Huntingdon, Selina Hastings (1707–1791), often has been placed on a pedestal with the condescending titles of Patriarchess and Queen of the Methodists. Permitting her to remain in the shadows of the Wesleys and George Whitefield, writers made of the Countess what they wanted and what their image of women allowed. Most chose to grant her her lady's place as a patroness, even while they acknowledged her role as a leader of Calvinistic Methodists. Consequently, she is known as a benefactor of evangelicals within the established church and later, of declared Methodist dissenters; a direct supporter of George Whitefield; a staunch advocate of religious education and the founder of Trevecca College; the central director of a "connexion" that numbered more than sixty chapels, complete with ministers and itinerants; an upper-class zealot who relentlessly endeavored to convert her peers from their folly; an "enthusiastick" in the most opprobrious connotation.[1]

But Selina Hastings was far more than a zealous benefactor. That complex upper-class woman of eighteenth-century England was a direct leader in religious and social reform and a connective, transitional figure between the Old and the New World. Stepping outside the prescribed female role of submission and modesty, she sought to lead her decadent Old World along the progressive path to Christian perfection, and in time, she extended her efforts to the New World of colonial British North America, particularly as a protagonist of frontier and Indian missions.[2] Never visiting the colonies, she nevertheless joined the two worlds in an indomitable spirit and a missionary endeavor that increasingly became more reformist.

But the Countess bridged Old and New Worlds in another way, also. For almost fifty years she pioneered in attempting to reform her class and in forging new religious roles for women in that class. Deriving power from her social and economic status, she was able to exert secular influence, however marginal, that normally would have been denied her gender. Gifted with intelligence and a personal charisma, she advanced to a religious leadership role as a founder of a reformist, renewal movement that stressed lay participation and granted women space for assuming authority and responsibility.[3] Religious endeavor clearly afforded talented, determined women such as the Countess with opportunities to build independent identities and to draw strength—even power—from associations in formal and informal networks.[4] Women of high status, seemingly more affected by their dependent roles than those of other classes, found autonomy and usefulness in working for religious reform among their own ranks.[5] Further, they extended their influence by going outside their rank and gender to foster evangelical efforts among other classes and among persons of different races.[6] As a result, the Methodist movement itself was altered. Selina Hastings offers a well-documented example of a woman who, in mid-life, was able to formulate a new and important identity. An examination of her life, particularly the years of her widowhood, reveals that she set upon a path that led to a "new world" for eighteenth-century women and at the very least offered a counterargument to the notion that pious women are always passive and submissive.[7]

Born in Leicestershire in 1707, Selina Shirley was the middle daughter of three born to the second Earl Ferrers and his wife, Mary Levinge. A serious child, she became religiously sensitive after an emotional experience during a funeral and thereafter prayed and meditated regularly. Highly intelligent, she improved her mind by reading and conversation and soon found new opportunities for learning.

At twenty-one, Selina Shirley married the ninth Earl of Huntingdon, Theophilus Hastings, a descendant of Edward IV, and thereafter she met many persons who were influential in court circles. Through frequent visits to her aunt, Lady Fanny Shirley, Selina had become acquainted with some members of this inner group which included the Lords Bolingbroke, Chesterfield, and Dartmouth. Lady Fanny had been a friend of King George I and was a close companion of Lord Chesterfield. Now Selina's associates increased in number and she made many female friends, among whom were her husband's pious sisters—the Ladies Elizabeth, Anne, Frances, Catherine, and Margaret Hastings. She amused herself with social activity, some of which revealed an interest in politics and introduced her to the female intellectual group of the era. Because Selina Hastings was one of the elite, she escaped the boredom of household chores and could intrude, however marginally, upon the male domain, even though only in conversation and knowledge. However, Lady Huntingdon did not escape frequent childbirth. From 1729 until 1739, she bore the Earl seven children; only one died in infancy. There is no record of any birth after the year 1739, when Lady Huntingdon was thirty-two; yet the records indicate that she and the Earl were especially close during the period between 1739 and his death in 1746.[8]

After the birth of their last child, Selina became increasingly involved in the religious activity of the Hastings, particularly those of Lady Margaret, who had been converted by Benjamin Ingham, an original member of Wesley's Oxford band. From late 1735 throughout most of 1736, cooperating with the Wesleys in the new colony of Georgia, Ingham had lived among the Creek Indians and worked in the Indian school established by Moravian missionaries of the Unitas Fratrum, even composing an Indian grammar for the use of the colony.[9] Called back to England, Ingham soon departed for a tour of Holland and Germany as an itinerant, preaching to the masses. Returning to his home in York, where even before his sojourn in Georgia he had initiated prayer services in his mother's home, Ingham began to preach. At that time, the Hastings were visiting their oldest sister, Lady Elizabeth, at Ledstone Hall in York. Out of curiosity, they went to hear the great itinerant and were converted to his cause. When in the summer of 1739 Ingham was prevented from using the established churches of York, Lady Elizabeth offered him the use of her chapel at

Ledstone Hall. He accepted and the sisters began to work with him among the poor. When Lady Elizabeth died in late 1739 and Ledstone Hall became the property of Lord Huntingdon, the other sisters returned to Donington Park.[10]

A true convert, Lady Margaret Hastings encouraged her sister-in-law the Countess to meet many religious activists and soon enticed her to join the Wesleyan-supported Fetter Lane Society, founded in 1739. At first exhibiting only moderate devotion, Lady Huntingdon donated increasing time and effort to the work of the reforming society. Through Lady Margaret and Benjamin Ingham, who were married in late 1741 at the London residence of Lord Huntingdon, Selina became aware of the value of itinerancy and the need for mission efforts in the New World, as well as in the Old World she knew so well. Then a serious illness in late 1741 or early 1742 precipitated a crisis and prompted the crucial conversion of a soul ostensibly already saved. Near death, Selina Hastings self-diagnosed her illness as spiritual poverty, and after offering a prayer of dedication, she was at once at peace with herself.[11]

Her health immediately improved, and the countess threw herself into intense religious activity. Beginning with her servants, she soon tried to convert everyone she saw. She opened her kitchens, purse strings, and schools for the poor in the area; and then she advanced to an attack on the London elite. The Countess recognized that her peers often ignored the poor and that the masses were estranged from the established church. Working with the Wesleys, she gave them her support freely and worked directly and indirectly to persuade John Wesley of the value of lay and itinerant ministers. Each social engagement furnished a splendid pulpit—particularly receptive were her female peers. The death of two children in the early 1740s served only to accelerate her evangelism.[12]

Lord Huntingdon, while not converted to her belief, went occasionally to meetings and did not object when she opened their home to the Wesleys and others. The Earl, although reticent, was not obstructionist. He gave his wife the gift so few receive: Even above love, wealth, and prestige, he gave recognition of and respect for her independence and moral support for her causes.

Lord Huntingdon supported his Countess even in death. In

1746, he left his thirty-nine-year-old wife in virtual control of the family fortune and their remaining four children. The Countess, ill with grief at his death, intensely rededicated herself to the work of the Gospel and soon was on her way to recovery. The following year when her eldest son, Francis, reached eighteen, she promptly gave him the Earl's estate in Donington Park and moved to a less ostentatious dwelling nearby. Relieved of social duties, she reduced her staff of servants and gave all her time to the revival of the church. Giving generously to reforming ministers, she turned her home into a gathering place where distinguished guests heard sermons from equally distinguished evangelists. She held special meetings for women and soon was leading a female network. Selina Hastings then initiated an unusual activity for women of her time: She sponsored a missionary group to Wales consisting of select bands of like-minded women and proven evangelists, the first of many excursions she and her friends undertook.[13]

On her return from Wales, Selina invited George Whitefield, just back from his third colonial visit, to preach in her home. She had decided to employ a chaplain to hold regular services for the nobility, and after hearing his sermons on two occasions, the Countess asked Whitefield to become her chaplain.[14] He accepted the employment and accordingly met many important persons, including Lord Chesterfield, whose wife and sister had been converted by the Countess.[15]

For the next twenty-two years, until Whitefield's death in 1770, the Countess of Huntingdon and George Whitefield, the nominal Anglican with no organized religious sect, were informal partners. Their work was coordinated and their ideas complementary. During this period the activities of the Countess in both the Old and New Worlds intensified and became more closely connected. She and Whitefield became fund raisers as well as savers of souls. Selina Hastings emerged as manager of what, in modern times, would be termed a foundation. Long nurturing the desire to convert his Bethesda Orphan House, near Savannah, Georgia, into "a college of pious youth," Whitefield felt his desire quicken after beginning his association with the Countess, as did his special interest in the training of "new-creature ministers."[16] The Bethesda operation was crucial to Whitefield's work and offered him not only a base but a symbol, predestined to last long after his death. During the 1750s he laid plans to put Bethesda on a sound financial basis in preparation for its conversion into a college.[17] The Countess, on the other hand, was laying her own plans. She was fast becoming the leader and coordinator of the group of Dissenting ministers who, while still connected, were known as Calvinistic Methodists. She acted as their mentor and counselor and was generous with property and financial aid.[18] She also concentrated on developing the elite network that sustained her and on broadening the female circle to include many of the nobility, such as Lady Mary Wortley Montagu and others of an intellectual bent. During the decade of the 1750s, Selina befriended poor as well as noble debtors and increasingly called upon her wealthy friends for donations to her projects.

When in 1757 her son Henry died, the Countess increased her already exuberant efforts and again recovered from grief by rededication. She inaugurated a relentless campaign to reform the established church by converting the upper class and encouraging its members to become aware of the poor and unreached. She sold her jewels and, for Whitefield's use, built a small chapel near her home. Opened in 1761, this chapel was the first of a large number that were either built or remodeled from old buildings at fashionable spas frequented by the nobility. The Countess, however, did not abandon the use of her drawing room. She held evangelical soirees more often and introduced her company to the oratory of Whitefield, John Berridge, William Romaine, the Wesleys, and others. She held prayer meetings for women, and soon those women were holding similar gatherings in their own homes. Among her converts were Lady Mary Hamilton, Lady Jane Nimmo, Lady Frances Gardiner, Lady Fanny Shirley, the Countess of Leven, Lady Chesterfield, and the Countess Delitz, Lord Chesterfield's sister.[19]

Selina Hastings rebuked the members of the aristocracy who were not easily converted to church reform. Among those who felt her sting were Frederick Cornwallis, the Archbishop of Canterbury, and his wife, who supposedly held gay social affairs on Sundays. When they ignored her rebuke, she persuaded King George III to reprove them. The Countess feared no man or woman and even tried to bring to repentance her cousin, the psychopathic Lawrence Shirley, the fourth Earl Ferrers, who was imprisoned for murder in the Tower of London. Working through the governor of the Tower, she cut the earl's wine ration, prevented him from gambling, and even forbade him to see his mistress lest he die in adultery. But neither her frequent visits nor those of George Whitefield converted the mentally ill earl.[20] Despite much ridicule, the Countess of Huntingdon was taken seriously by more and more people of her class and was able to gain the support of a number of notables, including the Lord and Lady Dartmouth.[21]

The Countess used her networks to place political pressure on people who were able to right the wrongs done to enthusiastic ministers. She was influential in gaining the release of Nonconformists pressed into military service and often intervened to secure the dismissal of charges (and fines) against reforming ministers accused of disturbing the peace. She was known as a defender of civil liberties for itinerants, to whom she gave generously. She not only supported their work but established a pension fund for the wives of those who died in poverty. She continued to open chapels for the use of ministers who preached reform.[22]

During the 1760s, however, the Countess became aware that she had more chapels than trained ministers. She longed for the realization of Whitefield's plans for a college, and she solicited the aid of Lord Dartmouth and others whom she had converted. Meanwhile, she tried to remain content in directing and counseling her group of itinerants and chaplains and in donating to such colonial enterprises as Moravian missions to Indians, Eleazar Wheelock's Indian school, the College of New Jersey, and, of course, the Bethesda Orphan House. She and Lord Dartmouth, who was then head of the Board of Trade, gained support for the college charter for Bethesda, and Whitefield presented the proposal to the Privy Council in 1764. But Thomas Secker, the shrewd Archbishop of Canterbury, delayed action until her friends in the Rockingham ministry had been forced to resign in political defeat. Whitefield then withdrew the proposal and resolved to build support in Georgia, in the hope of having an act passed through the colonial legislature.[23]

In 1768, seven tradesmen's sons who were attending Oxford at the recommendation of the Countess, and partially at her expense, were expelled for religious enthusiasm. The Countess then opened a theological school in Trevecca in South Wales, to train ministers for the Church of England, or for any other Protestant denomination. The school attracted evangelicals and was the pride of the Countess, who visited often and for several months at a time. She was more than a patroness; she was an overseer who required rigorous training and high standards in return for her sponsorship.[24]

The Countess became increasingly convinced of the value of proper education for ministers and continued to encourage Whitefield's efforts to establish a college in the New World. Her plan was to offer basic education for the poor in addition to higher education for the ministry. In 1770 Whitefield completed his plans for Bethesda, a college that would educate both boys and girls, and he presented it to the Georgia Common House. After securing the support of Governor James Wright and several prominent Georgians, Whitefield embarked on a tour northward, from which he never returned alive. At the time of his death in Massachusetts in 1770, the matter of Bethesda College was still pending.[25]

Selina Hastings inherited the Orphan House, but she soon despaired of transforming it into a college. Going beyond Whitefield's goal, the Countess envisioned using Bethesda as a center for the evangelization of the southern colonies by missionaries and itinerants trained at Trevecca. Encouraged by Lord Dartmouth, when Whitefield's estate was settled in 1772, she prepared her students for their mission. Summoned from England, Wales, and Ireland, they met at Trevecca where plans for the frontier mission movement among settlers, Indians, and Negroes were discussed. The Countess hoped that Georgia would endow the plan if she supplied the enthusiasts. After a week of religious services held all across Great Britain, the small band sailed, with a minister, a chaplain, and the Countess' housekeeper. The exuberant missionaries, on their arrival in Georgia, combed the countryside for converts. They were so successful that they earned the wrath of the regular clergy, who complained to London.[26]

Despite its initial success, the mission met obstacles that all but destroyed it. In 1773 the Orphan House burned, and thieves and inefficient management set it back further after the Countess had rebuilt it. When the American Revolution erupted, the mission's president, the Reverend William Piercy, immediately abandoned Bethesda and fled to Charleston and then to London. The mission's slaves were stolen (and recovered); the property was seized and damaged by the British and was in a poor state when the Americans seized it in 1782.[27]

But Piercy's actions were the most devastating. After his arrival in Cork Harbor in January, 1781, the Countess questioned Piercy's behavior and soon discovered his dishonesty. Piercy had contacted Whitefield's London executor and informed him that he had been forced to draw funds on the Countess in order to finance his family's voyage to England. The Countess, who had not heard from Piercy in years, refused to be responsible for these and other bills incurred by Piercy. She informed him that his brother had told her that Piercy had driven forty-one of Bethesda's best slaves to Boston for sale, and she requested an accounting. Piercy sent lame excuses, but no accounting. The Countess even aided him during an illness that winter, but she grew impatient when she discovered that Piercy had written to Georgians and others with accusations against Bailie, the resident manager at Bethesda, and that Piercy had threatened suit against her. The Countess then had the property tallied by people in Georgia, but affairs were still in disarray. Anxious to clear the legacy of Whitefield from ill repute, the Countess asked Lord George Germaine, then a secretary of state, and Governor James Wright for advice. These British officials suggested that she empower Georgians to audit the property, but she had done that already.

The Countess realized that she needed more assistance from the American side, and at this juncture she was fortunate in becoming acquainted with Henry Laurens, who had been imprisoned in England during the last stages of the Revolution and was recuperating in Bath. Laurens' father had been an adviser to Whitefield, and his daughter and the Countess were good friends. The Countess introduced the ailing Laurens to many influential dignitaries, and she and he also became good friends.[28]

Admitting her fears that Bethesda's confused financial state would be used against her by enemies of her plan to make it an evangelical mission center, the Countess persuaded Laurens to conduct her affairs in the New World and straighten out the Piercy-Bethesda entanglement. Anxious to clear her own name as well as that of Bethesda, the Countess still maintained a sense of justice toward her adversary Piercy. On June 30, 1783, she wrote Laurens that she needed to clear the matter up soon and needed his advice as to "the best means thought on to exculpate" her from charges of neglect, but that she insisted on learning the truth. Even "the best or the worst have a right to the impartiality of all our actions to them," she wrote, "whatever all our actions to them, whatever their meaning or practice has been or may be to us."[29]

Her sense of justice appealed to Laurens, who undertook what must have been a severe imposition on his precious time and health.[30] Seven months later, while delayed in London receiving treatment for what he called "gout" of the head, Laurens wrote the Countess that he had attended to her affairs in London and had apprised the proper attorney there that Piercy had misrepresented the facts.[31]

When he returned to the United States in the summer of 1784, Laurens carried with him full authority to investigate affairs at Bethesda. Unfortunately, all affairs in the colonies were deeply confused at that time, including those of Laurens. From necessity he turned her affairs over to a lawyer, but he warned the Countess that the process probably would not be completed within the year. He added that she could not conclude that her Georgian contacts were remiss in not contacting her, since everyone in the colonies was faced with financial confusion, including himself.[32]

Almost in the same packet, a letter arrived from the Countess' former housekeeper who had gone to Bethesda in 1772 with the Trevecca itinerants. This account made the matter clear. Evidently Piercy had misrepresented himself in Georgia, telling the people there that he had an independent income. He had lived a life of "grandeur and Parson's pride" at Bethesda: He had relieved the housekeeper from duty, hired his brother as a replacement, and used the former housekeeper as a singer to entertain his company.[33] Through Laurens and those he retained, as well as the witness of the housekeeper, the

Countess finally clarified the financial situation, but even Henry Laurens was unable to settle other grave matters concerning Bethesda.

The Countess moved to regain her estate in order to convert its revenue into an Indian mission; upon receipt of suitable Indian lands, she planned to complete her negotiations. She entreated George Washington and several governors for aid in her scheme, sending her plea by James Jay, the eldest brother of John Jay. James was then in England acting as agent for King's College in New York. She desired a location that would be adjacent to Indians and at the same time be suitable for a colony of several hundred families. Washington replied in 1785 with discouraging news—her foreign status would impede her petition for lands in the western area. Despite her friendship with Laurens and his own testimony, which affected her "deeply," she could not understand the frustrating confusion in the aftermath of the American Revolution.[34] The general mood of the new nation was not receptive to giving lands to a British subject, for whatever reason.

The state of Georgia, however, did act to show special respect for the Countess. In June 1786, John Habersham wrote the Countess of the state's attempt to set up "a regular system of education," informed her that it had set aside certain properties for the purpose of public schools and a university, and inquired about her wishes regarding her property, in the hope that they would coincide with the wishes of the state of Georgia. His letter to the Countess was ever tactful—not so her reply.[35]

She denounced the charter of the University of Georgia (which Habersham had enclosed for her perusal) for opening opportunities to "all professions of Christians" and, seemingly irate, suggested that "even Popish Bishops of Satan" could become the instructors and "guardians of youth." Contending that such latitude would end in "wretched slavery," the Countess withdrew her services unless it could be shown that her interpretation was in error. Her strong letter must have been disappointing, but it did not prevent the Georgia legislature of 1788 from acting to permit her to continue as a trustee of Bethesda. This law allowed the Countess to hold the property, offered additional monies for its support, and designated Georgia trustees of the land to be used for the "Bethesda Orphan House or College."[36]

The Countess took the hint and reverted to Whitefield's old goal of combining the Orphan House with a college to train "new-creature ministers." Her intent was to provide education for the worthy poor and orphaned, as well as to create another college like Trevecca. But once again poor management coincided with apathy to prevent success. Bethesda simply drifted along. In desperation, the Countess sent over a Dissenter trained at Trevecca College, John Johnson, whom she knew to be loyal and efficient. But this time, loyalty and efficiency were not enough. The Reverend Mr. Johnson immediately antagonized the Georgians when he insisted upon educating and converting Negroes, and the enterprise suffered as a result. Johnson was acting manager when the Countess died on July 3, 1791, and in December, the Georgia legislature interpreted the act of 1788 to infer that the Countess lost the trust of Bethesda at her death and that, acting through a board of trustees, the state of Georgia was to assume control. But Johnson refused to yield until he was arrested and imprisoned.[37] Thus in 1792, Selina Hastings' fundamental role in George Whitefield's Bethesda came to an end. The new Georgia was no more interested in an Indian mission than the new nation had been. Both repelled the utopian aspirations of the Countess of Huntingdon.[38]

At the time of her death in 1791, deepened evangelistic zeal was evident in both the Old and the New World, and the Countess' role in the Methodist contribution to that zeal had been outstanding. She had founded and endowed a college, guided its students, and acted as placement director for its graduates, thus helping to diffuse religious knowledge and train Nonconforming religious leadership. She had been, as historians insist, a patron and a central director of a connection that numbered more than sixty chapels, many of which she founded and endowed, complete with ministers and itinerants. Her effort to convert the British aristocracy was ahead of its time; she had helped to initiate a social reform that would reach its heights in the next century. She had aided both the poor and the rich.

The true stature of the Countess as a religious leader

nonetheless has failed to be recognized on several accounts. In particular, while she led and directed the Calvinistic Methodist group that gave George Whitefield his major support, and while for all practical purposes she coordinated that great minister's work in both Old and New Worlds after 1748, she continues to be unrecognized as a major wielder of economic and political influence in Whitefield's behalf.[39]

Additionally, her adroit use of power did not depend totally upon her class position and wealth, as commentators sometimes imply; her superior managerial skills in planning, implementing, and checking also were crucial. Through determination and hard work, she initiated and ran Trevecca College to serve several purposes simultaneously. Only through careful planning was she able to finance her mission endeavors to the poor. In much the same way, she designed the conversion of her own class. She did not wish to convert the British nobility simply for their own sake, but also for their potentially great role in the perfection of society. She sought to enlist their support in aiding the poor, whose suffering she noticed, and the Indians, whom she never had seen on their native soil. She hoped to channel the frustrations and estrangement of the masses into revivalism and to redirect the upper class, wasting its time and energies on amusements and gambling, into social and religious reform.

As serious history of churchwomen develops, Selina Hastings deserves to be widely recognized as a pioneer, in both the Old and New Worlds, of female religious leadership. The evangelical Christian renewal movement of Calvinistic Methodism afforded the wealthy Countess the opportunity to assume an authority and responsibility normally denied her gender and to extend her influence by fostering social and religious reform both at home and abroad. Throughout this endeavor the Countess effectively used a female network that gave women self-confidence and support. She instigated prayer meetings and formed discussion groups. She encouraged women to express themselves on matters of the soul, if only to each other and in the privacy of their homes.[40] Through her sponsored excursions with itinerants, she provided them with opportunities for missionary activity, with herself as a role model.

Selina Hastings did not hide her knowledge, as her contemporary Lady Mary Wortley Montagu lamented women often must, but used her mind and her gift of persuasion.[41] Having gained a new identity during her widowhood, she was scarcely an adornment for Methodist men, as described by Abel Stevens three generations after her death, but a leader and thinker in her own right—one who innovated in the use of lay ministers and itinerants and who set policy whenever it was possible for her to do so.[42] A creature of the Enlightenment even though she embraced an "enthusiastic" religion, she believed in unlimited progress for all—for Indians, whom she saw as infidel children of nature, and for women, whom she saw as socially underdeveloped and underutilized.

Despite her striking successes, the Countess obviously was restricted because of her sex. Her historical importance within the Methodist revival has been underestimated for the same reason. In her lifetime, she was derided for having stepped out of her role as a woman, although eventually she was taken more seriously. She overlooked much discrimination, ignored the powerful weapon of derision, and through her deep religious commitment and the self-made support system which sustained her, was able to overcome the insecurity and discomfort caused by criticism. Selina Hastings did not see her aims and labors as feminist in intent, but she must have recognized their implications for women's religious leadership. Secure in her own spiritual and social identity, she used her marked talents in a planned, self-assured manner that offers a model for later women evangelists and activists in Methodism. A determined leader in missions, the Countess of Huntingdon stands as a powerful transitional figure connecting the Old World and the New.

AMERICAN INDIAN WOMEN

Frederick A. Norwood

One of the most significant themes in the history of Christian interaction with American Indians is the interplay of social forces as the two major cultures came into contact and conflict. Until recently, most white Christians easily assumed that religious and cultural influence simply went one way: Christian civilization was a blessing to be bestowed upon the benighted savage. They tended to ignore the strong enduring characteristics that were widely shared in the various Indian cultures—articulate oral communication, profound philosophies of life based on understanding the ways of nature, and strong tribal loyalty and responsibility. The relative failure of the mission to the Indian may be attributed in large part to the failure of missionaries, and white people generally, to understand Indians and their way of life.

There were exceptions. Occasionally an explorer or missionary penetrated deeply enough to develop an appreciation of what the Native American had to offer and to understand the reasons for their lack of response to white values and incentives. Missionaries knew better than did most other whites the destructive effects of the Westward Movement and the consequent disruption of Indian life. They saw at first hand the terrible things the white man's culture could do. It brought despoilment of the forests and near extinction of the buffalo, the rifle and the Colt revolver, diseases, liquor, and greed.

Missionaries and teachers lived and worked, most of them with selfless commitment, in the midst of this immense one-sided conflict. They fought against the liquor dealer, the land shark, and the legal cheat, even as they tried desperately to bring the Christian message and to "civilize" the Indians, sometimes confusing Christianity and civilization.

All this must be said also of the white women—the wives and mothers, the missionaries, teachers, and camp workers. They too were caught up in a vast process they could not wholly comprehend. The women shared the limitations and blind spots held by male missionaries. They, also, caught an occasional flash of truth, perceiving the injustice and oppression that accompanied westward expansion and discovering unexpected strength in Indian character, culture, and religion. They could view these things far more clearly than could most of their secular associates.

Here we will focus primarily on the interaction between American Indian women and women of the northern and southern Methodist Episcopal churches from the mid-nineteenth century until 1939, when the two denominations united to become The Methodist Church. The principal sources that document this interaction are the missionary journals of the two denominations and certain early histories of the women's work. Turning first to the work of white women missionaries and the projects that were developed through the women's home missionary societies, we will capsule the wide scope of programs initiated by the societies of the two denominations and supported by the general mission boards of the churches. We will study the crucial roles women played, demonstrating that much of the early work actually was begun by women's organizations and that pioneer female missionaries often were the first emissaries of Christianity to Indian Americans.

Second, we will convey a picture of Indian women themselves and the effect of Christianity upon their lives. Except in a group of matriarchal tribes, women were kept in submission. Conversion to Christianity sometimes enabled them to better accept themselves and served as a catalyst to raise their status in relationship to the males of Indian society. The journals further document the growing role American Indian women came to play in the women's missionary societies, as they increasingly assumed positions of responsibility formerly held by white female missionaries and members of the missionary societies of the northern and southern

177

Methodist Episcopal churches. A weakness lies in the inability to recover accounts by Indian women from sources other than the Protestant missionary literature. Any negative reactions Indian women may have had to the impact of missions are not directly discernible in such sources, which emphasize the positive influences of Christianity.

Organized work by Methodist Episcopal women among American Indians was officially begun in the 1880s, when home missionary societies were organized in both the southern and northern churches. Although a Miss Archibold was among the teachers in the early Shawnee mission in Kansas in 1850, the Woman's Home Missionary Society of the Methodist Episcopal Church (WHMS) was not organized until 1880. From its beginning, as one of its five specific emphases, it stressed concern for Indians, as well as for freed black people of the South, Mexican Americans, Mormons, and Chinese. (See, e.g., *Woman's Home Missions* 3 (1886): 138; 4 (1886): 59; 5 (1888): 89; 6 (1889): 148-9.) A justification of Methodist women's work among Indian tribes published in 1938 might well have been written by WHMS leaders in the 1880s: "The Indians in the Territories and in Alaska are the victims of our injustice and wrong, and have claims upon us for Christian civilization not to be surpassed by heathen of foreign lands."[1]

The northern women's society approached Indians through three action bureaus: the Indian; the New Mexico and Arizona, which extended also to the far west; and the Alaska. The first concentrated on classic "frontier" locations in Indian Territory; the second, on southwestern tribes; and the third, on Aleuts and Eskimos. In every case the early days were filled with uncertainty, privation, frustration, loneliness, and stark fear.

With audacity, Harriet McCabe, Jennie Fowler Willing, and Lydia H. Daggett, the bureau secretaries, planned unprecedented projects and sent women out alone or by twos or with their husbands, to start from scratch Christian missions among Indians who, if no longer warlike, still were resentful and resistant to the enterprises of white missionaries. This resentment was balanced, however, by the gratitude of some American Indians—especially women—who felt a sense of acceptance and affirmation for the first time in their lives.

178

The loneliness and isolation felt by many of the female missionaries was expressed by Sarah Moore, one of two young women assigned to open a mission among the Jicarilla Apaches in New Mexico in 1889:

Two Mexican families live within a radius of a half mile; also two men at the Agency. . . . Amargo is our P.O., six miles distant. Agency men are kind enough to carry our mail. We would have to go in a southeasterly direction more than 100 miles, to Antonito, before reaching a church, and in a northwesterly direction about 80 miles, to Durango. . . . In other directions it is open country for I don't know how far. The nearest school is, so far as we know now, the Indian school on the Ute Reserve at Ignacio, about 50 miles distant. The police regulations amount to but little. There is an Indian police force whose duties consist in keeping peace around the agency. . . . So far as we know yet there are only Mexican settlers in the adjacent country. The Jicarilla Apaches live in tents which they move frequently. . . . Among the whole tribe, numbering nearly 800, about 20 houses have been begun during the past year, but will not be finished this season. One of the police lives in a house something like a civilized being, only one in the whole tribe.[2]

A survey of the projects developed by the WHMS among Native Americans gives some idea of the involvement of those women. By the mid-1880s, a number of projects were already underway—missions to the Pawnees, Poncas, and Osages in Oklahoma, and the Apaches and Navahos in New Mexico. At the end of the decade, the WHMS began work among the natives of the Aleutian Islands. This operation came about before any work was accomplished by the general mission board of the denomination.

The WHMS of the northern Methodist Episcopal Church was most active in the Indian Territory in the present states of Oklahoma and Kansas. In July 1885, Frances L. Gaddis and her young son, who was about fourteen, arrived on the reservation of the Pawnees. The first missionary to the Pawnees, she came in response to a call from Harriet McCabe, who had learned of the desire of the Woman's National Indian Association to transfer its new mission to a denominational sponsor. The Association was a nondenominational organization which had been formed in Henry Ward Beecher's church in Brooklyn to

179

help plant missions that then would be taken over for development by some denominational missionary group.

Frances Gaddis and her son settled on a small farm with a cottage, a barn, and a pony, and they struggled for about two years to establish roots in the unfamiliar culture. One of Mrs. Gaddis' successful efforts was a sewing class attended by some eighty women.[3] There were also an active Sunday school, worship services, and recreation classes for children two evenings each week. By 1887, a church was organized with twenty-seven members, including three chiefs. Mrs. Gaddis also supplied an amateur medical service. This mission continued under WHMS sponsorship until 1907, when the Baptists took it over under comity arrangements, and the Methodist efforts were transferred to the Ponca and Pottawatomie missions.

When Frances Gaddis left Pawnee in 1888, she went to Pawhuska, the Osage agency. With characteristic energy, she began a mission and school in her little house. Although the Roman Catholics had begun work there, Gaddis was convinced that a Protestant voice was needed, and with the help of the agency and with federal funds, she successfully developed a school which enrolled fifteen girls the first year. Mrs. Gaddis left the mission at the end of the decade because of ill health, but the project continued and later became the Adelaide Springer Osage Mission.

The Ponca Mission at White Eagle, also begun through the work of Frances Gaddis, was another of the enterprises inherited from the Woman's National Indian Association. In 1888, young Emma Clark began work with the Poncas. She must have experienced a powerful culture-shock. These Indians were poor and nomadic, had not given up their traditional habits of polygamy, lacked sanitation and modesty, and in addition, had acquired the white vices of drunkenness and gambling. Clark did not yet have a barn or fenced lot, and soon after she arrived, her pony, on which she, like other early missionaries, was dependent for basic transportation, ran away. But she persevered on foot, visiting the Indian women, teaching the children, tending the sick, and even, together with the medicine men, burying the dead. As described in a WHMS *Annual Report:* "The heathen rites were actually suspended, and the dusky warriors stood in silence while the fair young girl knelt in their midst and pleaded for the blessing of the God of nations!"[4] Conditions improved somewhat when a Methodist minister was appointed government agent for the tribe and Clark became the new matron of the government school. In 1929, the mission built a substantial community building, and nine years later, just prior to Methodist reunification, regular preaching services were being held and a weekday religious education program had been established in the Ponca boarding school.[5]

Considerably later, another mission, serving the Pottawatomie tribe near Mayetta, Kansas, came under the wing of the WHMS. This work had been started at the beginning of the twentieth century by the Kansas Annual Conference of the Methodist Episcopal Church and in 1903 was transferred to the woman's society. The first missionary, Flora York, worked for two years without salary. Her experience suggests that in its eagerness to begin projects with or without funds, the WHMS sometimes exploited its missionaries and occasionally failed to give them even elemental support.

Sarah Moore and Maria Clegg, two of the first female missionaries in the New Mexico and Arizona area, began work among the Jicarilla Apaches at Dulce, New Mexico, in 1887. For several years they lived in a tiny two-room log house. Then three rooms were added to provide separate spaces for worship and education. A Methodist minister occasionally came thirty miles to preach and conduct sacramental services. In 1892, Thomas Harwood, superintendent of the New Mexico Spanish mission of the denomination, organized a class meeting at Dulce. A small chapel and schoolroom were constructed. When Moore accepted the position of field matron, a governmental post, Mary A. Tripp joined the two missionaries as teacher. However, the mission was closed in the first decade of the twentieth century.

With considerable hesitation, the WHMS sent Mary Eldridge and Mary Raymond to embark upon a mission to the Navahos in 1890. The bureau secretary Jennie F. Willing had reported in 1888, "A visit to the Navaho Reservation convinced your Secretary that it is not safe to send ladies alone to that tribe."[6]

But her successor, Mrs. E. W. Simpson, decided to take the chance, for the opportunities were great: The Navahos were more numerous than other tribes and had developed a higher culture. The main problem was isolation. The first mission was located seventy miles from any railroad. Soon after their arrival the two women were able to move from their tent into a small one-room house, which was promptly filled with curious Indians interested in the promise of medical care and industrial training. As soon as another room was added, Eldridge and Raymond began religious and educational projects, and a class meeting of about fifteen persons was organized.

At the time of Raymond's death, Eldridge became governmental field matron and Mary Tripp was added to the staff of the Navaho mission; a day school was underway and a dormitory for boarding students was built. At the turn of the century, the whole mission moved to a new site near Farmington, New Mexico, where adobe buildings were constructed, including a school for the first six grades. For ten years the mission continued and grew, but as the result of a disastrous flood in 1911, a new site had to be chosen. This, too, grew impressively: New buildings were added in 1926 and the school was expanded to include the seventh and eighth grades. In the mid-1930s the educational goal of the mission was reached with the opening of a four-year high school, which graduated its first class in 1939.[7]

Farther west at Yuma, where the National Indian Association had begun work in 1904, the WHMS assumed control in 1907, with support from the Southern California Annual Conference. After a flood in 1916, new buildings, including a school and a parsonage, were situated on a hilltop. The church, dedicated in 1920, was a fine well-equipped structure. This mission has continued to grow and expand its services, especially to the Indians of the Colorado River Valley.

In the Pacific Northwest, the WHMS undertook projects in California and in Washington. The Ukiah Indian Mission among the Diggers was opened in 1891 with support from the California Annual Conference. There were churches and government schools at each of three locations. The male missionary struggled against many problems, some in the native culture, such as nomadism and polygamy, and others derived from the white population, especially alcohol. When the government schools were closed in 1905, a mission school was organized. The next year the whole project was placed under the California Annual Conference.

Another project was started in central Washington among the Yakima Indians, building on the work of the famous "Father" J. H. Wilbur. The interest of Dr. and Mrs. Daniel Dorchester, members of a well-known New England Methodist family, was aroused, and they sent a medical doctor, Emily C. Miller, to serve a mission about twenty-five miles from the railroad. She won the friendship of the Yakimas, who gave her a cottage and garden. When Mrs. Dorchester died in 1895, the mission became a project of the WHMS, and a forty-acre plot was acquired. Although Miller left the mission in 1902, the work continued under the Washington Annual Conference.

At about the same time, the WHMS founded the Stickney Home in Lynden, Washington, as a home and school for Indian children.[8] In 1901, the boarding school became a day school, and industrial and craft training were added. The woman's society continued sponsorship until the Board of Home Missions and Church Extension assumed control in 1927.

A separate bureau of the WHMS promoted and directed work in Alaska. The women opened a mission there several years before any were begun by the general missionary society of the denomination. All early work of the Methodist Episcopal Church in Alaska was concentrated on the Aleutian Islands, the area assigned to it by cooperative Protestant comity arrangements. Dr. Sheldon Jackson, the capable Presbyterian founder of Christian work in the new Alaska territory, was not interested in wasteful denominational competition.

The most significant project begun by the women and supported by the denominational mission board was the Jesse Lee Home at Unalaska, founded in 1889 after several years of planning and financing. John A. and Mary P. Tuck, husband and wife, began by taking in two little Aleutian orphan girls. Soon there were twenty-five, all of them living in a small one-and-a-half story house. They received help upon the arrival of Agnes L. Soule, but when Mary Tuck's health failed after seven years, the pioneer couple returned to San Francisco. In

1897 and 1989 new facilities were opened, though with considerable difficulty.[9]

For several years, the mission at Unalaska was the only place within hundreds of miles where Protestant services were held regularly. Agnes Soule's new husband, Albert Newhall, was a young medical doctor who served also as minister and government teacher. Agnes Newhall died in 1917, but her husband continued his work until the mid-twenties, when the home was moved to Seward. One of the new missionaries was Anna Gould, who had been raised in the Jesse Lee Home. Her brother, P. Gordon Gould, was the first resident of the home to graduate from college and become an ordained minister. The cottages at Unalaska were exchanged for three large new buildings in Seward, each three stories tall, with large dormitories in two and general facilities in the other. Here a boarding school, hospital, and home for children were combined. After being damaged in the great earthquake of 1964, the institution was moved to Anchorage where it became a home for the care of emotionally disturbed children.[10]

Other projects sponsored by the WHMS included the Hilah Seward mission at Sinuk, near Nome, begun in 1906. Its purpose and development were much like that of the mission at Unalaska and, with joint support from Sheldon Jackson, were directed toward the Eskimo population. A reindeer herd was obtained for economic development, and a small orphanage was opened. In 1919 it was destroyed by fire and its twenty-two residents were housed temporarily in Nome and in 1925 were sent to the new Jesse Lee Home in Seward. The WHMS efforts had been extended to Nome itself after population pressures of the gold rush in 1900 disrupted Eskimo society.

In the Methodist Episcopal Church, South, work among American Indian women began prior to the Civil War. Several young women shared in the earliest efforts by the new general mission board to develop schools and academies among the transplanted tribes in Indian Territory. One of the most successful and durable schools was Bloomfield Academy for Chickasaw girls, opened in 1853 by the Reverend John H. Carr. Carr's wife served as matron and as teacher, along with the Misses S. Johnson and Ellen J. Downs. In 1857 they were joined by another teacher, Elizabeth Fulton, eighteen years old and the daughter of a Methodist missionary. Two years later she married, but she did not allow this domestic arrangement to interfere with her missionary calling. During the Civil War, Elizabeth Fulton Hester taught a class of twelve Indian boys, all of whom became chiefs, and she later became active in both foreign and home missionary societies.[11]

Southern Methodist women's work with the American Indians was first launched through an as yet undifferentiated Woman's Missionary Society (WMS) established in 1878 and rechartered as the Woman's Foreign Missionary Society (WFMS) about 1890. Supported by the WMS, the work remained under the Woman's Board of Foreign Missions until 1910, when that body merged into the Woman's Missionary Council and American Indian work was turned over to the new Home Department.

Another girls' school, the Harrell International Institute, was founded by the general board in 1881 at Muskogee in Indian Territory. The Reverend Theodore Brewer served as its first president, and Indian Methodist leaders were among its directors. In 1886 the school became a principal project of the Woman's Board of Missions. Women were related to the Harrell Institute, as to other educational institutions, as missionaries, wives of missionaries, and teachers. Brewer's wife organized a local Woman's Missionary Society at Harrell in 1882 and four years later founded such a society in the Indian Mission Conference.

The general board also founded The Seminole Academy, a boarding school at Sa-sak-wa in Indian Territory. In 1882 the Woman's Board raised $600 to support a woman teacher, Mrs. S. J. Bryan; in 1883, it doubled the amount; and in 1884 it assigned another teacher, Jennie Wolfe.

Prior to the 1880s, all Methodist work in Indian Territory was concentrated among the relatively settled tribes of eastern Oklahoma that earlier had been moved forcibly from their homelands east of the Mississippi River. No one had had the temerity to approach the native nomadic tribes of western Oklahoma, the so-called wild tribes. Toward the end of the decade, the Reverend J. J. Methvin, a member of the Indian Mission Conference of the southern church, volunteered and was appointed "missionary to western tribes." He was prepared to go alone, but his wife insisted that the family, including all five children, undertake the venture together. They moved to Anadarko and existed for two years in a small shack. Methvin described one of his first experiences, a significant encounter with a notable female Indian religious leader:

About 11 o'clock pulled up in Kiowa village. Interpreter not there. Found Virginia "Stumbling *Bear*," an old Carlisle student, rather averse to filling the office of an interpreter, finally consented, gathered a congregation together and in the smoke of a teepe sang and prayed and preached. Virginia Stumbling Bear nursed two children and interpreted at the same time. . . . Had an interesting meeting after all, God blessed the services and the Indians were impressed, and my own soul was refreshed.[12]

Methvin developed a church and a school with a vigor characteristic of all his actions. From the beginning, the WFMS provided funds and support for the school, and between 1888 and 1890 became owner and sponsor. Many women participated in the work of the Anadarko mission in its early years, particularly in teaching and in aiding Indian women. Among those who have been identified are Mrs. M. B. Avant, Helen Brewster, Elizabeth Gregory, Mrs. J. J. Roland, Irene Lindsay, Liffie Shirk, Sallie G. Davis, Emma McWhirter, Hattie Jones, Lottie Davis, and Ida May Swanson, who was Methvin's second wife.[13] The pupils included some whites and Mexicans, but most were of the Kiowa, Apache, Comanche, Caddo, or Delaware tribes.

By 1893, white children were taught separately, with Sallie Davis assigned to the "white school."[14] She also was active among the Indians, however, a twelve-year-old girl, Blanche Kokom, serving as her interpreter. Many Indian women wore clothing characteristic of white women by this time, but Davis reported, with approval, that some Christian Indian women still clung to native dress.[15]

One of Methvin's most aggressive and courageous co-workers was Helen Brewster, whose special assignment was "camp work." She went into Indian camps, wherever they happened to be set up, and visited and lived with the Indians in their own cultural surroundings. Brewster learned more than one Indian language, though she used interpreters when they were available. "Miss Brewster's camp work," Methvin wrote, "is the most difficult work we have in all this field, I suppose, but it is a very essential factor in successful missionary operations here."[16] She helped organize missionary work at both Fort Sill and Mt. Scott. Methvin described the latter in this way:

Miss Brewster, in her work as Bible woman and teacher down among the Comanches, excites my continual admiration. So far as her own race is concerned, she is alone, being twenty miles away from any white. She goes into the homes of the Comanches and Mexicans, reads and talks and prays with them, eats with them, and in a kind, patient, cheerful way has won their affection. She has learned their language and can already speak it. She has begun a day-school and has a regular patronage of ten pupils.[17]

On these expeditions to Indian camps, Brewster became well-acquainted with important Indian leaders, one of whom was the formidable Chief Quannah Parker, who lived with his six wives and a whole wagonload of children. Helen Brewster seemed well able to take such polygamous customs in stride.

By the late 1890s, nine missionary societies—six for adults and three for children—had been organized in Indian Territory by the WFMS of the Methodist Episcopal Church, South. These missions continued into the twentieth century after Oklahoma became a state, although they were increasingly encroached upon by the expanding white population. Their efforts were disrupted but not destroyed by the dissolution of the separate Indian Mission Conference in 1906. It was reestablished in 1918, and much of the activity then took the form of rural church support. In this capacity, for example, in 1938 Mary Beth Littlejohn worked in small churches in the Indian Mission Conference, as a deaconess under appointment from the Woman's Missionary Council.[18]

Paucity of sources makes the recovery of attitudes and experiences of Indian women most difficult. Outlines of their lives may be drawn from their own words and the words of female missionaries found in official journals, however. These provide insights into the status of Indian women in domestic and public life, their marital relationships, the effect of Christianity on their lives, and their contribution to the church and leadership in religious life.

The general picture of the daily existence of Indian women that emerges is one of degradation and hardship. In her annual report from the Bureau of Indians to the WHMS of the northern church in 1884-1885, Harriet McCabe described the condition of Pawnee women as deplorable. "They are bought and sold for wives when barely beyond childhood." Though there was a government school attended by about sixty boys, girls were rarely admitted. McCabe attributed this situation to the fact that Pawnees did not see fit to educate women and that the government had done nothing to change their attitude or to uplift women. She appealed to churchwomen to take up the cause of the Pawnees, particularly the needs of the women, by evangelizing, educating, and teaching the basic skills of sewing. She saw no hope from the government:

Agent Bowman appealed to the government for the women and girls, saying nothing could be done for the tribe while girls and women were left in this condition. That was four years ago, but nothing has been done yet. Excellent words spoken by President Cleveland and Secretary Lamar lead to the belief that a short time will find many of these wrongs righted. The government supplies them with clothes, but the women and children are poorly clad, and there is much suffering, sickness, and death. If the Indian is dying out it is for want of the instruction we can and should have supplied centuries ago as to providing for himself and how to do it.[19]

One of the missionaries' primary concerns was the base condition of women in marriage, which they hoped that conversion to Christianity and nurture in the faith could alleviate. The southern *Woman's Missionary Advocate* described the discovery of the Reverend Methvin in Anadarko upon receiving two young women into church membership: Both women were married to the same man. They came to the missionaries for counsel, but Methvin's answer is not given in the historical record. He was sure, however, of the general benefit of Christian influence: "Marriage . . . will be a more sacred thing hereafter, and Christian marriage means Christian homes."[20]

One of Helen Brewster's good friends at Anadarko, a man named Horse, said disconsolately, "I would love to be a Christian, I earnestly long to be one; but you know how I am all tangled up by having two wives. I say to you younger men, Don't let your life get tangled up in that way."[21] The old habit of bargaining away young daughters as commodities was hard to discourage. The missionaries hoped that when the stubborn older generation died off, customs would change. "The younger women are quite different. Christianity and education are doing much for the present and rising generation."[22]

Christianity brought inner relief to some Indian women, and the strength to bear the burdens of marriage. Such was the experience of one aged woman in the face of approaching death. "Poor Sarah's" words, quoted here in length, present a convincing testimony:

I go sorrow, sorrow all day long. When the night come, husband come home angry, beat me so, then I think, oh if Sarah had friend, Sarah no friend. I no want tell nabor I got trouble, that make only worse, So I be quiet, tell nobody, only cry all night and day for one good friend. One Sunday, good nabor come, and say, Come Sarah, go meetin. . . . When got there, minister tell all about Jesus; how he was born in stable, go suffer all his life, die on great cross, bury, rise, and go up into heaven, so always be sinner's friend. He say too, if you got trouble go to Jesus. He best friend in sorrow, he cure all your sorrow, he bring you out of trouble, he support you, make you willing suffer. So when I go home, think great deal what minister say, think this the friend I want, this the friend I cry for so long. . . . When Sunday come, want go meetin 'gain. Husband say, you shant go; I beat you if you go. . . . When get home, husband beat me, 'cause I go meetin—don't stay home work. I say, Sarah can't work any more on Sunday, 'cause sin 'gainst God. I rather work nights when moon shine. So he drive me hoe corn, that night, he so angry. I want to pray great deal, so go out hoe corn, pray all the time. When come in house, husband sleep. Then I kneel down and tell Jesus take my bad heart—can't bear bad heart; pray give me Holy Spirit, make my heart soft, make it all new. So great many days Sarah go beg for a new heart. Go meetin all Sundays; if husband beat me, never mind it; go hear good nabor read Bible every day. So after great while, God make all my mind peace. . . . Only sorry 'cause can't read Bible—learn how to be like Jesus; want to be like his dear people Bible tell of. So I make great many brooms, go get Bible for 'em. When come home, husband call me fool for it; say he burn it up. Then I go hide it; when he gone, get it, kiss it many times 'cause it Jesus' good word. Then I go ask nabor if she learn me read; she say yes. . . . So, Misse, I learn read Baptist Hymn; learn spell out many good words in Bible. So every day take Bible, tell my children that be God's word, tell em how Jesus die on cross for sinner; then make 'em all kneel down, I pray God give them new heart; pray for husband too, he so wicked.[23]

Some male missionaries were deeply aware of the impact that the Christian message should make upon the condition of Indian women, as well as its ability to provide them spiritual comfort. Similarly, they recognized that it was their responsibility, as missionaries, to bring that gospel to bear upon the everyday lives of Indian men and women. Writing of his experience among the Indians on Grape Island off Quincy Bay, Massachusetts, the Reverend W. C. Case described the condition of the women:

The Indian females, like those of every barbarous nation, are found in a very degraded and humble condition. In some tribes their sufferings are exceeding great, so that their lives are even a burden to themselves. The woman is obliged to endure the severest hardships in travelling, and to perform the drudgery of the family so soon as they halt for rest and refreshment. She bears the covering of the wigwam on her head in the journey, and sometimes is added the burden of a heavy child. I have seen them labouring under these excessive burdens until they fainted and fell to the ground. When they halt, it is expected she will build the wigwam, bring wood, and light the fire; and having prepared the meat for her husband, she retires until he finishes his repast. She is then permitted to eat of what remains. These are her burdens while she has strength to support her in her hardships; and when she becomes sickly or aged, it is not unfrequently the case that she is abandoned by her relatives as incurable, and given up to die.[24]

Case held that without Christianity, woman would be treated on a level with the beasts. He believed that the basic truths of Christianity should raise women to "equal partnership" with men, investing them with "first place in our houses, at our tables, in our hearts." He endeavored to apply this message to the everyday lives of the Indians, explaining to the men that they "should lift the burden from their oppressed wives, and treat them, not as slaves, but as companions and friends." Hosting the Indian families at breakfast, he explained to the husbands that they should invite their wives and daughters to sit beside them at meals. Though the men were at first reluctant, after further urging they gave the invitation.

The sisters took their seats, perhaps for the first time, beside their husbands at the table—There was much smiling with the women when the invitation was given, and all seemed happy and cheerful, and enjoyed the season finely. I had the pleasure of serving them at the table, saying that I also had a female friend who prepared my meals, and always sat with me at the table.[25]

A female missionary, who instructed the Indian women in housekeeping along with biblical teachings, was a part of the missionary team on Grape Island.

Other missionaries also reported that conversion to Christianity brought marked changes in the meaning of marriage in Indian villages. As early as 1820, Methodist workers among the Wyandots at Upper Sandusky in the Ohio Conference had written that the old custom of "putting away their wives for very trifling considerations" had been a source of great evil among the braves. Indians who had been converted to Christianity had disavowed this practice, however, "and they now desire to be lawfully married, so as to be joined together for life, thereby setting an example of connubial happiness to others of the Indian tribes."[26]

Missionaries were sensitive, too, to the evils that American settlers had introduced into the lives of Indians and felt it imperative that they lead the Indians away from the vices of liquor and gambling. Mrs. Bowden, who worked in Indian Territory, wrote in her diary that she found groups of from six to twelve women gathered in tents, gambling on the ground. The square game, as it was called, was played with plum seeds, and the winner carried home all the calico, beads, or whatever the women may have had in their shawls. The missionary recorded her stern words of admonition: "I told them that it was wrong and that Jesus would be angry with them, and by doing this they were serving the evil spirit and would go to hell." While some were ashamed, others were bold in their response. "One woman said she did not care if she did go to hell."[27]

One of the most important influences of Christian missions was in helping to raise the status of American Indian women within the home. Most Indian women were first of all wives and mothers, and it was a major contribution of the Christian message to persuade some tribes to grant them a more humane existence. The Indian Mission Conference of The Methodist Church took note of this in 1952, dedicating the conference to Methodist Indian women. The tribute read on that occasion must be seen as a result of the understandings that missionaries had endeavored to impart to the Indians with whom they had worked during the past century.

Man regardless of race or creed, seem [sic] to consider, man alone, to be honored. There are few men under this tabernacle on Jimmy Creek at this hour who would be worthy to profess, I am a man of God, were it not for the spiritual influence of a good woman.

We exhort all men to cling to the fountain of decency, common honesty, high morality and loyalty as exemplified, by the quiet, worthy and great Indian Mother. They possess a reserved culture all their own. No other group of mothers in the world deserve more praise and have received less than Indian Mothers.

We beseech our eternal Father on this beautiful sabbath morning, that we dedicate this conference to the Methodist Indian women. May we resolve, in the innermost recesses of our hearts, from this moment to have a firm and lasting determination to honor and pay tribute to Indian women.

Devout Indian women are a treasure of great wealth, as a source of lasting inspiration. This mountain of towering strength that has endured the ravages of time is because most of our Indian women talk only when it is necessary to speak. Protect them God from becoming loose and careless with their tongues never let them imitate the foolish constant babbles.

As a united people this God blessed characteristic has been a power in protecting Indians in America from many forces of evil. May God continue to bless our people with these high and noble qualities.

May our heavenly Father guide the footsteps of Indian women so long as the sun rises in the east and sets in the west so long as fish swim and birds sing. God, let us glorify, this day Our Mothers.[28]

Beyond uplifting women's role within the home, Christian missions also endowed them with greater dignity and worth by providing outlets for service and leadership in the church. First, missionaries welcomed Indian women to their services of worship; clearly, such equal participation in the public life of the village was atypical for most tribes. One missionary among the Comanches in Indian Territory, W. A. Brewer, reported that he and his wife alternated in filling the pulpits at headquarters in Ft. Sill and at his second appointment, West Cache. Brewer praised the response the Comanches were making to the Christian movement, attributing much of the enthusiasm to the presence of Indian women:

Numbers of the squaws and papooses attend; two months ago not one would come. At almost every service the chapel is filled. We will have to start plans to build a large church. "Praise the Lord, O my soul!" Seven months ago there was, from a human standpoint, not one hope for the Comanche Mission; now I am often bewildered at the grandeur of the movement. Jesus is walking among the *tepees*. . . . I am endeavoring to lead an entire tribe of people "to the Lamb of God which taketh away the sin of the world."[29]

Certainly one of the most important roles played by the Indian women was as a bridge between home and church. One of the earliest of whom there is record, Mrs. Samuel Checote, was the wife of a Creek chief who was also a Methodist pastor and a hero of the Confederate army. Although she did not speak English, Mrs. Checote was a very able person and made her home a center for Methodist life for both Indians and missionaries in the years before she died in 1873. Another early Methodist was Mary Stapler Ross, second wife of the famous Cherokee chief and lay Methodist, John Ross. She, however, was white. Since Ross was away from home much of the time, during the Civil War, and afterward on tribal and political business, she was lonely and spoke of "the warm welcome I the lonely white stranger received far from my childhood's home."[30] In the 1850s she and her family were active in missionary work, and she helped bring her influential husband into closer contact with Oklahoma Methodism. Only after a long struggle did Indian women begin to gain experience for responsible positions beyond the family circle.

A veritable dynasty of church leaders was begun when Virginia Stumbling Bear, daughter of a powerful Kiowa chief, married Luther Sahmaunt. Virginia had been raised under Christian influence and educated at the Indian school in Carlisle, Pennsylvania. Her first service, as interpreter for the missionaries in Anadarko, was crucially important, both for the mission and for herself.[31]

Luther and Virginia Sahmaunt had two children—a son, Joel, and a daughter, Nannie Susan. In 1908 Nannie married Guy Quoetone, a Kiowa educated at Methvin Institute and the son of Jimmy and Rekobeah Quoetone. Guy joined the Indian Mission Conference in 1921 and served as a Methodist minister and tribal leader during the remainder of his long life. Nannie had been born in 1893 near Mt. Scott in the camp of her grandfather, Chief Stumbling Bear. She grew up in the

Methodist church there and also studied at Methvin Institute. The Quoetones struggled to keep the Methodist work going in Mt. Scott after the Oklahoma Conference closed that mission, persevering until it was revived. Nannie died in 1935, leaving her husband and six children—one of whom, Charles, became a United Methodist minister.[32] Another son, Allen, entered government service but remained active in the affairs of the church; he was a member of the United Methodist General Commission on Archives and History from 1976 until 1980.

Joel Sahmaunt, Nannie's brother, married Guy's sister, Carrie Quoetone, in 1922. Carrie enjoyed a long life and occupied many positions of leadership in Methodism. In the Woman's Society of Christian Service and in United Methodist Women, she held local, district, and conference offices. A product of Ft. Sill Indian School and Haskell Institute, Carrie Sahmaunt was respected throughout the Indian Mission Conference. In 1976 she was honored as Oklahoma Indian Mother of the Year. Among her ten children was Virginia (Mrs. Ray) McGilbray, who was a school teacher in Oklahoma and on the Navaho Reservation and received a Master of Arts degree from Northern Arizona University. Virginia McGilbray represented the Women's Division of The United Methodist Church in 1980 at the World Conference of the United Nations Decade for Women, in Copenhagan, after long service in local, district, and conference offices of United Methodist Women.[33] The Sahmaunts' daughters and sons have remained active at various levels of United Methodist work.

Another Kiowa Methodist family was that of Delos Lonewolf, a local preacher in the 1920s. His daughter, Hazel, graduated from Methvin Institute, married Matthew Botone, and helped him, and later their son, through the General Conference course of study for the ministry. Active in the Woman's Society of Christian Service, she served that organization in the Indian Mission Conference as president, vice-president, and spiritual life secretary. She played the piano in church meetings, taught Sunday school, and encouraged active participation by women in the life of the church and in society. When Matthew Botone died in 1961, Hazel continued his ministry as a local preacher until her retirement in 1971.[34]

Our findings have shed light on emerging understandings of

the interaction between Methodist women and American Indian women during a highly formative ninety-year period of missionary work. They document the essential functions that were carried out by female representatives of women's missionary societies as agents of the church on the frontier. They performed the roles of ministry that, in more settled areas of that day, usually were delegated to ordained men—preaching, visiting parishioners, and consoling the sick and dying. In addition, women were primarily responsible for the establishment and early development of the institutions that led to more settled communities—Sunday and weekday schools, hospitals, and homes and recreational facilities for children.

The faith that Methodist women brought to American Indians was embedded in an Anglo-American culture that often intruded on traditional Indian folkways. Efforts to civilize and uplift Indians were sometimes accomplished at the cost of violating customs more central to tribal life. Here we have illustrated the more positive aspects of Christian missions—those that helped to elevate the status of women and open wider opportunities within tribal life, notably in the family and in the church. This invites further study of the ways in which Indian culture in turn affected the whites who carried the Christian mission to the frontier, a next necessary step in understanding the genuine interaction between the two cultures whose destinies were altered and shaped on the American frontier.

For literature in the field, see Francis Paul Prucha, ed., *A Bibliographical Guide to the History of Indian-White Relations in the United States* (Chicago: University of Chicago Press, 1977); also his *Churches and the Indian Schools, 1888–1912* (Lincoln: University of Nebraska Press, 1979); works by Angie Debo, R. Pierce Beaver, Robert F. Berkhofer, Jr., Robert W. Mardock, and Vine Deloria, Jr.

For initial mingling of home and foreign concerns in missionary societies, name changes, and rechartering, see Mrs. F(rank) A. Butler, *History of the Woman's Foreign Missionary Society, M.E. Church, South* (Nashville/Dallas: Publishing House of the M.E. Church, South, n.d.); Mabel Katharine Howell, *Women and the Kingdom* (Nashville: Cokesbury Press, 1928); Noreen Dunn Tatum, *Crown of Service* (Nashville: Board of Missions, Woman's Society of Christian Service, 1960).

For development of American Indian work by WMS and WFMS, see Butler, *History of the WFMS*. Tatum, *Crown of Service,* sheds light on the 1911 transfer of Indian work.

11

SISTERHOODS OF SERVICE

Anastatia Sims

"Since Eve—the first human mother was made, *nothing else has been made*. The lesson is plain. The work of perfecting the human race was delegated to woman."[1] Thus stated North Carolina clubwoman Sallie Southall Cotten in an address to the Mothers' Club of Winterville, North Carolina, more than sixty years ago.

Mrs. Cotten was among hundreds of thousands of American women who, in the late nineteenth and early twentieth centuries, joined together in religious and secular organizations to better themselves and society. "The work of perfecting the human race" included activities that ranged from planting flowers and distributing religious tracts to winning the right for women to serve on school boards and promoting interracial cooperation. All women's groups, however, shared certain assumptions about the world and about woman's place within it. Women believed that through their clubs, they could oversee the moral and physical welfare of their communities just as they looked after the moral and physical well-being of their families. The notions of inherent feminine virtue and domesticity that lay at the heart of the ideal of southern womanhood became the basis for women's organized efforts to extend their influence beyond their homes. They argued that the exigencies of life in modern America demanded that women apply their uniquely feminine skills to problems of the public, as well as of the private sphere.[2] An examination of the social service programs of female voluntary associations reveals some of the ways those women adapted an antebellum role model to the conditions of twentieth-century life.

The spirit of voluntarism touched American women of all regions, races, and religions. Here, however, we will consider

196

only white women in two organizations—the North Carolina Federation of Women's Clubs and the Methodist women's missionary societies—in one state, North Carolina. While the activities of national and regional groups have been well documented, less information is available about clubs that functioned on a smaller scale. Specifically, little is known about how closely the rank and file of clubwomen adhered to the policies of national and regional leaders. Records of local organizations are scarce, but state records—published minutes and reports, official correspondence, and in some cases, personal papers of statewide leaders—are plentiful and often contain references to the work of the local groups as well as the statewide, or in the Methodist case, conferencewide organizations. A state study, therefore, can shed some light on the nature of women's public activities within individual communities. North Carolina was chosen because of the availability of material and also because the Tarheel State was reputed to be one of the most advanced southern states during the Progressive era—a prime example of the potential of the New South.[3] A comparison of the social service programs of Methodist women and of clubwomen can help us evaluate the contributions of organized women to the Progressive movement. It also can enable us to assess the impact of evangelical Christianity on southern women's attitudes toward reform.

In authorizing the establishment of a woman's organization to raise funds for the construction and maintenance of parsonages, the 1886 General Conference of the Methodist Episcopal Church, South, hoped to further the church's missionary program in the American West and at the same time answer the women's demands for a meaningful role in home mission work.[4] Male Methodist leaders believed that the Woman's Department of Church Extension provided an appropriate outlet for women's desire to serve. Since the prevailing feminine ideal proclaimed woman's domain to be the home, it seemed proper that women should assist the church in building homes for its servants. In 1890, the women's organization was granted the power to build parsonages. Women leaders in North Carolina and elsewhere, however, had developed a broader vision of their place in the church's home mission program. In 1896 the president of the Woman's

Parsonage and Home Mission Society of the North Carolina Conference described women as "worthy and capable of occupying responsible positions as co-laborers with men in the work of the church," while another writer called on women "to help save America to save the world."[5]

Despite the dedication of a few women to furthering organized work for home missions in North Carolina, Methodist women's home mission societies were slow to take root in the Tarheel State. Attempts to organize began almost immediately after the General Conference authorization in 1886. A representative of the General Conference, attending the North Carolina Conference meeting in Reidsville that year, appointed several women to develop a Woman's Department of Church Extension within the state. None of the early auxiliaries survived and little is known of their activities. However, Lillie Moore Everett, historian of the first fifty years of Methodist women's mission work in the North Carolina Conference, reported that the women raised $63 in 1888 and over $300 in 1889.[6] When North Carolina was divided into two conferences in 1890 (North Carolina and Western North Carolina), efforts to engage Methodist women in home missions continued, but with limited success.

Part of the problem in the eastern part of the state stemmed from a dispute within the Woman's Home Mission Society (WHMS) itself. In 1898 the organization adopted a new name and a new constitution, which provided that all funds be disbursed through the general society, rather than through the state branches. This provision displeased many North Carolina women. The president and corresponding secretary of the North Carolina Conference society resigned in protest and circulated five hundred copies of a letter criticizing the new constitution. Thirty years later one woman recalled:

This letter was widely distributed and caused much dissatisfaction in the Conference. So, in fact, to such an extent that a number of auxiliaries disbanded and it was through faith in God that a few auxiliaries, ever loyal and true, and with dauntless courage the new officers took up the work and pushed forward, but the opposition naturally retarded the growth of the work.[7]

Only five women attended the meeting of the conference society in December 1898.[8]

Lack of support from Methodist ministers also slowed the growth of women's home mission work in North Carolina. In 1901 six clergymen were asked to preach at the annual meeting of the North Carolina Conference WHMS before one finally consented.[9] Despite these obstacles, the WHMS survived, slowly increased its membership, and in keeping with policies set forth by the society's leaders, gradually expanded its scope to include social reform as well as benevolence.

Beginning in the 1890s, WHMS auxiliaries assumed many of the functions of Ladies' Aid societies. They visited the sick, collected food, clothing, and fuel for the poor, and distributed books, magazines, and religious leaflets.[10] After 1900 the societies undertook more ambitious projects as well, inspecting county jails and holding religious services for inmates, sponsoring community clean-up campaigns, and establishing playgrounds.[11] Printed minutes reveal that at annual conference-wide meetings, WHMS officers listed the aggregate accomplishments of the local groups, commended specific auxiliaries for outstanding achievement, and urged the societies to expand social service programs within their own communities. Further, they reminded the delegates of the importance of "connectional" work—support of institutions sponsored by the WHMS or by the church as a whole. Women in the North Carolina Conference were especially interested in the Methodist orphanage in Raleigh. The conference society collected money and supplies for the orphanage, and each auxiliary was asked to sponsor one child. Western North Carolina women considered Brevard Institute, a Methodist school in Brevard, their special charge. They asked that part of their conference society's pledge to home missions go to the Institute, and they also funded several scholarships there. In addition, they contributed money to missions in Asheville, Cooleemee, Greensboro, and Winston-Salem. City missionaries—usually young unmarried women—performed the same services in mill districts that WHMS members performed in more affluent communities. They visited the sick, held religious services, and distributed food and clothing. Most of the city missions also organized Sunday schools and mothers' clubs. At Cooleemee and Winston-Salem, Methodist home missionaries began to organize day nurseries for young children of working mothers and night schools for older children who worked in factories.[12]

Most local, conference, and denominational projects were aimed at alleviating the symptoms of society's ills, rather than at seeking out their underlying causes. A few leaders, however, in North Carolina as well as in the rest of the South, attempted to identify and eradicate the roots of social problems. They focused their reform efforts on four major areas: elimination of the double standard of sexual morality, prohibition of liquor, creation of laws and programs to benefit children, and improvement in the living conditions of southern blacks.[13]

The dual code of sexual behavior, which required feminine chastity while condoning masculine promiscuity, had long been a grievance of southern women. Before the Civil War they expressed their resentment of the system obliquely in popular literature, and more bluntly in their diaries.[14] By the 1890s North Carolina women were openly voicing their discontent and calling for a single standard of morality that demanded masculine as well as feminine purity. Methodist women confronted the issue in several ways. First, the WHMS supported schools for "wayward" and delinquent girls, to provide both a refuge and the foundation for a fresh start in life.[15] Second, they attacked public refusal to condemn men who became involved in illicit sexual liaisons. A poem published on the woman's page of the *North Carolina Christian Advocate* lamented the world's unequal treatment of "fallen" women and their male counterparts:

They scorned the woman, forgave the man;
'Twas ever thus, since the world began.[16]

In 1915 the superintendent of social service for the Woman's Missionary Society (WMS) of the North Carolina Conference reminded delegates to the society's annual meeting that "there is no fallen woman without a fallen man." She continued, "But the man hides his sin and holds his place in the world; the woman can only bear her shame and sink lower in the scale of existence. The time has come to open the door of hope to her or to compel him, too, to wear the scarlet letter."[17]

A year later the conference society adopted a resolution

advocating "that we seek to mould public sentiment in favor of a single standard of morality." In 1919 Western North Carolina Conference women suggested stronger action, calling for a law requiring men to pay for the education of their illegitimate offspring.[18] Finally, the women devised what they deemed to be practical measures to eliminate the problems of illegitimate births and the double standard. The social service committee of the Western North Carolina Conference WMS recommended that parents cultivate "purity of knowledge and thought concerning matters of sex" in their children, while the women of the North Carolina Conference endorsed a law raising the age of consent.[19]

Like other American reformers in the Progressive era, North Carolina Methodist women considered liquor the cause of many social problems. They cooperated with the Woman's Christian Temperance Union and other temperance forces to secure statewide prohibition in 1908.[20] After that success, women in home mission societies began campaigning for the enactment of national prohibition. In 1916 the social service committee of the North Carolina Conference WMS urged that the society "take a definite stand for National Prohibition and use our influence to promote any measures looking toward that end." Once the Eighteenth Amendment was ratified, North Carolina Methodist women repeatedly passed resolutions demanding its strict enforcement, and society officers advised local auxiliaries to press for observance of the law in their communities. After women won the ballot, WMS leaders suggested that they vote only for candidates who were strongly committed to prohibition.[21]

Most Methodist women subscribed to the prevailing notion that "the crown of womanhood is motherhood." According to popular mythology, maternity brought responsibility as well as honor. Victorian Americans believed that maternal influence was the single most potent force in a child's intellectual, physical, and moral development.[22] In the late nineteenth and early twentieth centuries, American women translated the individual mother's obligation to her own child into a collective duty of all women to all children. Methodist missionary societies, along with other female voluntary associations of the era, took a special interest in a variety of issues related to children—education, health, juvenile delinquency, child labor.

The WHMS supported several schools for underprivileged children, and society leaders also encouraged members to investigate conditions in local public schools.

To improve the children's health, Methodist women worked for the establishment of playgrounds and recreational facilities, advocated state-supported hospitals for crippled children, and in the 1920s, endorsed the federal Shepherd-Towner Bill for maternal and child care. A few auxiliaries provided milk and meals to undernourished school children. Social service superintendents of the WMS also urged Methodist women to organize day nurseries for children of working mothers and classes in nutrition and child care.[23]

Concern for the moral as well as the physical welfare of children led North Carolina Methodist women to support censorship of movies and literature and regulation of cigarette and drug sales to minors. In addition, local and conference societies investigated the causes of juvenile delinquency and the way the state was dealing with the problem. The WMS joined with other women's organizations—the King's Daughters, the North Carolina Federation of Women's Clubs, and the Woman's Christian Temperance Union—to recommend the establishment of a juvenile court system and homes for delinquent children.[24]

More important to WMS leaders than these activities, however, was the crusade to regulate child labor. Restriction of child labor was one of the "two great causes" to which the Woman's Missionary Council, the governing board of the WMS, had committed itself in 1916. Because of the large number of textile mills in North Carolina, women there had witnessed firsthand the consequences of the employment of children. At their annual meetings, the societies of both conferences repeatedly passed resolutions calling for "higher standards for state and federal control of child labor." The members sought the revision of North Carolina labor laws to increase the number of children covered by provisions that limited hours and the implementation of a compulsory education law; they also urged passage of the child labor amendment to the United States Constitution.[25]

Securing "greater opportunity for education and justice for

the Negro in the South in health, morality, recreation, and living conditions" was the other "great cause" the Woman's Missionary Council adopted. At a time when white southerners based their racial attitudes on assumptions of the inherent inferiority of the black race, southern Methodist women attempted to "work with not for" blacks.[26]

The task the women had set for themselves was not easy. It required that they not only challenge the values of others, but question their own beliefs as well. Only three years before the Woman's Missionary Council pledged itself to improve opportunities for southern blacks, the social service superintendent of the Western North Carolina Conference WMS had reminded Methodist women of their responsibility to "the negro on our hearthstones, with his childlike faith, horrible superstitions, debased ideals, and brutality."[27] That statement was more representative of the paternalism the Woman's Missionary Council wished to eliminate than of the spirit of interracial cooperation it was hoping to foster.

Other Methodist women in North Carolina, however, did recognize the need for new patterns of race relations. Beginning in 1915, some leaders encouraged WMS members to work with black women to form Bible classes, Sunday schools, and mothers' clubs. In the 1920s, conference society leaders, following the directives of the Woman's Missionary Council, recommended that each auxiliary organize a committee for interracial work. The committees were to contact local black leaders and work with them to achieve desired goals. They hoped to raise the standards of black elementary schools to equal those of whites, make high schools available to all black children, establish hospitals and playgrounds, improve streets, and start day-care centers. In that same decade, black and white Methodists in Winston-Salem joined to support a settlement house for blacks, which the Western North Carolina Conference WMS adopted as one of its projects in 1930. In 1931, both conference societies endorsed the movement to outlaw lynching.[28]

Despite conference resolutions favoring work with blacks, few local auxiliaries carried out the Woman's Missionary Council's programs for interracial cooperation in their own communities. In 1922 only two of the 549 auxiliaries in the

203

North Carolina Conference reported special work with blacks, and the number continued to be small in subsequent years. Conference social service superintendents complained that many auxiliaries refused even to use the interracial literature the council provided. In 1927, not a single auxiliary in the Western North Carolina Conference studied the recommended text on race relations, although thirteen had formed committees on interracial cooperation.[29]

Three years earlier, Lillie Moore Everett, superintendent of study and publicity for the North Carolina Conference, had reported: "The Inter-Racial subject was not a popular one, but our women who used the books on this subject, put aside prejudice and personal distaste, to do so, and many expressed enjoyment of the course after it was finished."[30] Her statement suggests a reason for the rejection of the literature: Most WMS members were unable to "put aside prejudice and personal distaste." The majority of North Carolina Methodist women in the early twentieth century found the Woman's Missionary Council's plans for interracial cooperation too radical. They could not accept a policy that challenged the system of race relations that lay at the heart of the southern social structure.

Although Methodist women did not recognize it at the time, their work with blacks ran counter to southern mores in a more subtle way, as well. Unlike their participation in other reform efforts, the promotion of interracial cooperation did not fall within the boundaries of the southern lady's traditional sphere. It was not founded on ideas about feminine moral superiority or the maternal instinct. It stemmed instead from a genuine commitment on the part of a few women to live by a Christian precept—the God-given equality of all persons. The small group of women who were attempting to ease racial tensions in the South transcended the debate on woman's place in society. They were acting on principles that applied to men and women alike, and few of their contemporaries, male or female, could follow their example.

The reluctance of North Carolina Methodist women to follow WMS policies in their communities was not limited to the area of race relations. To a lesser extent, it was evident also in their approach to other social problems. Women who readily endorsed reform resolutions while cloaked in the anonymity of a conference WMS meeting found it difficult to initiate reform programs at home where they were surrounded by family, friends, and neighbors who might eye such activities with suspicion and disapproval. This is not to suggest that these women were cowardly or lacking in conviction. They lived and acted at a time when the vast majority of Americans of both sexes believed that woman's place was in the home, not meddling in public affairs. By approving the council's demands for social change while confining their local activities, for the most part, to fund raising, charity, and civic improvement, North Carolina Methodist women exercised their prerogatives as society's moral guardians without violating the southern code of feminine behavior.

The clubwomen of North Carolina in the early twentieth century also managed to espouse social reform while maintaining a ladylike demeanor. They were concerned with many of the same problems that engaged their Methodist contemporaries: poverty, illiteracy, vice, exploitation of workers. But they differed somewhat both in the issues they emphasized and in the solutions they proposed. The North Carolina Federation of Women's Clubs (NCFWC), which by 1924 represented more than fifty thousand women, did not support institutions such as orphanages, city missions, and schools as extensively as did the Woman's Missionary Council; clubwomen looked to the government to inaugurate social service programs.[31] The federation functioned as a pressure group, attempting to influence both public opinion and public policy.

The WMS and NCFWC differed significantly in their origins and structure, as well. Unlike the Methodist home mission auxiliaries, which were formed under the direction of male Methodist leaders at the conference and denominational levels, women's clubs originated locally, and from the beginning they were run exclusively by and for women. Most began as literary societies, to develop "self-culture" among their members, but many quickly incorporated social service into their programs. In 1902, delegates from seven clubs met at Winston-Salem to found the NCFWC.[32]

In comparing the work of the NCFWC with that of Methodist women's missionary societies, it is important to remember that the former was a federation—a coalition of diverse groups. While the WHMS and WMS were regional organizations with local auxiliaries, the NCFWC was a representative body composed of several different types of groups—reading circles, civic betterment associations, home demonstration clubs. Most of the individual Methodist societies were expected to follow programs prescribed by denominational leaders, but local NCFWC affiliates acted independently, becoming more active in their communities than were their Methodist counterparts.[33] Working for beautification of their neighborhoods and improvement of living conditions, they sponsored clean-up campaigns, installed trash cans on public streets, planted trees and flowers, and equipped playgrounds. To improve health standards, they conducted "better baby" contests, distributed literature on disease prevention and nutrition, and hired public health nurses.[34] Although the WMS endorsed such activities, conference records indicate that few auxiliaries initiated similar projects. Instead, their attention was centered on charitable work, an area most women's clubs neglected.

Like missionary society women, North Carolina clubwomen took a special interest in issues related to children. In 1907 the NCFWC joined with the King's Daughters, a nondenominational association of Christian women, to raise money for a cottage at the state-supported Stonewall Jackson Training School for delinquent boys.[35] The federation also participated in a campaign to erect a similar institution for girls. In 1919 the chairman of the Department of Social Service declared, "Our greatest effort has, and will be, to establish a home in North Carolina for the delinquent girl." Clubwomen felt that the opening of the home at Samarcand a year later was due in large part to their efforts.[36] The NCFWC also agreed with the WMS on the need for a juvenile court system. Finally, clubwomen, like Methodist women, sought to protect the morals of youth by calling for the establishment of a board to censor motion pictures.[37]

Concern for the problems of industrial workers and minorities developed among North Carolina clubwomen later than it had among southern Methodist women. Although a few federated clubs operated day nurseries and reading rooms in the mill districts during the first decade of the twentieth century, their work never equaled that of the church's city missions. In later years, the NCFWC began to take more interest in the working conditions of women and children. It endorsed restriction of hours for women and children and prohibition of factory work for children under fourteen. In 1929 the federation joined other women's organizations in sponsoring a federal Department of Labor survey of working conditions in the state's mills. The governor canceled the proposed survey, however, when mill owners protested.[38]

Like Methodist women, the clubwomen acknowledged the need for interracial cooperation but were reluctant to act to ease tensions between whites and blacks. A few clubs conducted sewing and cooking classes or organized civic clubs for black women, but for the most part, clubwomen ignored the federation's directive to "give more thought and time to the study of Negro Welfare" and to improve the standard of living in the black community.[39]

Women's clubs sponsored a wider range of activities than did missionary societies. Clubs included departments of fine arts to encourage the study of art, literature, and music among their members. Home economics was also a prominent feature of club work. Many club programs centered around housekeeping techniques, budgeting, nutrition, and child-rearing. The area of greatest interest to clubwomen, however, was education, in the widest sense. In the early twentieth century, educational opportunities were limited for all southerners, but especially for women. The ladies of the NCFWC not only tried to expand their own knowledge, but also endeavored to improve the public schools and to make educational resources available to every member of the white community.

Women's clubs played an important role in the movement to obtain public libraries in North Carolina. Perhaps because of their efforts to educate themselves, clubwomen all over the state crusaded for the establishment of public libraries in towns and traveling libraries in rural regions. Four of the sixteen clubs at the first NCFWC convention included library extension among their goals. The Goldsboro Woman's Club, one of the oldest and largest in the state, maintained eleven traveling libraries in 1902, and in 1906, listed the establishment of a "Free Circulating Library" among its accomplishments. Other clubs followed Goldsboro's example.[40] In 1909 the NCFWC helped persuade the North Carolina General Assembly to set up a library commission. The federation's department of library extension remained active through the 1920s.

Women's clubs promoted higher education by funding and administering scholarships. Although they offered some financial assistance to men, they were interested primarily in increasing educational opportunities for young women. At the fifth NCFWC convention, while the federation itself was still struggling for financial stability, delegates voted to support a scholarship at Salem Academy. In addition, North Carolina clubwomen cooperated with the General Federation of Women's Clubs in its efforts to establish a program to enable American women to study at Oxford University.[41] In 1911 the NCFWC supported fourteen scholarships, in addition to those funded by individual clubs. Two years later, the federation voted to honor its founder, Sallie Southall Cotten, by creating the Sallie Southall Cotten Loan Fund "for the benefit of North Carolina girls seeking higher education."[42]

The belief that education could provide the solution to many vexing social problems, combined with the conviction that education of children was a feminine responsibility both at home and at school, led North Carolina clubwomen to seek improvements in the state's system of public education. A number of clubs donated books, magazines, and pictures to the public schools. Others sought to insure that school buildings were properly maintained, with adequate lighting and ventilation and sufficient facilities and equipment for recreation.[43] The NCFWC advocated compulsory education, longer school terms, and higher salaries for teachers.[44]

The clubwomen's interest in education had an unexpected consequence: It heightened their awareness of the legal disabilities of the female sex. North Carolina women did not receive the vote until the ratification of the federal woman suffrage amendment in 1920, but in the first decade of the twentieth century, few women seemed to find disfranchisement a liability. In 1910, Mrs. Al Fairbrother, a prominent clubwoman and journalist, proclaimed: "For be it known that the women of the South, those who belong to clubs and those who do not, are alike agreed that they do not need and do not wish the right of suffrage, realizing that they stand on higher ground and occupy a more commanding position without it."[45]

Within two years, events prompted Mrs. Fairbrother and other women of North Carolina to reevaluate their situation. In 1911, NCFWC president Sallie Southall Cotten launched a campaign for legislation to enable women to serve on school boards, only to encounter an unexpected obstacle: A North Carolina constitutional provision that limited board membership to voters. "Must we all become suffragists?" a despairing Mrs. Cotten wrote in her diary after a conversation with the state's attorney general.[46] The 1913 General Assembly waived the requirement and passed legislation making women eligible to serve on school boards, but the discovery of this heretofore unsuspected restriction aroused in NCFWC members a new interest in their relationship to the law. The 1912 convention appointed a Committee on the Legal Status of Women, which published its report in 1914. In 1918 the NCFWC, after an "animated" discussion, adopted a resolution calling for equal suffrage, since enfranchisement would enable women to serve as superintendents of public instruction and improve the status of women in the teaching profession.[47]

At the same time North Carolina clubwomen were campaigning for eligibility for school board membership and debating woman suffrage, southern Methodist women were attempting to win laity rights within the church.[48] In pursuing these ends, both groups of women were attempting to assume roles in the making of public policy that were unprecedented. Yet they argued for expansion of feminine power in the same terms they used to justify their social service programs—that women could make a unique contribution to the work of church and state. They believed that the combined qualities of domesticity and moral superiority gave women perspectives and expertise that men lacked. In 1911, Sallie Cotten asserted that serving on school boards was "eminently" within woman's domain because it dealt with the welfare of children.[49] Thirteen years later, after the ratification of the Nineteenth Amendment, NCFWC president and former suffragist Cornelia Jerman told clubwomen: "It is the duty of every wife and mother who holds the home and family sacred to vote at every election for officers who will safeguard that home and protect the children through laws governing health, education, social relations and labor."⁵⁰ North Carolina Methodist women contended that they were entitled to laity rights because "there is a complementary difference in the sexes, and the church should take advantage of it and utilize it."⁵¹ Because women's expansion of their sphere did not lead to redefinition of the feminine role, their participation in new fields would continue to be colored by old notions of woman's nature.

By 1930, female voluntary associations had propelled women into public life to a greater extent than had seemed possible in 1890. But southern women's fundamental assumptions about themselves and their role had changed little. By increasing opportunities for women within the context of the domestic ideal, women's organizations left intact the ideology that would undergird the feminine mystique. Their accomplishments must not be minimized, however. Their shared belief in woman's special talents and responsibilities led clubwomen and Methodist women alike to tackle some of the most difficult social problems of their day. While adhering to the traditional model of southern womanhood, they became leading advocates of Progressive reform in North Carolina.

12

CIVIL RIGHTS, 1920–1970

Arnold M. Shankman

The civil rights movement of the twentieth century has brought about some of the most profound changes in American history. Although there are hundreds of books and articles about the activities of those brave blacks and northern whites who struggled to promote integration and to improve race relations, relatively little has been written on the role of the southern white woman in promoting tolerance. No discussion of liberalism in Dixie would be complete without mention of the work of the Commission on Interracial Cooperation and its successor, the Southern Regional Council. From 1920 until 1970, three Methodists—Carrie Parks Johnson, Jessie Daniel Ames, and Dorothy Rogers Tilly—dominated the women's work of these two organizations. A study of these three women not only spans five decades, but reveals much about the way the South slowly came to grips with its racial problems.

Carrie Parks Johnson is the most obscure of the three women. A woman whose grandfather, father, uncle, and husband were clergymen in the Methodist Episcopal Church, South, she was born in Georgia, probably in Cuthbert, on September 16, 1866.[1] Information about her childhood is meager; even her place of birth is uncertain. It is known that she was president of the young adult missionary society of her father's church and that in 1883 she graduated from LaGrange College, a well-respected Georgia women's school, on whose board of trustees her father served.[2] Intelligent and devout, Carrie Parks hoped to be either a lawyer or a missionary to China. Because law was considered an undignified profession for ladies and missionary service too taxing for Carrie's fragile health, she was encouraged to devote her talents to church work in Georgia.[3]

211

At about the year 1888, Carrie Parks married Luke G. Johnson, seven years her senior and then minister of the First Methodist Church of Decatur, Georgia. Three children were born to the Johnsons, of whom one died in infancy. Carrie Johnson became so devoted to their remaining son and daughter that while they were small, she refused to involve herself in church work that took her more than an hour's distance from her home.[4]

Despite her desire to be with her children, her talents as a gifted speaker and tireless worker caused her to be noticed at the local woman's missionary society. In 1899 she was elected recording secretary of the North Georgia Conference Woman's Home Mission Society (WHMS). Four years later she was in charge of press work for the WHMS of the Methodist Episcopal Church, South. In 1910 she became one of ten managers on the general Board of Missions. She was also named secretary of the board of trustees of Scarritt College in Nashville.[5]

Increasingly, Carrie Johnson found herself devoting more time to church work. According to one close friend, "The church was her life, and she gave to it more energy than she could well afford. She was a dynamo of activity." Mrs. Johnson became acquainted with Belle Harris Bennett, prominent missionary administrator and stateswoman, at a Methodist conference and was so captivated by her extraordinary personality that she became her disciple. It was said that Carrie Johnson was to Belle Bennett what Luke had been to Paul in New Testament Christianity. Bennett was a genuinely saintly woman who was both a feminist and a crusader for better treatment of blacks.[6]

Carrie Johnson and Belle Bennett first demonstrated their capacity to work well together in the crusade for laity rights for women in the church. They directed the successful nine-year campaign for women's voting rights, and through it all, Carrie Johnson displayed impressive ability and stamina. After the battle was won, she was chosen a delegate from the North Georgia Conference to the 1922 General Conference of the Methodist Episcopal Church, South, the first General Conference open to women.[7]

In 1920 Carrie Johnson began her most ambitious task, the

betterment of southern race relations. At the annual meeting of the Woman's Missionary Council in Kansas City, she was unanimously selected to head a standing committee to study the race question and to develop ways for black and white women to work together. Her selection was extremely popular. Wilma Dykeman and James Stokely have observed of Carrie Johnson: "The strong features of her countenance indicated her inner strength of character. Her energy for any cause in which she believed made some friends wonder if she suffered from a hyperthyroid condition. Perhaps her ceaseless activity came instead from a hyperconscience."[8]

This action of the Woman's Missionary Council was bold for 1920. Racism was prevalent in the South, where even Bibles in courtrooms and soft drink bottles were segregated, such was the strength of the taboo on "race mixing." Lynchings were frequent, and anti-Negro riots had disgraced the streets of numerous northern and southern cities in the summer of 1919. Moreover, the Ku Klux Klan was enjoying increasing popularity. This was an awkward time for southern Methodist women to champion better race relations, since many of them lived in rural communities where blacks outnumbered whites. However, buttressed by her religious faith, Carrie Johnson accepted the challenge and controversy involved in trying to improve communication between the races.

Will W. Alexander, a founder of the Commission on Interracial Cooperation (CIC), and Lugenia Hope, a black social worker and the wife of the president of Atlanta University, offered Mrs. Johnson help in arranging a meeting with Negro women. Since the biennial conference of the National Association of Colored Women was scheduled to be held in Tuskegee in July 1920, Mrs. Hope suggested that Carrie Johnson and Sara Haskin, editor of *Laity Rights,* a leading Methodist woman's periodical, be present. Even though neither woman had ever before heard of the organization, they agreed to attend and asked that after the conference, they be permitted to meet with a small group of representative black women.[9]

The two white guests were given segregated housing and dining facilities at Tuskegee, but in no other way were they accorded preferential treatment. Their very presence made many of the eight hundred black delegates uneasy. When it was learned that the whites would meet with ten women after the conference to discuss race relations, several of the blacks assumed that they would be asked to suggest ways to acquire more reliable domestic help.[10]

The meeting took place in the study of Margaret Washington, widow of Booker T. Washington. Immediately, Carrie Johnson sensed that there was a "gulf of mistrust and suspicion":

I wanted to speak to them [the black women] but I didn't know how. I wanted to invite their frankness and their confidence. . . . Only after an hour spent in the reading of God's word and in prayer [was it possible to have] a discussion of those things which make for better civilization, for justice and righteousness and for Christian relations.[11]

When the blacks finally spoke, Carrie Johnson found it "painful at times" to listen, but listen she did.

Lugenia Hope observed that there would be no progress in the South until blacks could live in Dixie unashamed and unafraid. Carrie Johnson was profoundly moved. "My heart broke," she wrote, for she saw "colored women . . . of education, culture and refinement. I had lived in the South all my life but I didn't know such as these lived in the land." At that moment Carrie Johnson resolved that she would work to make southern white women aware of their obligation to their black sisters. She therefore asked the blacks to draw up a list of rights to which they believed they were entitled.[12]

Reaction to the meeting was favorable, and blacks were optimistic that progress could be made. Will Alexander was equally pleased. Even before the Tuskegee meeting, the CIC had decided to assemble representatives of various southern women's church groups to consider racial questions. He easily persuaded Carrie Johnson and Sara Haskin to organize the meeting in October and to invite a few black guests to address the whites.[13]

Maintaining a low-key atmosphere seemed essential if the meeting were to succeed. Newspaper coverage was avoided. The Memphis YWCA, a relatively inconspicuous location, was selected for the conference. Representatives of the Methodist, Baptist, Presbyterian, Episcopal, Disciples of Christ, YWCA, and state women's groups were invited.[14]

The conference at Memphis was as revealing—even as traumatic—for the 92 white women delegates, 68 of whom were Methodist, as the Tuskegee meeting had been for Johnson and Haskin. Carrie Johnson was determined that the assembly be productive, and therefore she encouraged candor from the blacks, even though it might offend some white delegates: "We're here for some frank talk. . . . In your own way tell us your story and try to enlighten us. You probably think we're pretty ignorant, and we are, but we're willing to learn."[15]

Speeches from Margaret Washington and from Jennie Moton, wife of Tuskegee president Robert Moton, were well received and noncontroversial. Charlotte Hawkins Brown, an eloquent black educator from North Carolina, abruptly changed the tone of the conference. En route to Memphis she had been rudely evicted from her pullman berth and forcibly marched to the "Negro car." She bitterly recounted this episode and further startled the white women when she discussed the subject of lynching: "All [Negro women] feel that you can control your men. . . . So far as lynching is concerned, if the white women would take hold of the situation, lynching would be stopped, mob violence stamped out, and yet the guilty would have justice meted out in due course by law and would be punished accordingly."[16]

When the meeting concluded it was decided to create a continuation committee of seven white women to carry on interracial work. The women were to affiliate with the CIC, which was then composed totally of men.[17]

Carrie Johnson was sure that the women showed "determination to face the issues involved with calmness, good will, sympathy, and Christianity." Margaret Washington was somewhat more reserved in her evaluation. Nonetheless she concluded that most of the whites had been polite and that many were sympathetic and interested.[18]

On November 16, 1920, the continuation committee met at Atlanta's Ansley Hotel and requested formal affiliation with the CIC. The committee members were admitted to the commission the next day, and Carrie Johnson was named director of women's work. As she accepted her new position, she warned that "the race problem can never be solved as long as the white man goes unpunished and loses no social standing while the negro is burned at the stake."[19]

During the next three years, in all the southern states except Florida, Mrs. Johnson organized women's groups to study race relations. Curiously, she found that it was necessary to defend herself from allegations that she was not a true friend of blacks. Female Negroes expected to be admitted to the commission, but in November 1920, the question of their membership was tabled. This outraged blacks and some whites, but not until March of 1921 were black women permitted to join.[20]

Even more distressing was another controversy. As noted, at Tuskegee, black women had been asked to draw up a position paper listing the desired rights for their race. A bold and frank document was prepared, but Jennie Moton gave Carrie Johnson a version of this paper that omitted its controversial preamble. The missing section requested, among other things, voting rights for black women. Further modifications were made in the document by either Mrs. Moton or Mrs. Johnson, and at Memphis, Carrie Johnson, before reading the section on lynching, commented that it was deplorable that some acts of Negro men excited mob spirit.[21]

Black women, especially Lugenia Hope, were furious with the modified document. Hope's anger intensified when she learned that the revised document was to be printed as the official statement of the black women who had met at Tuskegee. Carrie Johnson met with some of the angry black women in March 1921, and some minor compromises were made. In the end, the CIC published parts of the Tuskegee statement, and the Southeastern Federation of Colored Women's Clubs published a more complete version of the same document.[22]

Black women may not have trusted Carrie Johnson completely in 1921 because of the unfortunate dispute over the Tuskegee statement, but they believed that she was sympathetic to their goals. They realized it would take time for her to appreciate fully the concerns of black women. These hopes were not misplaced, for by 1922 Mrs. Johnson had become so bold in denouncing race prejudice that historian Henry Warnock stated that "one might have easily supposed [that she was] a member of the race for which she was making her appeal."[23]

Carrie Johnson inspired women's groups in the CIC and in Methodist missionary societies to pass resolutions concerning race relations. She was disgusted that often these resolutions were not publicized, but she doubtless realized that the statements reflected a boldness that might have been absent if hordes of newspaper reporters or spectators had been present. However, the press sometimes covered the results of her work. For example, newspapers reported that after the beating of a black woman, a Georgia Methodist group declared itself "for the protection of all womanhood of whatever race" and observed that "no falser appeal can be made to Southern manhood than that mob violence is necessary for the protection of womanhood." Such resolutions were gratifying to Mrs. Johnson, for they were passed by "thoroughly representative" white women, who not only condemned lynchings but began to familiarize themselves with other problems, such as black health-care and education, and the mistreatment of black prisoners.[24]

Carrie Johnson was a prominent speaker also at national bodies of churchwomen. When outside Dixie, she was more free to express her own sentiments than when she addressed conservative southern ladies. Perhaps her boldest speech was delivered in Indiana in 1922 to a convention of the Disciples of Christ. In that talk she pointed out that Americans had no right to criticize Europeans for treating their colonial peoples poorly until they abandoned their "attitude toward treatment of the Negro." She further stated that whites should stop pointing out the alleged immorality of Negro domestics and consider "the immorality of our own race which has so helped to degrade Negro womanhood that our blood is today mixed in the millions of mulattoes in our land."[25]

Active as she was with the CIC, Carrie Johnson remained devoted to church work. She served on the executive committees of Scarritt College, which was located at Kansas City, Missouri, until 1924, when it moved to Nashville, Tennessee; and of Paine College for blacks at Augusta, Georgia.[26] Women of the Methodist Episcopal Church, South, had given long-time assistance to both institutions.[27] In 1922 she worked with Belle Bennett to reorganize the missionary activities of the denomination. Through their efforts a department of women's work of the general missionary board was created, and Carrie Johnson was named chairwoman. This job enabled her to focus the attention of southern Methodist women on race relations, and she did a superb job. Methodist women denounced lynchings as murder and raised funds for Negroes to attend church school institutes. After the Congressional defeat of the Dyer Anti-Lynching Bill, some missionary societies called for effective state legislation, to prove that a federal statute was truly unnecessary. But southern Methodist women were unwilling to question the desirability of segregation. Even so, they probably did more to promote racial harmony than any other Christian group in Dixie, and Carrie Johnson deserves much of the credit.[28]

But there was a price to be paid for Johnson's activity. Commission and church duties required constant travel, and sometimes she was on the road for five or six weeks. Once she joked that she had not been home in more than a month and needed to become reacquainted with her husband. Increasingly she was told by her doctors to give up some activities or risk health problems. Margaret Washington once wrote that "Mrs. Johnson . . . is going to kill herself, I know, and who will take up her work? People who are capable should go slow, so they can round out their work."[29]

In April 1925, giving no advance warning, Carrie Johnson resigned as director of women's work in the CIC.[30] She had not had a vacation in four years. Commission officials made every effort to persuade her to reconsider, but she refused.[31] Maud Henderson, her assistant, also a Methodist, was named as her successor. Mrs. Johnson devoted the remaining four years of her life to church work, supporting the same causes—improved race relations and human fulfillment for both blacks and whites.[32] Her focus on church work, after the abrupt termination of her leadership in the commission, suggests less a retreat than that her achievements in the CIC always had been crucially interlaced with her base in Methodist women's work.

At the time of her death in 1929, Mrs. Johnson had won the respect of nearly all southern black women. A few probably knew that she had told a friend, "I have nothing to be ashamed of when I associate with my colored brothers and sisters. I am seeking to help." Mrs. H. L. McCrorey, a black, wrote Lugenia Hope that "Mrs. Johnson was . . . a *Christian Hero.*" Jennie Moton eulogized her as "a fearless and far-seeing friend," and Johnson's daughter, Zillah Johnson Merritt, assured Mrs. Hope that "[mother] was deeply interested in every phase of your activities, and I am sure that now . . . she is pleading for the cause before the Father's throne."[33]

Despite her diligence and sincerity, Maud Henderson, Johnson's successor, was a more custodial than innovative director of women's work for the CIC. In 1928 she resigned, and a committee was asked to find a more energetic replacement. According to commission minutes, "The machinery is all set for a program capable of reaching almost the last woman in the South. It only awaits intelligent direction and the development of the necessary power." Jessie Daniel Ames was to prove the needed ambitious successor to Carrie Johnson.[34]

Jessie Ames and Mrs. Johnson came from very different backgrounds. Born Jessie Daniel in Palestine, Texas, on November 2, 1883, Mrs. Ames grew up in Georgetown. Her father had not been a Christian and had joined the church only in his later years. Her mother, on the other hand, was a devout Methodist who saw to it that her children received religious instruction. Unlike Carrie Parks, Jessie Daniel did not have a pleasant childhood. Her parents favored her older sister, Lulu, and did little to encourage Jessie to develop socially or intellectually. When she graduated from Southwestern University in Georgetown in 1902, she had no prospective husband and no marketable job skill.[35]

Three years later Jessie Daniel married Dr. Roger Ames, an army surgeon and a pioneer in the battle to eradicate yellow fever. Dr. Ames spent most of his time abroad while Jessie and their three children, two daughters and a son, remained in the United States. Dr. Ames' premature death in 1914 terminated an extremely unsatisfactory marriage that very likely would have ended in divorce.[36]

Early in her life, Jessie Ames had learned that in Texas, a wife was an extension of her husband, "an ornament of society." As a widow, however, she became interested in the suffrage movement and displayed formidable leadership and political talents. Soon she was one of the most politically active women in Texas. In 1940, she recalled that her neighbors in Georgetown were amazed that despite "the neglect on the part of their mother—who was so busy trying to reform Texas," none of her children was arrested or sent to a "state institution."[37]

In the 1920s Ames became interested in interracial work. She was impressed by a speech given by Nannie H. Burroughs, the distinguished black clubwoman, calling on white women to demand an end to lynching. The speech caused her to believe "the responsibility was put on me." From the activities of the Ku Klux Klan and her study of conditions in black schools, she concluded not only that lynching was bad but that there was a need for interracial work if the South were ever to make social progress. On March 21, 1922, she was one of twenty-five women who met with Carrie Johnson at the Dallas YWCA to form a Texas woman's group of the CIC. At that organizational meeting, Jessie Daniel Ames was elected chairwoman and began more than two decades of work for the commission.[38]

Nearly all the state women's committees of the commission were poorly organized. The notable exception was the Texas committee, and the reason for its success was Jessie Daniel Ames. In 1924, Mrs. Ames became a paid regional field worker for the commission in the Southwest, and increasingly she took over the tasks that Carrie Johnson no longer could perform. More and more she was persuaded that there was a unique role for women in correcting racial injustice. Once she wrote Johnson, "A woman can be borne down . . . with the making of gingham dresses and darning stockings in her few leisure hours instead of keeping fit in order to be able to go before the people in a none-too-popular cause and convert them to her belief." Ames would not be borne down with the making of gingham dresses.[39]

Mrs. Ames was the obvious choice to replace Maud Henderson. This distressed Will Alexander, for he thought an aggressive and tough-minded Texas suffragette was unsuitable for the position of director of women's work; others also felt that the job should go to a more gracious southern lady. Alexander tried to talk Mrs. Ames out of the job, but this was the opportunity she had long sought; and further, she needed

220

the money to support her family—especially her daughter Lulu, who had been crippled by polio.[40]

Alexander later would regret that he had been compelled to hire a director with such a strong, motivating personality. Alice Spearman Wright recently spoke of Ames' emotions as being "like the great out of doors. There were no limits set on them. . . . [She] didn't mind telling it like it is. She did not go out of her way to offend people . . . but if people were offended, so what? . . . She was really the kind I have never seen before or since."[41] She combined "ladylike manipulativeness and pugnacity." Mrs. Ames admitted, "I have never learned . . . to keep my mouth shut when something offends either my sense of justice or fair play or vitiates the principles of democracy and Christianity." Alexander soon found that he had employed a woman who would prefer to do away with the woman's committee of the commission entirely and "get us right into the mainstream."[42]

Unwittingly, Alexander provided Mrs. Ames with a golden opportunity to expand her activities and run her own show. After a dramatic upswing in the number of lynchings in 1929 and 1930, Alexander established a commission of prominent southern men who were to study lynchings and publish their findings. Mrs. J. W. Downs, a Methodist leader, soundly criticized him for excluding women from the commission.[43] Thereupon, Alexander came to Mrs. Ames to ask if she would agree to be a member of the committee. She refused, for she felt that a token female member would have no impact on the final report. Instead, she asked for and received permission to present a proposal to the CIC Administrative Committee on Women's Activities that an independent group of southern white women be organized to combat lynching.[44]

On October 4, 1930, Mrs. Ames met with the committee, which had three black members, and secured approval for her plan. There were to be two organizational meetings: one in Atlanta, for women living east of the Mississippi, and another five days later in Dallas, for those who lived in Arkansas, Texas, Louisiana, and Oklahoma. Since Mrs. Ames considered lynching a woman's issue, she determined to use her meetings to create a new organization—one more suited to her skills than the unappreciated work she was doing for the CIC. Southern historian Jacquelyn Hall has perceptively observed, "A women's campaign against mob violence would allow her to fuse her feminism with her perception of racial inequity and to pit her skills as an organizer and publicist against a phenomenon she associated . . . with arbitrary power."[45]

At the meetings in Dallas and Atlanta, Mrs. Ames called attention to the upsurge in mob violence and commented that in only a few cases was rape the actual motive for the lynching. Unless women agreed to make eradication of the crime of lynching their personal crusade, she insisted, there would be no getting rid of this "crown of chivalry which has been pressed like a crown of thorns upon our heads."[46] According to Hall, Mrs. Ames carefully "linked the language and assumptions of evangelical reform with the pragmatic issue-oriented style of the secular movement for women's rights."[47]

Out of these conferences came a new group, composed exclusively of southern white women, and later named the Association of Southern Women for the Prevention of Lynching (ASWPL). The CIC would provide funds for the association, but the memberships of the two organizations would be completely separate.[48]

Formal organization of the ASWPL took place in January 1931. The group was formed as a temporary structure that would dissolve when there were no more lynch mobs. Ames was in charge of the association and was its only salaried officer. "As Southern people," she later wrote, "we feel keenly our responsibility in having made somewhat respectable the crime of lynching, so we are now assuming the task of undoing the past." Education and action could "undo the past." Mrs. Ames resolved to accumulate evidence "to dissipate the claim that lynchings grow out of the failure of the courts to act."[49] The men might write studies, but she believed that the women would halt the barbaric practice.[50]

The association was run by a central council which met once a year, an executive committee to deal with routine problems, and state councils and executive committees. Members of the association signed the following pledge:

Lynching is an indefensible crime destructive of all principles of government, hateful and hostile to every ideal of religion and humanity, debasing and degrading to every person involved. . . . We pledge ourselves to create a new public opinion in the South which will not condone for any reason whatever acts of mobs or lynchers.[51]

By 1942, the pledge had been signed by more than 43,000 women, many of whom lived in rural areas with histories of racial violence. When a lynching was reported, Mrs. Ames checked her files to find the women in that vicinity who had signed the pledge, and those women were asked to investigate the crime and file a report. When news of a potential lynching reached Atlanta, women in the designated locality were asked to visit law enforcement officers and demand protection for the potential victim.[52]

Jacquelyn Hall has drawn an interesting profile of an association leader. She might be Episcopal, Jewish, or Catholic, but she was more likely to be Methodist. Methodists represented 29 percent of white Protestants in the South, but they constituted 55 percent of the leadership in the ASWPL, and they distributed more than half its literature. The association leader was active in her church or synagogue and usually belonged to several voluntary organizations. Often she was college educated, of middle- or upper-class background, and married to a professional. Not all were liberal—some were segregationists who viewed the association as a means to promote social control.[53]

These leaders conducted various activities to educate the public about lynching. Literature on race relations was sent to sheriffs in counties where the population was more than 10 percent black, and the lawmen were asked to sign pledges that they would tolerate no lynchings in their counties. Within ten years, 1,355 peace officers had signed these documents. Antilynching institutes were held, and the association sponsored contests for plays on lynching. Members also monitored the activities of the southern press. Women were encouraged to register their disfavor with newspapers that invited violence or that gladly published gruesome details of crimes.[54] In 1936, Mrs. Ames addressed the Southern Newspaper Publishers Convention and urged its members to circulate only the genuine facts regarding lynchings and to give that material front-page coverage. Only then, she stated, would the public realize that lynchings were motivated by illiteracy, poverty, and provincialism.[55]

Though prevention of lynchings was her major goal, Mrs. Ames also took advantage of the association to demand better education for blacks, to call attention to the problems faced by black domestics, and to demand that qualified Negroes be permitted to vote. In 1941, both the Woman's Division of Christian Service of The Methodist Church and the ASWPL condemned the white primary. Evidence indicated that fewer lynchings than anticipated took place in communities where there were many association members.[56]

As might be expected, there was a reaction. Few questioned the interracial work of Carrie Johnson, but extreme conservatives sent threats and nasty letters to Mrs. Ames on a regular basis. Others cancelled their subscriptions to *World Outlook,* a Methodist missionary periodical, when it called for better race relations. One particularly hostile writer called Mrs. Ames a "damn yankee" and added:

Your epidermis may be white, but your "innards" must be black—or you prefer the blacks. I have heard that some white women do but I could never bring myself to believe any such thing—though people as your outfit surely shake one's faith. . . . You may have yourself a nigger if you want one, but do not force them on others.[57]

Laura Daniel, then living with her daughter Jessie, became frightened. Jessie told her, "Mother, you'd better get on your knees and pray for our safety, because I'm not going to stop." Perhaps the most vocal opponent Mrs. Ames faced was Mrs. J. E. Andrews of Atlanta, founder of the Woman's National Association for the Preservation of the White Race, who accused the association of promoting rape and declared that encouraging college students to practice social equality was part of a communist plot to destroy the white race.[58]

Few took Mrs. Andrews' rhetoric seriously, and her criticism was easily answered. It was harder to respond to black women who felt left out—women who could attend association meetings but could not become members. They probably sensed that Mrs. Ames never fully accepted them as equals. It may be that Mrs. Ames worked so hard for blacks because she thought they were too weak to take care of themselves. Keeping blacks out of the association denied that group the very participants who could have kept its membership informed of the desires and goals of black women. Certainly Negro members would have objected to literature assuring readers that the legal process could be as quick and certain as a lynching.[59]

When Mrs Ames announced her opposition to the Costigan-Wagner federal antilynching bill, it caused many blacks to wonder whether she actually was a friend.[60] Though the association officially was neutral and the CIC endorsed the bill in 1935, Jessie Ames was hostile to a federal antilynching statute. "I cannot get it out of my mind," she wrote, "that an attempt by the Federal Government to interfere drastically in the problems affecting the two races in the South would increase racial prejudice and bring disaster to the Negroes in the small towns and rural communities."[61] Mrs. Ames objected to the $10,000 penalty that would be levied on any county where a lynching took place, and she believed that southern sheriffs would claim that prosecuting lynchers was not their job, but that of federal marshals. Moreover, Ames saw no need to champion a bill that was not likely to be passed. Her endorsement, she claimed, would alienate conservative rural women in Dixie, who then would have nothing more to do with the association. In 1935 she told Janie Porter Barrett, a black Virginia educator, that pressure for her to support Costigan-Wagner was "intense" and that if she were compelled to endorse the bill, "I would of necessity have to withdraw from active work on this program against lynching."[62]

Ames refused to testify in behalf of the bill or to release helpful information to the National Association for the Advancement of Colored People (NAACP), the chief lobbyist in its behalf. She also wrote Texas Congressman Tom Connally a letter encouraging him to filibuster against it. This was made public, and Walter White of the NAACP demanded her resignation and an apology. She not only refused to apologize, but succeeded in convincing Mary McLeod Bethune, the nation's most prominent black woman, that she genuinely sought the end of lynching. Mrs. Ames weathered the storm.[63]

Some historians contend that consciously or unconsciously,

Mrs. Ames opposed Costigan-Wagner because it would mean the death of the ASWPL. Plainly, she overestimated southern hostility to a federal law. On March 13, 1934, the Woman's Missionary Council of the Methodist Episcopal Church, South, unanimously endorsed the bill. In 1937 a poll showed that two out of three southerners favored a congressional antilynching law.[64] One year later, even the program committee of the association showed willingness to support the bill if it passed Congress.[65] Jessie Daniel Ames, however, remained unmoved. She observed in 1940, "Whatever daring stands I have taken that involved the Negroes . . . were inspired as much by my love for the South as my devotion to justice and fair-play and equal opportunities for all people regardless of race."[66]

Even if there had not been a Costigan-Wagner Act, the ASWPL would have been headed toward dissolution. The reason was simple: The association had removed the last traces of respectability from the crime of lynching, and the number of these brutal murders had declined dramatically. The ASWPL held its last executive meeting in 1941, and one year later it ceased to exist. Jessie Daniel Ames had foreseen its demise when in 1937 she had convinced reluctant leaders of the CIC to change her title from director of women's work to general field secretary.[67]

As CIC officials began to absent themselves from Atlanta to take government jobs during World War II, Mrs. Ames assumed more and more duties. Without formal authorization, she commenced publication of *The Southern Frontier,* which called for more rights for blacks. She encouraged Gordon Hancock, a black professor, to summon a meeting of Negro leaders to formulate a statement of reforms. After a series of conferences, the CIC was terminated and in 1944 was replaced by the Southern Regional Council.[68]

Jessie Daniel Ames had done much to bring the Southern Regional Council into being, but she was to receive no reward for her efforts. Many officials of the CIC had never liked or trusted her and were upset that her ASWPL had captured more of the nation's attention than any other commission-sponsored activity. Moreover, they considered her too independent and ambitious. Will Alexander and Howard Odum were eager to remove her from the Southern Regional Council even if it was necessary to humiliate her in the process. When her salary was cut in half and her title stripped away, she had no choice but to resign. This was a bitter blow to a woman who in the past had turned down lucrative job offers from private industry because she "would much rather work with people in changing their social outlook than in assisting corporations to maintain their present status."[69]

Rather than seek new employment, the over-sixty Jessie Daniel Ames purchased a home in Tryon, North Carolina. To one friend she wrote, "I am not retiring but just changing my status from a professional basis to a free lance one." To another she stated that she could criticize more constructively at a distance than if she were "tied down by an official staff position" in Atlanta. She chose North Carolina rather than her native Texas because she felt that the most important racial battles would be fought in the Southeast. In Tryon she was elected superintendent of Christian Social Relations for the Woman's Society of Christian Service in the Western North Carolina Conference of The Methodist Church. She became more interested in the institutional church in her last years, and she participated in the civil rights revolution, helping to register black voters in the 1950s. When she died on February 21, 1972, at eighty-eight, her contribution to the elimination of lynching had been almost completely forgotten.[70]

Dorothy Rogers Tilly was the next woman to assume charge of women's work for the Southern Regional Council. Her background more closely resembled that of Carrie Johnson than that of Jessie Ames. She was born Dorothy Rogers in Hampton, Georgia, on June 30, 1883, the fourth of eleven children. Her father, a Methodist minister and educator, was a scholarly man with great compassion for others; her mother, a college graduate, shared Mr. Rogers' love of learning and his interest in helping the less fortunate. Both parents taught their children to be fair to all. Devoutly religious, Dorothy became president of the children's missionary society of her father's church. She graduated with honors from both Reinhardt Junior College, of which her father was president, and two years later, in 1901, from Wesleyan College, her mother's alma mater. In 1903 she married a chemical salesman, Milton Tilly, from

Atlanta. The Tillys had one son, but because of her fragile health were advised not to have more.[71]

Milton Tilly encouraged his wife to become involved in church activities. Like Carrie Johnson, Dorothy Tilly first accepted positions of responsibility in her local church's missionary society. Her ability and energy were recognized, and soon she was elected to high office in the women's society of the North Georgia Conference. From 1918 until 1931 she was in charge of children's work for the conference, a task she performed with such skill that her activities were viewed as a model for others to emulate.[72]

Increasingly, Dorothy Tilly's attention centered on ways to improve relations between black and white youth. Her hope was "that when our children are grown a better understanding will exist between the two races that live side by side." Milton Tilly approved of his wife's activities and helped to expand her vision. At the onset of the depression, he drove her to the rear entrance of a fashionable Atlanta hotel, where they saw famished Negro children raiding garbage cans for food. When Dorothy protested that she did not wish to witness such horrible things, Milton Tilly chided her and urged her to mobilize others to improve the living conditions of southern blacks. He promised her financial and moral support if she would "get involved."[73]

That episode influenced the rest of Dorothy Tilly's life. At Paine College, she became active in summer leadership conferences to prepare Negro women for positions of responsibility in their churches, and by 1933 she was named director and dean of women for the conferences. Those summer leadership seminars did much to encourage mutual understanding and respect between white and black Methodist women in Georgia.[74]

Dorothy Tilly joined the ASWPL in 1931 and soon was named secretary of the Georgia chapter. Since the association operated out of CIC offices in Atlanta, she often accompanied Jessie Daniel Ames to investigate lynchings in Georgia.[75] From Mrs. Ames she learned to gauge public sentiment in racially troubled communities by stopping at filling stations and talking with the attendants. She also became experienced in working with various religious groups on cooperative ventures.

Although Mrs. Ames greatly influenced Dorothy Tilly, the women, though friendly, were not especially close. Their personalities differed greatly. Ames was argumentative and aggressive, too much a feminist for the soft-spoken, introspective Tilly. Whereas Mrs. Ames relied mainly on her own strength and that of her friends to resolve difficulties, Mrs. Tilly was religiously motivated and constantly prayed for divine assistance. Both were earnest, and despite their different natures, or perhaps because of them, they worked well together.[76]

During the decade before Mrs. Ames' forced retirement, Dorothy Tilly served as chairwoman of an association committee to study the effects of disfranchisement on blacks and was president of the Georgia chapter of the Committee on the Cause and Cure of War. She also campaigned successfully for the funding of a school for delinquent black girls in Georgia. Methodist women elected her secretary of Christian Social Relations in the Southeastern Jurisdiction. During World War II she was in Washington for a year as chief lobbyist for the Emergency Committee for Food Production. When Mrs. Ames moved to North Carolina, Dorothy Tilly became a field worker for the Southern Regional Council.[77]

In 1946, Mrs. Tilly became aware of the extent of racism in Dixie. During that winter, she was sent to Columbia, Tennessee, to investigate a race riot and there she saw innocent blacks put on trial. Later that year she went to Monroe, Georgia, to study the senseless lynching of two black women and their husbands and discovered that no sincere effort was being made to apprehend the murderers. In December 1945 Dorothy Tilly had been the only southern woman named to serve on President Truman's Commission on Civil Rights. Her work for that commission further demonstrated to her the need to find ways to lessen racial tension.[78]

For nearly two years Dorothy Tilly, now appointed director of women's work, and other officials of the Southern Regional Council had been planning a successor to the ASWPL, and in December of 1949, a new organization, The Fellowship of the Concerned, was formed. Members were to sign the following pledge:

I am concerned that our constitutional freedoms are not shared by all our people; my religion convinces me that they must be and gives me courage to study, work and lead others to the fulfillment of equal justice under the law. I will respond to calls from the Southern Regional Council to serve my faith and my community in the defense of justice.[79]

Outwardly, the Fellowship of the Concerned was similar to the ASWPL. It had no paid staff except Mrs. Tilly, charged no dues, met irregularly, and strongly condemned lynching. The fellowship, however, was interracial in composition from its inception and was particularly interested in courtroom justice. Its members were asked to attend trials of blacks accused of serious crimes, and their visits brought about changes. Embarrassed officials ordered the courtrooms cleaned, and lawyers, conscious of the prominent women who attentively watched the proceedings and took notes, were careful not to insult Negroes by calling them boy, uncle, or auntie. Spectators were also more circumspect in their behavior, and jurors began to take their jobs more seriously.[80]

As lynchings declined in the 1950s, the Fellowship of the Concerned took on a new function: It became a supporter of desegregation of schools and public facilities. Mrs. Tilly held workshops for the organization in Atlanta and elsewhere. Early meetings were concerned with schools and the courts; later workshops focused on the United Nations, juvenile delinquency, alcoholism, and open housing.[81]

In the spring of 1954, when the Supreme Court outlawed school segregation, Dorothy Tilly urged churchwomen to accept the decision as final. She wrote a pamphlet, *Christian Conscience and the Supreme Court Decision on Segregated Schools,* liberally quoting from the Bible to show that racial prejudice was harmful to youngsters. In time, she hoped, everyone would realize that May 17, 1954, was a milestone in the liberation of humanity.[82]

Not all members of The Methodist Church were reconciled to integration. Clergy sometimes refused to meet with Dorothy Tilly or asked that she curtail her activities; a church elder implied that she was sympathetic to communism. One man wrote a minister to suggest that she be investigated by the House Un-American Activities Committee. Former church friends shunned her, and she was subjected to threatening telephone calls.

These incidents distressed Dorothy Tilly, but they did not stop her. She believed that Methodism's mission was to promote justice and harmony and that clergymen unwilling to encourage tolerance were in the wrong profession. As for the ugly phone messages, she kept a record player on her telephone table. Whenever cranks called, she would loudly play the Lord's Prayer and that usually silenced her critics. Even when the Ku Klux Klan threatened to bomb her house, she did not abandon her work.[83]

The fellowship members faced intimidation from the Klan, from hostile newspaper editors, and from white citizens' councils. In Alabama, photographs of fellowship women and their husbands' business connections were published in segregationist newspapers; similar harassment took place in Mississippi. Dorothy Tilly comforted the women involved by noting that "reprisals have a way of striking back." But she knew that many did suffer and that some even came to fellowship meetings without the knowledge or approval of their husbands.[84]

The 1960s were trying years for Dorothy Tilly. Her devoted husband died, militant blacks alleged that she was patronizing them, and Southern Regional Council leaders became annoyed with her insistence that alcohol not be served at their functions. Furthermore, though hardly a feminist, she resented the fact that male council leaders seldom consulted her about matters of policy. Worst of all, Dorothy Tilly, who never had been in good health, was troubled by various ailments. After entering a nursing home in 1969, she died there on March 16, 1970, and with her death, the Fellowship of the Concerned was terminated.[85]

For fifty years three Methodists had dominated the efforts of southern white women to seek racial harmony in Dixie. Each woman was a product of her time and did as much as realistically possible to advance conditions for blacks. Carrie Johnson grew up during Reconstruction and came to adulthood in the period called the nadir of American Negro history. It is not surprising that she never openly questioned segregation, for had she done so she would have become a social outcast. She sought, instead, to educate white women about the inferior status imposed upon their black sisters. Her orientation was primarily religious, for she felt that if injustice prevailed in Dixie, it would be impossible for missionaries to spread the gospel abroad to nonwhite peoples. By modern standards her goals were tame and even paternalistic, but she was almost alone when she castigated the practice of lynching and denounced the racial and sexual double standards. Carrie Johnson could not have been bolder without losing her base of support. Southern women in the 1920s would have turned a deaf ear to advocates of integration. But because of Mrs. Johnson, white women studied the race problem objectively. She planted the seeds that ultimately eradicated segregation. The facts of Carrie Johnson's life suggest that if she had lived until the 1960s, she too would have favored integration.

Jessie Daniel Ames was less religious than either her predecessor or her successor, but she also believed that lynch mobs in the South negated missionary efforts in foreign lands. Mrs. Ames was a superb organizer and public relations expert and led one of the most important women's crusades in American history. If she sometimes seemed aggressive and militant, perhaps it was because unlike Mrs. Johnson and Mrs. Tilly, she had no husband to provide for her, her children, and her mother. Since she was highly capable, it is natural that she would resent the fact that mediocre men were recognized for modest achievements while her own were largely ignored. It is true that the Association of Southern Women for the Prevention of Lynching was closed to blacks, but Mrs. Ames felt that the crusade could succeed only if it were led by women who personified the alleged justification of lynching. Her main opposition to a federal antilynching law stemmed from her honest belief that education—not coercion from Washington—was the only way to persuade the South to abandon that barbaric practice. Insofar as the times allowed, she pointed out the evils of segregation. Publicly she was known for her antilynching campaign, but she also led white women to study the poor educational opportunities available to blacks, the exploitation of Negro domestics, and the effects on all blacks of disfranchisement. Unlike Carrie Johnson, she faced detractors who called her a traitor to her race. But such accusations did not overwhelm her. Living to witness the civil rights movement of the 1950s and 1960s, she spent her last years helping southern blacks register to vote.

Perhaps Dorothy Tilly's task was hardest of all. It was her job to promote integration in southern society. World War II made racism unfashionable, but many in the South still resisted integration. Through years of work with black women and service on President Truman's Civil Rights Commission she realized that integration was inevitable and desirable, and she possessed an uncanny ability to determine how far public opinion would permit her to go. Through Dorothy Tilly, southern women came to recognize that they had a role in bringing law and order to their region and that the South could never advance if it kept half its population out of decent schools and out of voting booths. For these views she was regularly called a communist, even though her accusers well knew that her motivation was the gospel of Jesus Christ, not the writings of Lenin or Stalin. Fortunately Dorothy Tilly lived long enough to witness the enactment of civil rights laws and to receive recognition from some who once had been her detractors.

Scholars increasingly are realizing the importance of historical research into American race relations. Only when the roles of such women as Carrie Parks Johnson, Jessie Daniel Ames, and Dorothy Rogers Tilly are studied can there be a proper appreciation of the way southern "ladies" helped to prepare their region for integration and better race relations.

Section Three
Foreign Missions and Cultural Imperialism

13

THE CASE OF
ANN HASSELTINE JUDSON

Joan Jacobs Brumberg

By 1845, in those American homes where Protestant evangelical religion predominated, it was unlikely that any individual—adult or child, male or female—except perhaps on the more remote frontiers, had not at least heard the names of Adoniram and Ann Hasseltine Judson. "For more than thirty years his name has been a household word," wrote Hannah Chaplin Conant from Rochester, New York, after Adoniram's death in 1850. "A whole generation had grown up familiar with the story of his labors and sufferings, not one of whom had ever seen his face." In fact, Mrs. Conant was describing her own generation, born after 1800, which regarded Judson as "a sort of Christian Paladin, who had experienced wonderful fortunes, and achieved wonderful exploits of philanthropy in that far off mythical land of heathenism."[1] Judson's life, including his forty years of foreign missionary work, were memorialized in numerous antebellum tributes—both poetic and prosodic—in the secular and religious press during his lifetime and in posthumous biographies which continued to be written well into the post-Civil War period. Later generations of subscribers to the Pioneer Series of the Woman's Foreign Missionary Society of the Methodist Episcopal Church, for example, could read of Judson's exploits in Burma in Pamphlet no. 3, written by Mrs. O. W. Scott.[2]

For many antebellum evangelicals, however, it was Ann Hasseltine Judson, rather than Adoniram, who initially took center stage in the emerging drama of American foreign missions.[3] In fact, the literary evidence suggests that after her untimely death in 1826, Ann Judson became a central and established figure in the female hagiography of the nineteenth century and that the importance she assumed as a popular cultural heroine provides some explanation for the enthusiasm with which so many nineteenth-century women embraced the foreign mission movement. At the same time, the ethnological perspective developed by Ann Judson and the popular cause she represented mitigated the nascent domestic movement for woman's political equality.

Wherever one looks in the American woman's popular literature of the nineteenth century, one can find the name of Ann Hasseltine Judson. Young women such as Pamela S. Vining, a student at Castle Hall seminary in Catskill, New York, wrote poetry in Ann Judson's honor, and each verse was carefully copied from periodicals into personal albums.[4] Others, of particularly pious evangelical families, followed the Judsons' missionary exploits in the religious newspapers. Ministers and women editors, aware of the didactic potential of Ann Judson's story, extolled her virtues and the manner in which her glory reflected on her Christian sisters in all the Protestant evangelical denominations.

The most popular of all the antebellum Judson books was James D. Knowles' posthumous biography of Ann, first published in Boston by Lincoln & Edmands in 1829. A year later the interdenominational American Sunday School Union brought out a second edition. Knowles' *Memoir of Mrs. Ann H. Judson, Late Missionary to Burmah* went through ten editions by 1838 and was reissued on an almost yearly basis until 1856, and again in 1875.[5] Unitarian Lydia Maria Child referred to it as "a book so universally known that it scarcely need be mentioned."[6] Knowles' biography appears on almost every antebellum reading list designed for the self-education of young Christian women. Members of the women's organization of a Congregational church in Vermont, for example, were able to borrow it from their association library.[7]

Ann Hasseltine Judson's biography was included in at least a dozen antebellum collections of "women of worth," including Lydia Maria Child's *Good Wives* published in 1833 and Sarah

Josepha Hale's *Woman's Record,* published twenty years later. The Episcopalian Mrs. Hale, editor of the popular Godey's *Lady's Book,* wrote that Ann Judson, "as the first American woman . . . to leave her friends and country to bear the gospel to the heathen," merited "the reverence and love of *all* Christians."[8] Another biographer said of her: "If [Judson] had lived in legendary instead of historical times, she would have ranked with Saint Agnes and Saint Cecilia; but as plain truth is now spoken of the good, the devoted, and the martyrs, she will be remembered for ages, as one deserving of high praise in *all* the churches."[9] Without doubt, Ann Judson's reputation transcended the limits of any single denomination; hers was a story that earned her a place in the pantheon of American Christian womanhood.

While Ann Hasseltine, Adoniram's first wife, was always the most popular figure among the Judson women, there were some biographers—like Arabella Stuart Willson—who chose to "embalm in one urn" the memory of all Judson's wives (the third of whom survived him). Mrs. Willson's book of collective biography, first published in 1851, sold at least 28,000 copies by 1856 and by 1875 had been reprinted six times.[10] Interest in Ann and her successors was so high that in the 1850s, Daniel C. Eddy, a Baptist minister in Boston and a biographer of Adoniram, made something of a second career by writing about the women in the Judson family. Eddy produced three volumes on female missionaries. The text was basically the same in each edition—only the titles changed. In 1850 and 1855, respectively, he gave his book the generic titles *Heroines of the Missionary Enterprise* and *Daughters of the Cross.* By 1859, probably in response to a persistent market for Judson material and the popularity of the name, Eddy renamed his book *The Three Mrs. Judsons, and Other Daughters of the Cross.*[11]

Adoniram and Ann Hasseltine Judson were, in fact, one of the two first American missionary couples to begin evangelization in foreign lands.[12] In the summer of 1812 they left Salem, Massachusetts, aboard the ship *Caravan* for an undetermined location in the Orient. Judson, at the time, was twenty-four; his wife of one week was twenty-three. They were accompanied by another young missionary couple, Samuel and Harriet Newell (Harriet was only eighteen), and the unmarried Luther Rice.

The men had known one another as students at Andover Theological Seminary; Ann and Harriet had been classmates and friends at the Bradford Female Seminary and had been converted at approximately the same time in a revival that had taken hold of their hometown in 1806. This youthful band of foreign missionaries was sponsored by the Congregational Church through its newly formed agency, American Board of Commissioners for Foreign Missions (ABCFM).

The inception of the ABCFM in 1812 and the departure of the five young people marked the beginning of the American foreign mission crusade, the single largest organizational aspect of evangelical Christianity in nineteenth-century America, and soon the special preoccupation of women in all the major Protestant denominations.[13] By 1850, the major Protestant churches were increasingly committed to the work of foreign evangelization; each had its own foreign missionary structures, and some had special training schools.[14] By 1871, separate women's foreign mission boards had become the order of the day within each denomination and were enormously successful.[15] In 1890, the Woman's Foreign Missionary Society of the Methodist Episcopal Church alone had 3,000 auxiliary groups and counted more than 100,000 members.[16] These women's boards published their own newspapers and magazines, supported the operation of schools and orphanages abroad, and trained medical missionaries, zenana workers, Bible women, and schoolteachers in ever-increasing numbers throughout the century.

The effort that had begun in 1812 as a strictly Congregationalist program quickly expanded to include other denominations. While the historical reasons for this are complex and beyond the scope of this essay, a significant portion of the story of the evolution of the foreign mission crusade is related to the remarkable events that befell Adoniram and Ann Hasseltine Judson and the publicity that accompanied those events.

In the first place, the Judsons caught the attention of the American religious community by an audacious act of biblical interpretation. On board ship, even before they had decided on Burma as their destination, both Judsons became convinced that there was no scriptural authority for their baptism as infants in the Congregational Church. As soon as they reached

Calcutta, they joined the Baptist denomination and were both rebaptized. The news of their decision, which spread throughout the United States "like the sound of a trumpet," horrified the Congregationalists and required careful attention from the Baptists, who virtually had the couple dropped in their lap. The Judsons' rejection of infant baptism certainly would not have pleased Methodists, who frequently contended with their Baptist fellow-evangelicals over just this issue. Within months of the receipt of the news, American Baptists responded with the formation of the Baptist Society for Propagating the Gospel in India, a missionary society that committed itself to raising funds to support these runaway children of New England orthodoxy. By 1814, the Baptists had organized twenty-two different missionary auxiliaries throughout the Northeast and South. In the interim, the story of the Judsons' change of heart was transmitted beyond the circle of people who had known them in Bradford and Salem, through the pages of the *Massachusetts Baptist Missionary Magazine.* Judson's letters explaining why he had abandoned pedobaptism appeared in the March 1813 issue of the magazine, just two months after the first news arrived. Ann Judson's letter to a friend, a very personal explanation of her new belief, was published the following May: "Can you, my dear Nancy, still desire to hear from me, when I tell you I have become a Baptist?"[17]

For more than a decade, the letters of Adoniram and Ann Judson to their family and friends and to their new denominational sponsors were published in at least a half-dozen different Baptist periodicals, providing readers with firsthand accounts of their labors and emotional responses to life among a non-Christian people.[18] Secular papers in communities where Baptists comprised a significant portion of the readership also reported on the events of the Judsons' Burmese mission. Since most nineteenth-century periodicals were circulated among friends and neighbors, extending their readership far beyond actual circulation figures, it is no wonder that the Judson name became a household word in antebellum America.

If the Methodist press neglected to cover the celebrated couple in Ann's lifetime or to mention Dr. Judson before 1846, it was due less to denominational rivalry (though that was real enough in the period) than to a combination of the founding dates of leading Methodist periodicals and Methodist official-dom's overwhelming concentration on internal missions until at least 1845.[19] Some farsighted clergy, somewhat interested in overseas work, founded the Missionary Society of the Methodist Episcopal Church in 1819.[20] But "from several quarters opposition to the new society was formidable." The argument was pressed that American Methodism was by its very nature a missionary movement and that a separate missionary society would be superfluous.[21] The society was recognized by the 1820 General Conference, but reflecting these pressures, the report of the Committee on Missions "set forth . . . the claims of the American continent on immediate missionary effort, involving postponement of effort over-seas."[22] In light of this, it is not surprising that "the society grew slowly. Volunteers were rare. The society [itself] had only advisory and auxiliary powers" and "could claim only spare-time attention from its officers until 1836." Indeed, just before the 1844 division of the church, Methodism reportedly "had some 360 missionaries in the homeland but a bare handful in its one overseas mission . . . Liberia," begun in 1833.[23]

Yet if Methodist bishops and clergy were focused on the evangelization of settlers and Indians, Methodist Episcopal women, like their sisters in other denominations, seem to have been drawn to foreign missions. As early as 1819 they began to form auxiliaries and join interdenominational efforts. Al-though scarcity of sources makes direct evidence nearly impossible, it is unlikely that foreign-mission-minded women among the Methodists failed to follow news of Ann Judson and later read her biography, even if Methodist/Baptist rivalries inhibited public announcement of their interest. Members of the strong and enduring Female Missionary Society of New York (1819–1861) would in due time have been interested also in Sarah and Emily Judson, as might members of the Ladies' China Missionary Society at Baltimore after 1847.[24]

Within a year of its establishment in 1845, the *Missionary Advocate* of the Methodist Episcopal Church began to cultivate Judson interest among Methodists by featuring the work of Adoniram in its pages. Excerpts from the widower's account of his second wife's death at sea and of her missionary work were the first entry. Later in 1846, the *Missionary Advocate* twice printed Judson's remarks during his triumphal visit home after thirty-four years. In 1847, the newspaper introduced the third Mrs. Judson to readers and in 1848 ran two of her items. In 1850, it printed part of *Malcom's Travels in Burmah,* including a visit to the Judson mission in 1838, which attested: "His labours and sufferings for years, his mastery of the language, his translation of the whole word of God . . . make him the most interesting missionary now living."[25]

While this explicit Methodist interest postdates Ann Hasseltine Judson, it was her flair for publicizing the mission during its first fifteen years that set the pattern for ongoing public interest in Adoniram and his wives. From the outset, it was Ann—not Adoniram—who acted as the dramatist of the mission. Adoniram's published accounts addressed method-ological questions of the best way to go about evangelization. Since he had had no preliminary conversations with his Baptist sponsors, correspondence must have been peculiarly impor-tant. Almost all his published papers were therefore profes-sional, rather than personal. Ann's letters, in contrast, focused on her emotional reactions to Burmese culture, the care and management of her family, and the Burmese she employed and taught. In a straightforward and artless manner, the young missionary provided the basic narrative structure of the Burmese mission story and at the same time revealed her own joys, fears, and sorrows. The intimate style of the Judson correspondence and the manner in which their story unfolded captured the attention of the American reading audience.

In the December 1814 *Western New York Baptist Missionary Magazine,* the home audience learned from Ann Judson's letter of the death of Harriet Newell, the other young woman in the original missionary band. For Ann, it was an enormous loss, which she described poignantly by personifying death itself: "Harriet is dead. Harriet, my dear friend, my earliest associate in the Mission, is no more. O death, thou destroyer of domestic felicity, could not this wide world afford victims sufficient to satisfy thy cravings, without entering the family of a solitary few, whose comfort and happiness depended much on the society of each other?"[26] Ann Judson's loneliness was a constant preoccupation; when Luther Rice, another of their original associates, departed for the United States because of illness, Ann wrote: "Mr. J and I are entirely alone. There is not one remaining friend in this part of the world." In July 1813, when the Judsons had finally reached Burma and made their first home together in a house deserted by British missionaries, Ann wrote of the future: "I should have no society at all, except for Mr. J for there is not an English female in all Rangoon."[27] On the death of her eight-month-old son, born in the summer of 1815, Ann Judson poured out her heart in a letter that received wide circulation in the religious press of the United States:

Death, regardless of our lonely situation, has entered our dwelling, and made one of the happiest families wretched. . . . Our only little darling boy was three days ago laid in the silent grave. Eight months we enjoyed the precious gift, in which time he so completely entwined himself around his parents' hearts, that his existence seemed necessary to their own. When we had finished study, or the business of the day, it was our exercise and our amusement to carry him around the house or garden, and though we were alone, we felt not our solitude when he was with us.[28]

Denied all "bonds of sisterhood" by Harriet Newell's premature death, Ann Judson stood, a lone Christian woman, in an alien geographical and cultural landscape. As a result, evangelical women were sympathetic and interested both in how she fared and in what she had to report about the relative positions of women in Christian and heathen societies.[29]

In addition to conveying the harsh emotional realities of the mission, Ann Judson's letters were consistently filled with information about the social and economic life of Burma. American readers learned that the Burmese lived principally on rice and fish. "There are no bread, potatoes, and butter and very little animal food," wrote the appalled daughter of New England.[30] In a very real sense, Ann Judson was practicing a rudimentary form of cultural anthropology, for her letters plied the American Christian reading audience with various details about the Burmese diet and language, their family patterns and sex roles, the nature of Hindu religious practice and belief, and the forms of native architecture and clothing. All Ann's reports, however, were informed by a Christian perspective and by her feeling that she was an agent for moral

241

transformation through Christian conversion. In one of her earliest published letters from the field, she articulated her aims as a missionary:

I desire no higher enjoyment in this life, than to be instrumental in leading some poor, ignorant females to the knowledge of the Saviour. To have a female praying society, consisting of those who were once in heathen darkness, is what my heart earnestly pants after, and makes a constant subject of prayer. [I am] resolved to keep this in view; as one principal objective of my life.[31]

Repeatedly Ann described the need for general education and immediate Christian conversion. She wrote with spirit in an early letter to her sisters in Bradford, Massachusetts:

Good female Schools are extremely needed in this country. I hope no missionary will ever come out here, without a wife, as she, in her sphere, can be equally useful with her husband. I presume Mrs. Marshman [of the English mission at Serampore] does more good in her school, than half the ministers in America.[32]

From the heart of "heathendom," Ann Judson reported that the elevated moral status of women was a characteristic feature of Christendom and that heathen women were in a desperate and deplorable condition. Her early religious feminism expressed in her published letters did much to define the nature of Christian service to heathen women throughout the nineteenth century. According to Ann Judson, the simultaneous spread of literacy and the gospel were the best antidotes to the immorality of heathen social practices, particularly those that victimized women—the zenana, the harem or seraglio, polygamy, female infanticide, child marriage, and suttee.[33]

In the Hindu practice of suttee, a widow's self-immolation on her husband's funeral pyre, American readers found the perfect symbolic representation of the moral gulf between Christianity and heathenism. Stories of female degradation and suttee carried to America by Ann Judson became pervasive in the periodical literature read by antebellum Christian women. In the introduction to the 1838 *Christian Keepsake and Missionary Annual,* suttee figured prominently in the first two verses of Lydia Huntley Sigourney's poem:

THE CASE OF ANN HASSELTINE JUDSON

Tint the red flame, and paint the gazing throng
Where sultry India rears the funeral pyre;
Plead for the widow, ere the thundering gong
Drowns the last wild shriek of her death of fire.[34]

Lydia Maria Child, in her 1835 *History of the Condition of Women,* reported the case of a Koolin Brahmin who had more than 100 wives, 22 of whom—between the ages of 16 and 40—were consumed with his corpse. Child claimed that 19 of the victims had seldom seen the husband with whom they consented to perish.[35] Sarah Josepha Hale put the question in Godey's *Lady's Book:* "How can the heathen woman/Her hopeless lot endure?"[36]

When Ann Judson returned to the United States in 1822 for recuperative purposes, she continued to elaborate on the moral gulf between women in Christian and those in non-Christian cultures. In a series of meetings in Salem, Boston, Bradford, New York, and Baltimore, the ailing missionary—who was being treated with large doses of mercury—reiterated the ethnological themes she had set forth in her published letters.[37] American women, she believed, would mobilize for action if they knew the truth about their "tawny sisters on the other side of the world." Judson stressed the advantages American women enjoyed, as compared with their illiterate, degraded sisters in the East. Of course, this perception reinforced, rather than undercut their belief in the "cult of true womanhood," a collective hyperbolic statement of the perfection of Christian women in America.[38] Concern for the uplift of heathen women became the central fund-raising appeal of the women's foreign mission crusade.

As a result, this concentration on the "other" worked against the domestic movement for woman's political equality by emphasizing the greater social and educational privileges of western women, siphoning off energies, and directing resentment abroad. Religious women who accepted the mantle of "true womanhood" because of its Christian underpinnings directed their attention to what they considered the pervasive ignobility of heathen women rather than to the social revolution implicitly threatened by the women at Seneca Falls.

The religious feminism of American evangelical women was

a cautiously constructed and tenuous ideology: Mistreatment of women was located abroad, rather than at home; criticism of men was levied only at heathens, infidels, alcoholics, and possibly slaveholders—not at practicing Christians. In the name of woman's uplift abroad and at home, antebellum women were able to develop careers as participants in Christian endeavor, as managers of the "benevolent empire," as teachers, and as missionaries. This "apostolate of women," as demonstrated in the life work of Ann Judson, absorbed the hearts and minds of evangelical women.[39]

On June 21, 1823, following a six-month period of recuperation, the publication of her letters in book form, and an appearance before the Baptist Triennial Convention in Washington, D.C., a rejuvenated Ann Judson returned to Burma for her greatest and final adventure. A letter from Adoniram published in July 1824 carried the happy news that Mrs. Judson and he had been safely reunited the previous December. But in February 1824, Ann Judson wrote from the capital city of Ava that "in consequence of war with the Bengali government, foreigners are not so much esteemed at court as formerly, I know not what effect this war will have on our mission."[40] That was the last letter Ann Judson would write for two years. The outbreak of the Burmese-British War drove almost all English-speaking people from Burma and severed communications with foreign countries. The fate of the Judsons, who had not come out of Burma with other refugees, was unclear.

American readers were kept as informed as possible by a conscientious Baptist press. An editorial in the *American Baptist Magazine* explained: "The state of our missionaries at Ava was by our latest accounts eminently perilous. The war seems to have been carried on with unusual ferocity. Should the exasperation against the English be extended to our missionaries, we cannot but tremble for the result." Observers in Calcutta reported starvation, chaos, and violence in Burma; in fact, the king and queen had been beheaded. The Baptist press prepared its readership for the worst: "Should the dear missionaries at Ava fall sacrifice to Burman cruelty . . . we must send others to supply their place, and to strengthen our hand."[41]

THE CASE OF ANN HASSELTINE JUDSON

In December 1825, information was received and published in the *American Baptist Magazine* that the Judsons were alive. However, the February 1826 issue stated that the good news had been, regrettably, premature. Throughout the spring of 1826, continued uncertainty as to the Judsons' fate was reported in the religious and secular press. In July, news of the termination of the Burmese War arrived, but it was not until October 1826, more than two years since Mrs. Judson's last letter, that foreign mission supporters read the headline: JOYFUL INTELLIGENCE. Two brief letters from Adoniram and Ann outlined the terrain of hardship through which they had passed. Said Ann, "I can hardly, at times, believe it a reality that we have been safely conducted through so many narrow passages."[42] With the home audience's appetite whetted, Ann Hasseltine Judson eventually would describe all the gory details in a letter of more than 14,000 words, published in the *American Baptist Magazine* in its entirety and excerpted in later memoirs and biographies. Of that letter, which took more than two months to write, James Knowles remarked: "Fiction itself seldom invented a tale more replete with terror."[43]

As the Judsons' letters began to appear, those who had waited out their captivity began to piece together a fascinating story of Christian fortitude in the face of heathen oppression, and it was readily apparent that the drama's major protagonist was Ann Hasseltine Judson. It was Ann who remained a relatively free agent while her husband was confined in a series of horrifying jails, and during that time, their second child, a daughter, was born. It was Ann who traveled into the dangerous Burmese jungle carrying the infant, to minister to the medical and nutritional needs of Adoniram and the other men who were suffering from the deplorable prison conditions. When the Christian prisoners faced certain death by execution, it was Ann who pleaded their case in the capital city of Ava and connived with Burmese officialdom for their reprieve. It was Ann who ultimately saved the Burmese mission by preserving unharmed the central focus of their missionary work: Adoniram's translation of the Old and New Testaments.

The Judsons' adventures in Burma obviously made good reading. When the publication of their war letters began, the

245

American Baptist Magazine experienced an increase in readership.[44] In fact, the Judson story had all the compelling qualities of a contemporary media event. The two-year news blackout followed by their serialized reports heightened public interest in the mission. In addition, the old lessons of religious piety, perseverance, and courage were newly animated against a colorful backdrop of exotic heathenism. The context of a non-Christian culture provided high dramatic overtones to the personal battles of illness, loneliness, and death that plagued the Judsons, and with which many readers could identify. And because the story was being created as it was being read, there was a measure of importance and urgency to each published installment.

When Ann Hasseltine Judson died shortly after the end of the war, as a result of a fever acquired during her recent deprivations, it was not, in fact, the conclusion of the Judson story. Their daughter died at about the same time, and Adoniram Judson remained in Burma, doing the solitary work of translator and lexicographer, and writing letters for publication in the Baptist press. In April 1834, at Tavoy, he married Sarah Hall Boardman, the widow of another missionary, and they had seven children. In 1846, after the death of Sarah while she was en route home for her health, Judson—now fifty-eight—arrived in the United States to a hero's welcome. William Learned Marcy, then Secretary of War, introduced him to President James K. Polk as "the Greatest Ecclesiastical Character now living."[45] Before returning to Burma, Judson married twenty-nine-year-old Emily Chubbuck, a "mistress of belles lettres" at the Utica Female Seminary and the literary sensation of the 1840s, who wrote under the pseudonym Fanny Forester.

Judson remained very much in the public eye throughout his forty-year career; in fact, his controversial third marriage to a popular fiction writer only increased his visibility. Each of Judson's wives would be lauded for her particular strengths: Ann for her courage and perseverance, Sarah for her constancy, Emily for her acuteness and wit. "Dr. Judson's two later wives were highly esteemed," R. Pierce Beaver has written, "but Ann possessed the love and veneration of churchwomen beyond all others. More biographies and sketches have been written about her than any other woman missionary."[46] Ann Judson's death in British Burma in 1826 provoked countless tributes from every corner of the evangelical empire. One secular reviewer claimed that one could "search the annals of Greek or Roman medieval or modern heroism, and . . . find no name worthier" than that of Ann Judson.[47] The Anglican Bishop of Calcutta regarded Ann Judson as a symbol of "an order of American women to whom . . . the pen of history will do justice as having been the glory of the nineteenth century."[48]

Evangelically inspired writers throughout the century repeated for women and girls of all ages the courageous story of "Ann of Ava." Convinced of the energizing or motivational power of the lives of great Christians, didactic writers made Ann Judson's biography a stock item in the popular culture of nineteenth-century America. As for the generation of women who actually followed the serialized exploits of Mrs. Judson in the religious papers, their keen identification with her intensified the appeal of foreign missions. This perhaps explains in part the full flowering of the women's foreign mission crusade after 1850. It is not coincidental that both Sarah Hall Boardman and Emily Chubbuck laid their first interest in foreign missions at the feet of Ann Hasseltine Judson, confirming the evangelical axiom that literature does indeed influence behavior. At age nineteen in eastern Massachusetts, Sarah Hall had been inspired to become a missionary after hearing and seeing Mrs. Judson on her 1822 visit to Salem.[49] Emily Chubbuck, growing up in Hamilton, New York, knew the Judson story through the religious papers that were read aloud in her family. Upon hearing about the death of Ann Hasseltine Judson in 1826, ten-year-old Emily cried out, vowing that she too would consecrate herself to the missionary life.[50] If there is truth in the theory that we carry around in our head a collection of story plots, and tend to see and shape our life according to those plots, then the wide dissemination of the biography of Ann Judson has particular importance for the history of American religious women.[51]

While Congregationalists revere the memory of Judith Grant and Elizabeth Dwight, and Methodists rightly extol the achievements of Ann Wilkins, Isabella Thoburn, and Clara

Swain—Ann Hasseltine Judson was nevertheless the premier model of American female missionary work through her striking adventures, and through her own and antebellum Baptists' promotional skills. In addition, Ann Judson's early articulation of religious feminism foreshadowed the approach of every major Protestant women's foreign mission board. A great proportion of religious women throughout the century would thereafter eschew involvement in the domestic struggle for woman's rights to concentrate their efforts instead on the uplift of women abroad. Finally, the pervasive posthumous use of Ann Judson's biography made her a figure of extraordinary significance. The fact that she continued to be known and admired by pious women throughout the century suggests the existence of a self-perpetuating women's culture that transcended denominational lines. For this reason in particular, we have lifted Ann Hasseltine Judson out of denominational history as it is narrowly conceived and pushed her onto the ecumenical stage of the history of American women, appropriating her significance for nineteenth-century women's lives and for American evangelicalism generally.

14

DOING MORE
THAN THEY INTENDED

Adrian A. Bennett

The shifting aspirations and roles of women within a particular society are regarded by many as hallmarks of a major social revolution. Social revolutions are virtually impossible to see or to analyze firsthand with any precision; as with most developments, they are most clearly seen at a distance and even then with difficulty. The changing role of women is a social revolution that has developed over the past two centuries, and the end is not yet in sight, particularly if one includes similar developments in the non-western world. Women's history, chronicling these changes, is a relatively new field of inquiry; hence, while a little is known of the shifting aspirations and roles of women in the West, less is known of the non-western world. One of the more fascinating areas of study is the role of women in the revolutionary process in twentieth-century China.[1] Here are found women who were trapped in a traditional concept of second-class status, both in theory and in reality, for more than a thousand years, but who in the course of the last century have moved to positions of equality, at least in theory if not yet in complete reality.

One recent published study, for example, notes the prominent part young women played in the revolutionary movement, particularly as militant schoolteachers during the first decade of the century. Another discusses the appearance and function of newspapers by and for women at the turn of the century. Closely tied to the rising national sentiment that swept China after 1900, those periodicals "intended to arouse women to a consciousness of their oppression and its relationship to the fate of the nation."[2] Few of the studies offer speculations as to the origins of this transformation of women's place in that society. Generally, western attitudes, ideas, and examples prior to 1900 are seen as being significant influences in changing the concept of the status and role of women in China, but nothing definitive is offered. One possible connection between western influence and the rising aspirations of Chinese women is found in the late nineteenth-century western female missionary effort, itself a product of an ongoing transformation of women's roles in the West.[3]

The missionary endeavor in China focused on bringing Christianity to the Chinese; in a broader sense, however, the missionary brought western civilization and all its values, perceptions, and attitudes. In a word, missionaries were cultural imperialists: They promoted the values and ideals of their own society as superior to those held by the indigenous population, with the intention of changing those people. While this label is applied from a twentieth-century perspective, some missionaries did recognize that they were, in effect, anticipating a change in the host culture. Alexander Duff, an eminent Scotch Presbyterian pioneer missionary in India, whose views were circulated widely in American missionary circles, noted: "It may be safely laid down as an undoubted axiom, that every individual who receives a thorough English education, whether he becomes a convert to Christianity or not, will, with it, imbibe much of the English spirit—*i.e.* become intellectually Anglicized."[4]

In 1881, Young J. Allen, superintendent of the China Mission of the Methodist Episcopal Church, South, and a missionary to China since 1860, also recognized missionaries as being cultural imperialists in their promotion of a transformation of Chinese women, and in addition, he testified to the broader nonreligious impact of the missionary movement. The seclusion of Chinese women was changing, according to Allen, because of "the presence of a superior civilization on the shores of China, one of the chief elements of which is woman enthroned in the family, with liberty of entrance and egress, and . . . a more intimate acquaintance with foreign ideas, manners, and customs, especially on the subject of the family and social relations."[5] Such attitudes and actions have been regarded as arrogant and damaging, but cultural imperialism also may be seen as a force for change, motivating traditional societies, or groups within those societies in directions of "progress" that could be approached only slowly without such stimuli. Moreover, recent scholarship argues that the intellectual and psychological impact of the West—the core of cultural imperialism—was a greater cause of socioeconomic change in early twentieth-century China than was the well-documented economic impact.[6]

The women's endeavor mirrored the general missionary movement, but with one vital difference. Women could not preach at home or abroad, and thus they could assist only in supportive work, which tended to be "in the direction of the family circle," as Allen put it in 1882.[7] This "circle" was largely the more secular arena of outreach, either to other women through home visits and health-care programs, or to youth through educational programs where missionary teachers discussed or displayed, either consciously or unconsciously, aspects of western civilization that were other than strictly religious. Thus female missionaries were more culturally imperialistic than were their male counterparts: Women were forced into direct confrontations on several levels, whereas males generally found themselves engaged in more circumscribed evangelical work—primarily, preaching. The impact of the women's missionary movement must be considered, therefore, in terms that encompass more than purely religious issues and that reach beyond statistics on the number of converts or pupils enrolled.

Here we will explore the relationship between one American women's missionary organization—the China mission of the Woman's Missionary Society of the Methodist Episcopal Church, South, during the last two decades of the nineteenth century—and the emergence of Chinese women as a political and social force for change. There were far more influences promoting the transformation of Chinese women at the turn of the century than the presence of western female missionaries. Population explosion, political inertia in Chinese leadership circles, military defeat by Japan in 1895, economic change, urbanization, overseas education, and especially rising national consciousness—all functioned in the impetus toward change. The female missionary movement was a factor, however, and it needs careful study.

Origins and Philosophy

When compared with other similar organizations, the women of the Methodist Episcopal Church, South (MECS) established their society relatively late. By 1878, thirteen other woman's missionary societies were already operating, the Woman's Foreign Missionary Society of the Methodist Episcopal Church having been organized in 1869. Southern Methodist women, however, were not inactive. In fact, since 1854 Mrs. James W. Lambuth (Mary McClellan), the wife of a missionary, had been teaching Chinese children and contacting their mothers. But most important, she stimulated "the interest of the women at home until they formed organizations to aid in her work."[8] At the same time, the male missionaries of the church themselves requested, with increasing frequency after 1870, that female missionaries be sent to the China field. They needed women to reach and convert Chinese females, since the latter were inaccessible to male missionaries due to the strict separation of the sexes in traditional Chinese society.

No doubt the activities of other women's missionary societies, and their own support work, as well as the appeals from their own male missionaries, inspired the women of MECS to organize formally into a missionary society. Their primary motivation, however, resulted from a strongly felt need that was sweeping through postbellum American southern women. Anne Firor Scott, a historian of the women's movement in the American South, claims that in the 1870s, "Women all over the South were seized with a simultaneous impulse" to organize missionary societies, study geography, raise money, and recruit people to go to remote parts of the globe.[9]

The original object of the Woman's Missionary Society (WMS) was "to enlist and unite the efforts of women in the work of sending the gospel to women in heathen lands, through the agency of female missionaries, teachers, and Bible-readers."[10] The primary goal in China was to reach adult females, in hope of converting them to Christianity by visits, discussions, and literature, and thus promoting a fundamental change. The missionary movement recognized, in the words of Young J. Allen, that "the family, and not the individual, [is] the unit of population . . . or, in other words . . . 'The family is the institution on which is based the whole social and political edifice of China.'"[11] Many missionaries assumed that if the mothers could be reached with the Christian message, then Christianity would gain a crucial foothold in the land.

The evidence indicates, however, that adult Chinese females were not easily reached. This was due to a variety of factors, one being that even female missionaries were not welcomed by female Chinese. More important, to really do "woman's work" in China required that the missionary be proficient in the language, a process that required a minimum of two years' serious study. Few acquired the skill necessary to visit homes or teach without the assistance of a translator.[12] The inability to either learn the language or reach the women of China was partially the result of the high turnover among the missionaries themselves, due to illness, death, or marriage, all of which required a good deal of internal transferring in the field. As a consequence, few missionaries remained long in any one location or assignment. It was only in 1896 that the China mission assigned Mrs. Julie A. Gaither to develop woman's work for the first time on a sustained basis.[13]

To compound the situation, the society had inherited an educational focus from the wives of missionaries in the field prior to 1878 that proved difficult to lay aside.[14] In fact, by 1880, only two years after its constitution was framed, the society had amended its initial objectives to read: "The objects of this Society shall be to enlist and unite the efforts of women and children in sending the gospel to women *and children* in heathen lands, through the agency of female missionaries, teachers, *physicians,* and Bible-readers."[15] The society could thereby undertake the education of young males as well as females and also engage in health programs, in addition to hiring Bible women.

Methods: Bible Women

Reaching and converting adult Chinese women remained the primary focus and purpose of the Woman's Missionary Society. As already suggested, the traditional social structure of China, the lack of interest by Chinese women, and the tremendous language barrier proved nearly insurmountable hurdles. Despite the frustrations, females were not ignored, but a less direct approach was used—that of using Chinese Bible women.

The idea was not new—the practice of training indigenous women in the Scriptures so that they could visit other indigenous women was well-entrenched in most missionary circles and had been in use in the Methodist Episcopal Church, South, since the 1850s. The society seized upon the concept immediately and its first annual report in 1879 described the role of Bible women: They visited from house to house, reading and explaining the Scriptures to Chinese females "in their own homes, since in the East, women are almost inaccessible to the gospel in any other form." After visiting a number of homes, according to the report, the Bible women would then try to arrange a meeting for those interested in further conversation and prayer, so as to draw the women "by degree" out of their homes and into the chapels where female missionaries could talk with them, and eventually male missionaries could preach to them. Such a hope was theoretical at best, because in reality the Bible women were illiterate and had to be taught to read. Hence their own understanding of the Scriptures was not the best, and their reading skills were such that few could "interest a hearer for long." Moreover, these women were poor, widowed, and most of them were elderly. Due to social barriers, they could not therefore approach the upper-class women of China, and some who had families could not devote full time to their work.[16]

Nevertheless, the society did collect some fascinating statistics on the work of their Bible women. In 1879 the Shanghai station had six Bible women, who in the previous year had made 972 visits, addressed 3,708 people, found 2,240 more or less glad to hear, sold 36 books, gave away another 72, and had 935 female visitors coming to hear the gospel read. In 1883, a station in Nantziang had two Bible women, who talked with 1,327 people, of whom 682 were either "glad to hear or seemed to understand," and more than 20 knelt in prayer.[17] During the 1880s there were, at most, ten Bible women (in 1882) for the entire mission, and usually three or four. Later the number increased, reaching twenty-four by 1898, and the number of visits increased accordingly.

Despite their lack of social status and understanding of Christianity, the Chinese Bible women, although with a good deal of imperfection, clearly performed the central task of the society. They were a key link in reaching the women of China and by the 1890s, were of "greater importance, and likely to do more good," a "more effective way of spreading the good news and having the gospel truths explained." Moreover, by 1890 the Woman's Missionary Society (shortly to become the Woman's Foreign Missionary Society) had arrived at a conclusion common in missionary circles—"few heathen women receive or assimilate the truth as it comes to them in public services." Face-to-face contact was absolutely vital to bring about conversion. At the very least, it made the women "feel that the message . . . is personal to them." The society also knew that such work required a great amount of patience and tact on the part of the Bible women and, because of the continuing lack of interest on the part of the Chinese, a good deal of "boldness to push ourselves into towns and homes where we are not known or wanted."[18]

With such conclusions, it is not surprising that Bible women, even with their inadequacies, loomed ever larger in the plans of the society. By the 1890s, society members began to request schools to effectively educate their helpers. In 1890, Laura Askew Haygood, the dynamic, serene, capable, and confident coordinator of the work in China from 1885 until her death in 1899, argued: "We need Bible schools for women . . . schools where women may come and live for two or three months . . . and be taught the truth . . . and to read the Bible." It was not until 1893, however, that a Bible training institute received recommendation, and even then it was another four years before such a school actually was established.[19]

To assess the significance of such work is difficult. The number of home and village visits increased throughout the 1890s to more than 3,500 visits a year. Undoubtedly, the sending of half-literate, half-trained Chinese women into neighboring homes and villages generated a great deal of chaff and little wheat. Over a period of time, however, such efforts produced relatively knowledgeable Christians among the Bible women themselves, and no matter what else is said of such work, it must be admitted that those women behaved differently from their peers. That individual Chinese women moved through a city or village advocating anything was perhaps as challenging to tradition as were the ideas they advocated. But in this case the ideas were more threatening. After all, these Bible women were promoting a foreign religion which incorporated such concepts as virgin birth, Communion, baptism, monotheism, a Son of God, his death on a cross, sin, salvation, and perhaps more secular ideas such as equality between the sexes and vague notions of democracy. Moreover, some quarters of Chinese society suspected Christianity of promoting rebellion, due to its entanglement with the major internal threat to the peace of China in the nineteenth century, the Taiping Rebellion (1850–1864). All of this made Christianity questionable, threatening, frightening, and provoking. When Chinese women attempted to discuss such a religion with various levels of understanding and competence, no doubt additional fears were raised, and one can understand why Chinese leaders perceived Christianity as a threat to the very foundation of their society. Bible women were, in this sense, symbols of new roles or value-systems that females could assume or hold.

Methods: Education

Since 1848, when the Methodist Episcopal Church, South, first sent male missionaries to China, education had occupied the center of attention. While day schools for boys were quickly established, it was recognized that young women also needed an education, and the wives of missionaries soon found themselves running girls' day schools. Such support institutions were auxiliaries to the main focus of the mission—that of winning adult Chinese to Christianity by preaching and distribution of leaflets. The missionaries discovered, however, that the schools were important avenues in themselves, offering potential for an enduring impact on Chinese society. This was especially true since the boys' schools aimed at producing Christian young men, and ideally, they would need Christian young women as wives. These couples would produce Christian children, and a large step toward winning China to the cross would be accomplished. By 1883, the corresponding secretary of the society believed the schools were "nurseries for the engendering of pure principles, and homes for the development of womanly virtues. To make Christian wives and mothers of heathen women will be the acme of missionary effort in the marvelous unfolding of this unrivaled age."[20]

More immediately, the missionaries assumed that daily contact with Christian influences in the schools would, if not convert the pupils, at least send new ideas, values, and influence into traditional Chinese families. Young J. Allen claimed in 1883 that the "schools are influencing the whole town, male and female," and "a large number of parents are drawn to [the schools] and hence a wider field . . . is opened to woman's work." After that date, numerous reports noted the potential influence of such institutions: "Through the children we reach the families," even to the extent of expecting the children to witness "for Christ in their homes"; "we gain entrance to the home through the sons"; and "day school work in China gives a fine opportunity for woman's work and for mother's meetings."[21] By inviting the mothers to visit the school and by visiting the children in their own homes, contact with adult Chinese women could be made and hopefully maintained. However, as already noted, few missionaries had the time for home visitation. It was the Bible women who pursued this avenue of the "women's work."

When the society sent Lochie Rankin as its first missionary to China in 1878, her initial assignment was to take over several day schools around Shanghai that had been established by the wives of missionaries. Within two years she started a boarding school. Rankin held the longest service record of the society in China, retiring in 1928 after forty-nine years as a teacher in a variety of schools. As far as can be ascertained, she never did "woman's work" in the narrow sense. In fact, she became so convinced of the evangelistic "importance of day schools" that she maintained one out of her own pocket.[22] The pattern begun by Miss Rankin continued throughout the 1880s and 1890s, leading to annual reports which claimed that visitation was not done due to the pressing business of running schools. Alice S. Parker, wife of missionary Alvin P. Parker and active worker for the Woman's Missionary Society since 1877, typified the frustrations of "woman's work." In 1885, she argued that the society was not fulfilling its own objectives unless "the mothers [of the pupils] are visited and instructed as far as possible; but *that* work no one has been able to carry on."[23] Laura Haygood commented further in 1887: "Of Woman's Work, I am profoundly sorry that I have so little to report. It has been impossible during the year to do the work for mothers and families that we had hoped and planned. Our hearts have ached more than we can tell you, as again and again, in physical weakness, we have been obliged to turn away from open doors."[24]

The inability to reach the women of China caused the Woman's Missionary Society to redefine "woman's work" itself. As early as 1886, Bishop A. W. Wilson of the MECS argued while on a visit to China that woman's work *"is the right arm of our power in the work of evangelization.* Every child brought into your schools opens the way into a household; first for the ladies, and then for our preachers, and secures attendance of some or all the members of the family upon the ministry of our missionaries."[25] By 1889 the missionaries themselves had arrived at a similar conclusion. Dora Hamilton, in China since 1885, claimed in 1889, "The longer I work at [teaching], the more deeply I feel that it is truly woman's work for women. Through our pupils we reach the mothers in a way that claims at once their confidence and respect."[26] Thus woman's work was no longer primarily reaching adult females but reaching the children of China in order to reach the adults.

This emphasis on education is quite clear from a breakdown of the yearly appropriations. The society's budget for China increased rapidly. It had begun with $5,000 and one missionary in 1879, but it averaged $24,000 and 18 missionaries throughout the 1890s.[27] In some years the appropriation was doubled, due either to the purchase of land or the erection of new buildings. Virtually the entire amount went for educational purposes; a small fraction was designated for the training of Bible women and their salaries, and a slightly larger fraction for medical work. About one-half of any one year's appropriation covered salaries of women who were teachers, except for one or two medical personnel, and even these taught medical students on a part-time basis.

If schools became a primary focus of the society, what did such institutions offer, and who were the pupils? It is difficult to make a precise statement as to the curriculum because of the variations in the several schools. Generally there were three categories of subject matter: Christianity, homemaking, and language/mathematics/science. Clearly, Christianity was the major emphasis, with catechism, readings, hymns, and church services. This material was prepared in Chinese so that students could learn Christian ideas and at the same time, learn to read, although some pupils already had attended traditional Chinese schools. Among the texts used were *The Three Character Christian Primer, The True Doctrine Primer* (including *Henry and His Bearer*), portions of the *Old* and *New Testaments, Peep of Day, Line Upon Line, Streaks of Light,* and *Two Friends.* Some of these were written especially for the missionary schools, while others originally were used in Sunday schools in America and had been translated into either the local dialect or Mandarin.[28]

Another category in the curriculum was homemaking, where students were "taught to cut and make their own clothes, to knit, embroider, cook and wash."[29] In the boarding schools, pupils did the housekeeping, assisted with the cooking, and served the meals. These courses were designed to train the students for "duties that await them as wives, mothers, and home makers."[30] This was the most practical portion of the curriculum and the least offensive to China's traditional view of women.

There was one additional category, described at first only as "instruction in ordinary branches of education." These "branches" included the Chinese language and Chinese classics, English (in a few of the schools), as well as geography, arithmetic, physiology, and music, which were standard items in boarding-schools, and to some extent in day schools. In addition, with increasing frequency during the 1890s, the pupils were offered "universal history," geology, chemistry, zoology, and astronomy. Since no standardized texts were readily available, each district managed as best it could. Among the more frequently mentioned are Dr. Lucy Hoag's *Primary*

Physiology, Mrs. Alice S. Parker's *Arithmetic,* and Lyman Dwight Chapin's *Advanced Geography.* These correspond with the standard course offerings. Other texts noted on occasion include Calvin Mateer's *Arithmetic,* Mr. Pilcher's *Primary Geography,* and Young J. Allen's *Science Primer.* Overall, these texts were by no means satisfactory, since each appeared in a different Romanized Chinese dialect; moreover, they were in short supply. Despite these problems, the general purpose of such materials was clear: "to arouse [the pupils'] intellects and give them some idea of the world they live in"—the world as the missionary viewed it—thus helping to undermine the traditional cosmology of the Chinese.[31]

Day schools focused on "disseminating a knowledge of gospel truth, of planting it in youthful minds and through them, of conveying it to their parents and friends."[32] Hymns, catechism, Scripture, arithmetic, and geography formed the usual curriculum. During a year, approximately 150 to 260 pupils attended the 14 to 21 day schools that were in operation during the 1880s. The 1890s found between 30 and 45 day schools operating, with the number of pupils increasing dramatically, from 647 pupils in 1890 to 1,259 by 1898. Perhaps even more significant, two to three times as many males as females were enrolled in any one year during the same period, a reversal of figures from the preceding decade. In 1890, there were 429 males in day schools, compared to 218 females; in 1898, 970 males and 289 females. There are several explanations for this change. Most important, China itself was changing, especially in the area of Shanghai where the China mission was centered. As the city became more commercialized, opportunities for employment increased, particularly for young women, in the cotton mills and silk filatures. For such jobs, they did not need an education. "If any door be opened," wrote one missionary in 1888, "whereby the girls can earn a cash more than the dinner you give or the embroidery you teach be worth, that instant the child is lost to the school."[33] At the same time, young men were beginning to recognize the importance of learning basic mathematics and rudimentary English in order to qualify for jobs.

These enrollment figures, however, cover up an important fact. The turnover rate among the pupils in day schools was quite high. Few pupils remained longer than two or three years, or beyond the age of thirteen. Therefore the exposure they received to Christian literature, Chinese language, English, arithmetic, and scientific subjects was short and fragmentary. Moreover, staffing of the day schools was a serious problem because of the society's reliance on Chinese teachers. In 1881, Young J. Allen, arguing for more direct western supervision, claimed that because of the lack of "necessary personnel" the schools were "in an almost unqualified sense, immense failures." Laura Haygood, writing seven years later, felt that "to secure the best possible results from our day schools, there should be closer foreign [western] supervision and more foreign teaching than we have hitherto been able to give."[34] The day schools continued to suffer from an inadequate teaching staff throughout the 1890s, even though in 1891 the society had begun to train teachers specifically for that purpose. There were just too many schools for the capable teachers available. But because the schools did provide contact with the mothers of the pupils, the society could not abandon them, despite the evidence that for most pupils, the exposure provided but a momentary glimpse of another world.[35]

Between 1878 and 1898, the society operated three boarding schools for females and one for males, although the latter did not open until 1898. The schools for girls provided instruction in all the fields noted earlier and the society believed that they were developing strong Christian "wives and mothers [who] would be the center of Christian influence in the sphere of power with which Christ has gifted them [the family]." However, should the students remain unmarried or find themselves widows, they were recognized as "the best possible material for teachers of day schools, or the work of Bible women."[36] In the first decade, the average enrollment was 30 pupils per school, while in the second decade the figure dropped to 25. The pupils stayed longer, having been essentially contracted for three to five years, and many did not leave until age eighteen. Since the missionary women provided the instruction, these students were under constant western influence.

In 1890, the purpose of the boarding schools changed. Institutions originally intended to provide Chinese females with a Christian education became institutions specifically designed to train teachers, although with a decidedly Christian emphasis. Reality stimulated this change: Many of the girls who graduated from the boarding schools did marry Chinese Christians, but they also became teachers in the day schools of the Methodist Episcopal Church, South, or of some other denomination. Even as early as 1881, the society hired its own pupils from the Shanghai boarding school to teach in day schools. One society member argued that "the general opinion . . . seems to be that a number of useful schoolteachers, personal teachers, Bible women, and of earnest, consistent Christian women have been educated in [our schools]."[37] In 1891 a report noted that one of the first pupils of Mrs. J. W. Lambuth (1870s) now had two daughters of her own enrolled in a boarding school. Of more significance, that same early student became a "leading woman of the congregation" of the Methodist Church in Shanghai and by the 1920s, was serving "in the capacity of local preacher."[38] By 1900, in a graduating class of three from a recently established school, two began to teach immediately, while the third went to Staunton, Virginia, for further study.[39]

Here we have concrete examples of the Chinese women who were moving into nontraditional roles. The Chinese female teacher in a Christian day or boarding school may well be the prototype of the teacher who appeared after the turn of the century. As we have seen, these students studied a variety of topics, with an emphasis on Christianity, and by the late 1890s, even were translating Hans Christian Anderson into Chinese.[40] The curriculum was by no means revolutionary in design or intent, but the schools, by their very nature, were radical. The learning system was alien to the traditional Chinese, for women in particular, especially since the students boarded under foreign supervision. As those women became adults and moved into careers, particularly as teachers, the values and attitudes they possessed, even their presence, was an implicit challenge to traditional China.

Methods: Medical Missionaries

The original goal of the society—to reach the adult Chinese woman directly—was never forgotten. As has been indicated, however, educational activities absorbed so much of the missionaries' energy that little time was left for other aspects of the work. In fact, education itself became woman's work. Despite recognizing this inability to follow woman's work as originally defined, the society did pursue the goal by two alternative avenues—through Bible women, already discussed, and through medical missionaries.

The society recognized female medical personnel as a key part of its missionary work almost from the inception of the organization. The corresponding secretary of the society summed up its rationale in 1882:

The distressed millions of our sex in heathen lands, shut off from all ordinary means of relief from physical suffering, appeal eloquently and loudly to Christian women to come with gentle tone and touch, and all the modern appliances of science and knowledge, to minister to their bodily infirmities. Along with medical skill and practice is mingled the oft-repeated never-wearying story of redemption for the sin-dwarfed soul, and thus is rendered a two-fold service that only woman can give to woman in the land of the Orient.[41]

Female medical missionaries clearly would serve a need—they could minister to the physical ailments of Chinese families while providing a direct contact with the Woman's Missionary Society.

As it turned out, medical work also proved relatively attractive to the Chinese. At first the people "would have nothing to do with us," wrote Sue Blake Crozier on her first tour of the countryside in 1892, "and would beckon us to pass on and not stop at their homes. . . . [But] when told we had medicine it was amusing to see how quickly their manner toward us changed. . . . They came to the boat for help, where they received the gospel."[42] But to persuade the women to come to the clinics, or especially to stay in a hospital, was much more difficult. The society recognized "the reluctance of the women to leave their families, and come for a time into a strange place, with strangers about them, and put themselves entirely at the mercy of a foreigner."[43] One of the primary difficulties was the missionaries' overriding concern with the spiritual welfare of the patients. Anne Walter Fearn, the doctor in charge of the society's medical program from 1893 until 1896, pointed out the essential thrust of this work in 1895: "While the medical work is of undoubted importance, it is after all but means to an end, a key to unlock the doors of homes otherwise closed against the gospel. . . . It is our great desire to be able to follow each patient to her home and keep them always under our Christian influence."[44] The use of female medical missionaries was seen as a way to do woman's work when other avenues were closed.

The work, however, began slowly. By 1881 one female, Mildred Philips of Missouri, was studying at the Woman's Medical College in Philadelphia, with the intention of working in China upon completion of her studies. Not until 1888, with the opening of a hospital for women and the arrival of Dr. Philips, did the society finally put into practice its medical-care program. Later, in 1896, a children's hospital was built. It is apparent that the Chinese females who came to the hospital or clinic were, in essence, a captive audience. In the treatment room, the doctor diagnosed and prescribed, while in the waiting room, a male pastor preached, or a Bible woman read Scripture, or another member discussed a tract.[45]

The impact of this aspect of the society's program is difficult to assess. It did help Chinese females who were in need of medical attention; the number of patients increased from 2,300 in 1889 to more than 7,000 by 1896. And some of those patients apparently pursued additional contacts with the society. In 1889, one year after it opened, Mrs. J. P. Campbell, acting as an administrative assistant at the hospital, noted that she had entertained at least two hundred women in her own home, "the greater number of them being those who came in from hospital clinics. After our talk in the chapel and having their diseases diagnosed, they often enjoy coming in and sitting awhile when we can become acquainted over a cup of tea and talk more freely."[46] Whether any of these women continued such visits, were converted, or otherwise found the spiritual message helpful, is unrecorded.

In 1890, the medical program of the society began to train Chinese females as nurses. Initially, three women were enrolled and over the decade, the program expanded until there were eleven students. But the entire course was taught in English, primarily because the doctors had no time to study

Chinese, so few Chinese could participate. The students who did take the program were well trained, according to the doctors. As there was a high turnover among the doctors—due to fatigue or marriage—several reports are available on the quality of the nurses, and all contain high assessments. The actual program included "all branches taught in America." Courses were offered in conjunction with a medical program for Chinese males sponsored by the MECS general Board of Missions although there were curtains to divide the sexes.[47] In 1893, the society began to train women as doctors, and the first graduates appeared in 1896. One of the doctors, Dora Yui, went to Korea when the society opened that field in 1896; the other graduate, Zak Fok-me, served as resident physician at a society hospital until her death from tuberculosis in 1898.[48]

Once again, on a limited basis, the Woman's Missionary Society had promoted a program to train Chinese females in roles that were in stark contrast to the accepted norms of traditional China. This was not a deliberate effort, but one that evolved from the need for assistants in the women's hospital. Upon graduation some nurses continued in further training, but most were employed immediately in situations that required stamina, skill and, at times, courage to go against conventions. One nurse kept the hospital open during a period when there were no western doctors, cared for more than 300 patients, and had "good results." Another nurse went about the city of Shanghai during an epidemic when a western doctor was unavailable, "and out of nearly two hundred cases treated by her, fully one-half that number were cholera patients." The significance of these efforts was not lost on the society: The annual report of 1896 noted that "only those who know of the secluded lives led by Chinese girls can appreciate the true courage . . . shown in their conduct."[49] Thus the society's medical training program directly confronted the traditional views of the station and capability of Chinese women and no doubt played an important part in changing those views.

Conclusion

In assessing the overall impact of the Woman's Missionary Society in view of its intended goal—Christianizing the women of China—one must conclude that it was essentially unsuccessful. The number of converts were few. This lack of success was due not so much to its methods, however, but to the message itself and the serious implications of conversion for the Chinese. The society was well aware of the revolutionary nature of such an act for the students in its schools: "To become a Christian means to them, not only to be disinherited and driven from home, but to go out almost wholly unprepared to support themselves, and bearing the stigma of [being unfilial]."[50] It is not strange that relatively few Chinese were converted. Thus the Woman's Missionary Society effort to bring Christianity to China met the same fate as other missionary efforts.

As noted earlier, however, the impact of the missionary endeavor must be analyzed in broad terms, beyond the scope of any the missionaries may have envisioned. For as one American historian has argued, the revolution one intends may not be the revolution that occurs.[51] This phenomenon is particularly relevant to the Woman's Missionary Society program and to the entire American missionary effort in China. They may not have succeeded in converting many Chinese, but they did introduce many new cultural values, ideas, and institutions, and it is here—in viewing the missionaries as cultural imperialists—that we may look for the influence on Chinese women. By 1890, the society itself was aware of the effect of its own efforts, but its view was within a Christian framework and only dimly did it perceive its impact in other areas:

Indirectly woman's work in China touches many lives. Thus there is through it more appreciation of female education among Chinese Christian men, and an impulse has been given in its favor, shaking the belief that women are helpless creatures without brains, who cannot be taught. And with this higher ideal of womanhood an impulse has also been given toward moral and social reforms. For where Christianity comes it must create in those who receive it and their families a sentiment against infanticide, bound feet, early betrothals, and early marriages, and it will put the relation of mother and daughter-in-law in the right light, by teaching that "a woman's duty is not that of slavery to another woman."[52]

The society produced role models that undoubtedly served as prototypes for a new generation of Chinese women. By the early 1900s, three of the most influential women in twentieth-century China had passed through one of the society's boarding schools in Shanghai. Ai-ling Soong, the eldest, married H. H. Kung, China's minister of finance from 1933 until 1944; Ch'ing-ling Soong married Sun Yat-sen; and Mei-ling Soong married Chiang Kai-shek. The last two couples need no introduction. Moreover, as of 1920, of the twenty-nine Chinese women sent to America for further education on Boxer indemnity scholarships (established in 1908), thirteen had received earlier education at Woman's Missionary Society institutions.[53]

But it was individual missionaries who became even more significant models for many Chinese women. After all, the missionaries were usually young, unmarried, and educated. Many of them were strong-willed and independent, and they often were placed in charge of educational and medical institutions. Thus these women engaged in negotiations over building sites, oversaw the erection of new buildings, and handled all types of problems relating to their students. Moreover, they taught, exhorted, and lectured, as well as nursed and performed operations. They represented a revolutionary concept of womanhood. Here may be the western influence with the widest and most profound impact, and one that remains the most difficult to trace. In summary, the Woman's Missionary Society, by sending female missionaries to China and by promoting programs to educate the youth of China in western ways and to train Chinese women as Bible women, teachers, nurses, and doctors, helped lay the foundations of a sociopolitical-economic revolution with an impact we are still witnessing today.

THREE AFRO-AMERICAN WOMEN

Sylvia M. Jacobs

Afro-Americans, since their arrival in the United States, have felt an ambiguous alliance with Africa. While they accepted the reality of their heritage, they endorsed the western image of Africa as a "dark" continent. This helps to explain why, during the late nineteenth and early twentieth centuries, many black Americans supported mission work in Africa, believing that this religious and cultural exposure would help make the continent acceptable to the world. This self-imposed duty, along with the perpetuated myth that Afro-Americans were immune to African fevers, convinced some blacks that it was their "special mission" to "civilize" and Christianize Africa, and they felt they could best fulfill their obligation to the continent of their forefathers by becoming missionaries. As one Afro-American clergyman emphasized, "Negroes of America, God calls you to duty; He calls you to service and He calls you now."[1]

The majority of missionaries assigned to Africa were men, although they usually were accompanied by wives who shared in missionary duties. Women who went to Africa either as missionary wives or as commissioned missionaries generally aided in upgrading the lives of African women and children, since the mores of that day dictated that women missionaries be employed in capacities designated as "women's work." Studies of three women—Amanda Berry Smith, Sarah E. Gorham, and Fanny Jackson Coppin of the American-based African Methodist Episcopal Church—dramatically illustrate the role that women played in the "civilizing mission" in Africa.

The Missionary Society of the Methodist Episcopal Church was formed in 1819 for the work of evangelizing at home and abroad. On March 8, 1833, Melville Beveridge Cox inaugurated the Liberian Mission, the first overseas mission. Regrettably, Cox died only four months later, after uttering the stirring and prophetic cry: "Though a thousand fall, let not Africa be given up."[2]

The African Methodist Episcopal (AME) Church was organized as a separate branch of Methodism in 1816. Its foreign mission outreach began in Africa in 1820 when Daniel Coker, a representative of the American Colonization Society, organized the first AME Church in Sierra Leone. That church, however, was abandoned when Coker died in 1835. The first official foreign missionary of the church, Charles Butler, was appointed in 1822, but he never took up his assignment. John Boggs is thought to be the earliest AME appointed missionary to reach Africa. He arrived in Liberia in 1824, but there is no available information on the extent of his work.[3]

In 1844, the General Conference of the AME Church authorized the organization of the Parent Home and Foreign Missionary Society as the central agency for the operation of missions, but the society did not begin to function actively until 1864, when a Board of Missions was established and a Secretary of Missions elected. Ultimately, there were two women's auxiliaries. In 1874, the Woman's Parent Mite Missionary Society was organized in Philadelphia, and in 1898, as a result of Bishop Henry McNeal Turner's visit to South Africa and the southern AME women's dissatisfaction with northern leadership in the Mite Missionary Society, the Woman's Home and Foreign Missionary Society was organized in South Bend, Indiana. The Woman's Parent Mite Missionary Society supported the work of the church in Haiti, Santo Domingo, Liberia, Sierra Leone, Barbados, Demarara, the Bahamas, the Virgin Islands, Trinidad, and Jamaica; and the Woman's Home and Foreign Missionary Society supervised AME missions in southern Africa.[4]

Africa was set apart as a foreign mission field by the General Conference of the AME Church in 1856, and John R. V. Morgan was appointed missionary-pastor to Liberia. Little is known of Morgan except that he returned to the United States because his work was not supported by the church. The first permanent mission in Africa finally was established in 1878. In that year Samuel F. Flegler led a group of thirty Afro-Americans from Charleston, South Carolina, and a church and school were built at Brewersville, Liberia.[5]

The permanent work of the AME Church in Sierra Leone dates from 1886 when John Richard Frederick was appointed the first missionary, though he did not arrive in that country until 1887. There he founded Bethel Church and Allen AME Church. Frederick also was faced with lack of moral and financial support, and in 1899 he withdrew from the AME denomination and joined the British Wesleyan Methodist Church.[6]

In November of 1891, Bishop Turner reached Freetown, Sierra Leone, and organized the Sierra Leone Annual Conference in the Zion AME Church, the first annual conference of the church established in Africa. Two weeks later, he initiated the Liberia Annual Conference in Muhlenberg.[7]

The years betwen 1892 and 1900 also witnessed the rise and growth of the AME Church in South Africa. In 1892, a schism occurred in the South African Wesleyan Methodist Church, resulting in the organization of the independent Ethiopian Church. The Ethiopian Church petitioned the AME Church for membership in 1896. This request was granted and the South African Ethiopian Church united with the American church. The following year the Cape Colony Conference was organized, and in 1898 Bishop Turner established the Transvaal Conference. In 1904, Bishop Levi J. Coppin reported the creation of three more annual conferences.[8]

By the beginning of the twentieth century, the AME Church was definitely mission-minded, united in an effort to support the cause of missions in Africa and elsewhere.[9] Three women who went to Africa during this period of missionary zeal exemplify the sincerity of the church in aiding in the "development" of that continent.

Amanda Berry Smith

Amanda Berry was born on January 23, 1837, in Long Green, Maryland, to slave parents Samuel and Miriam

Matthews Berry. When Amanda Berry was quite young, her father bought his own freedom and eventually earned enough to buy the freedom of his wife and five of his thirteen children. After the entire family was free, the Berrys moved to Pennsylvania, and their home became one of the main stations of the Underground Railroad. In March of 1856, Miss Berry joined the AME Church in York, Pennsylvania. She married Calvin M. Devine, who was killed in the Civil War, and then James H. Smith, a member of Philadelphia's Bethel AME Church. In November 1869, Smith died, and Amanda Smith later commented, "Since then I have been a widow."[10]

Amanda Berry Smith announced that she had received a call from God, and in October 1870 she began evangelistic work. Since the AME Church did not license women to preach, she participated in revivals and conducted seminars in churches, and her fame became national. Although her parents had talked about Africa when she was young, Mrs. Smith did not consider becoming a missionary until, at a Methodist camp meeting in 1872, she was told the story of Melville Cox. She remarked, "This was the first of my thinking of going to Africa."[11]

In July 1878 Mrs. Smith left the United States for England as a traveling evangelist and remained out of the country for twelve years. After twenty months in Europe, she volunteered with an English friend to become a missionary to India, where she worked for nineteen months. Later she stated that God had sent her to India to better prepare her for mission work in Africa. During those twelve years she was financially supported by the Methodist Episcopal Church.[12]

On December 24, 1881, Amanda Smith sailed for Liberia from Liverpool and arrived in Monrovia on January 18, 1882. In 1878 the AME Church had established mission stations in Brewersville, Monrovia, White Plains, and Carysburg. Although Mrs. Smith was not a commissioned missionary of the AME Church, she was a member of that church and worked with it. While in Monrovia, she established a boys' church school, which consisted of Bible readings and Sunday morning meetings.

In February 1885 Amanda Smith arrived in Cape Palmas.

There she held Bible readings, preached at many denominational churches, taught in the children's Sunday school, organized female and prayer bands, supervised young men's prayer groups, gave addresses, conducted temperance meetings, and established a course of Christian training for children. About eighty persons were brought to Christ in Cape Palmas as a result of her efforts.[13]

During her eight years in Africa, Mrs. Smith came to feel that it was her "duty" to help everyone she could by founding missions and schools. She referred to all Africans as "my people," but she particularly hoped to improve the condition of women:

The poor women of Africa, like those of India, have a hard time. As a rule, they have all the hard work to do. They have to cut and carry all the wood, carry all the water on their heads, and plant all the rice. The men and boys cut and burn the bush, with the help of the women; but sowing the rice, and planting the casava, the women have to do.[14]

Amanda Berry Smith also saw the need for a system of education. She noted that there was no government school in the entire country of Liberia:

There is great need for good books. In this the government is very slack; and until we do our whole duty in this our country is *doomed*. Education is our country's great need. There is so little attention paid to the education of girls; not a single high school for girls in the whole republic of Liberia. It is a great shame and a disgrace to the government.[15]

Before she left Africa, Mrs. Smith visited Sierra Leone and Nigeria. She confided, "I calmly looked over all my mind, and my work in Africa. I felt that while there was so much to be done, and I had only done a little, yet that I had God's approval that I had done all I could. I went to Africa at His bidding, and did not leave till I was sure I had His sanction."[16]

Mrs. Smith arrived in New York on September 5, 1890, and devoted the remainder of her life to the Amanda Smith Orphans' Home for Colored Children in Harvey, Illinois, a suburb of Chicago. Ground was broken for the orphanage in

1895 and it was completed on June 28, 1899. Mrs. Smith died in 1915 at the age of seventy-eight.[17]

Though she was born in slavery and poorly educated, Amanda Berry Smith stands out in the history of Methodist missions in Africa because of her concern for education. Her efforts in behalf of African women were also particularly encouraging. In the United States, she had a comfortable living standard and a wide circle of friends, but she had left that secure life to labor among "her people" in Africa. Although she was not an appointed missionary of the AME Church, she has been included in this study because her efforts surely affected church sentiment toward women missionaries and possibly could account for the appointment of Sarah Gorham in 1888 as the first AME woman missionary.

Sarah Gorham

Sarah Gorham was born on December 5, 1832, in Fredericksburg, Maryland, the native state of Amanda Smith. Little is known of her life before 1880. At that time, however, she visited some relatives who had emigrated to Liberia. There she observed the people and country and traveled throughout the republic, preaching and comforting the needy and destitute.

After a year, Miss Gorham returned to the United States and settled in Boston, Massachusetts, where she joined the Charles Street AME Church. She was active in humanitarian work in the church and also was employed as a social worker by the Associated Charities of Boston. Having become interested in African work while on her visit, in 1888 she was moved to offer her services as a missionary upon the urgent appeal of S. J. Campbell, who was touring the United States seeking volunteers for the AME Liberian Mission. She originally planned to go to Liberia but was convinced by the Reverend Frederick to join him in Sierra Leone.

Miss Sarah Gorham, at fifty-six years of age, became the first woman missionary of the AME Church appointed to a foreign field. Sponsored by the Woman's Parent Mite Missionary Society, she left the United States in 1888. She insisted that God had directed her to Africa, and she was determined to go, believing that her labor would be best employed for "the heathens" of her fatherland. In spite of her age, she traveled to Africa to make her contribution to the "development" of the continent.[18]

After her arrival in Sierra Leone, Miss Gorham traveled to Magbelle, one of the leading AME missions, on the banks of the Scarcies River, one hundred miles from Freetown. There she was active in the Allen AME Church and worked among the Temne women and girls. She also established the Sarah Gorham Mission School, which would become a powerful force in AME missionary work in Sierra Leone. The school gave both religious and industrial training; the girls were taught domestic science and the boys learned about gardening. The Sarah Gorham Mission School was one of the first on the African west coast and by 1899 could boast 250 to 300 pupils.[19]

In 1891, Miss Gorham visited the United States to regain her health, and while in this country, she made appeals for recruits for the Sierra Leone Mission. After she returned to Sierra Leone, she spoke of her dedication to African mission work in a letter dated May 28, 1894: "With all I am suffering and all I am enduring I would not give up this work under any condition." She emphasized the need for financial support: "Surely God will bring the people of the [AME] church to judgment for denying the heathen the lamp of life. I have a great and mighty piece of work here before me, and you all must help me all you can. God gives the reward."[20]

In July of 1894 Sarah Gorham became bedridden with fever and, despite the efforts of an able physician, died on August 10. She was buried in Kissy Road Cemetery in Freetown, where her tombstone bears the following inscription: "She was early impressed that she should go to Africa as a missionary and that her life work should be there. She crossed the ocean five times, and ended her mission on the soil and among the people she so much desired to benefit." Frederick eulogized Miss Gorham: "I have frequently been astonished at the wonderful power of endurance she possessed, and above all the extraordinary spiritual gifts and graces by which she was endowed. She was indeed mighty in word and deed."[21] The Woman's Parent Mite Missionary Society of the AME Church later rebuilt the by then

274

dilapidated Sarah Gorham Mission School at Magbelle as a memorial to her efforts in West Africa.[22]

Although very little is known about the AME Church's first appointed woman foreign missionary, Sarah Gorham holds an exalted position in the church because of her unswerving dedication. She demonstrated that women were able to work in missions, and this led the church to appoint other unmarried women as missionaries to the foreign field. Her contribution to the Sierra Leone Mission, although limited because of the short time she spent there, nevertheless had reverberations in the establishment of homes and schools for children.

Fanny Jackson Coppin

Fanny Ann Jackson, one of America's first black women college graduates, was born a slave in Washington, D.C., in 1837. After gaining her freedom, she went to school in Massachusetts and Rhode Island and then earned a bachelor's degree from Oberlin College in 1865. From 1865 until 1902 she taught at the Institute for Colored Youth in Philadelphia and eventually became principal there. She also introduced teacher-training into the educational system of that city.[23] During that period, she was greatly involved in efforts to further the educational opportunities of Afro-Americans. In 1900 Coppin State College in Baltimore, Maryland, was named in honor of her achievements.

In 1881, Fanny Jackson married Levi Jenkins Coppin, who had been born free in Fredericktown, Maryland, in 1848. Levi Coppin was licensed to preach in the AME Church in 1876, and from 1888 until 1896 he edited the *A.M.E. Church Review*. Fanny Jackson's marriage ultimately led her to an increased concern for religious teaching in Africa. Mrs. Coppin became president of the Woman's Parent Mite Missionary Society in 1883 and remained in that position until 1892. As if fate had ordained it, Fanny Coppin, who had taught blacks for thirty-seven years in the United States, ended her career by educating blacks in Africa.

In 1900, Levi Coppin was elected the first bishop of South Africa and was assigned to the Fourteenth Episcopal District (Cape Colony and the Transvaal). His main responsibility was to unite the Ethiopian Church in South Africa with the AME Church in America. Levi Coppin arrived alone in Cape Town, South Africa, on February 19, 1901, and departed for the United States on December 26. It was a common practice in the AME Church to assign a certain portion of the missionary duties to wives. Accordingly, in 1902 Mrs. Coppin, who had retired as principal of the Institute for Colored Youth, prepared to return to South Africa with her husband.[24]

On November 30, Levi and Fanny Coppin disembarked at Cape Town to begin their work among black South Africans. Here Mrs. Coppin, more than sixty-five years of age, began a second vocation. In spite of the often-experienced hardships, she worked as feverishly at this task as she had at teaching in the United States. She confessed, "Here my 'special' work began."[25] Many are not aware that in addition to Fanny Jackson Coppin's contribution to black education in the United States, she also had an impact on early twentieth-century South African womanhood.

Levi Coppin described mission work in South Africa as being in the primary stage, requiring intense and vigilant dedication. Missionary headquarters were located in Cape Town, although Bishop and Mrs. Coppin frequently traveled into the interior. Mrs. Coppin maintained that she and her husband were concerned least of all with their own comfort and that their "one absorbing thought was, how shall we accomplish the work for which we left our home?"[26]

Before her journey to Africa, Fanny Coppin had confessed that she viewed Africa as a place devoid of any religious development. She later admitted that she was surprised to find that Africans had engaged in theological thought before the arrival of a single missionary. She therefore felt that the major role of missionaries was to improve on the African ethical, spiritual, and moral life: "Our religious training is, in a sense, but an explanation of [Africans'] own religious impulses." Seemingly dedicated to preserving the indigenous culture, she asserted that it was the task of missionaries to structure religious training around the patterns that already existed.

While her immediate concern was with religion, Mrs. Coppin also was involved in other aspects of African life: the conditions of black South Africans in Cape Town; the development of indigenous women's organizations; the establishment of a school and mission house in Cape Town; the impact of white minority rule upon the lives of black South Africans. The living and working conditions of blacks who had left their villages to find employment in Cape Town evoked sympathy from Mrs. Coppin. The situation in Cape Town was worse than that in the rural areas, since most urban blacks were uneducated, unskilled, poor, and generally exploited by their white employers. She continued to work among the black Cape Town residents in an effort to raise their standard of living.[27]

During her stay in South Africa, Mrs. Coppin directed most of her attention to organizing black South African women into Woman's Christian Temperance Union Societies and Woman's Mite Missionary Societies. Although she was not successful in establishing strong groups in Cape Town, societies were inaugurated at several nearby towns where mission stations were located. In the interior, where a great portion of her time was spent, Mrs. Coppin held religious and various other meetings for women and formed small missionary groups among the wives of black South African ministers.

At the South African Conference held in Port Elizabeth in January 1903, Mrs. Coppin presided over a session devoted to the concerns of black South African women. At the gathering, emphasis was placed on the founding of additional missionary societies. Through a number of women who participated in that conference, and with the assistance of ministers' wives, Mrs. Coppin was able to expand the influence of AME work among women.[28] One permanent result of the Coppins' missionary stint in Africa was the establishment of Bethel Institute, an old building in Cape Town that had been converted into a school and mission house. Mrs. Coppin also used the institute as a meeting place for the women of Cape Town to discuss their work in the temperance movement.[29]

The Coppins, like many black Americans working in Africa during this period, questioned the benefits of European rule. Mrs. Coppin believed that the British, who earlier had suppressed a Boer bid for independence in the Anglo-Boer War (1899-1902), were also attempting to crush the hope of black South Africans for equality. She asserted that under British rule, black South Africans remained uneducated, lived in

277

dilapidated homes, and were exposed to all kinds of disease because of the unsanitary living conditions. Mrs. Coppin also noted that in the interior, indigenous chiefs no longer held sovereign rule over their people, as they had before the coming of the white man, and no portion of that country remained the same after the imposition of colonial rule.

While they did not become politically involved in South Africa, the Coppins nonetheless were under constant surveillance by British officials. Mrs. Coppin claimed that government spies were observing the behavior and speeches of black American missionaries because of the British fear that religious and educational training would promote uneasiness among black South Africans and result in revolt against white rule. She predicted that these administrators soon would realize that their suspicions against Afro-American missionaries were unfounded. Her prognostication was somewhat naïve, however, because after the Zulu uprising of 1906, which the British claimed was initiated and sponsored by black Americans, Afro-American missionary activity was restricted. She was aware, though, that repercussions might be expected when colonial subjects became educated and more knowledgeable of their inferior position in their society:

I think, however, the authorities finally came to understand that we were missionaries pure and simple, and not politicians, and if there was any cause for alarm it must grow out of the fact that enlightenment does indeed enable people to see their true condition, and that they do sometimes become dissatisfied when convinced that injustice and a general lack of the Christian spirit of brotherhood, is responsible for much of their misery.[30]

In truth, Mrs. Coppin believed that education, while it allows for the development of certain skills, is also a vehicle for the expression of discontent among oppressed peoples.

Although Levi Coppin was assigned as a missionary to South Africa and has received much of the credit for results there, Fanny Coppin's contribution to the religious and educational growth of black South Africans is equally laudable. Levi Coppin admitted that his wife's presence had been a source of inspiration for the women of South Africa. He asserted that Mrs. Coppin's prior experiences as a school teacher and public speaker, together with her compassionate sympathy for black South Africans, had perfectly fitted her for their work.[31]

The Coppins left South Africa in 1904 and again made their home in Philadelphia. Mrs. Coppin did not return to teaching, but spent that time writing about her life's work. She continued her interest in Africa, however, constantly beseeching blacks to return to the continent to help in the process of education and particularly urging women into the mission field. Mrs. Coppin insisted that the African people needed the help that only trained black Americans could provide.[32]

Fanny Coppin referred to her work in South Africa as her "special duty." She saw missionary work as an indication of the continued interest among black Americans for the "redemption" of Africa. Mrs. Coppin summarized her experiences: "My stay in Africa was pleasant, for I did not count the deprivations, and sometimes hardships." Fanny Jackson Coppin died on January 21, 1913, less than ten years after her return home. A Fanny Jackson Coppin Girls' Hall was named in her honor at Wilberforce Institute in Evaton, South Africa.[33]

Conclusion

Three women, all members of the AME Church, went to Africa as missionaries: Amanda Berry Smith, to Liberia; Sarah E. Gorham, to Sierra Leone; and Fanny Jackson Coppin, to South Africa. These women, with similar motives, had much in common. All were born in the 1830s, and all may have been born slaves (we know very little about Miss Gorham's birth or early life). Two were born in Maryland and one in Washington, D.C., possibly within one hundred miles of one another. All were more than forty years of age when they first arrived in Africa, having spent most of their former lives working in some outreach capacity. Mrs. Smith was the only woman of the three who had done mission work in other areas of the world.

The women were interested in the "development" of Africa. Generally, they adhered to the need for a "civilizing mission," and they went to Africa to accomplish that end. Each was active in her area in efforts to improve the lives of women and children: Mrs. Smith began a church school for Liberian boys;

Miss Gorham established the Sarah Gorham Mission School in Sierra Leone; Mrs. Coppin organized South African branches of the Woman's Christian Temperance Union and Woman's Mite Missionary Society, and also helped to establish Bethel Institute at Cape Town.

Although their stays in Africa were short, varying from two to eight years, their long-term influence on the women and children of Africa was surely considerable. Most important, as pioneer Afro-American missionaries, these three women exemplified the role women could play in the "redemption" of their fatherland. In the final analysis, they were representatives of many black Americans of that period, both male and female, who saw their "special mission" in Africa.

16

CHARLOTTE MANYE MAXEKE

Carol A. Page

The *African Yearly Register,* a "who's who" of the African continent compiled by T. D. Mweli Skota in 1931, contains an extraordinary number of biographical sketches of political and social leaders in southern Africa.[1] The *Register* contains a mere handful of women, but of those profiles, one of the longest is devoted to Charlotte Manye Maxeke, an educator and civic leader who remained a staunch member of the American-based African Methodist Episcopal (AME) Church throughout her life.

Charlotte Maxeke typifies the educated, early-twentieth-century South African whose belief in Christian brotherhood and the virtues of British constitutionalism remained unshaken in the face of imperial betrayal and Union legislative onslaught.

The educated black elite's incredible optimism toward its position within the new Union of South Africa is attributable in part to its strong ties with mission educators and liberal advisers. Though more often than not those relationships were paternalistic at best, European influence over the elite was nonetheless strong. And these ties insured that African thrusts toward the redress of grievances—the franchise, land, education, and labor—took the form of prayers, petitions, and delegations, rather than direct mass action.

However, Charlotte Maxeke was doubly unique: She was actively engaged in her people's struggle for human dignity during the crucial Hertzog era at a time when African women were still primarily on the veld rather than in the urban areas; and her connection to her missionary mentors extended across the Atlantic into black America.[2]

Little about Charlotte's early family life has been recorded, but it appears that her father, a Basuto, migrated from the Transvaal to the Cape, was converted, returned to the

Transvaal, and promptly placed his two daughters in a Congregational mission school in Uitenhage. When the family moved to Port Elizabeth, Charlotte continued her education in local mission schools. When she was grown, she moved to Kimberley and taught for a time in a Wesleyan school where she achieved a local prominence of sorts as a singer.[3]

Charlotte Manye caught the eye of J. H. Balmer, an enterprising Englishman living in Kimberley who had been inspired by the financial success of an Afro-American choir, the McAdoo Jubilee Singers, whose 1890 tour of the Transvaal and Cape had been highly publicized. He organized a troupe of African Jubilees.[4]

Manye began her odyssey in 1893 at the age of twenty-four as a member of the African Jubilees which toured the British Isles between 1890 and 1892, and subsequently Canada and the United States. The American tour proved unsuccessful and the group was disbanded. The plight of the young people was brought to the attention of the AME Church, which appealed to the benevolent among its members to come to their aid. Several of the singers were invited to attend AME schools. Charlotte accepted the offer and entered Wilberforce University in January 1895. She was "adopted" by the Woman's Parent Mite Missionary Society of the Third Episcopal District, which paid some of her school fees, the remainder being picked up by the church in general.[5]

Manye entered Wilberforce at a particularly heady time in the history of the AME Church. Within this most aggressive of the black churches involved in Africa's evangelization in the waning years of the ninteenth century, there was a clique led by the senior bishop, Henry McNeal Turner. That group was engaged in a campaign designed to emphasize the African/Afro-American connection, in contrast to leading spokesmen such as Booker T. Washington and the assimilationist Frederick Douglass, who tended to deemphasize it. Together with its sister black churches, the AME denomination considered Africa its special domain for evangelization that would "redeem" and "uplift" the heathen while vindicating the capacity and ingenuity of their American "kith and kin."

In any case, Wilberforce seems to have been a focal point of much Africa-oriented activity. For several years the university's annual essay contest winners submitted essays on Africa-related topics, and a number of resident African students were made highly visible at various school and church functions.[6]

Manye was so impressed by her surroundings that she wrote to a relative in Johannesburg boasting about Wilberforce and about the AME Church, its schools, its churches, and its publishing house—all owned and operated, she emphasized, by blacks.

Through Manye's correspondence, Mangena Mokone, the Transvaal leader of the breakaway Ethiopian Church, became acquainted with the AME Church and its education programs. The two churches merged in 1896 and this was the origin of the AME connection with South Africa.[7]

Manye's activities during her sojourn in the United States are somewhat hazy. We know that she was an exemplary student and made a number of lifelong friends, one of whom, Nina Gomer DuBois, was the wife of W. E. B. DuBois. We also know that she supplemented the funds given her by the church through occasional lectures at black churches and clubs on the condition of blacks in South Africa.[8] Not only did this experience stand her in good stead in her later public speaking career, but it offered the skeptics in her American audiences positive proof that black Africans were not the lip-smacking cannibals they may have expected. Notwithstanding the difficulties of language and new environment, Manye graduated from Wilberforce in 1901 with a Bachelor of Science degree and shortly after, returned to South Africa to work in the church's nascent education program.

Charlotte Manye was the first black woman in South Africa to earn a university degree. Moreover, she was one of a very few college-educated blacks in South Africa at the time of Union. And it is likely that her inclusion as a witness before various government commissions and her membership on agencies that tackled Bantu "problems" were more a result of her educational qualifications than of any conscious desire to hear a woman's point of view.

On her return to Africa, Manye was assigned to the Transvaal, where all educational facilities were inadequate, even those for whites. For blacks, they were abysmal, and as a result, perhaps one in a hundred Transvaal Africans was literate. Unfortunately, due to travel restrictions imposed by the Anglo-Boer War, Manye was confined to the Cape, but she put her time to good use by organizing Mite Missionary societies and writing to remind her American supporters to honor the financial pledges they had made.[9]

When travel once again was possible Manye relocated in the northern Transvaal, where she successfully organized day and night classes for boys at Pietersburg, as well as several Christian Endeavor societies. Once the foundations had been laid, however, Manye was replaced in 1903 by a male Wilberforce graduate, Marshall Maxeke, whom she later married.[10] Marshall Maxeke had been a firm British supporter during the recent conflict and had used American podiums and newspapers to preach the benefits Africans would derive from British hegemony in the two republics.[11] However, once that hegemony had been effected, Maxeke was harassed by British authorities in the Transvaal because he belonged to the AME Church, which they suspected of being seditious.[12] In addition, he raised the ire of the South African Native Affairs Department by insisting that African ministers who belonged to independent churches should be given exemption certificates to spare them the humiliation of submitting to the onerous "pass" laws.[13] He also led the agitation against the forced removal of Transvaal Africans to segregated locations. There was, then, a history of activism on the part of both Charlotte and Marshall Maxeke.

For the next several years, the Maxekes crisscrossed the Transvaal, establishing schools. During this period they organized the nucleus for Wilberforce Institute, an AME facility that still exists in Evaton Township near Johannesburg. Eventually they were called to the Cape to open a private school in the Transkei, the success of which caught the attention of the Tembu paramount chief, Dalindyebo, who recruited them to establish a school for his royal family. Charlotte Maxeke not only taught at that school but became an influential member of the chief's inner circle of advisers and was said to have wielded a great deal of influence over him. Again, it is likely that her educational qualifications overrode any possible objections the chief might have had because of her gender. When her work in Tembuland was interrupted by illness, she returned to Johannesburg, renewed her mission work as president of the Woman's Mite Missionary Society, and became increasingly involved in the activities of the African National Congress (ANC).

That Charlotte Maxeke became involved with the congress is predictable; a number of staunch AME members were associated with it. The organization had been formed in 1912 by some of the educated elite who recognized the need for a Union-wide, multiethnic pressure group committed to finding constitutional means to press for their rights and protect their particular interests. Indeed, in her very first public address upon her return to South Africa, Charlotte Manye had cautioned her audience against ethnic divisiveness. She deprecated the distinctions made between Xhosa and Fingo and declared, "How much grander it would be to say that we all belonged to the African nation!"[14] Even had she not held these sentiments before she arrived in America, it is difficult to imagine that she was not influenced by the AME Church's credo that "the African races are one, whatever their tribal differences may be or whether they live upon the continent of Africa, or in Asia, America, Europe or upon the Isles of the Sea."[15] And certainly while in the United States, she must have kept abreast of the activities of the church in South Africa, where Turner had specifically warned his ministers to avoid ethnic squabbling, because "the African, regardless of tribe or local situation should be one people and one man."[16] In any case, the establishment of an African unity that would transcend all ethnic and regional considerations became her personal crusade.

While remaining a central figure in the AME Church, in 1913 Charlotte Maxeke helped organize the Bantu Women's League as the female arm of the African National Congress.[17] The league was designed to focus on the problems of black African women in a rapidly industrializing South Africa.

The ANC had adopted "passive action" as the vehicle for its propaganda efforts to educate popular opinion about African grievances. As early as 1913, African women in the Orange Free State had pursued a course of passive resistance by openly defying the pass laws, thereby becoming liable to arrest and imprisonment.[18] These demonstrations marked the first time Africans had resorted to such a tactic. Before the campaign could expand, however, World War I erupted, and in what was to become a characteristic move, the women halted their activities and rallied around the Union Jack.

The campaign against the passes was resumed in 1918 during a period of particular agitation in the African community. This time the thrust came from the Transvaal. The women now had a national leader in the person of Charlotte Maxeke, president of the Bantu Women's League. Under her direction, league members met with Prime Minister Louis Botha to protest the proposed issuance of passes to women in the Orange Free State, sent off countless petitions calling for an end to the extension of the pass laws to women, and called public attention to the demeaning medical inspection of domestic workers as a prerequisite for employment.[19]

Through her church work and her activities with the league, Maxeke caught the eye of South Africa's white liberals. She became their expert on African women's problems and was a fixture at the various joint councils of English-speaking Europeans and middle-class Africans that proliferated during the 1930s. Though these conferences, since they emphasized patience and moderation, tended to neutralize the influence of the small number of direct-action supporters within the ANC and other African organizations, Maxeke avidly supported them and called for the creation of more. Because she was a product of mission schools and had studied in an American institution which counted among its leaders several colonial-born bishops who were almost embarrassingly Anglophile, Maxeke was a firm believer in the alleged British sense of fair play and the Christian ideal of the brotherhood of all men, Hertzog's Segregation Bill notwithstanding. In an atmosphere of increasing political and social segregation, these joint councils were an important vehicle through which black African grievances were aired, although the majority of whites in South Africa chose not to hear. Those who did listen had neither the power nor perhaps the inclination to make full restitution.

Charlotte Maxeke testified at a number of government

commission hearings, "native" councils, and interdenominational conferences regarding the problems that plagued the African community as a whole, but it was the concerns of urban women that led to her real prominence among Union whites.

Though her own life belied it, Maxeke held the traditional view of woman's role in society. A woman was first and foremost a wife and mother. She alone was responsible for instilling in her children the "right principles and teachings of modern civilization."[20] As such, it was necessary that the home be orderly, clean, and Christian. Like the nineteenth-century women who engaged in so-called social uplift in rural black America, and like white women with whom she came in contact in South Africa, she stressed the tenets of Victorian morality: temperance, sexual chastity, and hygiene.

To be sure, Maxeke accepted the mission stereotypes of the precolonial African woman—that she was a commodity bought and sold through the system of lobola, or bridewealth, which rendered her the absolute slave of her husband. She firmly believed that European missionaries had freed African women from what she called the hideous practice of polygamy.[21] Yet for all that, she held a wistful, almost romantic reverence for precolonial, preindustrial rural society. And well she might. Industrialization in South Africa had brought African men and women—particularly women—alienation and dislocation.

Therefore in the various government commissions before which she testified and in the interracial councils on which she served, Maxeke discussed the deleterious effects of capitalist development on African family life. She railed against the segregationist government policies which fostered that development, yet she did not seem to connect the two. She seems to have understood the relationship between land restriction and labor, between the migrant labor system and the destruction of family life, and though ideally she wanted African women in the home, she knew that the ultralow wages paid black African laborers necessitated that women leave the home to supplement the family income.

As for female employment opportunities, domestic service was practically the only legal occupation open to uneducated urban African women, and Maxeke fully endorsed their entry into this field. There were obvious economic reasons for her encouragement of domestic work, but she had another reason as well, and that had to do with her theory that domestic work builds character. It is good practice for keeping one's own home tidy.

The major alternative to domestic employment for urban African women was the home brewing of beer, which was far more remunerative than housework, and mothers could stay home with their children. However, after 1929 it was illegal, and Maxeke, with her strong temperance bent, firmly believed that the liquor business set black African women and children on the path to perdition. Perhaps she advocated domestic service also because she operated a domestic placement bureau.[22]

At any rate, Maxeke saw the correlation between absentee mothers and fathers and the growing delinquency among urban youth. Yet her solutions to the myriad problems of her people—landlessness, family dislocation, low income, malnutrition, and so on—became mired in her belief in the efficacy of constitutionalism, in a situation where her people had no access to the state.

Because she was a recognized authority on the African urban woman's needs and problems, the Native Affairs Department created, especially for her, the post of Welfare Worker for Johannesburg women. She also held the position of probation officer for African women at the Johannesburg Magistrate's Court and was chaplain for the African women's prisons. In this capacity she visited the prisoners, combining her AME mission work with her secular responsibilities. For many who drifted in and out of the Johannesburg court system, Maxeke acted as a kind of surrogate mother, on occasion taking the children of imprisoned women into her own home.[23]

Though one is tempted to say that Maxeke was myopic in many respects, there is no doubt that she was an inspiration to African women, and to men. Through her efforts a number of black South Africans were encouraged to seek higher education, and some made their way to Wilberforce University. She was, after all, its most celebrated African alumna. Among those she inspired was the celebrated physician and ANC president, A. B. Xuma. After dutifully paying tribute to

Maxeke's culinary and housekeeping talents, which seem to have been prodigious, Xuma continued:

Charlotte is an argument for the education of African girls to lead exemplary lives as wives and as leaders of our womanhood. . . . To me she is a daily inspiration and reason for hope about the future of African womanhood. She is our pride and hope whenever she takes the platform anywhere, because we know that our case will be well stated. Africa thanks God for Charlotte![24]

Section Four
Professions in the Church:
Individual and Corporate Responsibility

17

ORDINATION OF WOMEN*

James E. Will

While the licensing and ordination of women as elders in full connection has been recognized as a legitimate part of Methodist polity since 1956, the struggle to achieve that gain dates back much farther. Both the Methodist Protestant Church and the Methodist Episcopal Church dealt with the issue of ordaining women, though the former initially was more progressive. As early as 1880 the Methodist Protestant Church had begun to accept women as ordained clergy, but the idea was not widely accepted and did not survive into the twentieth century. The General Conference of the more conservative Methodist Episcopal Church, although it authorized the licensing of women as lay preachers in 1920, never approved their ordination.[1] This action was taken by the unified Methodist Church in 1956.

By contrast, in the Church of the United Brethren in Christ during the nineteenth century, women made significant gains in entering the ordained ministry as members with full status. In the 1840s the United Brethren Church was still fairly small (it counted an estimated 25,000 members in 1840), and like a number of other denominations of the mid-nineteenth century, it still segregated men and women on opposite sides of the church.[2] This practice gradually disappeared, however, and was of little significance by the early 1850s. It was during that era that United Brethren women made their first attempts to

---

*An earlier version of this essay was published in *Woman's Rightful Place*, ed. Donald K. Gorrell (Dayton, Ohio: United Theological Seminary, 1980), and is included in this volume by permission.

become ordained clergy. Their successes were at best moderate, although there was nothing in either the constitution or the *Discipline* that definitively barred women from clergy rights.[3]

The earliest known attempt by a woman to apply for what might be called a license to preach occurred in May 1841. At a session of the Scioto Annual Conference, a committee was appointed to review the application of Sister L. Courtland, who reported that she felt "an impression to read and comment on the Scriptures." Uncertain as to whether this impression came from God, she requested counseling from the conference, together with a permit to do whatever work the conference might assign. A resolution was then brought to the floor of the conference recommending that a committee be formed to "advise Sister L. Courtland as to the course she is to pursue with reference to her impressions as the conference cannot determine whether she is called to preach, teach or exhort."[4]

A similar matter came before the Scioto Conference two years later in April 1843. This time the request came from Louisa P. Clemens, who possibly was petitioning for ordination, although the available documents are very sketchy. The matter was to be deferred to the next annual conference, but the proceedings for 1844 make no note of it.[5]

On May 10, 1845, the General Conference convened at Circleville, Ohio, then a major center of the United Brethren Church. Circleville was the home of the publishing establishment and the center of the Scioto Conference, perhaps the most influential conference in the church.[6] At the May 15 session, several petitions were brought to the floor of the conference, including one presented on behalf of Louisa Clemens by the Reverend J. Montgomery, a representative of the Scioto Conference. The matter was referred to a committee, which reported five days later. Clemens' petition was rejected for three reasons: She was not a member of the church; she was not a member of the annual conference; and the committee felt that the gospel did not authorize "the introduction of females into the ministry in the sense in which she requests it."[7] Based on the committee's report, it would appear that Louisa Clemens' petition was doomed to failure because she did not meet even the basic requirements. One wonders why the Scioto Conference itself had not raised these issues, but it is significant that the General Conference still felt it necessary to add that women could not be introduced into the ministry.

Despite that General Conference action, in January 1847 Charity Opheral applied to the White River Conference for a license to preach. After consideraton, the conference "resolved that Charity Opheral receive a note of commendation to liberate to public speaking."[8] Although the resolution is vague, it is generally thought that Opheral's "note of commendation" was the first annual conference license granted to a woman in the United Brethren Church.

During the 1850s the issue of licensing women to preach came into clearer focus. Until that time, a woman theoretically could have been licensed by any annual or quarterly conference, providing she met the criteria that had been established for men. But in a rather surprising action, the General Conference of 1857 passed a resolution prohibiting women from being licensed to preach.[9] The action had little immediate impact and was of slight concern until 1876.

But the ruling did have at least some effect on the aspirations of Lydia Sexton. On May 3, 1851, she had been granted the first quarterly conference license by the Iroquois Circuit of the Illinois Conference. The license was subject to annual renewal, which Sexton indicated was an occasional inconvenience, but it was easily obtained, even after 1857. The real problem facing Lydia Sexton was that she was not permitted to receive an annual conference license.[10]

Sexton's autobiography suggests that Bishop David Edwards may have been favorable to the idea of licensing women to preach. Because of the General Conference action, he had no legal right to issue an annual conference license, but he suggested that a letter of recommendation to preach could be provided. Such a document carried with it rights and responsibilities similar to those of a license, although technically it was not a license.[11]

It was in this context that on April 2, 1859, the Upper Wabash Conference issued Sexton a letter of recommendation to preach:

Whereas, Sister Lydia Sexton is regarded among us as a Christian lady of useful gifts as a pulpit speaker; and
Whereas, She has been laboring among us in the gospel of Christ; therefore,
Resolved, That we, the members of the Upper Wabash Annual Conference of the church of the United Brethren in Christ, do hereby recommend her to the churches as a useful helper in the work of Christ.[12]

The crisis-filled decade of the 1860s saw the progress of the women's movement halted, both within the church and outside it. The age that had resounded with the names of Harriet Tubman, Dorothea Dix, Sojourner Truth, and Susan B. Anthony, as well as those with whom we have made a brief acquaintance, had come to an end.[13]

Beginning in the 1870s, however, the role of women in the United Brethren Church began to expand rapidly. Perhaps the most significant development was the formation of the Women's Missionary Association on October 21, 1875, by representatives of nine major annual conferences.[14] Within two years, it had begun to send missionaries into the field. Growth was rapid between 1880 and 1900, and perhaps this in itself encouraged women to seek clergy rights again. In the meantime, Union Biblical Seminary had been founded and admitted its first class in the fall of 1871.[15] Within a few years women were attracted to the seminary, and a small number graduated into the work of the denomination. Thus women with special religious training became an active part of the church's ministry, alongside the Women's Missionary Association.[16]

Meanwhile, a practically unnoticed event had taken place. On May 23, 1874, at a meeting held at Pleasant View Church near New Albany, Indiana, a woman by the name of Maggie Thompson (1848–1924) received a quarterly conference license to preach, the first issued since Lydia Sexton's. Thompson began serving as an evangelist the following year, and continued in that role for fourteen years.[17] On August 23, 1876, at a session of the Indiana Annual Conference, her name and the names of nine men were referred to the Committee on Applicants.[18] The following day, this report was adopted by the conference:

Your Committee on Applicants having examined Sister Maggie Thompson find her clear and satisfactory on all the points of doctrine as proposed to applicants in our *Discipline*. We recommend that she receive a letter of commendation as a worthy Christian sister and a profitable laborer in the vineyard of the Lord to be signed by the Bishop of this Conference.[19]

Maggie Thompson was born near New Philadelphia, Indiana, on September 5, 1848, one of twelve children. She attended Indiana's Marengo Academy before becoming actively involved in the work of the church. On September 11, 1877, she married John Elliott, a minister in the Indiana Conference, and they lived at Corydon, Indiana, for nearly twelve years before moving to Illinois in 1889. The move was occasioned by Maggie Elliott's transfer to the Central Illinois Conference.

But at this point the focus of our attention shifts to the General Conference of 1889, probably the single most important conference in the history of the United Brethren Church. It dealt with a number of issues—the first and most well known concerned modifications in the constitution. When the changes were adopted, the smaller conservative faction led by Bishop Milton Wright withdrew in protest. The remaining delegates then took up the questions of lay delegation and the licensing and ordination of women. The issue of lay representation had been discussed on and off since 1857, and the consensus had been that the church was not ready. The matter was discussed in some detail at the General Conference of 1873, but had become bogged down in debate over an amendment dealing with pro rata representation. This issue seemed to divide the supporters of lay delegation into two groups—larger conferences that favored pro rata representation, and smaller ones that favored a fixed ratio.[20] Although there had appeared to be a majority favoring lay delegation, the whole matter was dropped and was not reconsidered in any substantial form until 1881.

By contrast, the question of licensing and ordination of women, which had been prohibited by the 1857 General Conference, had not been seriously examined in the intervening decades. Both the Methodist Protestant Church and the Methodist Episcopal Church were debating similar issues during the 1880s, and the United Brethren Church clearly was interested in their discussions, as reflected in the floor debate of the 1889 General Conference, as well as in the denomination's weekly periodical, the *Religious Telescope*.[21] In addition, the continued growth and influence of the Women's Missionary Association may have made the conference more receptive to the idea of extending clergy rights to women.

Thus the General Conference of 1889 simultaneously considered the issues of lay delegation (for men and women) and the licensing and ordination of women. Both items were approved. The text of the decision on women's ordination states:

Not wishing to hinder any Christian, who may be moved by the Holy Spirit, to labor in the vineyard of God for the salvation of souls, it is ordered, that whenever any godly woman presents herself before the quarterly or annual conference as an applicant for authority to preach the gospel among us, she may be licensed to do so . . . and may be ordained after the usual probation.[22]

On September 13, 1889, within four months of the passage of that resolution, the Central Illinois Conference ordained the first woman minister in the United Brethren Church. She was Ella Niswonger (1865–1944), a native of southern Ohio and one of the first graduates of Union Biblical Seminary.[23] Before her ordination, Niswonger had served for two years at a mission station in Streator, Illinois, and thereafter served at a number of other locations in Illinois and Kansas.[24] In 1901 she became the first woman ministerial delegate to General Conference, representing the Central Illinois Conference.[25]

Following in Ella Niswonger's steps were literally hundreds of women pursuing the same goal. Maggie Thompson Elliott, whom we met earlier, was ordained in 1890 by the Central Illinois Conference; then followed Visa Bell in 1891, by the Indiana Conference; and Ellen Runkle King in 1892, by the East Ohio Conference. With the door opened to ordination, significant numbers of women were ready to respond to a ministerial calling. By 1901 ninety-seven women at one time or another had been listed in the United Brethren ministerial directory, and the number continued to grow.[26]

Ordained women remained a small but vital section of the

ministry of the United Brethren Church until November 1946, when the denomination merged with the Evangelical Church to create the Evangelical United Brethren Church. The Evangelical Church and its predecessor bodies had never ordained women, and consequently in the union of the two denominations, there arose a clash of traditions.

As the merger negotiations proceeded, clergy rights for women were quietly abandoned. Prior to union there had been no indication that women would lose their right to be ordained. The official weekly papers of the two denominations were silent on the matter, and the respective General Conference minutes were, at best, vague. Remarks made at the 1941 General Conference of the Church of the United Brethren in Christ suggest that the issue was not being addressed openly. After Bishop G. D. Batdorf reported on the progress of the merger negotiations, he was asked whether or not women would be ordained. He responded that the matter was "sort of a sub rosa subject," but added that "the door is not closed completely."[27]

Actually a final decision had been reached more than a year earlier, according to a report read at the 1946 General Conference of the Evangelical United Brethren Church. Bishop George Edward Epp, secretary of the Joint Board of Bishops, reported several items from their meetings. The following is of particular interest:

The question as to whether there was record of any action regarding the status of women in and for the ministry in the Evangelical United Brethren Church was discussed at length. It was pointed out (a) we have committed ourselves to the position that church union as such will not change or take away the ministerial status of any man or woman in such ministry at the time of union, and (b) that at the Indianapolis meeting of the Joint Commissions on Church Union it was voted: "Another recommendation, to the effect that in the new Church there be no ordination as ministers granted to women, was likewise adopted." (Indianapolis, Nov. 11, 1939)[28]

The minutes of the Board of Bishops of neither the Evangelical Church nor the United Brethren Church made a record of this action, and there are no extant files of the Joint Commissions on Church Union.[29]

While detailed reasons for ending women's ordination in the

Church of the United Brethren in Christ cannot be found in official records, the practice ceased with the creation of the Evangelical United Brethren Church in 1946. Thus several decades of ordained ministry by women faded into history as the women already ordained passed from active service. But for more than one-third of its denominational existence, the United Brethren Church had been enriched by the ministry of ordained women while the great majority of Protestant denominations had refused to allow that ministry.

Women in the Church of the United Brethren in Christ (1889–1894)*

Date	Conference	Name	1889	1890	1891	1892	1893	1894
1889	Central Illinois	Ella Niswonger	#	0	0	0	0	0
1890	Northern Michigan	Mrs. S. E. Drake		x	0	0	0	0
	East Ohio	Ellen Runkle King[30]	=	0	0	#	0	0
1891	Tennessee	Mrs. A. L. Billheimer		#	0	0	0	0
	Central Illinois	Maggie T. Elliott[31]		**	0	0	0	0
	Arkansas Valley	Maria Friend[32]		x	0			#
	Lower Wabash	Mrs. H. J. Musselman		x	=	0	0	
	White River	Amanda Williams[33]		x	=	0	0	
1892	Indiana	Rose Knipe[34]			x	0	0	#
	East Ohio	Jennie B. Metsker[35]		x	=	0	0	#
	Illinois	Nettie M. Churchill[36]				0	0	0
	Central Illinois	Cassie Niswonger				0	0	0
	Northern Ohio	M. Agnes Percival			x	0	0	#
	White River	Allie Sipe[37]			x	0	0	#
	Lower Wabash	Mrs. C. A. Stevenson[38]			x	0	0	0
	White River	Nettie Valentine[39]			=	0	#	0
	West Africa	Lida M. West				0	0	
1893	Northern Ohio	Sulie Miller					0	0
	White River	Carrie M. Boose[40]				x	0	0

	Conference	Name				
	East Ohio	Mattie J. Mumma				0
	Arkansas Valley	Ella L. Tharp		=		0
	Upper Wabash	Minnie Thorn				0
	Kansas	Emma J. Weller[41]		x		0
	Tennessee	Mary L. Westcoat				0
	White River	Emma Wright Miller		x		0
1894	Erie	Anna H. Allen		x		#
	Indiana	Visa Bell[42]	**	#		0
	Kansas	Ella Caldwell				#
	Miami	Sarah Dickey			#	0
	Indiana	Fannie H. Fix		x	x	#
	Wisconsin	Jennie Hatch				0
	Wisconsin	Ida Richards				0
	Minnesota	Anna Talbott		=		0
	Lower Wabash	Sadie B. Whistler		x		0

* James Will, "A Collection of Basic Data Concerning the Issue of the Ordination of Women in the United Brethren Church 1872–1900," 1978. Private collection.

0   Listing in ministerial directory of *U.B. Almanac-Yearbook*

Year of ordination

x   Year of reception into indicated annual conference

=   Year of licensing

**   Year of licensing and reception into annual conference

MAGGIE NEWTON VAN COTT

Janet S. Everhart

Margaret Newton Van Cott was an American Methodist evangelist whose preaching career spanned almost half a century, from the mid-1860s until the first decade of the twentieth century. "Widow" Van Cott, who devoted herself full-time to evangelical endeavors after her husband's death, is generally recognized by Methodist historians as the first woman licensed to preach in the Methodist Episcopal Church. This study, based mainly on church periodicals, tells the story of Van Cott's preaching license and her subsequent relationship to the Methodist Episcopal Church. The aim is twofold: to piece together some of the scattered fragments of information about a remarkable woman, and to provide a glimpse of nineteenth-century Methodism as it struggled to define the role of women in a changing church and society.

The only book about Maggie Van Cott, *Life and Labors of Maggie Newton Van Cott,* was published in 1872 and again in 1876 under a different title, *The Harvest and the Reaper.* According to the preface of the first edition, Van Cott narrated her experiences to John O. Foster, a member of the Illinois Conference, while she was recuperating from an attack of "erysipelas," a fever she contracted during a speaking tour of Illinois.[1] Although the book was written near the beginning of Van Cott's long career, it is invaluable for the information it provides about her childhood, marriage, and early experiences as an evangelist.

Margaret Newton was born in New York City on March 25, 1830, to an English father and a mother of Scottish descent. William K. Newton was a man of some stature, a real estate manager for John Jacob Astor and other wealthy New Yorkers. Maggie's parents were Episcopalian, and she was confirmed in that church at age eleven; her introduction to Methodism was through her maternal grandfather. When Maggie was about twelve, her younger brother died from an attack of apoplexy, and the Newtons moved to Brooklyn and then to the family home in Williamsburg, Long Island, which stood near the Gothic Methodist Episcopal Church located at the corner of Ewen and Grand streets. Mrs. Newton forbade her daughter to attend services there, but Maggie liked to hide in the cupola of the house and listen to the songs and prayers.

In 1847, at one of the Newtons' frequent parties, Maggie met Peter Van Cott and married him less than a month later. Revealing her characteristic independent streak, she recalls that she paused when the minister came to the word *obey* during the marriage ceremony. "Maggie had determined to skip that word, but the mother had been in consultation with the minister, and three times was the question asked before the trembling bride said, in a very low voice, 'obey.'"[2]

Peter Van Cott was a druggist, and from the beginning, Maggie helped in the store. Early in their marriage the Van Cotts lost the elder of their two daughters to scarlet fever, and soon afterward, Peter was struck by the first of many maladies. Maggie was forced to carry on the business, making long treks to visit other druggists, obtain orders, and conclude sales. It was during one of those trips that a painful inward religious struggle finally was resolved and Maggie was "soundly, powerfully converted" as she was walking past John Street Methodist Episcopal Church in New York City. Immediately after she had experienced "light [from heaven] streaming in upon her soul," she remembers hearing Satan suggest to her that God would take her husband away. But she replied, "'Though he slay me, yet will I trust in him.' Yea, I will praise him; for he is MY God. Glory be to his holy name!"[3]

Shortly after her conversion experience, Maggie Van Cott began to attend the Wednesday evening prayer meetings at the Duane Street Methodist Episcopal Church. At one of those meetings, she experienced a blessing which she later interpreted, in a manner reminiscent of her contemporary Phoebe Palmer, as the "fullness which God promised in Joel: 'I will pour my spirit upon all flesh; and your sons and your daughters shall prophesy.'" From that hour, Van Cott felt "that her lips had been touched as with a live coal from the altar of Jehovah."[4] That experience may have been what the Holiness people would call entire sanctification; certainly the ecstatic joy that passed through Van Cott that night marked the beginning of a long and impressive career as an evangelist.[5] Thereafter, she often rose to give testimony in the Wednesday prayer meetings, a fact her husband's brother John mentioned rather pointedly one night during dinner. John soon had reason to regret his remark, for Peter Van Cott replied calmly, "If she never does any thing worse than that I will rejoice." And Maggie herself announced firmly, "I believe my tongue is my own, John, and I will use it when I please, where I please, and as I please."[6]

Van Cott began to read various works published by the Methodist Book Concern, including the "lives of Wesley, Fletcher, Cartwright, Finley, Bishop Asbury, Stevens's History of Methodism, and the Bible." During this period (probably in the early 1860s) Peter Van Cott died. Although she grieved deeply, Maggie's religious convictions helped her through this time, as they had not when her daughter Rachel died. As she left the church after her husband's funeral, her brother put his arms around her, "but the 'everlasting arms' of Jesus were felt even more precious."[7] Shortly after her husband's death, Van Cott joined the Methodist Episcopal Church.

With a daughter to support, Van Cott determined to continue her husband's business. At the same time, she was asked to lead some Sunday school classes. Reluctant at first, she became very popular and soon began to lead singing and to speak at the Five Points Mission in New York City. At her instigation, Sunday evening prayer meetings were organized at the Sixth Ward Mission and, depite predictions to the contrary, were very successful. Within a few weeks the meetings were filled to overflowing, and the pastor took over the meetings himself, encouraging Van Cott to begin yet other meetings on Thursday nights.

Through this leadership Van Cott began to acquire a reputation as an exciting evangelist and received invitations to speak elsewhere in the area. In 1868, with the encouragement of New York pastors A. C. Morehouse and William O. V. Brainard, Van Cott gave up her business and devoted herself wholly to evangelistic work. The same two ministers, both connected with the Duane Street Church, presented her with a certificate of commendation, affirming that "we are convinced that God has *called her to the work of an evangelist in his Church.*"[8] With this and other letters of recommendation in hand, Van Cott embarked upon her career as a traveling evangelist, responding to invitations to lead revival services and prayer meetings. Sometimes her daughter accompanied her, but more often Sarah stayed with family or friends.

Despite the scarcity of funds, Van Cott continued to prove her effectiveness as a preacher, and at one of the meetings in early 1869, she was handed an exhorter's license dated September 6, 1868, for the Windham Circuit of the New York Conference. According to her biography, this "ecclesiastical formula" had been obtained without her knowledge.[9] Pastor Morehouse, who signed the license, explains in his autobiography that he and the Prattsville presiding elder, T. W. Chadwick, had decided to give Van Cott an exhorter's license and later, if her work continued to be successful, a preacher's license, since "many were inquiring if persons without a license were allowed to preach."[10] Accordingly, about a month later when Van Cott was working at Stone Ridge in the Ellenville District of the New York Conference, Presiding Elder A. H. Ferguson and the Stone Ridge pastor, Charles Palmer, asked her to appear before the quarterly conference, and after the required examination, she was duly awarded a preacher's license, signed by Ferguson on March 6, 1869. For many evangelists, the license to preach would have been a natural result of their efforts and activities. However, the license awarded to Maggie Van Cott, though she herself "valued it very little," caused a great stir within sections of the Methodist Episcopal Church.[11]

The Church's Reaction to a Licensed Female Preacher

The controversy began in earnest at the 1869 session of the New York Conference, held at Sing Sing. The conference minutes note only that "on motion of M. D'C. Crawford, the matter of licensing females was referred to a committee, to report at next Conference."[12] But the *New York Times* of April 25, 1869, gives a much more descriptive account of the conference discussion:

Our readers will remember the excitement caused in the late New-York Methodist Episcopal Conference, held at Sing Sing, by the announcement of the Presiding Elder of the Ellenville District, that the Quarterly Conference of his District had licensed a female preacher, one "Widow VAN COTT." The Conference immediately became greatly agitated over the subject, about one-half being in favor of continuing the "widow" in the good cause of converting souls, while the other half were strenuously opposed to such a proceeding, avowing openly and above-board that it was a female suffrage movement with which they would have nothing to do.[13]

The *Times* article continues by reporting that a motion to disapprove the licensing of female preachers failed, as did a motion to censure Mr. Ferguson. However, the *Times* quotes one clergyman as saying, "It is secretly understood that the 'Widow VAN COTT' will not have her license renewed."

Following the New York Conference session, which Van Cott apparently did not attend, she kept up a busy schedule of revival activities, mainly in New York and New Jersey. During the spring of 1870 she supplied the pulpit of the Trinity Methodist Episcopal Church in Springfield, Massachusetts, while the pastor was ill. Springfield was the site of the New England Conference session in April 1870, and many ministers of the conference heard her preach, as reported in *The Methodist*:

The novelty of a woman in the pulpit still continues to create a sensation, and to draw crowds in Springfield and vicinity. Probably Mrs. Van Cott never addressed so august or critical an assembly as on Tuesday evening, March 22d. The preachers of the New-England Conference had just arrived, and, in consideration of her rising fame, signal success, and the probability of her being proposed for admission as a probationer to the New-England Conference, they all rushed to Union-street Methodist Episcopal church to hear her.[14]

Reports of the conference indicate that "Sister Van Cott" and the Troy Praying Band conducted meetings between sessions and led revival services at the Union Methodist Episcopal

Church in town. The extent of Van Cott's visibility during the conference is evidenced by the frequent appearance of her name in the conference journal; however, the journal does not record any recommendation for her admission as a ministerial member. Although several local papers had predicted that she would be presented for orders, the New York *Christian Advocate* reported after the conference that "The application for the admission of Mrs. Van Cott was prudently withheld by the Presiding Elder of the District where she has labored largely, and a resolution commending her Christian work, and recommending her as a worthy and successful evangelist, was laid upon the table."[15]

The Presiding Elder referred to is almost certainly David Sherman, whose essay "Woman's Place in the Gospel" appears as an introduction to Van Cott's biography. Although Sherman moved from Springfield District to Lynn District, Trinity Church in Springfield continued to affirm Van Cott's work. In contrast to the failure of the annual conference to recognize her, in early April 1870 the "Quarterly Conference of Trinity church . . . voted to continue the license of Mrs. Van Cott as a local preacher." The official board of the same church also adopted resolutions acknowledging Van Cott's "valuable and useful services" and commending her as an "efficient laborer in the work of saving souls."[16]

Just as the New England Conference avoided any official recognition of Van Cott's work, the New York Conference committee appointed to discuss the issue of licensing females requested at the 1870 conference session that it be "excused from the further consideration of the subject."[17] The reluctance of these two conferences to confront the issue of women's participation in professional ministry is consistent with the response of the larger Methodist Episcopal Church.

Although regional editions of *The Christian Advocate* followed Van Cott's activities, the New York edition, largest of the weekly periodicals, was strangely silent. Finally, an 1873 article in the New York *Advocate* declared its frustration at the church's failure to take a stand on Van Cott's activities. The writer of the article, probably the editor, Daniel Currey, explained that while the name Van Cott was seen frequently in both religious and secular papers, the New York *Advocate* had "been greatly at a loss what to say about the whole subject, not from any lack of definite convictions, but because we have felt the delicacy of the whole affair. And even now we approach it with reluctance, and only because it is forced upon us by circumstances that we cannot control." Near the end of the lengthy article, which attempted to recount the history of Van Cott's relationship with the church and its conferences, the author remarked in frustration that "the Bishops observe a dead silence about it, the Annual Conferences avoid it, the Church press fight shy about it, most of the ministers keep clear of it, but a few admire the 'wonderful woman,' flatter her, puff her up in the papers, and generally make much of her."[18]

While official representatives and organs of the church seemed reluctant to deal with the subject, regional papers such as *Zion's Herald,* edited by activist Gilbert Haven, discussed the issue and spoke out in favor of Van Cott's ministry and ordination. In April 1870 the New York *Advocate* complained that *Zion's Herald* was abusing its editorial freedom by pushing for Van Cott's ordination. The *Herald* responded by pointing out that

the brother who held her [Van Cott's] recommendation and who is the official leader in this act, and is warmly in favor of it, is Rev. David Sherman. *The New York Advocate* does us too much honor, in assigning to us the chief place in advocating the admission of Mrs. Van Cott to the New England Conference.[19]

Despite this disclaimer, however, the *Herald* was outspoken in support of Mrs. Van Cott, taking frequent opportunities to chide the New England Conference for its failure to officially recognize her ministry. Gilbert Haven's support of Van Cott was not limited to his own paper; he also wrote a glowing introduction to her biography, heralding her as "without doubt, to-day, the most popular, most laborious, and most successful preacher in the Methodist Episcopal Church. She has more calls, does more work, and wins more souls to Christ than any of her brothers."[20]

In addition to Haven, a strong abolitionist, Van Cott found support and admiration among some black pastors and churchgoers. After overcoming her own strong racial prejudice when she was faced with the prospect of associating with black people near the Five Points Mission in New York, Van Cott worked with black Methodists on occasion in her revival efforts. She was twice invited by Joseph C. Hartzell, a leading proponent of black rights in the church, to hold revival meetings at Ames Chapel in New Orleans. Hartzell, who, like Haven, was elected to the episcopacy, gave Van Cott excellent press coverage in the *Southwestern Advocate,* a paper he established in 1873. In one editorial, Hartzell supported Van Cott's ordination:

Paul has been quoted against women speaking in public, but if he could attend a few of the meetings now in progress in Ames Church in this city, conducted by Mrs. Van Cott, and he had the power to do it, he would strike every word out of his epistles that could in any way be made to silence the voice of women calling sinners to Christ. . . . Mrs. Van Cott as a regularly licensed preacher in the Methodist Episcopal Church is entitled to ordination, and we advocate it, in her particular case. . . . Eligibility to ordination depends on the spiritual power of the candidate to do good.[21]

Despite the support of activists like Hartzell and Haven, however, the General Conference, governing body of the Methodist Episcopal Church, was not ready to support women's ordination or even to approve the licensing of women as local preachers. At the 1872 session, a report of the Committee on Woman's Work in the Church conceded that more than two-thirds of the church membership was female, but noted that

to define and designate the exact character and fields of their labor is not an easy matter. . . . In regard to woman's preaching we must wait for further developments of Providence. We rejoice in the indications that women are called to be teachers of the Word of Life, and yet the instances are not sufficiently numerous to justify any new legislation in the Church on this subject.[22]

The continuation of Van Cott's preacher's license after 1870 has not been documented, although it may have been renewed in the California Conference in 1874. There is, however, evidence that her admission into an annual conference was still being explored, either on her own initiative or at the instigation of interested pastors. During 1874 Van Cott was in California for several months, conducting revival meetings, and the issue of her ordination was raised there. In July of that year, the *Pittsburgh Christian Advocate* reported that

Mrs. Vancott [sic] was at late accounts laboring at the Powell street church, San Francisco. She has united with the Powell street church, and a correspondent of the California *Advocate* says, it is expected that she will be recommended to the Annual Conference for election to orders as a local preacher.[23]

Interestingly, just one week later, the *Northwestern Advocate* noted that "Mrs. Van Cott does not ask for 'ordination,' but for simple liberty to 'take a text.'"[24] In any case, whether or not Van Cott herself sought ordination, she was recommended by the San Francisco District Conference on September 2, 1874, for ordination as a deacon. The recommendation was brought before the California Conference but was refused by Bishop Stephen M. Merrill on the grounds that "the Board of Bishops did not recognize that any quarterly or district conference had a legal right to grant women licenses to preach."[25]

Bishop Merrill's refusal to recognize Van Cott as a validly licensed local preacher was consistent with the views of other Methodists who opposed the licensing and ordination of women. The New York *Christian Advocate* had contended in 1873 that quarterly and district conferences had no authority to license women. Noting that a local preacher is eligible for deacon's orders after holding a license for four years, it stated that Bishop Levi Scott's refusal to consider Van Cott for ordination in the New England Conference "must have been on the grounds that the candidate was not, because she could not be, a local preacher of the Methodist Episcopal Church."[26] On the other side of the question, a Methodist who wrote to the *Northwestern Christian Advocate* in 1874 pointed out that the affirmation of "women's zeal in the evangelization of the masses" by the 1872 General Conference contradicted the apparent episcopal decision to block the licenses of females.[27] Such protests, however, did not carry much weight with the bishops, who seemed to stand together on this issue; in 1875

Bishop Thomas Bowman of the North Indiana Conference echoed Bishop Merrill's opinion, noting that the "whole tenor of Discipline was against the licensing of women to preach" and that "license to preach implies the right of ordination."[28]

Despite the equivocations of the 1872 General Conference, the presence of preaching females within annual conferences forced church officials to debate both the licensing of women and the corollary question of women's ordination. Several annual conferences hoped to obtain some ruling on the issue from the 1876 General Conference. That conference received an appeal of Bishop Merrill's refusal to ordain Mrs. Van Cott in California and was presented with a report from the California Conference on the granting of local preacher's licenses to women. The report and appeal were referred to the Committee on Revisals, which also received a resolution instructing it to look into "the expediency of so changing the Discipline as to provide expressly for the licensing as preachers of such women as evince . . . that they are called of God to this work."[29] Despite the plea of several delegates that the presence of talented female preachers within the church indicated a need to officially recognize them with licenses, the appeal, the report, and the resolution resulted in no definitive action. The wording of the *Discipline* did not change until 1880, leaving annual conferences and bishops free to decide whether "person" should include women.[30]

Although the General Conference and the New York *Advocate* regarded women preachers as a rarity, for whom accommodating legislation was not necessary, Maggie Van Cott was not the only woman who was licensed and engaged in an active preaching ministry in the 1870s. Limited research has uncovered the names of fourteen other women who were granted local preacher's licenses during that decade, as well as that of Mrs. Emma Richardson, who reportedly received a preacher's license in the Canadian Methodist Episcopal Church in 1864, hence "outranking" Mrs. Van Cott by five years.[31] Other women were granted exhorter's licenses or simply preached without any official credentials. Perhaps in belated recognition of the growing number of women engaged in active ministry, finally the 1880 General Conference took a definitive stand. That conference, from which Anna Oliver sought a ruling permitting the ordination of women, adopted a report from the Committee on the Judiciary stating that "the Discipline of the Church does not provide for nor contemplate the licensing of women as local preachers." In 1884, the General Conference reaffirmed this stance by adopting another report which stated: "Your committee, to whom was referred the question of licensing women to exhort and preach, and also the question of ordaining women, beg leave to report that . . . it is inexpedient to take action on the subject proposed."[32]

A Broader View

Recent research in the areas of women in religion and women in the nineteenth century may help to cast some light on the controversy created by Maggie Van Cott's preaching career. Ann Douglas' pioneering work in these areas suggests that the lives of ministers and women of that time were connected in complex ways. As interest in church activities declined during the latter part of the century, ministers worked closely with women, who constituted the majority of churchgoers. They shared many activities: writing, nurturing, and generally living within a sphere removed from the exigencies of North American politics and business. Nineteenth-century culture supported the idea of a special sphere for women—the exalted arena of home and church within which they created a haven for their husbands, sons, fathers, and brothers who were functioning in an increasingly complex society—and ministers helped to create and maintain that exalted sphere as a bastion of religious values.

Douglas has shown that while nineteenth-century ministers were intimately involved with, and largely dependent on their female parishioners, this very dependency fostered an intense territorialism.

Clerical hostility was a form of territorial imperative springing from an uneasy sense of a too cramped space. Ministers suspected—and rightly—that women had more chance of capturing the church than the Senate; and they reserved their fiercest powers of resistance for such a possibility.[33]

Maggie Van Cott's successful evangelistic preaching en-croached upon clerical territory and doubtless touched on fears that women would invade yet another male bastion, the pulpit. An article on "Methodism and Revivals" featured in an 1870 edition of the New York *Advocate* seems to reflect these fears. Although it does not mention Van Cott, it is possible that she was one of the unofficial preachers against whom it was warning:

Hence it may be announced as a principle, that the Pastor of a Church is the only evangelist to be admitted to its pulpit; that the minister and members of a Church should conduct and carry on all its religious meetings; and that the regularly appointed means of grace are the principal kinds of services that should be held for the conversion of sinners.[34]

The protective note sounded by this article reflects concern about the growing number of evangelical and "holiness" preachers who were operating extensively both within and outside the Methodist Episcopal Church at that time.

In discussing and analyzing the controversy stirred by Van Cott's evangelical efforts, it is pertinent to ask whether she herself ever actively sought ordination or official recognition. According to her biography, which covers only her early career, she did not view either a preacher's license or ordination as necessary for her work. Both her exhorter's license and her preacher's license had been obtained at the instigation of interested Methodist pastors. When Ferguson handed Van Cott her preacher's license, this exchange reportedly took place: " 'Will this [preacher's license] make me more efficient in winning souls for Christ?' 'I cannot say that it will,' he replied. 'Well, then, sir, I value it but very little.' "[35] Gilbert Haven, in his introduction to Van Cott's biography, underlines her apparent diffidence toward attempts to secure official creden-tials, noting that it was with trepidation that she ever preached from a pulpit. In contrast to detractors who criticized her unwomanly aggressiveness, Haven remarks:

She never forgets her ladyhood in this boldness of daring. . . . She rarely does a new thing until it is suggested by others. . . . She refused to attend class-meeting until a few years ago, because she said it was a shame for a woman to speak in such places. They [ministers] say "You must be licensed as a local preacher." Again she objects, again submits. Thus every step in her public career has been forced upon her, and thus every step has been a victory.[36]

Yet another indication of Van Cott's possible indifference toward clerical credentials is the failure of her biography, which was published in 1872, to mention the 1870 renewal of her preacher's license.

Despite these observations, however, Van Cott's biography reprints her original preacher's license. And whether as an advertisement for the book or as an indication of genuine pride in the achievement, Van Cott's picture appears in the front with the caption, "The first lady licensed to preach in the Methodist Episcopal Church in America." Either Van Cott or Foster clearly took some note of the license, remarking that as a regularly licensed local preacher, her discourses could appropriately be referred to as sermons.[37]

With apparently conflicting evidence and the absence of any report from Van Cott's own hand, the question of her intentions regarding her official relationship with the Methodist Episcopal Church must be left unanswered. However, recent research on the Holiness movement of the nineteenth century provides some clues, since as an evangelist, Van Cott exemplified several of the characteristics identified with the Holiness people. If we consider her in relation to that movement in which institutional authority took second place to charismatic ability, it may help to explain the apparent ease with which she moved in and out of the Methodist Episcopal Church.

The Holiness movement "had a theology centered in experience," and a reader of Van Cott's biography and the newspaper reports of her work will realize that her conversion and subsequent ecstatic experiences were essential to her ministry. Van Cott's own criterion for success hinged on the conversion of souls.

Another characteristic of the Holiness movement was its experiential interpretation of Scripture. One can imagine that Van Cott would have pronounced a hearty Amen to Phoebe Palmer's insistence that "THE BIBLE, THE BLESSED

BIBLE, IS THE TEXTBOOK. Not Wesley, not Fletcher . . . not Mrs. Phoebe Palmer, but the Bible." Interpreting the Bible in light of experience, Holiness people "claimed Biblical authority, but they were not bound by literal interpretations" and thus did not find the ministry of women to be in conflict with the Scriptures. Although Van Cott never went so far as to argue, as some did, that the "women's-rights movement was . . . the culmination of New Testament teachings," she did view women's preaching as a natural outgrowth of the gospel. The concluding chapter of her biography is a biblical defense of woman's right to preach and sounds remarkably like Mrs. Palmer's argument.[38]

The Holiness movement also emphasized the work of the Holy Spirit, an emphasis which led "naturally to a charismatic concept of leadership and ministry."[39] Van Cott seemed comfortable with a charismatic style. Her preaching was not confined to Methodist churches, but took place in homes and camp meetings as well. Although significant numbers of people joined the Methodist Episcopal Church under Van Cott's watchful guidance, her concern was not primarily with denominational membership but with the number of souls converted. Articles about her revival meetings attested to her charisma and "free style": "It is amazing to see her bring people to the altar. She sets the meeting going and then flits all over the house, here and there, in pew or aisle, entreating, warning, praying, yet a lady always."[40] Van Cott's commitment to nondenominational evangelism is reflected in the fact that, unlike other women who were refused ordination in the Methodist Episcopal Church, she did not seek it elsewhere. Instead, she went about the Lord's work on the authority of her ability to convert souls to Christ.

Maggie Van Cott's ability to minister effectively without the endorsement of an ecclesiastical structure was a source of concern to some church officials. *The Christian Advocate* suggested in 1873 that someone should "forbid" her.[41] Just as some ministers were vehemently opposed to licensing or ordaining Van Cott, others apparently were eager to have her admitted to the clerical structure of the church. Were those pastors simply carrying out their convictions that women ought to share with men the privileges and responsibilities of the ordained ministry? Or were some of those supporters aware that Van Cott would create less of a disturbance and present less challenge to the church hierarchy if she, too, fell under the jurisdiction of a presiding elder and bishop?

To question the motives of those who supported Van Cott's ordination may seem grossly unfair; yet it is necessary, in light of recent studies which reveal the complexity of the relationship, the power struggle, between women and ministers in the nineteenth century. A closer look at the rhetoric used by Van Cott's supporters may be helpful. In an essay which appears at the beginning of both editions of Van Cott's biography, David Sherman suggests that "Christianity is emphatically the Gospel of woman. It takes the female type, and exalts the humaner and feminine virtues."[42] Gilbert Haven, in his introduction to the book, argued that the church should make use of women's unique gifts: "The theatre, the opera, the platform, are not the only sphere for woman. The Church must seize and sanctify this gift. . . . Offset the demon Woodhull with the saintly Palmer and Van Cott." By contrasting them with the radical feminist Virginia Woodhull, Haven assured his readers that women like Van Cott did not threaten the prevailing notion that the home was still women's chief sphere. The possibility "that woman, generally, will be called to this work, no one believes. . . . Her sphere is chiefly home, and will ever be. . . . But the . . . Holy Spirit will continue to call His daughters into His service."[43]

When we compare Van Cott's critics with her supporters, we see that both camps marshaled arguments based on the idea of woman's special sphere and influence. Her supporters praised her feminine qualities; her detractors faulted her for the lack of those same qualities. Ironically, the "sympathetic power of woman" was used both in defense of women's active participation in ministry and in favor of keeping women on the home front. Similarly, a corollary of this argument, the "persuasive power of women," was instrumental in finally winning the female franchise. Even in attainment of professional rights, women were still assumed to labor in a sphere different from that of their male counterparts!

It is beyond the scope of this paper to delve deeply into the motives of Van Cott's supporters and detractors. However, it is clear that some church officials preferred official recognition of women ministers to the unaccountability enjoyed by unlicensed preachers. In an article advocating the licensing of women, the Reverend J. W. Robinson suggested that they "should receive the church's license, and thereby be placed directly and fully under its direction and control."[44] Nearly twenty years later, the *Southwestern Christian Advocate* expressed a similar view in reference to Jennie Fowler Willing, a popular speaker and temperance leader who had received a preacher's license in 1873 from the Joliet District Conference of the Rock River Annual Conference. Admitting that Willing was an excellent preacher, the paper observed:

It is not certain how far the Church can with safety permit this class of impassioned orators to go free of all ecclesiastical restraints, save as laymen are restrained, and as their own fancy may direct. The time must yet and soon come when there will be some further and more definite action than any yet taken by the church upon this subject.[45]

The views expressed by these writers suggest that women preachers, forced to remain outside the ordained ministry, challenged the authority of the institutional church on a basic level and deeply threatened the authority of male ministers. On a much more overt level, the desire to integrate women like Van Cott and Willing into the church structure demonstrated a recognition of their effectiveness. At the 1874 California Conference session when Bishop Merrill had refused to consider Van Cott for ordination, two presiding elders noted in their district reports that her work had helped several churches reduce their financial liabilities.[46] Van Cott was also instrumental in adding thousands of members to Methodist Episcopal Churches. During one twelve-month period, from early 1871 to early 1872, an excerpt from her journal notes that she had "seen 3,085 seeking at the altar the Saviour's love, who have professed to have been blessed. Of this number I have been privileged to extend the right hand of love and welcome on probation in the Methodist Episcopal Church to 1113 souls."[47] In short, then, a complex variety of factors—ranging from cultural conditioning, to economic pragmatism, to simple jealousy—can be identified in the controversy that surrounded one woman's relationship to the Methodist Episcopal Church.

The furor over Maggie Van Cott's license to preach came at a time when other churchwomen were beginning to consider the possibility of ordained ministry. Within ten years of Van Cott's 1869 license, other Methodist Episcopal women had received local preacher's licenses, several had graduated from seminaries, and some, including Anna Oliver and Anna Howard Shaw, were actively seeking ordination. When Van Cott is placed within the framework of increasing agitation over women's role in the church, one might ask whether interested pastors hoped to find in her a logical and willing test case for women's ordination.

In many respects, Van Cott was a good choice for a test case. She was popular and well known, and she was not connected with the women's suffrage movement or other controversial issues of the day, although some of her detractors attempted to make that connection. By her own admission she had been a racist before the Civil War and hence certainly not involved with abolition. Van Cott's apparent indifference toward official credentials was appealing to those who feared that women in the pulpit would represent one more crack in the wall of woman's "special sphere." Clearly, some observers of the furor over her preacher's license and possible admission to the New England Conference did view her as a test case; a "New England Correspondent" writing to *The Methodist* in 1870 remarked, in reference to Van Cott, that "it is to be regretted . . . that the candidate . . . to be made the test case is not in every way unobjectionable."[48] Despite these observations, however, and no matter how ideal a test case for women's ordination Van Cott may appear from this vantage point, the evidence is insufficient to warrant more than speculation, and the question must remain open.

By now it should be apparent that the full story of Maggie Van Cott's relationship to the official ministry of Methodism is complex indeed and has by no means been exhausted by this study. Much of Van Cott's "life and labors" has been left untouched; the continuation of her preaching career into the early twentieth century is material for another paper. The portion of Van Cott's career considered here has shown that both as a woman and as a preacher on the fringes of the Holiness movement, Van Cott rocked the boat within the Methodist Episcopal system. She was an irregular preacher by virtue of both her methods and her sex, the latter probably posing the greater threat to the church.

Although she challenged church tradition and polity, Van Cott's call and abilities also presented the church an opportunity to deal with the question of women's role in professional ministry, a question that has not been completely resolved a century later. Her presence and popularity forced church officials to debate the issue of female clergy, thus setting the stage for the many women who followed her. Maggie Newton Van Cott probably would have asked any writer to mention both her preacher's license and the large number of people who first confessed Jesus Christ as Lord and Savior under her watchful guidance. And it is probably safe to say that she would chide an author for placing those two achievements in that order!

THE FUNCTION OF
FEMALE BONDING

Catherine M. Prelinger and Rosemary S. Keller

The Protestant deaconess movement in nineteenth-century America owed its institutional inspiration to the *Frauendiakonie* at Kaiserswerth, Germany, the first deaconess order in the modern world, founded in 1836 by Theodor Fliedner, the acknowledged Restorer of the Apostolic Office of Deaconess.[1] In 1849, Fliedner personally accompanied four deaconesses to Pittsburgh, at the urgent request of Lutheran pastor William A. Passavant, to transplant his work into American soil. Lucy Rider Meyer, founder of the second deaconess order in the United States, in 1887, gratefully attributed the lineage of her work to Kaiserswerth in her book *Deaconesses: Biblical, Early Church, European, American.*[2] Yet the transplantation of the diaconessate from Germany to America is a tale of paradox.

Passavant's Lutheran enterprise at Pittsburgh soon faltered, but Meyer's Chicago Training School and Deaconess Home, where the Methodist diaconessate originated, was by contrast a singular success. What enabled the Methodists to adapt the German precedent with such evident effectiveness, while the Lutherans failed?

The institutions founded at Pittsburgh and Chicago were alike in the external practices borrowed from their German model. Both trained young unmarried women in the essentials of nursing and the tenets of Protestantism for the purpose of ministering to the improverished and sick. Both offered a livelihood to their candidates: lodging, board, a small allowance, and meaningful work. Most important, both promised their members a lifelong community of women to work with, to live with, and to return to when their days of service were past. Beneath the surface, however, the two

American experiments were very different, and different as well from the German model they emulated.

We will first explore the foundation of modern deaconess orders laid by Fliedner's Kaiserswerth institution, focusing particularly on the unacknowledged role of women in its founding and early survival. We will argue that the spirit of female mutuality that lay behind the organization's facade was, in fact, essential to the institution's success.

We then will consider the varying modes of institutional adaptation in the Lutheran deaconess home at Pittsburgh and in the Methodist Chicago Training School. The Methodist experience suggests that both the imagery and awareness of womanhood and the strong female support-system that bound deaconesses to women in local churches were central to the life of the Methodist school, in contrast to the ill-fated Lutheran home. The evidence assembled here strongly underscores the significance of conscious self-understanding of female experience and mutual support in the vitality of a woman's organization—in this case the professional deaconess movement.

Theodor Fliedner departed radically from contemporary practice when he founded the mother house and hospital at Kaiserswerth with the intention of restoring the apostolic office of deaconess. His goal was to enhance the position of Protestantism, particularly in the Catholic Rhinelands, by employing the resources of women. Protestant philanthropy had been a male preserve in Germany; female charity was confined to local and highly transient activities, except in abnormal circumstances such as war. The Roman Catholic model for charitable endeavor had been consciously rejected by Protestant churches, since repudiation of the celibate life seemed to invalidate the possibility of charitable orders. The potential role of women in the visible life of the congregation was diminished further in the Lutheran Church of Germany because of its unquestioned emphasis on enunciation of the Word of God by male clergy, an emphasis that trivialized works of practical Christianity.

Fliedner first became impressed with the charitable potential of women through the example of the English evangelist Elizabeth Fry. As a young pastor traveling in England to raise money for his parish, Fliedner observed the work of Fry as she sought to improve the spiritual and material lives of British prisoners, particularly at Newgate.[3] He was more immediately convinced of the possible good women could exert through charitable enterprises, by his own wife, Friedericke. Before their marriage, she had yearned for a vocation in practical Christianity. She had accepted his rather forbidding written proposal of marriage, which included the injunction, "The will of the man has to be given precedence and the woman has to yield according to human and divine right," because she believed that Theodor's discipline and parsimony would provide a suitable environment for such work.[4]

The couple's first collaborative project was an asylum for women just released from prison. Essentially a *Magdaleneninstitut*, the asylum located in the Kaiserswerth rectory offered an opportunity for Friedericke and a close friend to demonstrate their talents in working with the needy and indigent by rehabilitating wayward young women.

The diaconessate was a direct outgrowth of that experiment. Although Fliedner's concept of the diaconessate embraced other functions as well, the nursing office at Kaiserswerth assumed a centrality related to the urgent demands of the times and the possibilities of fund raising. Early nineteenth-century hospitals were essentially poorhouses, and the problem of staffing was acute. There was little resistance, therefore, to Lutheran deaconesses when the motherhouse at Kaiserswerth offered trained personnel, at a modest cost, to municipalities that applied for their assistance.

Fliedner's annual reports record the rapid material success of the diaconessate. Within the first year of the institution's existence at Kaiserswerth, 15 women's auxiliaries were organized and contributions were received from 950 persons. By the sixth year of operation, 500 patients were treated annually at the hospital. Within 10 years of its founding, in 1846, 100 women were working as deaconesses at Kaiserswerth and at the 18 hospitals served by the motherhouse.[5]

Official reports of the institution do not explain why women were drawn in increasing numbers to seek deaconess orders. The reasons are apparent, however, from internal records at Kaiserswerth—the autobiographies that women seeking admission were required to submit as part of their application.

These statements reveal that the religious and social goals enunciated at Kaiserswerth corresponded with the needs of a precarious segment of German womanhood: young single women to whom the traditional economy no longer offered a secure existence.

The demographic revolution during the mid-nineteenth century overburdened the economy in rural Germany, increased the population by 38 percent in thirty years, set a previously stable population wandering, and dramatically elevated the rate of illegitimacy. It also stimulated enrollment at Kaiserswerth, for single women were the most vulnerable. Virtually all the candidates for the diaconessate came from large families. Many had lost one or both parents and had either raised or been raised by siblings. Some of those siblings had married, but the deaconess candidates had not. Some ascribed their circumstances to the loss of a family farm, to inadequate education, or to early placement in domestic service.

All the deaconess candidates had been deeply touched by the Awakening. They perceived themselves as sinners reborn in Christ. Disobedience to an employer or a parent often precipitated what was described as a struggle with the Devil, or the Enemy, who finally was subdued when Jesus appeared to the young women. Kaiserswerth offered these women not only a livelihood, but a chance to legitimate their conversion and atone for their evident and understandable belief that life had dealt them ill.

The application of Christine Klett expresses the intense religious faith combined with a sense of abandonment by family that was characteristic of many of these documents. She had fallen ill shortly after her conversion and had gone to her sister's home to recover but "was treated coldly and without love."[6] Another candidate, Luise Mann, put it this way:

O how many vexations and bitternesses would have been spared had I only learned a little bit to bend my own obstinacy. . . . In the year 1834 in November I had no quiet day and night. I realized that I had not yet reached a self-awareness that I had become a sinner. I cannot express in what anxiety of death I found myself and so with hot tears I sought my dear Redeemer. . . . After the passage of eight days at 9 o'clock I was freed from the bonds of Satan; it was in my heart just as though my dear Saviour had stood before me and washed my heart with his blood.[7]

That the diaconessate met the spiritual and material needs of the candidates is obvious. Their psychological needs, however, were met by a powerful though invisible and unacknowledged female support-system that gradually developed within the Kaiserswerth operation. That support-system manifested itself through three critical aspects of institutional procedure: recruitment, training, and domestic life.

The impact of female solidarity is apparent in the recruitment of the first deaconess, Gertrud Reichardt. Unlike later candidates, she actually did not need the job, since she was employed as an assistant to her father, a physician. When Fliedner asked her to visit Kaiserswerth shortly after the purchase of the mother house, she was discouraged by the empty building. But the appearance of a huge package of linen bedding and bandaging contributed by a women's auxiliary persuaded her to remain. To Reichardt, this was dramatic evidence that women in supporting churches were committed to making the diaconessate a reality.[8]

The working of an extended, though unorganized female network is even more apparent in the correspondence of Sophie Eberle, a deaconess of the 1850s. She described her sojourn with the family of another deaconess when she had made her initial trip to Kaiserswerth and told of the support she received from the girls she had known back in Württemberg when she had entered training. Clearly their example was consequential in her enrollment.

Training at the diaconessate was onerous. Sophie Eberle wrote that their day, which was divided among care of the sick, school lessons, and worship was "so apportioned that from mornings at five o'clock until evenings at six the powers of both soul and body are perpetually in motion."[9] After the evening meal, this round of activity continued until 10:00 at night, and every two weeks, each deaconess was on duty all night. Work was rotated among the various units of the hospital, including food preparation and laundry, as well as care of patients.

Theodor and Friedericke Fliedner related to the deaconesses in notably different ways, pointing up the significant supportive—even motherly—role of Fliedner's wife. The strict personal standards Fliedner established for the deaconesses compounded the rigor of institutional requirements. Most of the novices came from simple backgrounds; many could not write or calculate, and their knowledge of housekeeping was elementary. Fliedner's patience did not extend to their ignorance and unintentional lack of personal discipline, qualities he equated with sinfulness rather than with simplicity. His comments, which he kept in his record book, bear witness to this severity. Helene Osthoff, he wrote, displayed "a lack of self denial concerning herself . . . too little concern with cleanliness; because of infestation not combing the sick; not friendly enough, often sulky."[10]

Yet Helene was one of the first sisters to take charge of a hospital in the field. It is hardly surprising that of the fifty women originally accepted as novices, only twenty-nine completed probation and were accepted for consecration. Without the mitigating role of Friedericke Fliedner, the number surely would have been much lower.

Friedericke's insights were crucial to the survival of Kaiserswerth. As superintendent, she sought to mediate the requirements of the institution, recognizing that beneath the probationers' unwitting lack of cultivation, there was a willingness and commitment. Friedericke ascribed their clumsiness and naïveté to inexperience with life. She further recognized that the quality of Christian piety demanded by Theodor did not always accompany the qualities required in a good nurse.

Friedericke articulated her apprehensions that the subordination she owed to the institution's inspector, Theodor, as her husband could not be satisfied if she were to fulfill the duty of impartiality she owed to the deaconesses as their superintendent. Each week she was required to submit a report of her work, and this became a trial because, as she put it, he "could only measure with the eyes of a man what had happened with the eyes of a woman."[11] It was difficult to maintain the tenuous balance between their professional and personal relationships. Friedericke interpreted the centrality of her institutional responsibility as an expression of her devotion to Theodor, assuming a subordinate position for all discernible purposes. Hence the complexity of her work as superintendent did not become a matter of institutional record.

When Fliedner attempted to describe Friedericke's contribution after her death, conceptualization failed him and he eulogized her "masculine energy."[12] No wonder the value of female commitment went unrecognized! Under the superintendency of Fliedner's second wife, Caroline, the situation was exacerbated by the world prominence Theodor had acquired through his extensive travels. Public opinion identified the character of the institution with his personality, whereas in fact, Kaiserswerth's truer identity was derived from its members.

Domestic life at Kaiserswerth increasingly fostered and was nurtured by a spirit of female solidarity. In the house rule of the institution, Theodor relied heavily on the family model. His instructions for the superintendent counseled her to employ a motherly role. He enjoined her to be sure that the deaconesses lacked "nothing of importance so that they feel just as at home in the *Diakonissenhaus* as they did in the home of their parents."[13] Establishment of a surrogate family was directed effectively to the needs of the sisters. Their autobiographies reveal that they yearned for family life and that the diaconessate met their expectations. Sophie Eberle wrote to her mother of "the tender friendliness in the expression of [Caroline Fliedner's] face."[14] Coffee hour in the afternoon, when a special brew of roasted rye was served to the assembled sisters, became a cherished institution at Kaiserswerth. When Friedericke Bremer the Swedish novelist visited the institute in 1846, she exclaimed that she had never seen such a collection of "enthusiastic, friendly, satisfied expressions" as the deaconesses who chatted with one another over what she herself considered an almost unpalatable beverage.[15] The sisters in the field, however, wrote with nostalgia of the *Kaiserswerther Kaffee* and tried to duplicate the occasion in their service posts. Much of the giggling and gossip criticized by Theodor in his record book were precisely the qualities that nourished Kaiserswerth's existence.

Fleidner's reluctance or inability to disclose the interior life of the diaconessate deceived historian and male visitor alike. Gerhard Uhlhorn, historian of German philanthropy, concluded that the diaconessate resembled a military organization. Martin Gerhardt, Fliedner's biographer, writing during the

Nazi era, admired the institution as an early implementation of the *Fuhrerprinzip.*[16]

In the light of their confusion, the myopia of the young Lutheran pastor from Pittsburgh, William Passavant, is more understandable. Writing to his parents in 1846 concerning his visit to Kaiserswerth, Passavant exclaimed, "Building after building goes up and . . . the necessary means are always at hand. . . . Kings [and] queens . . . have seen . . . and approved of this institution. . . . Fliedner gave me all the reports [and] documents."[17] What Passavant admired were the external signs of success.

Adhering to what he believed to be the Kaiserswerth model, Passavant determined to introduce the office of deaconess to American Protestantism. He acquired an infirmary building in Pittsburgh, a legal incorporation, donors, and the promise of a visit from Fliedner. The German founder in fact did appear, consecrated the new building, delivered a sermon in German, and installed four deaconesses who had accompanied him.

In the five years following their arrival, Passavant's own newspaper, *The Missionary,* regularly devoted space to developments at the infirmary but neither the deaconesses nor their work were ever mentioned. Passavant married shortly before his visit to Kaiserswerth, but his wife apparently exercised no part in the new diaconessate. Only one American woman ever presented herself for consecration at the Lutheran home. A note of desperation is apparent in Passavant's appeal for applications. "Christian females!" he wrote. "Shall thousands upon thousands of young men rush to battle, and to death, when their country calls, and can you refuse, when Christ invites you to the peaceful conquest of souls?"[18]

The Pittsburgh infirmary clearly lacked both the imagery of women's experience and the reality of a female community; recourse to martial language only accentuated this deficiency. In 1853, two of the Pittsburgh deaconesses left to be married, and when a third departed somewhat later, the enterprise expired.

The next major effort to adapt the Protestant diaconessate to American conditions was a result of the effective initiative of Lucy Rider Meyer in Chicago. Under the auspices of the Methodist Episcopal Church, she established the Chicago

Training School for City, Home and Foreign Missions in 1885, and the deaconess order, which grew out of it, two years later. During Meyer's 34 years of leadership, at least 5,000 women were consecrated into the deaconess order. She and her graduates have been credited with founding more than 40 major Methodist institutions, including hospitals, orphanages, and homes for the elderly.[19]

As with Kaiserswerth, under the leadership of Theodor and Friedericke Fliedner, the Chicago Training School was a vital collaborative effort of Lucy Rider Meyer and her husband, Josiah Shelly Meyer. In Chicago, however, the wife held the primary position and received the strong support of her husband. Lucy Meyer was principal of the school and Josiah the business manager. Their past experiences uniquely qualified them for these roles: She had been field secretary of the Illinois State Sunday School Association; his background included training for the ministry and experience in business and in the YMCA.

While the initial focus of Kaiserswerth was upon nursing care and hospital administration, the emphasis of the Chicago Training School was on settlement-house work and visitation in the homes of the immigrant poor of Chicago's burgeoning urban ghettos. The training school often was compared to the nearby and more widely known Hull House under Jane Addams' direction. Addams' work was described as "social rather than spiritual evangelism," however, while Meyer sought Christian conversion as well as physical healing and economic uplift in the lives of the immigrants.[20]

Lucy Rider Meyer publicly acknowledged her spiritual and institutional indebtedness to the Kaiserswerth deaconess order. More vital perhaps to the effectiveness of her own enterprise was an unconscious, almost intuitive adaptation of the Kaiserswerth ethos. Meyer converted the primary but private motif of the German model into the major theme of her movement. She integrated the imagery and experience of women—motherhood and daughterhood, sisterhood and "true womanhood"—into the office of deaconess. This amalgam accounts in a large measure for the early success of the Chicago Training School and Deaconess Order.

The sources that best reveal the motives and concerns of

those consecrated at Kaiserswerth are the letters and applications of the deaconesses themselves and the notebooks kept by Friedericke and by Theodor Fliedner. Theodor's extended absences generated correspondence from both Friedericke and Caroline which also conveys a vivid sense of life at the institution. Theodor Fliedner made use of annual reports and the monthly periodical *Der Armen-und Kranken-Freund,* both widely circulated, however, to describe the formal progress of the institution, to raise funds, and to record his own travels. By contrast, the monthly journal published at the Chicago Training School, *The Missionary and Deaconess Advocate,* later shortened to *The Deaconess Advocate,* accurately reflects the spirit of the Methodist order, as well as its concrete achievements. Hence the absence of personal manuscript accounts does not preclude historical insights into the vitality of the movement. Reaching a wide circulation of female subscribers, the journal contained stories of the work of deaconesses and articles designed to increase support of their work by women in local-church missionary societies.

Publications of the Chicago Training School reveal that the role of motherhood was central to the work and support of the institution. Lucy Rider Meyer described the public service of deaconesses graphically:

The world wants mothering. Mother-love has its part to do in winning the world for Christ as well as father-wisdom and guidance. The deaconess movement puts the mother into the Church. It supplies the feminine element so greatly needed in the Protestant Church, and thus is rooted deep in the very heart of humanity's needs.[21]

As the deaconess movement established the principle and person of the mother in the church, the settlement house became the "professional home," the public refuge in the world. Through the settlement house, deaconesses sought to provide the care that private homes could not.[22]

The leading articles on the front page and the major proportion of space in each issue of *The Deaconess Advocate* were devoted to "Stories from Life" and "Field Notes" of deaconesses who had guided and supported abandoned or battered mothers, wayward young people, and neglected children. The accounts were personal experiences of deaconesses who had entered homes of destitute immigrants, worked with them on a myriad of personal problems, brought the message of Christian redemption, and sometimes found successful solutions to both physical and spiritual needs.

Many narratives centered around women who were forced to shoulder the entire responsibility of family care. Such was the account of "The Way to the Heart." On making her first call upon a poor family, the deaconess found the father out of work, the mother half-sick, and the house "a dismal, heartless, hopeless place to call home." She returned a few days later with food and clothing and proceeded to wash the dishes, clean the house, and talk and pray with the woman. When the deaconess made her third visit, the "woman was happily converted, and the deaconess hopes this may be the beginning of better times. 'Save the man,' some one has wisely said, 'and he will save his circumstance'; and perhaps the first step toward saving the man may be to save the woman."[23]

Alcoholism was a theme closely related to such a situation. Sometimes, as in the stories "Threw Out the Beer," and "A Skeleton in the Closet," mothers had been driven to drink because of the apparent hopelessness of their circumstances. Only through the intervention of the deaconess—and her gifts of physical aid, friendship, and the promise of forgiveness and new life in Christ—was the situation reversed.[24]

Stories of teen-agers in trouble were equally numerous in the monthy journals. A recurring theme was the need to develop social centers in the slums, where young women who did not have suitable homes could bring their dates, rather than going to saloons and dance halls. Often such conditions led to delinquency among teens as told in accounts of boys saved from drinking, placed in jobs, and sent to night school through the efforts of deaconesses. Some articles considered the need to change laws to keep youth in school, to censor movies, and to provide proper supervision of places of amusement.[25]

The deaconess' deepest concern was that young girls be saved from the evils of city life. There were many tales of innocent girls who had been met at the railroad station by "fine looking men," but who had been saved from a life of prostitution by the intervention of the deaconess. The editor of *The Deaconess*

Advocate was concerned that young girls who might read the magazine should beware of venturing to the city for supposed romance and excitement. One story told of a deaconess who had enabled two motherless girls to go to a small town in Germany to be cared for by a loving aunt. A characteristic word of advice read, "Don't come alone to the city, girls, to seek your fortunes. Better wear calico dresses and stick to the farm."[26]

While such advice might be thought humorous by readers in the 1980s, it was received with utter seriousness by subscribers at the turn of the century. The editor beseeched mothers in small towns and rural areas to identify with their counterparts in the slums of Chicago. The most effective means of developing such empathy was through accounts and pictures of needy children. On the front page of an 1895 journal was a photograph of a slum hovel, the home of Lena, nine years old, who slept on a bundle of rags and often had no food. Her father drank, and her mother could not always find work. "Poor little Lena! Poor little other children, so many of them, with homes no better than hers." Readers were urged to send food and clothing, so that the deaconesses might dispense them among the needy families. Clearly the key concern was to rehabilitate the individual family, and the plea to readers was to provide resources for that task. The appeal of a cover picture of a deaconess surrounded by twenty-five six-year-olds was moving. The caption read: "It is the divine right of childhood to be mothered, and no institution, however perfect, can stand in the place of a real mother. 'Our superintendent' may see that we are properly clothed and fed, but 'my mother' kisses the bumps and bruises."[27]

The leaders of the deaconess movement recognized that the settlement house must be a genuine "professional home" to take the place of the countless homes that never would be reconstructed. If its workers could not supply love and care equivalent to that of mothers, they could train daughters to be better homemakers when they were grown. The message was presented graphically in a picture of thirty little girls in housekeeping uniforms, standing erect and in marching order, with brooms held like rifles. Accompanying the photograph was this statement, reflecting the commitment and idealism of the deaconesses more strongly than any article:

TO-DAY AND TO-MORROW

TO-DAY

To-day, these children come from ill-kept, insanitary homes, the homes of the ignorant poor. But also

To-day, they are being trained in right methods of house-keeping by skillful, Christian workers. They are learning to do by doing.

TO-MORROW

To-morrow, we have faith and hope to believe, these same children, older grown, will put into practice the methods they have learned to-day.

To-morrow, we hope to have no *ignorant* poor.[28]

The "Stories from Life" and "Field Notes" of deaconess work were the strongest means of developing a program to support the work of the Chicago Training School. Through such appeals, the leaders consciously sought to develop the bonds of common "sisterhood-through-motherhood" among the thousands of women who received the journal and mailings. Isabelle Horton's dedication of *The Burden of the City* was symbolic of this purpose: "to the good women who, with hearts anchored to home and its duties, still look out pityingly into the big, sorrowful world beyond and long to reach out helping hands to their brothers and sisters."[29]

Lucy Rider Meyer and her associates went directly to those helping hands for financial contributions. Their initial effort was a Nickle Fund through which the women of their denomination would be drawn together to provide funds for building the second home of the deaconess order in the 1800s:

Can a Twenty-five thousand dollar Home be built out of nickles? There are one million of women in the Methodist Episcopal church of the United States alone. Some one pleads for a penny a day from each of these women for the cause of missions. I would not ask that—365 cents every year—but five cents from each, not once a year, but *once in a life-time*—five cents, the despised nickle that we hand out so readily for a street-car fare or the daily paper—and $50,000, twice the amount asked for, would be in our hands for this building.[30]

The returns from the Nickle Fund did not bring the desired $50,000, but it did account for $3,000 the first year and, with other contributions, was enough to begin construction.

Through similar appeals, the training school staff sought to bring women throughout the country into sisterly alliance with the deaconess movement. One program was the Do-Without-Band. There was no membership fee; a woman simply committed herself to the pledge: "I will look about for opportunities to do without for Jesus sake." Responses to the call for funds for an addition to the training school building in 1888 indicate the bonds of sisterhood the movement had created. Fifteen hundred letters were sent out, asking each woman to send ten cents for construction of the building and to mail copies of the letter to friends. Over $6,000 was received, along with responses such as this: "I am delighted to be able to form one link of this beautiful chain of loving sisters. Inclosed find a dollar to make my part good and strong."[31]

The call to sisterhood involved more than simply an effort to raise funds for a worthy cause. It was deeply rooted in the belief, inherent in the increasingly vocal feminist movement of the late nineteenth and early twentieth centuries, that mothers had an essential responsibility toward one another. Charlotte Perkins Gilman, a leading intellectual in the woman's movement of her day, meant to inspire and stir women to recognize this corporate identity when she wrote "Feeding the Wolves."

> Here is the failure of our motherhood,
> Our human motherhood, that should be strong
> To guard all infancy, make childhood safe,
> Raise up a great race to rebuild the world.
>
> We sit alone. Each other strives, alone
> To save her children, in a man-made world;
> A world where wolves are legally preserved,
> Game for the sportsman—and they must be fed.
>
> Mothers, together, working for the child,
> Will cleanse the world of all its beasts of prey;
> Will make the world a garden safe and fair
> Where childhood may grow grandly to its goal.[32]

Beyond helping women join together in early bonds of sisterhood to forge a corporate identity, the deaconess movement enabled them to expand their role without violating the socially prescribed position of their sex. A gauge of the innovativeness of the movement in opening new avenues of autonomy and power for women is the degree to which leaders of the deaconess order and ordained clergy of the Methodist Episcopal Church sought to restrict the sisters' function to the specified women's sphere or to use this newly created position as a step toward further enlarging women's rights and responsibilities in both church and society.

The Message and Deaconess Advocate established that deaconesses themselves and officials of the church saw the order as a part of the trend of the day toward "new womanhood." In one witty article, the writer made it clear that the "new woman" of Methodism was not the elaborately dressed lady of the day, whose "dress now occupies pretty much all the floor beneath her; her sleeves all the room beside her; her fan all there is in front of her; her hat all the space above her." There was simply no more room for her to advance—either up, down, forward, or sideways. "The only thing for her to do seems to be to back gracefully out . . . and leave the stage clear for our mothers, and our sisters, our cousins, and our aunts."[33]

Most bishops and pastors of the denomination concurred with a Dr. Bristol, whose address before the 1895 Rock River Conference was published in *The Advocate,* that the deaconess was "the culmination and the climax of new womanhood." Spokespeople stressed her particular suitability for a definite sphere of work. Women were better suited to serve in areas of poverty and ignorance, to establish rescue missions, to visit brothels and saloons, and to call on wives and mothers in the slums. By aiding such destitute women, deaconesses would help to improve men and would raise a stronger generation of boys and girls. The basic consideration was that she work among the urban poor. No woman was too cultivated for that field; indeed, refined women were needed to provide the greatest uplifting influence. These writers, who stressed the deaconess' place in the urban ghetto, were equally emphatic that the "new woman of Methodism" was to be the pastor's helper but not to assume pastoral duties herself. "One thing is certain," wrote William Nast Brodbeck in considering the future of deaconess work. "The deaconess is not a substitute for a pastor, and it will mean the destruction of the order for her to take up pastoral lines of work."[34]

It is doubtful that Lucy Rider Meyer would have supported such a position. It was necessary that she assume her place, however, both among officials of the church, who would closely constrict the position of women in denominational service, and among those who saw the deaconess movement as an opportunity to broaden the work of females. One such occasion was the dedication service of the Lake Bluff Orphanage in 1895. Meyer stated in her presentation that deaconesses were "trying to contribute something in womanly lines to the solution of these great problems that are so agitating the world." She was followed by Bishop Stephen M. Merrill, who categorically set the limits of those "womanly lines": "The present age is remarkable for the opening of doors for the activities of women. Her opportunities for usefulness are now so numerous that she does not *need* to get into the pulpit. There must be no clashing in regard to spheres or rights."[35]

The second graduation service of the Chicago Training School in 1890, in which eight ladies had received deaconess licenses, stood in contrast to the dedicatory service of the Lake Bluff Orphanage. Bishop Merrill had been scheduled to give the commencement address but was prevented by illness. Bishop William Xavier Ninde, former president of Garrett Biblical Institute, spoke in his place. Lucy Rider Meyer was so impressed with his speech that she concluded her book *Deaconesses: Biblical, Early Church, European, American,* which contained her own story of the Chicago Training School, with his address.

Bishop Ninde began in much the same way Bishop Merrill might have. "A sphere has been opened to consecrated womanhood. . . . She has found her place." The deaconess movement had gone a long way in helping to answer "the question the ages have been asking: What shall we do with woman?"[36] The implication was that women in the public life of the church were a problem and that the deaconess movement had provided a "safe" slot for them.

Then the tone of Bishop Ninde's words changed. Nobody had ever asked "What shall we do with man? A strange misunderstanding of Scripture [has] cruelly forced [woman] into a subordinate place . . . has given woman, intellectually and functionally, an inferior position to man." This condition had changed because "the hammers of the Wesleyan revival broke her manacles and gave her the largest spiritual freedom." The forward thrust of his message was contained in these words:

[The Christian must] seek the deeper meaning of those more radical passages, which describe our nature in its essential and unchangeable features; and here we find no unhappy discriminations against woman. . . . The sentiment of the Christian masses is rapidly rising to their level, and the enfranchisement and elevation of our Christian sisterhood will soon become complete. The crown of the age is the generous—rather, I should say, the righteous—parity it gives to woman. Parity in the churches—parity in the schools—parity in the learned professions—parity wherever her physical and mental conditions fit her to work.[37]

Bishop Ninde also recognized and affirmed that most women would continue to find their essential service through the home. His point, however, was that the Christian gospel liberated women, along with men, to serve in whatever way their talents and training were most suited. In its deepest meaning, the Christian faith broke down the barriers that limited women to any particular sphere.

This more expansive outlook also underlay the purpose of Lucy Rider Meyer and other leaders of the Chicago Training School. Through the pages of *The Deaconess Advocate,* they strove—sometimes directly, but always patiently and persistently—to enlarge the vision of their readers, not only to the service of women as deaconesses, but to the wider opportunities outside any sphere designated particularly for women. One subtle but significant way to make this point came in the addition of brief "fillers": "At the Columbian Exposition congress one of the speakers declared that 'no more important discovery has been made during the nineteenth century than when woman found herself.'"[38] An article describing scrubwomen going to work on the night shift in a large office building should have been suggestive:

334

Then in the darkness there came a startling sound—the sound of women's laughter. . . . The scrubwomen were going to work—and they went laughing! Yea, verily, the woman's place is the home! Women must be sheltered, protected! Womanhood is sacred! Woman's hands must be kept unsullied, her shoulders free from burdens! It was ten o'clock on the downtown streets. The scrubwomen were going to work—and they went laughing![39]

The story of the scrubwomen helped to convey an image of women who were working, strong, responsible, and happy. The editor of *The Deaconess Advocate* presented a picture of woman which defied the traditional image of the middle-class female that long had been engrained into her typical readers. Similarly, Lucy Rider Meyer urged any woman who still might feel that her "quiet influence in the home is greater than the influence of her vote at the polls," to reconsider in light of the recent "dry" victory in Illinois. Almost one thousand saloons in the state had been closed because, she contended, women had voted in an election, and "what they *did* spoke infinitely more loudly than anything they could possibly *say*!" Isabelle Reeves wrote with pride of the thirty-two people in the Chicago Methodist Episcopal Old People's Home who had exerted their right to vote for the first time, in the state elections that spring.[40]

Rather than circumscribe the deaconesses' function to a particular place in the urban ghetto, or to a sphere excluding the ministry, Lucy Rider Meyer presented their work as a liberating choice for women. The deaconess had erroneously been pictured as a woman who worked only amid the poverty and squalor of the inner city, "as a goody-goody kind of woman who goes softly up dirty back stairs, reading the Bible to poor sick women and patting the heads of dirty-faced children." Rather, it offered expansive options of service for females: "There is nothing a woman *can* do in the line of Christian work that a deaconess may not do. Her field is as large as the work of woman, and the need of that work."[41] Among deaconesses were found every kind of professional woman: physicians, editors, stenographers, teachers, nurses, bookkeepers, superintendents of hospitals and orphanages. As women began to vote in city and state elections, nothing could have been more appropriate than that a deaconess be chosen as an election judge. The significance of this selection as a means of enlarging the deaconess' role was pointed up by the editor of *The Deaconess Advocate:* "At the polls the white ties stood not for a departure in deaconess work but for a natural and desirable broadening of the deaconess 'sphere.'"[42]

With persistence, Lucy Rider Meyer pressed her point with the readers of *The Deaconess Advocate* that the deaconess movement was a step in opening wider doors to women in society, but particularly in the church. The church was making a grave mistake when it stood aloof from the woman's movement, Meyer contended in her column "Editor's Desk," and she quoted a lengthy article by an eminent British religious worker, Miss Lena Wallis. Miss Wallis argued that there was no logical reason for women not to be allowed to enter the ministry. In Christ there was neither male nor female, and the Spirit had been poured out equally, empowering sons and daughters alike to prophecy. She concluded the article with this telling statement: "I strongly deprecate the dividing of men and women into separate groups" (or she might have said "spheres"). The interests of men and women were bound together and they "must work together for the new time which is coming. For, after all, humanity is greater and deeper than sex."[43]

The monthly journals published by the deaconess order of the Chicago Training School provide significant insight into the way women working in the mainstream of a Protestant denomination sought to expand the role of women in the church. The conscious purpose of the deaconess movement was to fulfill the needs of the church and society in urban ghettos. Through deaconess orders, a new public "sphere" was opened to women, giving them greater autonomy and independence of action in the church and in the society than was previously possible. The new sphere was legitimated and accepted by large numbers of persons in religious institutions because it was an extension of the long-held socially prescribed domestic functions of women—particularly wives. Discharging their daily duties, members of the order embodied characteristics considered "wholly feminine" by society in the nineteenth century: motherliness, care, self-sacrifice, subordination. As "help-mates" to male ministers, Methodist deaconesses fulfilled many prescripts that Puritan, Enlightened, and

Victorian society in America had established for women, but they applied them in the public rather than solely in the private sphere. To send sisters two by two into the slums of the city—into homes, saloons, houses of prostitution, and train stations—was in effect to say that women have no sphere.

Nineteenth-century deaconess orders were, in fact, a radical departure for women, both in Germany and in the United States. In Germany the office of deaconess for the first time permitted Protestant women to engage in works of charity on a sustained and professional basis, rather than simply in moments of national emergency; to occupy, in other words, a space previously monopolized by men. By the end of the century, the concept of Theodor Fleidner's diaconessate had been transformed in the work of American Methodism. But the paradoxical thread of continuity remained unbroken. For while the American Methodists believed that it was the institutional edifice they had transplanted and perfected, it was in reality the spirit of sisterhood and female mutuality that enabled both the initial experiment at Kaiserswerth and its elaboration in the United States to prosper. At Kaiserswerth, the vigorous, self-conscious but unpublicized bonding among the early deaconesses—a product of shared gender life experience, and religious conviction—lay at the heart of the institution. This quality informed life at the motherhouse and enabled the sisters to survive and finally to conquer the demands of their field assignments. The same spirit, enlarged and enhanced in America as well as converted into a rhetorical device, permitted Methodist deaconesses to embrace an unfamiliar world—to reach out in the name of motherhood to women in distress. The Chicago deaconess order used its monthly publications to celebrate the identity of women in sisterhood and to advocate their wider responsibility—first for one another and, ultimately, for the larger society through the achievement of suffrage and ordination. The Chicago order anticipated a society that would transcend the doctrine of separate spheres altogether.

20

THE LEGACY
OF GEORGIA HARKNESS

Joan Chamberlain Engelsman

For women theologians and scholars, one of the most significant figures of our past is Georgia Harkness. Even prior to her death in 1974, she often was cited as a role model to encourage women to obtain doctorates in theology and to plan teaching careers. Since her death, Garrett-Evangelical Theological Seminary has named a chair in her honor, while the Board of Higher Education and Ministry of The United Methodist Church has created a number of fellowships in her name, available to women who intend to enter the ministry as a second career. Yet despite this recent acclaim, scholars are only now beginning to analyze Harkness' legacy to Methodism and to the liberal/social-gospel tradition of which she was a part. Here I take a step toward recovering her contributions. I will look at Harkness' biographical information, analyze the main points of her theology, describe the major influences on her work, and conclude with a brief examination of her comments on women and an evaluation of her legacy as a scholar and role model for contemporary women.

Georgia Harkness was born in upstate New York on April 21, 1891. She was a good student and active in the Methodist church to which her parents belonged. "Stirred to experience conversion once a year when the traveling revivalist came to town . . . she was distressed to discover doubt at the age of nine." That crisis of faith was short-lived, however, and she later claimed that it was "the only one of her life."[1] She won a state scholarship to Cornell University, graduated in 1912 with a Bachelor of Arts degree, and for the next six years taught in several upstate high schools. Unsatisfied in that occupation, she enrolled in the Boston University School of Religious

338

Education, obtained a Master's degree, and received a doctorate in philosophy of religion from that university in 1923.

Her lifelong interest in both ministry and education emerged in the period immediately following her stay at Boston. In 1923 she joined the faculty of Elmira College (for women) and three years later was named a local elder in the Methodist Episcopal Church. Since at that time women could not be ordained to full conference connection, we can only speculate whether she would have exercised that option. We do know that she was an early advocate of the ordination of women, although she refused to pursue it for herself after ordination was granted in The Methodist Church in 1956.

Her fourteen years at Elmira were fruitful. Her first major work, *Conflicts in Religious Thought,* was published in 1929 and set the literary style for the rest of her books. Writing for students who desired basic information on religious matters, Harkness says in her preface, "This book aims to give a simple statement of the major problems of religious thought with some suggestions for their solutions. It deals with the profoundest questions and conflicts in human thinking, and in the argument here presented the author's main objective, aside from the desire to state it truly, has been to avoid stating it profoundly."[2] Although she wrote a total of thirty-six books and numerous articles, Harkness continued to address the same readers—lay people—striving to communicate with them in terms they could understand.

Harkness' involvement in world problems and ecumenism began when she became interested in foreign missions while taking her undergraduate work at Cornell, and in the summer of 1924, a tour of "war-ravaged Europe made her a pacifist."[3] Her interest in ecumenism grew during the 1930s, taking her to her first international conference at Oxford in 1937. The following year she traveled to Madras, India, for a conference on international missions. There she spent a day in the home of Gandhi, and fourteen years later she recalled the visit as "one of life's most unforgettable experiences." On the same trip she felt privileged to meet Rabindranath Tagore, the Nobel Prize laureate.[4]

After several years at Elmira College, Harkness moved on to Mount Holyoke College in Massachusetts, which was then over one hundred years old. In her book *Women in Church and Society,* she praised those who founded the first colleges and seminaries for women, believing that they "paved the way for the emergence of women to greater service and freedom." She quoted with obvious approval the inscription on the grave of Mary Lyon, founder of Mount Holyoke. Harkness said, "As I passed her grave . . . I read repeatedly the inscription which epitomizes the determination of her life; 'There is nothing in the universe that I fear, but that I shall not know all my duty, or shall fail to do it.'"[5] Certainly Georgia Harkness shared the same determination. By the time she left Mount Holyoke she had published six books and had been a delegate to several major international conferences; yet her twin career as author and churchwoman was barely underway.

In 1939 Harkness left Massachuetts to begin her life as a professor of applied theology, the first woman at a major seminary to be so honored, and the next twenty-two years were evenly divided between Garrett Biblical Institute and the Pacific School of Religion. While teaching at the graduate level she continued her writing and church work, and in 1947 was named one of the ten most outstanding Methodists in America.[6]

After World War II, Harkness renewed her international activities. She was a delegate to the 1948 Amsterdam conference which established the World Council of Churches. Four years later she attended the ecumenical conference at Lund and in 1954 was a delegate to the World Council of Churches in Evanston, Illinois. Her commitment to American Methodism remained strong, however, and during the course of her life she was elected six times as a delegate to the General Conference of The Methodist Church.[7] Somehow in the middle of all this productivity, she managed postgraduate and sabbatical study at Harvard, at Yale, and at Union Seminary in New York. She also taught for a year at Union Seminary in Manila and visited the Far East. Harkness was a modern circuit rider; the world was her frontier.

Georgia Harkness never married, yet she had a strong sense of family and a high opinion of marriage and children. She believed the family to be "the matrix within which the highest human qualities of love and tenderness are experienced and nourished."[8] She could experience some of those qualities firsthand because of her long-term relationship with Verna Miller. In a book published the year before she died, Harkness said, "I wish, as always, to express my gratitude to Verna Miller, the friend with whom I have shared a home for nearly thirty years, whose love and encouragement sustains me in my writing and still more in the many aspects of our life together."[9] Twenty-one years earlier Harkness had dedicated a book to her, saying later that Miller gave "a practical and a spiritual undergirding to the enterprises of our common life."[10] The strengths Verna Miller brought to their relationship were acknowledged by Harkness in every book she published during their association.

The spiritual interests of Harkness were varied. She wrote several books on prayer and edited *A Devotional Treasury from the Early Church.*[11] Greatly interested in mysticism, she believed it was "a universal need of the religious life and . . . available to all." Harkness defined the goal of mysticism as being *communion* with God, perhaps because she was "temperamentally unable to experience" the mystic rapture others described as being part of *union* with God. Her mentor in prayer and spirituality was the noted Quaker Rufus Jones. She attended Friends retreats in the early 1940s, later describing herself as "a life-long Methodist of Quaker ancestry."[12] Unfortunately, she left us no spiritual journal, nor do we have many of her prayers and poems. The current United Methodist hymnal, however, does contain two of her lyrics: "Hope of the World" and the third stanza of "This Is My Song."

Even a cursory review of her works would reveal that Georgia Harkness achieved a remarkable balance in her life. She spent most of her professional career in colleges or seminaries, yet she also gave a great deal of time and energy to social and ecumenical causes around the world. She had a prominent public life and at the same time cultivated her inner and spiritual resources. She demanded a great deal of herself, her students, and her fellow Christians. Approaching her work seriously and with earnest purpose, she seemed nevertheless to regard her outstanding personal achievements with modesty and a sense of humor.

One vignette is illustrative of her light touch with respect to the high professional status she had achieved. In *The Modern Rival of the Christian Faith,* she described a dinner held during a meeting of the Northern California-Western Nevada Council of Churches. An Episcopal bishop presided, she said, and a minister of the Assembly of God sat at his right. A Salvation Army band and an operatic tenor provided the music, a Negro Baptist gave the invocation, and a Missouri Synod Lutheran pronounced the benediction. "And—beg pardon, St. Paul—a woman theologian gave the address."[13]

The Theology of Georgia Harkness

What kind of theologian was this woman? First, Georgia Harkness did not construct a systematic theology. Although she occasionally organized her material around a central theme— ethics, prayer, mysticism—she usually wrote overviews of general topics—faith, religion, knowledge. As a result, most of her books contain a bit of everything, and her views about God, Jesus Christ, Christian anthropology, the Holy Spirit, and the role of the church were presented in an unorganized fashion. Second, all her books were written in a simple, discursive manner and rarely with footnotes. Because she saw herself as a tutor to the laity, she avoided theological or philosophical terms that might be unfamiliar to the general reader. These two stylistic devices make her theology appear superficial and often confusing. For the sake of clarity, therefore, here I will attempt to delineate her concepts and present them in a more systematic form.

God. One of the clearest images to emerge from Harkness' many works is her understanding of God as Father. Although she recognizes that we must speak of God in symbols and similes, she notes that

the most familiar of those applied to God is that of Fatherhood. . . . The father symbol is not a full description of God: to know God fully one would need to be as omniscient as God himself. The symbol is merely the means of mediating to our thought the reality which lies behind the symbol; and the Christian faith asserts that our nearest approach to a grasp of the real nature of God is to conceive him in terms of self-giving love and protecting care. Hence, "our Father."[14]

This correlation of love and care with Fatherhood was vital for Harkness, and she maintained it until her death. Even after the Christian feminist movement had gained momentum, she rejected the possibility of calling God *she* or even *he/she*; both terms she specifically termed "ridiculous."[15]

In connection with the Fatherhood of God and his perfect love for his children, Harkness often mentions God's role as our Redeemer. "God is Redeemer and Father. Neither creativity, nor judgement, nor sovereignty is the attribute by which we know him best. It is as redeeming love that he comes closest to us."[16] One aspect of this redeeming love is God's willingness to limit his power to change the course of events. Harkness believed this self-limitation is a direct manifestation of God's infinite wisdom and goodness and is responsible for human freedom and the orderliness of creation. She rejected the idea that God is an "arbitrary determiner of all human destiny including its evil aspect."[17]

God's self-limitation is an important aspect of Harkness' theology because she believed God has "long purposes— purposes that will eventuate both in the setting up of a heavenly kingdom in this life and the continuance of man's moral task beyond the grave."[18] He and we "must work together to create a world conforming more nearly to God's will and purpose."[19] This structure of cooperation is emphasized, rather than dissolved, by her understanding that God desires to develop a race of moral beings who will *"achieve"* their own goodness rather than have it thrust upon them.[20] Although our failures cause God to suffer, he continues to limit his power because he loves us.

In general, Harkness' understanding of God modifies the ontological argument; the "objective reality" of humankind's highest ideals becomes the strongest reason for belief in God, as well as the best way to describe God.[21] Thus love, nurture, self-control (limitation), and work become the symbols of divinity and at the same time are even more firmly established as the goals of human existence.

Christology. Harkness' ontological argument is most strongly developed in her understanding of Jesus Christ. Thus, she states:

If we are to believe in a personal God we must think of him in terms of the highest personality we know. To Christians, God is most readily conceived as revealing his true nature in the personality of Jesus. . . . It is as "the God and Father of our Lord Jesus Christ" that we know God most perfectly. The essence of the doctrine of Jesus' divinity lies in the fact that in his life and teachings we learn what God is like.[22]

Harkness articulates her interpretation of the Logos she sees operating both in nature and in Christ. In nature the Logos shows forth God's creative word; in Christ it signifies God's redemptive love for persons. She further explains, however, that "the Creative Word is also the Redemptive Word, waiting to bring to fulfillment through Christ both God's eternal purpose for mankind and God's particular purpose of good for the life of every man."[23]

This understanding of Jesus Christ establishes him as a window through whom we see and know God. Although Harkness often mentions Jesus' divinity and refers to him as the Son of God, she "does not mean that Jesus *was* God."[24] Rather, Jesus Christ's significance lies in the way he functions as a role-model for Christians. Harkness incorporated this understanding of Jesus into her interpretation of Christian ethics as "the systematic study of the way of life set forth by Jesus Christ, applied to the daily demands and decisions of our personal and social existence."[25] It is not surprising, therefore, that she regarded the Sermon on the Mount as the epitome of Jesus' teachings and the most significant section of the Gospels.[26]

This emphasis on Jesus as the model for human behavior also flavored Harkness' comments on mysticism. She eschewed the idea that mysticism should produce a rhapsodic union with God. Instead she gave her own interpretation of the classical *Imitation of Christ* by Thomas a Kempis, praising it as encouraging "mysticism of a very high order," since it contains no ecstasies but only the calm joy of deep personal devotion to the will and way of Christ.[27]

Christian Anthropology. Harkness' doctrine of persons, which grows out of her understanding of God's relationship to us and expectations of us, is most significant. Since God is primarily Father, we are his children, and because God has limited his powers in this world, we can be free. Harkness believed that each person is the *"resultant* of heredity, environment and experience"; therefore everyone is free to act, to choose, to rise above both heredity and environment and use his or her past experience as a stepping stone to higher achievements. Thus "in a very real sense each individual is the master of his fate."[28]

This freedom of the individual is intended to be expressed in work—primarily work that will advance the kingdom of God on earth. Nowhere did Harkness' basic optimism shine through more clearly than in her belief that human beings have developed and progressed throughout time in such a way that God's kingdom is more a reality now than ever before. "Little by little man has moved forward in the direction of the supremacy of the spiritual over the carnal. In spite of temporary eddies in human progress . . . a long look over the past reveals a tremendous advance from the ideals and standards of former days."[29] Thirty years later, in 1957, she still maintained that "it is doubtful that there has ever been a period of such general high Christian intelligence or deep commitment to Christian social ethics as in our own time."[30]

There is, however, much more to be done, and Harkness put her hope in the laity. She believed that if a sufficient number of lay people understood the gospel and followed it, they could "transform society from its present predicament of conflicts and insecurity into a scene of harmony, peace and effective living."[31] This confidence in the ability of the laity may explain why Harkness wrote so extensively for the general reader and why her books frequently define the moral responsibilities of Christians. Underlying all her prescriptions is the conviction that if lay people are properly educated, they will see their duty and will follow it.

Work is such an important component of Harkness' theology that it even colors her understanding of life after death. Thus she writes that "man's moral task is endless. Within every individual there is the obligation to grow, and the capacity for growth has no upper limit. Nothing save the continuation of personal existence beyond the grave will give opportunity for the continuance of personal moral growth."[32] Immortality therefore is assured in order that we may continue to work and develop after death.

Sin plays a rather minor part in the cosmic drama, according to Harkness. She rejected the Pauline statements concerning original sin and preferred to say, instead, that all individuals have a biological tendency to self-centeredness. All sin is rooted in self-love and persons err when they ignore the greater good that should be chosen; in other words, when we willfully "choose to be ungodlike."[33] God continues to love his people, however; they do not need to feel helplessly burdened. "A sense of sin in due humility we must have; this does not mean we must be torn apart by the tortures of remorse or rendered impotent by a crushing weight of inferiority which induces unhappiness and inhibits action. It is a Christian duty to try and find release."[34] Harkness took much the same position vis-à-vis psychic suffering. Although she was not insensitive to the subject, she believed such suffering should be overcome, particularly when it is of a spiritual nature. In *Dark Night of the Soul* she indicates that this can be done by facing one's shortcomings, repenting without despair, making all possible amends to others, and embracing the eternal and encompassing mercies of God.[35]

Spirituality, Prayer, and Mysticism. Although the Holy Spirit plays no discernible role in Harkness' theology, she believed all Christians should cultivate their spiritual life to the fullest. She recommended the daily practice of prayer, setting down in several places what she regarded as its proper components: adoration, thanksgiving, confession, petition, intercession, commitment to act, assurance, and ascription to Jesus Christ. Prayer is not to be used for begging favors, but as an aid in achieving self-control and in promoting social and ethical behavior.[36]

Harkness was also a major exponent of mysticism, particularly as it manifests itself in the Quaker tradition of *communion,* rather than *union* with God. She believed that anyone can be a mystic:

All Christian living that is more than casual requires self-denial, the purging of the soul by penitence, the renunciation of immediate pleasures at the call of love, the dedication of the self to the will of God at personal cost. In short, this cost is the way of the cross. The reward is God's acceptance and an ensuing holy joy. This note underlies all authentic Christian mysticism.[37]

Prayer and mysticism are closely related, though not synonymous, in Harkness' thinking. Both these aspects of spirituality are important, not so much in their own right or as ends in themselves, but as means to achieve self-control, to endure suffering, and "to act in love, compassion and service toward others."[38]

The Church. God created human life to work with him in establishing the kingdom of God on earth. Georgia Harkness saw the church, the committed fellowship of Christ's followers, as the institution most able to work for realization of that kingdom. "A Christian is one who sincerely tries to be a follower of Jesus Christ"; however, the cost of discipleship "is a price that few in our time have begun conscientiously and realistically to pay." Being "as good as the next fellow" is not the same as being a Christian.[39] Harkness even notes a "division between those Christians who are committed to a social gospel because of the many-sided obligation to love and serve all men as sons of God, and those others who see the primary, if not the sole Christian obligation as winning others to *become* sons of God and hence heirs of eternal life."[40] Her antipathy to "those others" was strong: "It is my prayer that this study of Methodism's social concerns may be used by God to lead Methodists, and perhaps others, to a deeper and wiser commitment to the making of a Christian society in our time."[41] She hoped the church would renew itself by establishing the social gospel in America, fearing that if it did not, it would be engulfed by modern society.[42]

Social Concerns. Although concern for all social issues permeates Harkness' work, several of those issues should be given special emphasis. Preeminently there was her concern for world peace, particularly prior to World War II; racial justice, which was a vital issue for her long before the 1960s; and equality for women, including their right to serve God through the church in whatever capacity they feel called to fill, including that of ordained minister.[43]

In addition to advocating these and similar issues, Harkness also spoke out strongly against certain trends she believed are antithetical to the Christian life. She strongly opposed alcoholic beverages of any kind. She also objected to divorce, believing that even apart from the teachings of the Bible, Jesus, and the church, "Anything else but monogamy simply doesn't work!"[44] In her eyes, however, the greatest threat to the establishment of the kingdom of God on earth is secularism and its accompanying ills—nationalism, racism, fascism, capitalism, and communism. In *Modern Rival of Christian Faith,* published in 1952, and also in *The Church and Its Laity,* written ten years later, Harkness described American secularism, and although she never used the term *civil religion,* her observations are as accurate today as when she first set them down.

One other issue Harkness discusses at length, particularly in her early works, is the relationship between religion and science. She saw no quarrel between real religion and real science, but she was highly critical of pseudoscience—any science that is "dogmatic and claims to cover the universe, denying the reality of anything outside its province." On the other hand, she associated pseudoreligion with denominational quarrels, prudish restraints, Sunday school instruction that does not instruct, and dry sermons that fall on deaf ears. She noted with approval that "religion, masquerading under the guise of archaic creeds, and impossible literalisms, and ecclesiasticism indifferent to human needs, has brought about an inevitable and in many respects wholesome revulsion." True religion has but two functions, or goals: "to make men better and to make men stronger. Keenness of moral vision, and strength to meet the storms and battles of life—these have been the dual gifts of religion."[45]

Influences on Harkness' Theology

Georgia Harkness obtained her doctorate in the philosophy of religion, and that training had a lasting effect on her work. Since she believed that religious faith was a phenomenon common to all people, she was interested in all the major world religions, and no doubt this outlook also buoyed her interest in ecumenism. Despite her strong attachment to Methodism, she gave generous amounts of time and talent to the World and the National Council of Churches. Philosophy also reinforced Harkness' belief in rationality, which she saw as an essential feature of religion. Although she believed that religion "in its higher reaches has always a more than rational element," she did maintain that "religion is rational" and that faith is "a rationally grounded conviction of the truth of beliefs not wholly proved."[46] This relation between faith and reason also underlay her conviction that if a person is shown what is reasonable and right, that person is able to do what is reasonable and right. Because religion is essentially rational, it can be taught to intelligent people, who will then understand their Christian duty and carry it out. Thus, to Harkness, the human will seemed to be a servant of the brain, rather than an independent aspect of the human personality that might, in fact, prevent a person from doing what she or he wants to do.

The Bible was another major influence on Harkness' thought. Her works contain frequent biblical quotations, especially from the Psalms, the prophets of the Old Testament, and the Synoptic Gospels, particularly those concerned with social action and responsibility. The Sermon on the Mount was her favorite passage. Although Harkness was neither a fundamentalist nor a believer in biblical literalism, her work does not evidence much familiarity with modern biblical studies or criticism. Her hermeneutic consisted of judging each portion of both the Old and the New Testament on the basis of the words and mission of Jesus Christ, and the biblical texts she wove into her writing reflect this stance. Noticeably absent are frequent quotations from the parables of Jesus, the Gospel of John, and the letters of Paul.

The third and most important influence on Harkness' thought was the liberal/social gospel movement in the American church. Although her writing shows some familiarity with the mystical tradition of the Roman Catholic and Protestant churches (including some devotional material from the early church), her general knowledge of theology seems weak. Her terminology and her interests are confined almost exclusively to those that emerged among American theologians during the nineteenth and early twentieth centuries. Since Georgia Harkness herself can be described as an exponent of the social gospel, it is necessary to understand that movement in order to analyze her theology.

Harkness shared with liberalism the conviction that theology emerges from inner experience and investigation. Unlike Roman Catholics, who emphasize ecclesial authority, or fundamentalists, whose authority is "the Book," the liberal's basic authority is human experience. The role of reason and education is, of course, vital for evaluating that experience. While she defended liberalism from the attacks of neo-orthodox theologians such as Niebuhr and Barth, Harkness admitted that some of their criticisms were justified, although often "unfair."[47] For example, she did not agree that responsible Christian liberals 1) denied the sinfulness of humanity and the need for saving help from God; 2) believed in the automatic progress of the human race; or 3) made God so immanent that there is no transcendent holiness in God's nature.

Harkness did believe, however, that liberal theologians failed to stress some necessary points. They were overly concerned about the moral applications of the teachings of Jesus and too little interested in the saving act of Christ. Because they focused too much on the kingdom of God on earth, the eschatological note was often lost. Liberal thought was concerned with healing the breach between religion and modern science, but Harkness thought the social gospel proponents occasionally went too far, seeming to take their orders from science. Finally, she admitted also that liberals sometimes stressed general, rather than Christian religious education and experience, placing the Bible on the same value-level with other sources. It was "these under-emphases, always more characteristic of the lesser exponents of liberalism than its great leaders, [that] got it into trouble." And she maintained that during the late 1930s and the 1940s, these negations and underemphases had undergone "radical correction."[48] She may have been as optimistic in this regard as in other matters.

Theological Evaluation

Georgia Harkness' theology had many positive characteristics in harmony with social gospel thought. First, it was extremely ethical. Americans are very familiar with the concept of the work ethic. There should be no lazy Christians, but dedicated men and women striving to establish the kingdom of God on earth. Care for one's neighbor, interpreted in the broadest sense, was Harkness' overriding concern; the two major commandments of Jesus are intertwined—if persons truly love God, they will love their neighbor, and those who love their neighbor obviously love God. This love is shown by action and good works in all areas of life.

Second, her theology was always optimistic and forward-looking. Just before her death in 1974, Harkness said, "I believe very much that we are moving forward. I believe that this is our Father's world and that God is at work within it."[49] One of the most interesting ramifications of her optimism was her ability to welcome modern technological and scientific advances, integrating them into her religious consciousness. She believed that science had improved life for everyone and that conflict, such as that between Darwinians and Christians, was unnecessary.

Third, Harkness' theology was highly rational. Her belief in education, particularly religious education in its widest sense, never wavered. She wrote all her books for students and lay people with the intention of educating them in the basics of the Christian faith and in their Christian duty. She was an excellent synthesizer and popularizer of other people's ideas, with the ability to explain fairly complicated religious concepts in simple terms. Not surprisingly, her books were very popular, and several are still in print.

Fourth, Georgia Harkness was deeply concerned for the individual's spiritual welfare. This is evident throughout her writings, but it comes to the fore in her many books dealing with prayer and mysticism. Perhaps because of her own bout with mental illness in the early 1940s, she was particularly sensitive to psychological difficulties, and one of her most popular books, *Dark Night of the Soul,* deals directly with these problems. Her pastoral concern is evidenced not only in her more devotional tracts but in her intense desire for justice for all people.

Fifth, a mainstay of Harkness' thought was her belief in ecumenism. Although she was an active and highly visible

Methodist, she spent a major portion of her energies for interchurch groups. That interest is reflected in her books, which often include appeals for Christian unity. Moreover, this unity was not limited to institutional churches. Harkness believed in the partnership of clergy and lay people in ministry, and she advocated greater understanding between Christians and non-Christians.

Sixth, Harkness applied her Christian faith to contemporary social issues. Long before they became popular movements and entered the political arena, world peace, racial justice, ordination of women, nuclear weapons, and secularism and civil religion were central issues to Georgia Harkness. No doubt she was particularly sensitive to society's problems because of her ethical and pastoral concern, but the keenness of her prophetic vision often outstripped that of her professional colleagues, and many of her positions and commentaries are still pertinent today.

While there are many positive things to be said for Harkness' theology, there also are several negative aspects, common to most social gospel thinkers. Foremost is her understanding of Jesus Christ as a model whom human beings could and should emulate. As this position is the dominant, almost exclusive basis of her Christology, certain specific problems naturally arise. One of the most troublesome is the loss or diminution of Jesus' divinity.

The church always has struggled to maintain the delicate balance between Jesus' perfect humanity and his perfect divinity. Lacking a deep and careful theology at this point, Harkness tended toward an Arian, or at least a semi-Arian position, in which Jesus, rather than being a part of the Godhead, is the idealized person, the epitome of God's intention for each of us. As the eschatological note of Jesus' preaching disappears, one focuses on trying to live like and be like God. Ironically, the burden of this interpretation of the life and ministry of Jesus Christ can fall most heavily on the conscientious Christian who tries to live a Christlike life and is therefore constantly aware of his or her shortcomings.

When, however, there is an emphasis on the miracles of Incarnation—God becoming human; and Resurrection—

Jesus taking our sins upon himself, dying, and being raised by God as a sign of our new life now as well as after death—we can understand that our perpetual sins and failures cannot separate us from God's love. Without this stress on the forgiving nature of God and a keen awareness of the divine aspects of Jesus' mission, Harkness' theology tends to foster a sense of human inadequacy, if not guilt. Thus one must either endure this awareness of guilt and failure, or repress these feelings and become self-righteous, believing that since one emulates Jesus in moral and social behavior, one is like him in every way and therefore deserves God's approval and salvation.

The weaknesses in Georgia Harkness' Christology are repeated in her understanding of God as Father. Although she constantly refers to God as a loving and forgiving Father, she also believed that actual acceptance by God must be earned through work. The perfection of human nature, which she saw as an achievable goal, is attained through good deeds that must be performed both in this life and in the life to come. Even prayer and communion with God become vehicles for earning God's approbation. In practice, therefore, the image of a loving Father apparently masks a sterner figure, remote, demanding, and judgmental.

The concept of sinners in the hands of an angry God, which emerged during the Great Awakening, is not lost in Harkness' theology, but is recast. In social gospel thought, language about God becomes softer, and the parables about the lost sheep and the prodigal son become more prominent. For Harkness, however, the deeper reality of God is still dark. Furthermore, she never describes the fate that awaits those who do not do God's will. While most theologians would agree that faith in Christ is made manifest in good works, Harkness approaches a concept of works righteousness that limits the saving love of God to the deserving.

A third difficulty with Harkness' theology emerges in connection with her understanding of sin. Sin is the result of self-centeredness. She believed that we are born with a biological urge to think of ourselves first; she also believed that this tendency can be overcome through education and the will to improve. Linda Clark described this attitude in her Tipple

Lecture at Drew University: "I grew up in a school system and in a culture where sin was essentially seen as, or defined as, a problem of miseducation. That is, if only I got smart enough I would stop sinning."[50] This highly rational approach is reflected in all Harkness' work, and she never doubted that comprehensive religious education is the best way to eliminate sin. Because the doctrine of original sin was not acceptable to her, she showed little sensitivity to the classic dilemma often faced by many Christians: The good that I would, I do not, and that which I would not do, I do. For Harkness, the human will is not so recalcitrant, and human beings *can* do what they know they *should* do; even illness and adversity are ultimately unacceptable excuses for failure. Each human being must bear the responsibility for achieving Christian perfection, and the otherwise necessary grace of God becomes relatively extraneous in the process.

Harkness' optimistic view of human nature was reinforced by her understanding that Christianity and culture are advancing together. This concept of "theistic evolution" that permeates her work unfortunately also blinded her to some of the problems of modern life.[51] Putting her emphasis on education, recent social legislation, and national and international religious groups, Harkness rarely commented on the dark side of modern life represented by the Holocaust, racial strife, Vietnam, Watergate, technological "future shock," world hunger, poverty, or irresponsible business practices. Her eyes focused instead on modern social and technological improvements, as evidence that this age is better than any former age.

From the days of the Puritan settlement of New England, American Christianity has been enraptured with the possibility of establishing the kingdom of God in this new land. Believing they could build a new Jerusalem on these pleasant shores, it was necessary for the clergy to determine why the promise was delayed, when the reality did not occur. Liberalism and the social gospel movement shifted an earlier emphasis on individual failure to a more communal one. Social problems such as slavery, alcohol, poverty, slums, lack of education, and increased lower-class immigration became the impediments, and theologians used pulpits and pamphlets to call for changes that would remedy these ills. Surely, when they were cured, the kingdom of God would come to America.

Harkness shared this liberal view, and as a result, her theology is millennarian as well as highly social, ethical, and communal. Nevertheless, there is an undercurrent of despair in her work, reflected by an "if only" dimension. Other social gospel advocates had different solutions, but Harkness put her faith in the laity. Thus she said, "There are enough Christian laymen to transform society from its present predicament of conflict and insecurity into a scene of harmony, peace and effective living—if these laymen understood the gospel and took it seriously."[52] The deeper question—Is it appropriate for Christians to expect the fullness of the kingdom of God on earth?—never surfaces in her writings. Therefore her instructions and recommendations to the laity take on a desperate edge: Unless Christianity advances, it will "go under."[53] Unfortunately, in Harkness' theology, God's role of salvation within the historical process seems less important than our own.

Harkness and Women

Harkness' view of women in modern Christianity is not totally applicable to the 1980s. She was, of course, in favor of higher education for women and applauded the growing number of women in the professions. Continuing to speak against the patriarchalism of the church, she became an early and articulate advocate of the ordination of women. In 1942 she told a nationwide gathering of Methodists that "the church is the last stronghold of male dominance."[54] Yet despite this early sensitivity, her general understanding of women was essentially Victorian. She placed a strong emphasis on motherhood and family, believing that by Christianizing the home, women would Christianize the world.[55] Even in 1973 Harkness continued to stress the importance of "femininity" in women and to perpetuate stereotypical images—men work outside the home; women are housewives. Furthermore, despite an awareness that God's love can be like mother love, Harkness refused to consider female pronouns for God or any other alteration of the sexist language used in the church in reference to God and humanity.[56]

This rather conservative approach to women's issues was reflected in her preference that men speak out on these matters; she hesitated to take the podium herself.[57] In this regard she differed from some of her peers—Dorothy Sayers and Mary McCloud Bethune, for example—as well as from other women such as Margaret Mead and Eleanor Roosevelt. Harkness may represent the "honorary male" syndrome so accurately described by Caroline Heilbrun.[58] Since she had succeeded in a man's world through education and hard work, it was her opinion that other women could, too. At the same time, she stressed the basic equality of men and women; she criticized Karl Barth, both in print and in person, for his anthropology which implied that women were created second. However, she appeared to be unaware of the cultural and societal impediments that restrict the very equality she emphasized.

If Harkness' attitude was less supportive of women than is that of Christian feminists today, does her theology offer any specific help for our time? The answer is both yes and no. Liberation theology, particularly as it is articulated by women in this country, appears to have many ideals in common with social gospel thought. It focuses on transforming society in highly ethical and moral ways and concentrates on removing social ills—poverty, discrimination, war—which restrict the full development of the individual. Liberation theology also looks hopefully to a future world that will be more free and more Christian. This transformation will be achieved by means of education, legislation, and social action. Because women and minorities will have an equal say in its creation, the resulting culture will be more human than the one we presently know.

Much of Harkness' writing supports this agenda and some of her insights regarding church and society enrich the present discussion. Unfortunately, there are also some negative similarities between modern liberation theology and the social gospel. A review of Harkness' work, however, may help to point up the consequences of the depatriarchalization of theology through minimizing the Trinity and the concept of original sin. An alternative approach may be difficult to evolve, but in order to achieve a truly liberating theology, it may be necessary to balance social improvement with a more humble assessment of human nature and an awareness of God's role in creation and redemption.

Conclusion

The name of Georgia Harkness is probably as well known as that of any woman in the church, but the reality of her life and work raises some difficulties. She was not an original thinker—she is at her best when synthesizing and popularizing the works of others. Perhaps because she wrote primarily for the laity, her style and content seem superficial, particularly to the scholar; she is occasionally incorrect in her facts; and she rarely conveys a deep awareness of classical theological issues. Although she shares many of these characteristics with other social gospel writers, Harkness seems to be rather timid—for instance, in *Women in Church and Society*. For all her advocacy of social justice, she maintains a certain academic detachment. She is essentially a teacher who believes in reason and rational behavior and apparently does not want to offend anyone lest they turn aside from her instruction.

These criticisms are greatly modified, however, by placing Harkness in historical perspective. At the same time she obtained her doctorate, women were just receiving the right to vote, and when she went to Garrett Biblical Institute, she was the first female professor of theology ever to teach at a seminary. During the 1920s and 1930s, women made stunning achievements in other fields—sociology, literature, even law and medicine—while the church remained closed to them except as ministers' wives and Sunday school teachers. Yet Harkness overcame these limitations through her writings and her work in the Methodist church, and she did it primarily alone. Without many women colleagues, she depended greatly on men and their perceptions. What she would have said or done had she come to maturity in these more supportive times, we will never know. Finally, although Harkness' social gospel thought may be less than adequate for today, she was an active member of a dynamic religious movement which still influences the way we think and believe.

In summary, perhaps Harkness' greatest gifts to us are her position on a seminary faculty, her numerous publications, and her participation in many national Methodist commissions and international church conferences. Those of us who would like to succeed in those fields will find our lot easier because Georgia Harkness was there first. That is a legacy United Methodist women can always cherish.

NOTES

INTRODUCTION

1. John to Abigail, July 3, 1776, *Adams Family Correspondence*, ed. L. H. Butterfield (Cambridge: Harvard University Press, 1963), vol. 2, p. 30.

CHAPTER 1. John Wesley and Sophy Hopkey

1. Albert C. Outler, ed., *John Wesley*, A Library of Protestant Thought (New York: Oxford University Press, 1964), p. 14.
2. The impact of Williams' affidavit can be gauged by its mention in the preface of Wesley, *The Journal of the Rev. John Wesley, A.M.* (hereafter cited as *Journal*), ed. Nehemiah Curnock (London: Robert Cully, n.d.), vol. 1, p. 84; Wesley, *The Letters of the Rev. John Wesley, A.M.*, ed. John Telford (London: Epworth Press, 1931), vol. 1, p. 342; *The Weekly History* 11, 12 (April 1741), 70, 71 (August 1742). Its text can be found in *The Progress of Methodism in Bristol, or, The Methodist Unmask'd, by an Impartial Hand* (Bristol: n.p., 1743), as an appendix to the doggerel quoted farther on.
3. The *Charleston Gazette, Calendar of State Papers Colonial 1738* , vol. 44, no. 257. Although the bulk of *Gazette* copies for the period of time Wesley was in Georgia have survived, most issues for September to November have disappeared. The affidavit also appears in *Journal*, vol. 1, pp. 382-85.
4. Patrick Tailfer et al., *A True and Historical Narrative of the Colony of Georgia*, ed. Clarence L. ver Steeg, Wormsloe Foundation Publications no. 4 (Athens: University of Georgia Press, 1960), p. 70. Portions of the book are reprinted in *Journal*, vol. 8, pp. 304-307.
5. Tailfer, *Colony of Georgia*, p. 80.
6. Methodist Archives, John Rylands Library, Manchester, Wesley 4/2, 3/15. Parts of these narratives (hereafter cited as Georgia papers) were included in *Journal* in brackets or an appendix, but important parts were silently excluded. Hereafter, references to *Journal* are cited only when they are not identified in the text by date of entry. Professor Frank Baker will be publishing a harmony of the Georgia papers in the complete Oxford Edition of *Wesley's Works*, forthcoming. I am grateful for his direction in locating these documents and for other assistance.
7. *Journal*, vol. 1, p. 281.
8. Georgia papers, 4/2.
9. A recent example is Stanley Ayling, *John Wesley* (London: Collins, 1979), who regards Williamson as a recent contender, to whom Hopkey turned after she was "bruised" by Wesley's decision to defer marriage (pp. 80-81).
10. Georgia papers 3/15, ¶ 36.
11. *Journal*, vol. 1, p. 339.
12. *Ibid.*, vol. 1, pp. 385-86.

13. Georgia papers 3/4, March 8.
14. Earl of Egmont, *Journal of the Transactions of the Trustees* (Wormsloe: n.p., 1886), p. 18.
15. *Journal*, vol. 1, p. 338.
16. *Ibid.*, p. 356.
17. No bishop was in fact responsible for Wesley. The jurisdiction of the bishop of London had not been extended to Georgia as it had to other American colonies, and Wesley answered only to the Trustees for Georgia (W. W. Manross, comp., *The Fulham Papers in the Lambeth Palace Library* [Oxford: Clarendon Press, 1965], intro., pp. 148-49).
18. Wesley's predecessor in Savannah, Mr. Quincey, had had a religious society comprised exclusively of men (*Calendar of State Papers Colonial* [London: Public Records Office, 1963]), vol. 43, no. 302; A. W. Harrison, "New Light on Wesley and Whitefield in Georgia," *Proceedings of the Wesleyan Historical Society* 19 (1937-38): 21-22. For an example of English reluctance to admit women to religious societies, see F. W. B. Bullock, *Voluntary Religious Societies 1520–1799* (St. Leonards-on-Sea, Sussex: n.p., 1963), pp. 146-47.
19. Tailfer, *Colony of Georgia*, p. 69.
20. See Doris Mary Stenton, *The English Woman in History* (London: Allen & Unwin, 1957), pp. 222-25.
21. *Journal*, vol. 1, p. 346.
22. *Apostolic Constitutions,* vol. 8, pp. 19-20, trans. in Alexander Roberts and James Donaldson, eds., *The Ante-Nicene Fathers* (Grand Rapids: Wm. B. Eerdmans Publishing Co., 1951), vol. 7, p. 492.
23. William Cave, *Primitive Christianity* (London: Rickerby, 1839), vol. 1, pp. 174-75.
24. In 1862, more than 125 years later, the Bishop of London would reinstate the ancient order of deaconesses.
25. William Law, *A Serious Call to a Devout and Holy Life* (London: J. M. Dent, 1906), p. 35; W. K. Lowther Clarke, *A History of the SPCK* (London: S.P.C.K., 1959), ch. 4. Wesley may have been influenced also by the Puritan tradition, which taught that women, though inferior to men by nature, were equal (sometimes superior) by grace; see William and Malleville Haller, "The Puritan Art of Love," *Huntington Library Quarterly* 5 (1941-42): 235-72.
26. V. H. H. Green, *The Young Mr. Wesley* (London: Edward Arnold, 1961), p. 206.
27. Wesley quoted his mother's letter to this effect in *Journal*, August 1, 1742.
28. Jeremy Taylor, *The Rules and Exercises of Holy Living and of Holy Dying*, ed. C. P. Eden (London: Longmans Green & Co., 1872), p. 56.
29. See Marlene LeGates, "The Cult of Womanhood in 18th-Century Thought," *Eighteenth Century Studies* 10 (1976-77): 21-39.
30. Georgia papers 3/15, ¶ 31, 42; *Journal*, vol. 1, pp. 293, 315.
31. Green, *Young Mr. Wesley*, p. 211.
32. See Frederick E. Maser, "John Wesley's Only Marriage," *Methodist History* 16 (1977): 33-41. The author disputes a suggestion by Frank Baker that Wesley technically was married to Murray; although the documentary evidence is somewhat ambiguous, what we know of Wesley's psychology favors Maser.
33. See Martin Schmidt, *John Wesley: A Theological Biography,* trans. Denis Inman (Nashville/New York: Abingdon Press, 1973), vol. 2, pt. 1, pp. 160-71.

34. See the famous passage at the end of the first "extract" of the *Journal:* "I, who went to America to convert others, was never myself converted to God" (vol. 1, pp. 421-24).

CHAPTER 2. "The Sun in Their Domestic System"

1. Approximately 3,000 uncatalogued books published during the 19th and early 20th centuries by the Sunday School Union of the Methodist Episcopal Church in New York City are found in the Methodist Sunday School Collection at Drew University's Rose Memorial Library (Madison, N.J.). Many of the pocket-sized leather-bound books are undated; most list no author. Those that can be identified as published before 1855 are often by British evangelical writers such as Hannah More (1745–1833) or Mary Sherwood (1775–1851), or by Methodist clergy, British and American. Most British materials simply were reprinted unaltered, since there were no copyright laws and early American Methodist publications were heavily dependent on British sources. The contents include natural history, memoirs, sermonettes, missionary letters and travels, family narratives, and catechisms. The "stories" are thinly fictionalized biographical tales.

2. Nancy F. Cott, "'Passionlessness': An Interpretation of Victorian Sexual Ideology," *Signs* 4/2 (Winter 1978): 237-52, hypothesizes that as women became the majority in church membership during the evangelical period between the 1790s and 1830s, the image of woman as less carnal than man was transformed into a religious and societal ideal. This in turn was transformed later in the century into a concept of woman as the symbolic and practical agent of moral reform. See also Keith Melder, "'Ladies Bountiful': Organized Women's Benevolence in Early Nineteenth-Century America," *New York History* 48 (1967): 231-54; David Pivar, *The Purity Crusade* (Westport, Conn.: Greenwood Press, 1973). Among the foremost ideologues of women's moral superiority based on their "lesser" sexual drive was Catharine Beecher (Kathryn Kish Sklar, *Catharine Beecher: A Study in American Domesticity* [New York: W. W. Norton & Co., 1976]).

3. [A Minister], *Old Crag, or The Alison Family: An Authentic Tale of Rural and Factory Life*, ed. D. P. Kidder (New York: Sunday School Union of the Methodist Episcopal Church [hereafter cited as SSU/MEC], 1854), p. 30.

4. Marvin Meyers, *The Jacksonian Persuasion: Politics and Belief* (Stanford, Calif.: Stanford University Press, 1957), p. 44; Russell Blaine Nye, *The Cultural Life of the New Nation* (New York: Harper & Row, 1960). On the Second Great Awakening as an organizing process in the developing nation, see Dickson D. Bruce, Jr., *And They All Sang Hallelujah: Plain-Folk Camp-Meeting Religion, 1800–1845* (Knoxville: University of Tennessee Press, 1973); William G. McLoughlin, *Revivals, Awakenings, and Reforms* (Chicago: University of Chicago Press, 1978). On the function of evangelicalism as a culture-producing synthesis in the early 1800s, see Randall Collins, *The Credential Society: An Historical Sociology of Education* (New York: Academic Press, 1979). For a summary view of changing attitudes toward child-rearing in the 19th century, see Bernard Wishy, *The Child and the Republic* (Philadelphia: University of Pennsylvania Press, 1968). Anne M. Boylan, "Sunday Schools and

Changing Evangelical Views of Children in the 1820's," *Church History* 48/3 (September 1979): 320-33, analyzes factors influencing the content and organization of Presbyterian Sunday schools in the same period as some in my sample.

5. Meyers, *Jacksonian Persuasion*, p. 177.

6. Carroll Smith Rosenberg, "Sex as Symbol in Victorian Purity: An Ethno-historical Analysis of Jacksonian America," in *Turning Points: Historical and Sociological Essays on the Family*, ed. John Demos and Sarane Spence Boocock, supplement, *American Journal of Sociology* 84 (1978): S212-47. For a recent presentation of this, see Paul Boyer, *Urban Masses and Moral Order in America, 1820–1920* (Cambridge: Harvard University Press, 1978), pt. 1, pp. 3-54.

7. Monica Kiefer, *American Children Through Their Books, 1700–1835* (Philadelphia: University of Pennsylvania Press, 1948), p. 70.

8. In a typical example of this message, an entry in the diary of Rachel Stearns, Greenfield, Mass., September 14, 1836, identifies the "encouragement" and focus for her energies as well as the new sense of self-worth found in converting from New England Congregationalism to Methodism, quoted in Nancy F. Cott, "Young Women in the Second Great Awakening," *Feminist Studies* 3/1, 2 (Fall 1975): 28-29, n. 48.

9. Richard Carwardine, *Transatlantic Revivalism: Popular Evangelicalism in Britain and America, 1790–1865* (Westport, Conn.: Greenwood Press, 1978) quotes an early statistical history of American Methodism as reporting that with fewer than 10,000 members in America in 1780, Methodism had grown to more than 250,000 by 1820, and then had doubled again before 1830 (p. 110).

10. John L. Thomas, "Romantic Reform in America, 1815–1865," *American Quarterly* 17/4 (Winter 1965): 656-81. He uses the term *determinism* rather than *fatalism*.

11. Edmund S. Morgan, *Visible Saints: The History of the Puritan Idea* (Ithaca: Cornell University Press, 1965), p. 70. "Self-searching itself became the mark, the appearance of faith [for the Puritan]" (p. 76).

12. Carwardine, *Transatlantic Revivalism*, p. 160. Also see Thomas W. Laquer, *Religion and Respectability: Sunday Schools and Working Class Culture, 1790–1850* (New Haven: Yale University Press, 1976); Robert Wood Lynn and Elliott Wright, *The Big Little School* 2nd ed. rev. (Nashville: Abingdon; Birmingham: Religious Education Press, 1980). Two general articles describe typical collections of Sunday school books: F. Allen Briggs, "The Sunday School Library in the Nineteenth Century," *The Library Quarterly* 31/2 (April 1961): 166-79; Frank W. Keller, "A Poor But Respectable Relation: The Sunday School Library," *The Library Quarterly* 12 (July 1941); 731-39.

13. "The Influence of Sunday Schools," *The New Englander* 5/11 (1847): 162-74; for quotation, see p. 173.

14. "Sunday School Literature," *Methodist Quarterly Review* (April 1850): 280-91; for quotation, see p. 287.

15. It was reported to the Methodist Episcopal General Conference in 1804 that circuit riders carried with them, besides the Holy Bible, a volume of memoirs, a portrait of the apostle Paul, and Wesley's sermons. After 1812, when books for children were being published, itinerants were to leave behind—because the itinerancy was transient, but the Sunday school was "permanent"—such books as *Religion Recommended to Youth, The Youth's Manual, Scripture Catechism,* and *Instructions for Children.*

Shortly after the founding of the Methodist Sunday School Union in 1827, they were also commissioned to deposit a cache of library books at each stop (James Penn Pilkington, *The Methodist Publishing House, A History*, 2 vols. [Nashville: Abingdon Press, 1968], vol. 1, pp. 164-66). Belief in "the well-directed powers of our own press" was trumpeted by the Annual Meeting of the Methodist Episcopal SSU, 1845: "The doctrinal conflict of this century . . . is to be decided by that wonder-working weapon with which God has armed our church—the Press" (p. 47).

16. "Influence of Sunday Schools" places these figures in context: "No less than 200,000 [persons were] employed as teachers in the Sunday Schools of the United States" in all denominations in 1847 (p. 174).

17. Daniel Howe, "Overview," in *Victorian America,* ed. Daniel Howe (Philadelphia: University of Pennsylvania Press, 1976), pp. 1-28.

18. Laquer, *Religion and Respectability,* p. 102; Collins, *Credential Society,* pp. 100, 107.

19. Edmund S. Morgan, *The Puritan Family* (New York: Harper & Row, 1966), chs. 3, 4; Michael Zuckerman, *Peaceable Kingdoms* (New York: W. W. Norton & Co., 1970), ch. 2; Sacvan Bercovitch, *The Puritan Origins of the American Self* (New Haven: Yale University Press, 1975), pp. 2, 94.

20. Ruth H. Bloch, "American Feminine Ideals in Transition: The Rise of the Moral Mother, 1785–1815," *Feminist Studies* 4/2 (June 1978): 100-126).

21. Linda K. Kerber, "The Republican Mother: Women and the Enlightenment—An American Perspective," *American Quarterly* 28 (Summer 1976): 187-205. Also, cited in the preface to Anne Louise Kuhn, *The Mother's Role in Childhood Education: New England Concepts, 1830–60* (New Haven: Yale University Press, 1947) is an article from the first *Parents Magazine* (October 1840) titled "The Bearing of Parental Fidelity on the Millennium."

22. Bloch, "Moral Mother," p. 105; Kuhn, "Mother's Role in Childhood Education," p. 79. Original sources exalting this patriotic family role include [A. Mott], *Observations on the Importance of Female Education and Maternal Instruction with Their Beneficial Influence on Society* (New York: Marlon Day, 1825); John S. C. Abbott, *The Child at Home* (New York: American Tract Society, 1833); Mrs. A. J. Graves, *Woman in America* (New York: Harper & Brothers, 1844); and Lydia Huntley Sigourney, *Letters to Mothers* (Hartford: Hudson & Skinner, 1838).

23. Sigourney, *Letters to Mothers,* p. 47.

24. Cott, "Passionlessness," p. 225.

25. Sigourney, *Letters to Mothers,* p. 112.

26. *Ibid.,* p. 117.

27. Horace Mann, "The Necessity of Education in a Republican Government" (1838), in *Ideology and Power in the Age of Jackson,* ed. Edwin C. Rozwenc (Garden City, N.Y.: Anchor Books, Doubleday & Co., 1964), p. 151.

28. Anne Scott MacLeod, *A Moral Tale: Children's Fiction and American Culture, 1820–1860* (Hamden, Conn.: Archon Books, Shoe String Press, 1975) analyzes "secular" children's stories that were largely in this form. A more helpful definition of the "moral fable" form is found in Nina Baym, *Woman's Fiction: A Guide to Novels By and About Women in America, 1820–1870* [(Ithaca, N.Y.: Cornell University Press, 1978), pp. 33-34], although Sunday school authors would not have thought of themselves as writing "fiction" or "fable."

29. Edward P. Thompson, *The Making of the English Working Class* (New

York: Vantage Books, Random House, 1966) presents a view of the Methodist movement as repressive and emotionally constricting (pp. 350-400).

30. *The Praying Mother* (n.p., n.d.) includes a section from a missionary letter concerning an encounter with savage New Zealanders. The missionaries were saved from cannibalism, but the anonymous author relished the bloodthirsty details. In *Mother's Talks with Ellen Designed to Make Her a Good Child* (n.p., 1852), there was a similar insertion—a story about a missionary daughter from Hawaii who must be sent "back" to a Christian civilization. The most outspoken British attitude toward dark-skinned people was a story called "The African Widow," in Mrs. Sherwood, *Tracts: Consisting of Tales and Narratives*, (n.p., 1841), in which a black woman, bereft of husband and child, loiters around the "white" burying ground. She is called Sister by a white woman parishioner who thus converts her. The story ends with the poor widow becoming "a member in full communion . . . washed and *made white* in the blood of the Lamb" (p. 224, italics added).

31. *The Waldos, or Incidents of the American Revolution*, ed. D. P. Kidder (New York: SSU/MEC, 1849), pp. 17-18.

32. [Daniel Wise], *The M'Gregor Family, by a Methodist Preacher* (New York: SSU/MEC, 1845), p. 84.

33. John J. Mathais, *Mary, the Young Christian* (New York: SSU/MEC, 1851), p. 62.

34. *Ibid.*, p. 63.

35. *Annual Report of the Sunday School Union of the Methodist Episcopal Church* (New York: SSU/MEC, 1845), p. 6.

36. Rev. J. M'D. Mathews, *Letters to School Girls* (Cincinnati: Methodist Episcopal Church, Western Book Concern, 1853), p. 7.

37. Sigourney, *Letters to Mothers*, p. 92.

38. In *Making of the English Working Class*, Thompson discusses the admirable way the Protestant work ethic harmonized with Methodism in industrializing England, acknowledging that Methodism was not alone in promoting this, but was "the leading example of developments taking place in all English evangelicalism" (p. 348). Max Weber himself specifically wrote about Methodism and Puritanism: "The regeneration of Methodism . . . created only a supplement to the pure doctrine of works, [providing] a religious basis for ascetic conduct after the Doctrine of Predestination had been given up. The signs given by conduct which formed an indispensable means of ascertaining true conversion [in an individual] or even its condition, as Wesley occasionally said, were in fact just the same as those of Calvinism" (*The Protestant Ethic and the Spirit of Capitalism* [New York: Charles Scribner's Sons, 1958], p. 143).

39. Hannah More, "The Shepherd of Salisbury Plain," *Tracts* (New York: Methodist Tract Society, 1821), vol. 1, 24 pp. (not consecutively numbered).

40. Meyers, *Jacksonian Persuasion*, p. 44.

41. Rev. Asa Kent, *A Sketch of the Life of Lucy Kent* (New York: SSU/MEC, 1855), p. 99.

42. *The Wilmot Family, or Children at Home: A Picture of Real Life*, (New York: SSU/MEC, 1850), p. 59.

43. Rev. T. Rogerson, *A New Heart Sought and Found by a Child, or a Short Narrative of Thomas Rogerson*, rev. by D. P. Kidder (New York: SSU/MEC, 1848), pp. 32-33.

44. *Nature's Wonders, or God's Care Over All His Works* (New York: SSU/MEC, 1851), p. 3, italics added.
45. Ruth H. Bloch, "Untangling the Roots of Modern Sex Roles: Survey of Four Centuries of Change," *Signs* 4/3 (Winter 1978): 237-52.
46. *Social Progress, or Business and Pleasure* (New York: SSU/MEC, 1856), p. 224.
47. *The Week, or the Practical Duties of the Fourth Commandment,* 3 vols. (New York: SSU/MEC, 1829), vol. 1, p. 5.
48. *Ibid.,* p. 11.
49. *Ibid.,* p. 21, italics added.
50. *Ibid.,* p. 79.
51. (Minister), *Old Crag,* p. 30.
52. *Ibid.,* pp. 42-43.
53. *Ibid.,* p. 216.
54. *The Grove Meeting,* ed. D. P. Kidder (New York: SSU/MEC, 1852), p. 31.
55. In Cott, "Passionlessness," the rise of the ideology of that female sexual quality is correlated with a distinctly improved view of women's character and social purpose in the 19th century. Cott argues that women's power and self-respect increased when moral, rather than sexual motives were imputed to them, and when they were allowed increasing self-determination within the domestic sphere (pp. 227-28).

CHAPTER 3. Subversion of the Feminine Ideal

1. [A Mother], "Female Piety," *Southern Lady's Companion* (hereafter cited as *SLC*), 2 (July 1848): 86. On the southern feminine ideal, see Dorothy Ann Gay, "The Tangled Skein of Romanticism and Violence: The Southern Response to Abolitionism and Feminism, 1830–1861" (Ph.D. dissertation, University of North Carolina at Chapel Hill, 1975), pp. 33-45; Anne Firor Scott, *The Southern Lady: From Pedestal to Politics, 1830–1930* (Chicago: University of Chicago Press, 1970), pp. 3-21.
2. For idolization of woman in American culture in general, see Barbara Welter, "The Cult of True Womanhood: 1820–1860," *American Quarterly* 18 (Summer 1966): 151-74.
3. Gay, "Tangled Skein," pp. 1-32.
4. Alexis de Tocqueville, *Democracy in America,* 2 vols. (New York: Century Co., 1898), vol. 1, pp. 507-508; James Silk Buckingham, *The Slave States of America,* 2 vols. (London: Fisher & Son, 1842), vol. 2, p. 28; Thomas R. Dew, "On the Characteristic Differences Between the Sexes, and on the Position and Influence of Woman in Society," *Southern Literary Messenger* (hereafter cited as *SLM*) 1 (May 1835): 496.
5. Grayson, "The Character of a Gentleman," *Southern Quarterly Review* (hereafter cited as *SQR*) 23 (January 1853): 57-58; "Female Education," *SLM* 6 (June 1840): 452; W. H. Holcombe, "The Southern Man," *SLM* 31 (July 1860): 26.
6. Mary E. Bailey to Eliza Seawell Hairston, June 13, 1844, Elizabeth Seawell Hairston Papers, Southern Historical Collection, University of North Carolina Library, Chapel Hill (hereafter cited as SHC). Cf. diary of Martha Foster Crawford, October 18, 1849, Manuscript Dept., Duke University Library, Durham, N.C.; diary of Lucilla Agnes Gamble McCorkle, December 20, 1850, William P. McCorkle Papers, SHC. John Bayley, a Methodist minister from Virginia, cataloged women's complaints

against men in *Marriage As It Is and As It Should Be* (New York: M. W. Dodd, 1857).

7. *Minutes of the Annual Conferences of the Methodist Episcopal Church, South,* 1864 (Nashville: Southern Methodist Publishing House, 1870), p. 545.

8. O. P. Fitzgerald, *John B. McFerrin: A Biography* (Nashville: Southern Methodist Publishing House, 1888).

9. James Penn Pilkington, *The Methodist Publishing House: A History,* 2 vols. (Nashville: Abingdon Press, 1968), vol. 1, pp. 326-30.

10. *Ibid.,* pp. 317-18; "Close of the Volume," *SLC* 3 (March 1850): 265.

11. "To Agents," *SLC* 5 (February 1852): 366; "Lady Agents," *SLC* 4 (December 1850): 216.

12. "The Close of the Volume," *SLC* 5 (March 1852): 366; Bertha M. Stearns, "Southern Magazines for Ladies (1819–1860)," *South Atlantic Quarterly* 31 (January 1932): 82-83. The subscription figure is impressive when compared to those of better known and more prestigious southern magazines such as the *SQR* and *DeBow's Review.* The *SQR* began publication in 1842 and had a subscription list of only 1,700 in 1849 (Frank W. Ryan, Jr., "The *Southern Quarterly Review,* 1842–1857: A Study in Thought and Opinion in the Old South" [Ph.D. diss., University of North Carolina at Chapel Hill, 1956], p. 470). *DeBow's Review* began publication in 1846 and had a subscription list of between 3,500 and 4,000 in 1850 (Diffee W. Standard, *"DeBow's Review,* 1846–1880: A Magazine of Southern Opinion" [Ph.D. diss., University of North Carolina at Chapel Hill, 1970], p. 65).

13. The *Companion*'s critical attitude toward the aristocracy and the content of its housekeeping articles are indicative of its readers' social status. For comment on these matters and praise of the *Companion,* see Mrs. A. M. F. Annan, "A Folly Cured," *SLC* 3 (April 1849): 16-19; "On the Subject of Etiquette," *SLC* 3 (January 1850): 227-34; "The Embellishment of Dwellings," *SLC* 7 (March 1854): 366.

14. "Editor's Table," *SLC* 4 (June 1850): 72.

15. For a comparison with other southern magazines, see Jay B. Hubbell, *The South in American Literature, 1607–1900* (Durham, N.C.: Duke University Press, 1954), p. 367.

16. "Why Is It?" *SLC* 6 (February 1853): 347-48; "A Word to Patrons," *SLC* 5 (December 1851): 277.

17. Gay, "Tangled Skein," pp. 133-65.

18. On establishment of *Home Circle,* see "To Patrons and Contributors," *Home Circle* 1 (February 1855): 83. The *Circle* ceased publication in 1861 because of a paper shortage (Pilkington, *Methodist Publishing House,* p. 418). For more on the *Companion*'s career, see James L. Leloudis II, "The *Southern Lady's Companion,* 1847–1854: A Study in the Subversion and Modification of the Southern Model of Woman" (Honors essay, Dept. of History, University of North Carolina at Chapel Hill, 1977).

19. Stearns, "Southern Magazines," pp. 78-87.

20. Barbara Welter, "The Feminization of American Religion: 1800–1860," in *Clio's Consciousness Raised: New Perspectives on the History of Women,* ed. Mary Hartman and Lois W. Banner (New York: Colophon Books, Harper & Row, 1974), pp. 137-57; Martineau, *Society in America,* ed. Seymour Martin Lipset (New York: Doubleday & Co., 1962), p. 353.

21. Scott, *Southern Lady,* pp. 29-34; Olmsted, *A Journey in the Back Country,* 2 vols. (New York: G. P. Putnam's Sons, 1907), vol. 1, p. 232.

22. "Diary of Looking Glass Plantation," North Carolina Department of Archives and History, Raleigh, cited in Scott, *Southern Lady,* p. 60; Rosa, "A Complaining Woman," *SLC* 5 (December 1851): 269.

23. Mrs. C. E. M., untitled article, *SLC* 6 (August 1852): 153; Rosa, "Complaining Woman," p. 269.

24. Cited in Guion Griffis Johnson, *Ante-Bellum North Carolina, A Social History* (Chapel Hill: University of North Carolina Press, 1937), p. 97.

25. *Ibid.,* p. 153.

26. "The South Atlantic States in 1833," ed. Bernard C. Steiner, *Maryland Historical Magazine* 13 (September-December 1918): 319-20.

27. James Lane Allen, *The Blue-Grass Region of Kentucky and Other Articles* (New York: Harper & Brothers, 1892), p. 10; Johnson, *Ante-Bellum North Carolina,* p. 146.

28. Zeno, "A Piece of Real History," *SLC* 5 (July 1851): 105; Sylvanus Cobb, Jr., "The Husband's Present," *SLC* 6 (December 1852): 271-72.

29. "Effects of Intemperance," *SLC* 8 (May 1854): 61-62.

30. Johnson, *Ante-Bellum North Carolina,* p. 95.

31. Cited by Clement Eaton, *The Growth of Southern Civilization, 1790–1860,* New American Nation Series (New York: Harper & Row, 1961; Harper Torchbooks, 1963), pp. 190-91.

32. Francis Pendleton Gaines, *The Southern Plantation, A Study in the Development and Accuracy of a Tradition* (New York: Columbia University Press, 1925), p. 161.

33. J. H. Green, "The Gambler's Victim," *SLC* 2 (February 1849): 255-57.

34. Cited by Scott, *Southern Lady,* p. 53.

35. John D. Paxton, *Letters on Slavery, Addressed to the Cumberland Congregation* (Lexington, Ky.: A. T. Skillman, 1833), pp. 129-30.

36. Kenneth M. Stampp, *The Peculiar Institution: Slavery in the Ante-Bellum South* (New York: Vintage Books, 1956), p. 351.

37. Diary of Comer, January 2, 1862, SHC.

38. Quoted in Martineau, *Society in America,* p. 226.

39. Wendell Phillips, *Speeches, Lectures, and Letters,* cited in *Agitation for Freedom: The Abolitionist Movement,* ed. Donald G. Matthews, Wiley Problems in American History Series (New York: John Wiley & Sons, 1972), p. 38.

40. Stampp, *Peculiar Institution,* p. 357.

41. Chancelor Harper, "Memoir on Slavery," *Southern Literary Journal,* new series 3 (February 1838): 96-97.

42. Mrs. Jameson, "Thoughts on English Women," *SLC* 5 (March 1852): 358-59.

43. On submissiveness, see Gay, "Tangled Skein," p. 127; Scott, *Southern Lady,* pp. 3-8. For quotation, see Hon. Robt. Charlton, "Extract," *SLC* 2 (August 1848): 114.

44. Gay, "Tangled Skein," pp. 78-79.

45. Memminger (Lecture before the Young Men's Library Association, Augusta, Georgia, 1851), cited by William S. Jenkins, *Pro-Slavery Thought in the Old South* (Chapel Hill: University of North Carolina Press, 1935), p. 210.

46. Empie, "Advice from a Father to His Only Daughter," *SLM* 1 (December 1834): 187.

47. Gilman, *Recollections of a Southern Matron* (New York: Harper & Brothers, 1839), p. 256.

48. "Home Influence," *SLC* 6 (September 1852): 187; "Strive to Make Home

Happy," *SLC* 7 (September 1853): 179. See also [A Matron], "Rules for Married Life," *SLC* 2 (May 1848): 47.

49. Elizabeth H., "Another Chapter for Husbands," *SLC* 5 (May 1851): 48; "Home Influence," p. 187; Eva, "A Chapter for Husbands," *SLC* 4 (January 1851): 235.

50. Sallie Ann, "How to Avoid the First Cross Word," *SLC* 7 (June 1853): 80-81; "How to Spoil a Spirited Wife," *SLC* 7 (May 1854): 374-75.

51. Prairie Pen, "A Word to the Congress of Complaining Husbands," *SLC* 5 (March 1852): 362-63.

52. "Home Influence," p. 187.

53. Jones to Caroline Davis, August 4, 1859, Joseph Jones Collection, Manuscripts Dept., Tulane University, New Orleans, Louisiana, cited by Gay, "Tangled Skein," p. 10.

54. Sallie, "Home and Its Pleasures," *SLC* 7 (December 1853): 269.

55. Barnsley, "An Essay on Affections," George S. Barnsley Papers, SHC, cited by Gay, "Tangled Skein," p. 17; Simms, "The Social Principle," *SQR* 4 (July 1843): 246.

56. Bishop Andrew, "Woman in the Relation of Mother," *SLC* 5 (August 1851): 123; Valarian Bates, "Government of the Temper," *SLC* 8 (June 1854): 79.

57. Sallie, "Home and Its Pleasures," p. 270.

58. Allston to aunt, October 11, 1849, Letters of Mrs. R. F. W. Allston, South Carolina Historical Society, Charleston, cited by Gay, "Tangled Skein," pp. 25-26.

59. Cited by Gay, "Tangled Skein," p. 25.

60. Cited by Jenkins, "Pro-Slavery Thought," p. 210.

61. Rev. C. B. Parsons, "A Tract," *SLC* 2 (September 1848): 133.

62. Chesnut, "The Destinies of the South," *SQR* 23 (January 1853): 198, 187.

63. Mollie, "A Cheerful Spirit," 5 (August 1851): 142-43; Bishop Andrew, "Woman in the Relation of Wife," *SLC* 4 (August 1850): 98-99.

64. Mollie, "Cheerful Spirit," p. 142.

65. Compare John Bayley's warning that white Southern men could protect the patriarchal order of their society from the woman's rights movement only by "keeping the flame of love brightly burning" and treating their wives with "the most kind and respectful attention" (*Marriage As It Is*, pp. 112-26).

66. J. B. C., letter, *SLC* 6 (June 1852): 93.

67. Scott, *Southern Lady*, pp. 9-12, 45-79; Gay, "Tangled Skein," pp. 49-59, 112-22.

68. M. E. C., letter, *SLC* 6 (June 1852): 93.

69. Emily C. N. Correll, "Woman's Work for Woman: The Methodist and Baptist Woman's Missionary Societies in North Carolina, 1878–1930" (M. A. thesis, University of North Carolina at Chapel Hill, 1977), pp. 9-43; Scott, *Southern Lady*, pp. 135-63.

70. Noreen Dunn Tatum, *A Crown of Service: A Story of Woman's Work in the Methodist Episcopal Church, South, from 1878–1940* (Nashville: Board of Missions, Woman's Division of Christian Service, 1960), p. 36. The Woman's Missionary Council was organized in 1910 through a merger of the home and foreign missionary societies. For an overview of woman's changing role in The Methodist Church, see Norma Taylor Mitchell, "From Social to Radical Feminism," *Methodist History* 13 (April 1975): 21-44.

CHAPTER 4. Distress from the Press

1. James Monroe Buckley (hereafter cited as JMB), "The Spirit of the Age," *The Christian Advocate* (New York) (hereafter cited as *CA*) 57/15 (April 13, 1882): 1.
2. George Preston Mains, *James Monroe Buckley* (New York: The Methodist Book Concern, 1917), p. 24.
3. JMB, "Significant," *CA* (December 17, 1891).
4. JMB, "Crime-Encouraging Sentimentality Foiled," *CA* 62/9 (March 3, 1887): 1.
5. JMB, "Our New Vocation," *CA* 55/23 (June 3, 1880): 8.
6. Susan B. Anthony and Ida Husted Harper, eds., *History of Woman Suffrage,* 6 vols. (Indianapolis: The Hollenbeck Press, 1902; New York: Source Book Press, 1970), vol. 4, p. 207.
7. Mains, *Buckley,* p. 28.
8. Anthony and Harper, *History,* vol. 4, p. 842.
9. JMB, "Personals," *CA* 72/22 (June 3, 1897): 8.
10. JMB, *CA* 55/45 (November 4, 1880): 1.
11. JMB, *CA* 60/24 (June 11, 1885): 1.
12. JMB, *CA* 55/48 (November 25, 1880): 1.
13. JMB, "Women and Charity," *CA* 56/25 (June 23, 1881): 1.
14. JMB, *CA* 60/32 (August 6, 1885): 2.
15. JMB, "The Normal Activity of Woman," *CA* 61/2 (October 21, 1886): 1.
16. JMB, editorial, *CA* 56/45 (November 10, 1881): 2; "Answers to Inquiries," *CA* 60/24 (June 11, 1885): 5; "Woman Farmers," *CA* 62/36 (September 8, 1887): 15.
17. JMB, *CA* 59/3 (January 10, 1884): 3.
18. JMB, editorial, *CA* (April 28, 1881): 1; "Catholic Priests and Woman Suffrage," *CA* 60/39 (September 24, 1885): 2.
19. JMB, "A Question for Wives and Mothers," *CA* 59/45 (November 6, 1884): 1.
20. *CA* 55/24 (June 10, 1880): 377; JMB, "Letting in the Light," *CA* (October 2, 1890): 1. Miss Willard was president of the Woman's Christian Temperance Union 1879–1898, and a Methodist Episcopal laywoman from the Rock River Conf.
21. *CA* 55/24 (June 10, 1880): 377.
22. "The Pronouns 'He,' 'His,' 'Him,'" *Discipline of the Methodist Episcopal Church,* 1880, appendix, ¶ 22, pp. 409-10.
23. M. L. G., "What the General Conference Did for Women," *CA* 55/50 (December 9, 1880): 10.
24. JMB, "Answers to Inquiries," *CA* 55/28 (July 8, 1880): 6.
25. JMB, "Normal Activity of Woman," p. 1.
26. JMB, "Answers to Inquiries," *CA* 61/11 (March 18, 1886): 5.
27. JMB, "Answers to Inquiries," *CA* 57/5 (February 2, 1882): 6.
28. JMB, "Moreover!" *CA* 67/8 (February 25, 1892): 1.
29. *Ibid.*
30. JMB, "The Influence of the Cultivated Woman," *CA* 64/42 (October 17, 1889): 18-19.
31. JMB, "Voting and Writing on Women as Lawmakers," *CA* 66/31 (July 30, 1891): 2, 4.
32. JMB, "An Appeal," *CA* 66/8 (February 19, 1891): 1, 2.
33. JMB, "Practical Objections to the Admission of Women," *CA* 66/35 (August 27, 1891): 1-2.

34. JMB, "Transcendent Importance of a Full Vote," *CA* 65/42 (October 16, 1890): 1.
35. JMB, "Significance of the Vote," *CA* 66/2 (January 8, 1891): 2.
36. JMB, "Because They Are Women," *CA* 65/41 (October 9, 1890): 1.
37. JMB, "Prophesy Unto Us Smooth Things," *CA* 66/13 (March 26, 1891): 2.
38. JMB, "A Delusion," *CA* 66/16 (April 16, 1891): 1.
39. JMB, "Making Void the Law of God," *CA* 65/39 (September 25, 1890): 1.
40. JMB, "Making Manifest the Truth," *CA* 66/36 (September 3, 1891): 2.
41. JMB, "Significance of the Vote."
42. JMB, "A Real Crisis in Methodism," *CA* 66/7 (February 12, 1891): 1.
43. JMB, "Errors Refuted," *CA* 65/42 (October 16, 1890): 1; "Has the Scriptural Objection Been Met?" *CA* 66/32 (August 6, 1891): 2-3.
44. JMB, "A Real Crisis," *CA* 66/7 (February 12, 1891): 1.
45. JMB, "Practical Aspect of Women in the Methodist Ministry," *CA* 66/12 (March 19, 1891): 1.
46. JMB, "Woman," *CA* 68/15 (April 13, 1893): 1.
47. JMB, "Wounded in the House of Their Friends," *CA* 68/44 (November 2, 1893): 2.
48. JMB, "A Grievous Blunder," *CA* 67/23 (June 9, 1892): 1.
49. "May 26 Proceedings," *CA* 67/25 (June 23, 1892): 9-10.
50. JMB, "John Wesley and the Woman Question," *CA* 69/27 (July 5, 1894): 2.
51. *Ibid.*
52. JMB, "One or Two Errors Pointed Out," *CA* 69/33 (August 16, 1894): 1.
53. JMB, "Are We a Civilized Community?" *CA* 82/13 (March 28, 1907): 6.
54. JMB, "National and International Notes," *CA* 83/30 (July 23, 1908): 4.
55. JMB, "A Remarkably Attractive Class," *CA* 78/42 (October 15, 1903): 5.
56. JMB, "Oppressive Discrimination," *CA* 72/9 (March 4, 1897): 1; "Shall Adult Women Be Forbidden to Work in Factories at Night?" *CA* 81/32 (August 9, 1906): 5.
57. JMB, "Injudicious Leaders," *CA* 72/43 (October 28, 1897): 3; "An Impertinent Mockery of Womanhood," *CA* 81/26 (June 28, 1906): 4.
58. JMB, "Editorial Correspondence from the General Conference," *CA* 71/19 (May 7, 1896): 1.
59. JMB, "Editorial Letter," *CA* 71/21 (May 21, 1896): 1.
60. JMB, "The Reaction Recently Registered," *CA* 72/24 (June 17, 1897): 2.
61. JMB, "Editorial Letter," *CA* 75/20 (May 17, 1900): 4.
62. JMB, "Grist Brought to the Wrong Mill," *CA* 75/25 (June 21, 1900): 5.

CHAPTER 5. An Ambiguous Legacy

1. For the original medieval latitude concerning priestly marriage and its destruction by the Gregorian reformers at Rome, see Anne Barstow, "The Defense of Clerical Marriage in the Eleventh and Early Twelfth Centuries: The Norman Anonymous and His Contemporaries" (Ph. D. diss., Columbia University, 1979).
2. J. V. Langmead Casserly, "Clerical Marriage in Anglican Experience," in *Celibacy: The Necessary Option,* ed. George Frein (South Bend, Ind.: University of Notre Dame Press, 1967); Henry C. Lea, *History of Sacerdotal Celibacy,* 4th ed. rev. (Secaucus, N.J.: University Books, 1966), pp. 424-26.
3. See Frederick E. Maser, *Susanna Wesley,* pamphlet, United Methodist

Biography Series (Lake Junaluska, N.C.: Commission on Archives and History, The United Methodist Church, 1976), pp. 4-6.

4. Lea, *Sacerdotal Celibacy*, pp. 378-80; John K. Yost's useful article, "The Reformation Defense of Clerical Marriage in the Reigns of Henry VIII and Edward VI," *Church History* 50/2 (June 1981) appeared too late to be utilized in this study.

5. Walter G. Simon, *The Restoration Episcopate* (New York: Bookman Associates, 1965), pp. 12-13.

6. Lady Montagu to Edward Wortley Montagu, February 18, 1741, in Mary Wortley Montagu, *Letters and Works*, 3rd ed., with a new memoir by W. Moy Thomas, 2 vols. (New York: AMS Press, 1932), vol. 2, p. 88, quoted in Casserly, "Clerical Marriage," p. 88.

7. John H. Pruett, *The Parish Clergy Under the Later Stuarts: The Leicestershire Experience* (Urbana: University of Illinois Press, 1978), pp. 38, 173, 176-77.

8. Leslie Stephen and Sidney Lee, eds., *Dictionary of National Biography* (hereafter cited as *DNB*), 22 vols. (London: Oxford University Press, 1921-22), vol. 1, pp. 1151-53.

9. Jasper G. Ridley, *Thomas Cranmer* (London: Oxford University Press, 1962), pp. 47-48.

10. "Convocation" was the assembly of prelates and representatives of the lower clergy that governed the Church of England.

11. Henry Bettenson, ed., *Documents of the Christian Church* (London: World's Classics, 1943), pp. 330-31.

12. A. G. Dickens and Dorothy Carr, eds., *The Reformation in England: To the Accession of Elizabeth I* (London: Edward Arnold Publishers, 1967), p. 136.

13. *Ibid.*

14. For a study of the alternatives faced by the medieval church in condemning priests' marriages, see Barstow, "Defense of Clerical Marriage," esp. ch. 5.

15. A. G. Dickens, *The English Reformation* (New York: Schocken Books, 1969), p. 245. The statistic for Cambridgeshire is from Margaret Spufford, *Contrasting Communities: English Villagers in the 16th and 17th Centuries* (Cambridge: Cambridge University Press, 1974), p. 244.

16. Dickens, *English Reformation*, p. 245; Lea, *Sacerdotal Celibacy*, p. 398.

17. *DNB*, vol. 9, p. 1254.

18. Dickens, *English Reformation*, p. 246.

19. Lea, *Sacerdotal Celibacy*, pp. 407-408.

20. *Ibid.*, pp. 410-11.

21. *DNB*, vol. 2, p. 936.

22. A. G. Dickens, *Lollards and Protestants in the Diocese of York, 1509–58* (London: Oxford University Press, 1959), pp. 190-91; cf. Anne L. Barstow, "Attitudes towards Priests' Wives: One Aspect of the Medieval Church's View of Women" (Paper presented at the Fourth Berkshire Conference on the History of Women, Mount Holyoke College, August 1978).

23. F. O. White, *Lives of the Elizabethan Bishops* (London: Skeffington & Son, 1898), p. 28.

24. For Godwin, see *DNB*, vol. 8, p. 415.

25. Roland Bainton, *Women of the Reformation in France and England* (Minneapolis: Augsburg Publishing House, 1973), p. 170.

26. J. Strype, *Ecclesiastical Memorials*, 3 vols. (Oxford: Clarendon Press, 1822), vol. 3, pt. 1, p. 404.

27. For Becon, see Derrick Sherwin Bailey, *Thomas Becon and the Reformation of the Church in England* (Edinburgh: Oliver & Boyd, 1952), pp. 81-82. For renunciation, see Dickens, *English Reformation*, p. 278. These punishments were first introduced into England by Anselm at the Council of London of 1101 (Barstow, "Defense of Clerical Marriage," pp. 93-95). It is remarkable to find them resurrected 450 years later.

28. *DNB*, vol. 17, p. 947.

29. John Foxe, *Acts and Monuments of These Latter and Perilous Days Touching Matters of the Church* . . . (London: n.p., 1563); reprinted as *Book of Martyrs* (New York: A.M.S. Press, 1965), vol. 8, p. 296. In Elizabeth's reign, Mrs. Vermigli's bones were reinterred (Bainton, *Women of the Reformation*, p. 172).

30. Foxe, vol. 8, p. 301.

31. White, *Elizabethan Bishops*, pp. 42-44.

32. Lea, *Sacerdotal Celibacy*, pp. 421, 425; *DNB*, vol. 17, pp. 773-74.

33. Pruett, *Parish Clergy*, pp. 36, 38, 62, 75.

34. *Ibid.*, p. 177.

35. See Lawrence Stone, *The Family, Sex and Marriage in England, 1500–1800* (New York: Harper & Row, 1977), pp. 135-39.

36. *Certain Sermons or Homilies Appointed to Be Read in Churches* (London: n.p., 1547, 1562, 1623; Oxford: n.p., 1822; Philadelphia: n.p., 1844), p. 123 (1844 ed.).

37. *Ibid.*, pp. 446-58. The sermon bears much resemblance to Heinrich Bullinger's *The Christian State of Matrimonye*, trans. Miles Coverdale, 1541, soon taken to be the model for such works.

38. *Ibid.*, p. 456.

39. *Ibid.*, p. 448.

40. Joyce L. Irwin, *Womanhood in Radical Protestantism, 1525—1675* (New York: Edwin Mellen Press, 1979), pp. 70, 119; Bailey, *Thomas Becon*, pp. 111-12; Lea, *Sacerdotal Celibacy*, pp. 420-21.

41. Baxter, *A Christian Directory* (London: n.p., 1673), p. 480, quoted in Irwin, *Womanhood*, p. 112.

42. Baxter, *Christian Directory*, p. 488, quoted in Irwin, *Womanhood*, p. 119. In view of these teachings, the respect shown by the Reverend Samuel Annesley for his youngest daughter Susanna's independent spiritual life and strong intellect is the more striking.

43. For Quakers, see Elaine C. Huber, "'A Woman Must Not Speak': Quaker Women in the English Left Wing," in *Women of Spirit: Female Leadership in the Jewish and Christian Traditions*, ed. Rosemary Ruether and Eleanor McLaughlin (New York: Simon & Schuster, 1979). For Anglican church, see Richard Hooker, *Of the Laws of Ecclesiastical Polity*, 2 vols. (London: Everyman's Library, 1958), vol. 2, p. 441, quoted in Irwin, *Womanhood*, p. 160.

44. For 17th century: One among many outstanding women was Mrs. Yaxley of Kibworth Beauchamp, who in 1660 was thrown out of a parsonage by Royalists. Her husband went peaceably, but she resisted, throwing stones and threatening to burn down the house. The Royalists fired at her, blinding and disfiguring her (Pruett, *Parish Clergy*, pp. 16-17, citing J. Nichols, *History and Antiquity of the County of Leicestershire* [London: n.p., 1795-1815], vol. 2, pp. 650-52).

45. Rosemary O'Day, *The English Clergy: The Emergence and Consolidation of a Profession, 1558–1642* (Leicester: Leicester University Press, 1979), observes that the status of the clergy rose steadily because they were

accepted by the English people; they were accepted because they were no longer a special clerical caste, as in the Roman church. She makes only passing reference, however, to the part that priestly marriage played in breaking down the medieval distinction between clergy and laity.

46. My thanks to Fredrika Thompsett for conversations in which I worked out some of these ideas. For reports on clerical marriages, see William Douglas, *Ministers' Wives* (New York: Harper & Row, 1965); David and Vera Mace, *What's Happening to Clergy Marriages* (Nashville: Abingdon, 1980).

47. A typescript of the entire ms. of Josselin's diary, which he kept from 1644 until his death in 1683, is available at the Essex Record Office, Chelmsford, England. A much-shortened version was published as *The Diary of the Rev. Ralph Josselin, 1616–1683*, ed. E. Hockliffe, Camden Society Publication, 3rd series, vol. 15 (London: Camden Society, 1908).

48. This information is taken from Alan Macfarlane, *The Family Life of Ralph Josselin, A Seventeenth Century Clergyman* (New York: W. W. Norton & Co., 1970).

49. *Ibid.*, p. 107.

50. *Ibid.*, p. 108, brackets in original.

CHAPTER 6. Susanna Wesley

1. The most perceptive and best documented study of Susanna is John A. Newton, *Susanna Wesley and the Puritan Tradition in Methodism* (London: Epworth Press, 1968). The best popular life is Rebecca Lamar Harmon, *Susanna, Mother of the Wesleys* (Nashville: Abingdon Press, 1968). But Newton rightly says: "There is no life of her extant which is at all commensurate with the central importance she holds both in the life of John Wesley and in the development of Methodism" (p. 11). A definitive biography written from primary sources is now practicable. The chief manuscript sources are the letters and papers of members of the Wesley family in the Methodist Archives at the John Rylands University Library, Manchester (hereafter cited as Methodist Archives, Manchester), and three small manuscript volumes containing prayers, meditations, reflections, three letters, and part of Susanna's devotional journal, at Wesley College, Bristol (formerly at Headingley, Leeds).

2. The most reliable indicator of Samuel Wesley's birth is the record in the parish register of Winterborne-Whitchurch of his baptism on December 17, 1662. This accords with the inscription on his tombstone, which states that when he died on April 25, 1735, he was 72. Statements elsewhere that he was born in 1666 are based on the records of Exeter College, Oxford, where he is reported as being "aged 18" when he matriculated on November 18, 1684.

3. Newton, *Susanna*, p. 38. Defoe was Annesley's son-in-law and a member of his congregation.

4. *Ibid.*, p. 44. When baptizing either Susanna or her predecessor, Dr. Thomas Manton, another prominent Puritan, is said to have asked the present tally of Annesley's children, to which Annesley replied that he "believed it was two dozen, or a quarter of a hundred."

5. See *Ibid.*, pp. 43-54; for quotation, see Susanna to John Wesley, January 31, 17[26/]27, in John Wesley, *Letters, I, 1721–1739*, ed. Frank Baker,

Oxford Edition of *Wesley's Works* (Oxford: Clarendon Press, 1980), vol. 25, p. 211.

6. Wesley, *Letters,* pp. 163, 164-66.
7. Newton, *Susanna,* pp. 46, 65-66.
8. *Ibid.,* pp. 57-63.
9. H. A. Beecham, "Samuel Wesley Senior: New Biographical Evidence," *Renaissance and Modern Studies* 7 (1963): 85-86, 103-104. Cf. Luke Tyerman, *The Life and Times of the Rev. Samuel Wesley* (London: Simpkin Marshall, 1866), p. 79.
10. Frank Baker, "John Wesley's Puritan Ancestry," *London Quarterly and Holborn Review* 187 (1962): 180-86.
11. Beecham, *Samuel Wesley,* p. 106. The year and place of the marriage were unknown until this writer examined the Marylebone parish registers some 30 years ago.
12. Cf. *ibid.,* pp. 89-91, 106-107; the date for Samuel Wesley's death should be corrected to 1735 and Beecham's incorrectly based argument revised.
13. For many details, see "Wesley Family," *Encyclopedia of World Methodism,* ed. Nolan B. Harmon (Nashville: Abingdon Press, 1974).
14. See Frank Baker, "Salute to Susanna," *Methodist History* 7/3 (April 1969): 5.
15. Susanna to Lady Yarborough of Snaith, March 7, 1702, in the "Remains" of George Hickes, one of the nonjuring bishops, quoted in Robert Walmsley, "John Wesley's Parents," *Manchester Guardian,* July 2-3, 1953; cf. Newton, *Susanna,* pp. 86-93 (the Hickes manuscript is owned by Walmsley, of Manchester).
16. Adam Clarke, *Memoirs of the Wesley Family,* 4th ed., enlarged, 2 vols. (London: Tegg, 1860), vol. 1, pp. 198-99.
17. For quotation, see Susanna to George Hickes, undated; Susanna to Lady Yarborough, March 7, 1702, quoted in Walmsley, "John Wesley's Parents."
18. See John Locke, *Some Thoughts Concerning Education* (London: n.p., 1693), the most influential work on education in Europe and the New World for a century. Before John Wesley's death it went through 50 editions, and another 50 afterward, in 10 European languages (see Critical Ed. by James L. Axtell, [New Haven: Yale University Press, 1968]). Locke constantly repeated his basic themes that parents should harden the child's body by plain living and perfect its character by discipline rigorously and inflexibly exerted from early infancy, but relaxed gradually as the child's reason was able to take over habits of self-discipline, in order to achieve wisdom and virtue. One of *Education's* earliest readers appears to have been Susanna Wesley. It should be noted that she speaks of conquering a child's will—not breaking its spirit, which she, like Locke, deplored. Locke scorned physical punishment and material rewards, advocating instead praise (in public) and rebuke (in private)—motives which would enable seemingly stern parents to secure both reverence and affection from their children. Esp. § § 33-66, 99-108 of Locke's *Education* were frequently echoed by Susanna; by John, e.g., sermon no. 95, "On the Education of Children," § 16; and by Charles to his wife, September 30, 1753, on their year-old first born: "The most important of Locke's rules you will not forget; it is that in which the whole *secret* of education consists: make it your invariable rule to *cross his will,* in some one instance at least, every day of your life" (Methodist Archives, Manchester).
19. John Wesley, *Journal,* ed. Nehemiah Curnock, 8 vols. (London: Epworth

Press, 1909-16), vol. 3, p. 34; see also Susanna to John Wesley, July 24, 1732, in *Journal,* and cf. another version given in part in Wesley, *Letters,* pp. 330-31.

20. Clarke, *Memoirs,* vol. 2, p. 6. Locke's *Education* § 148 began: "When he can talk, 'tis time he should begin to *learn to read,*" italics in original.
21. Wesley, *Journal,* vol. 3, p. 36.
22. Newton, *Susanna,* pp. 108-109.
23. Wesley, *Journal,* vol. 3, p. 39.
24. *Ibid.,* p. 32.
25. John Whitehead, *The Life of the Rev. John Wesley,* 2 vols. (London: Couchman, 1793-96), vol. 1, pp. 38-42; cf. Clarke, *Memoirs,* vol. 2, pp. 75-76, with examples, pp. 76-88; Newton, *Susanna,* pp. 132-42.
26. See extracts from her journals, *Wesley Banner,* 1852, and the surviving originals in Wesley College, Bristol, as noted in Newton, *Susanna,* pp. 208-209. For quotation, see *Wesley Banner,* 1852, p. 185.
27. Susanna Wesley to neighboring clergyman, August 24, 1709, *Arminian Magazine* 1 (1778): 32.
28. Wesley, *Journal,* vol. 3, p. 38.
29. See extracts from Susanna to Samuel, 1704-1707, *Wesleyan Methodist Magazine* (1846): 459-66, 665-67, 769-72, 870-75; cf. Clarke, *Memoirs,* vol. 2, pp. 137-50; Whitehead, *Life of Wesley,* vol. 2, pp. 36-38; or preferably the important original, October 11, 1709, Methodist Archives, Manchester.
30. Newton, *Susanna,* pp. 124-25; Adam Clarke greatly admired this document, *Memoirs,* vol. 2, pp. 28-72.
31. See "A Religious Conference between M[other] and E[milia]. . . . Written for the Use of My Children, 1711/12," issued as Wesley Historical Society Publication No. 3 (London: Wesley Historical Society, 1898), p. 41, from the manuscript now at Wesley College, Bristol. Emly was nineteen at that time.
32. Wesley, *Journal,* vol. 3, p. 38.
33. Quoted in Newton, *Susanna,* pp. 111, 125.
34. Whitehead, *Life of Wesley,* vol. 1, pp. 47-48, a fuller version of the original than that given by Wesley, *Journal,* vol. 3, p. 33. The *Account* was by Bartholomaeus Ziegenbalg and Heinrich Pluetscho, *Propagation of the Gospel in the East; being an Account of the Success of two Danish Missionaries, lately sent to the East Indies for the Conversion of the Heathens in Malabar,* trans. A. W. Boehme (London: n.p., 1709). Samuel Wesley had offered to lead an abortive scheme for a mission to the East Indies about 1705, so he would have been especially interested to secure a copy of this work (see Tyerman, *Life and Times of Samuel Wesley,* pp. 295-97).
35. John to Susanna Wesley, February 28, 1731/2, in Wesley, *Letters,* p. 329.
36. For quotation, see Susanna to John Wesley, January 1, 1733/4, in Wesley, *Letters,* p. 363.
37. John to Susanna Wesley, January 13, 1735, in Wesley, *Letters,* pp. 411-12.
38. *Speculum Dioeceseos Lincolniensis sub episcopis Gul. Wake et Edm. Gibson, A.D. 1705–1723,* ed. R. E. G. Cole (Lincoln: Lincoln Record Society, 1913), pp. xix-xx, 157.
39. For servants: In that time and place young men and women were happy to receive bed and board and a small allowance in return for service in house, barn, or glebe.
40. Susanna to Samuel Wesley, February 6, 1712, in Whitehead, *Life of Wesley,* vol. 1, pp. 46-47, in many respects gives fuller evidence than the

edited version in Wesley's *Journal*, vol. 3, pp. 32-34, though this also retains the phrase "last winter," showing that Susanna's letter spoke of two different winters.

41. Inman was ordained deacon in 1692, priest in 1719, and became rector of Blyborough in 1720 (John and J. A. Venn, *Alumni Cantabrigienses*, 10 vols. [London: Cambridge University Press, 1922-1954]). He had one sermon on the duty of paying one's debts, which served for all texts. He even used this theme in preaching from Heb. 11:6, "Without faith it is impossible to please God" (Tyerman, *Life and Times of Samuel Wesley*, p. 346).

42. Printed in Whitehead, *Life of Wesley*, vol. 1, pp. 48-49, italics in original. Pilgrims who visit the Epworth rectory, restored to its original plan, though with the bricks turned inside out, are naturally dubious about the possibility that the traditional kitchen could hold two hundred people, even small eighteenth-century people. The gatherings led by Mrs. Wesley almost certainly took place in the "fore kitchen" rather than the "back kitchen," the fore kitchen apparently either being the same as or adjoining the "dining-room" or "parlour." In fact, much of the rectory's ground floor could have been used, since a large front hall opened into at least one other large room, which had what is referred to as a "partition," a "screen," and a "folding door" (for the use of all these terms by contemporaries in connection with the rectory ghost, about 1716, see Joseph Priestley, *Original Letters by the Rev. John Wesley and His Friends* [Birmingham: n.p., 1791], pp. 121, 138, 142, 144, 147, 156, 158, 165, 166, esp. p. 136 for Emly's letter using the word *fore-kitchen*).

43. Whitehead, *Life of Wesley*, vol. 1, pp. 50, 52.

44. *Ibid.*, p. 53.

45. Edward Cardwell, *Synodalia* (Oxford: n.p., 1842), pp. 770-71.

46. Whitehead, *Life of Wesley*, vol. 1, p. 54.

47. Susanna to Mrs. Alice Peard of Tiverton, August 5, 1737, *Methodist Magazine* (1829): 392; cf. Clarke, *Memoirs*, vol. 2, p. 106. For a perceptive study of Susanna's relations with her sons, beginning with the reading of John's 1738 "paper," see Newton, *Susanna*, pp. 159-75.

48. Wesley, *Journal*, vol. 2, p. 267.

49. See Frank Baker, "Thomas Maxfield's First Sermon," *Proceedings of the Wesley Historical Society* 27 (March 1949): 7-16, esp. p. 8.

50. Susanna Wesley, *Some Remarks . . .* (London: John Wesley, 1741). See Frank Baker, "Susanna Wesley, Apologist for Methodism," *Proceedings of the Wesley Historical Society* 35 (September 1965): 68-71.

51. Susanna Wesley, *Some Remarks*, pp. 7, 25.

52. Susanna to Countess of Huntingdon, July 1, 1741, Methodist Archives, Manchester, quoted in Baker, "Susanna Wesley, Apologist," p. 71.

53. Wesley, *Journal*, vol. 3, pp. 29-30.

54. Wesley, *Letters:* on humility, p. 178 (cf. pp. 168, 172, 174); on faith, p. 179 (cf. pp. 174, 186, 377); on predestination, p. 179; on philosophy, p. 217.

55. *Ibid.*, pp. 172, 199-200, 210.

56. Wesley, *Journal*, vol. 3, p. 34; cf. Newton, *Susanna*, pp. 121-22.

57. Cf. Wesley, *Letters*, pp. 384-85.

58. Newton, *Susanna*, pp. 132-44; for quotation, see p. 135.

59. *Ibid.*, pp. 136-37; Albert C. Outler, *John Wesley* (New York: Oxford University Press, 1964), pp. 107-108, 251-52.

60. Wesley, *Letters*, pp. 151, 153, 162, 168, 179, 183, 189, 211-12, 215, 344-45, 372, 385.

61. E.g., Susanna to John Wesley, October 25, 1732, in Wesley, *Letters,* pp. 344-46, recommending Scougal, *Life of God in the Soul of Man* (London: n.p., 1677) and Baxter, *The Saint's Everlasting Rest* (London: n.p., 1650), see forthcoming bibliography in Oxford Edition of *Wesley's Works,* vol. 32, nos. 93 (1744), 165.iii (1754).

62. Newton, *Susanna,* pp. 144-48; cf. Wesley, *Letters,* pp. 326-27, on the real presence of Christ in the Lord's Supper.

63. Newton, *Susanna,* pp. 148-58.

64. Susanna to John Wesley, February 14, 1734, in Wesley, *Letters,* p. 377.

65. See n. 48.

66. This probably occurred on July 15, 1712, when Wake held a confirmation at Epworth, matching the tradition that John was admitted to communion at age 8, although actually he would have been just 9 (see Frank Baker, *John Wesley and the Church of England* [London: Epworth Press, 1970], pp. 10, 342, n. 20).

67. John to Charles Wesley, June 28, 1755, Methodist Archives, Manchester; cf. his traditional words, "Church or no Church, we must attend to the work of saving souls" (*Proceedings of the Wesley Historical Society* 27 [1949]: 168).

68. Baker, *Wesley and Church of England,* pp. 120-36.

69. For meekness, see Wesley, *Letters,* pp. 354-55; cf. Susanna's words on p. 383: "Severity . . . may make him a hypocrite, but will never make him a convert."

CHAPTER 7. A Partnership of Equality

1. Anna Heubeck Knipp and Thaddeus P. Thomas, *The History of Goucher College* (Baltimore: Goucher College, 1938), pp. 43-44.

2. Mary Goucher's "hymn book" (words and tunes pasted on blank pages), Goucher Papers, Lovely Lane Museum, Baltimore, Maryland (hereafter cited as GP).

3. James M. Buckley, "It Was the Master Calling," *Christian Advocate* 77/52 (December 25, 1902): 6; see also "Mrs. Goucher Is Dead," *Baltimore Sun* (December 20, 1902): 12; Knipp and Thomas, *History,* p. 44; "Mary Cecelia Goucher," Baltimore Conference, Methodist Episcopal Church (hereafter cited as BC), *Minutes,* 1903, p. 62.

4. Diary of John Goucher, July 21, 1869, GP.

5. Frank G. Porter, "John Franklin Goucher," in *Minutes of the BC,* 1923, p. 377.

6. Diary of John Goucher, February 18, 1869, GP.

7. See David G. Wright and Calvin Corell, *The Restoration of Lovely Lane Church* (Baltimore: Trustees of the M. E. Church in the city and precincts of Baltimore, 1980), esp. "Building the Monument."

8. Porter, "John Franklin Goucher," p. 379; Buckley, "Master Calling," p. 7.

9. Porter, "John Franklin Goucher," p. 378.

10. Buckley, "Master Calling," p. 7.

11. *Ibid.,* p. 6.

12. Erwin H. Richards, "Report of the Inhambane District," in *Minutes of the East Central African Mission Conference,* 1901, p. 23.

13. Knipp and Thomas, *History,* p. 585, n. 23; "General Missionary Items," *Christian Advocate* 58/48 (November 29, 1883): 763.

14. Porter, "John Franklin Goucher," p. 379.

15. Knipp and Thomas, *History,* p. 49.
16. N. L. Rockey, "The Goucher Impetus to India," *Washington Christian Advocate* 44/34 (August 24, 1922): 5-6.
17. Porter, "John Franklin Goucher," p. 379.
18. Buckley, "Master Calling," p. 6.
19. Knipp and Thomas, *History,* p. 46.
20. Porter, "John Franklin Goucher," p. 379.
21. "Baltimore Notes," *Christian Advocate* 59/3 (January 17, 1884): 40.
22. James M. Buckley, "1884—The Completed Century," *Christian Advocate* 59/3 (January 17, 1884): 3.
23. Asbury Smith, "A Century of Developing Concerns," in *Those Incredible Methodists: A History of the Baltimore Conference of the United Methodist Church,* ed. Gordon Pratt Baker (Baltimore: Commission on Archives and History, The Baltimore Conference, 1972), p. 414.
24. *Minutes of the BC,* 1884, p. 54.
25. Goucher to Van Meter *et al.,* December 2, 1883, Knipp and Thomas, *History,* p. 6.
26. *Ibid.*
27. "Baltimore Notes," p. 40.
28. Knipp and Thomas, *History,* pp. 7-8.
29. *Ibid.,* p. 9.
30. *Ibid.,* pp. 8, 9.
31. *Ibid.,* pp. 9-10; WEA circular, February 11, 1884, GP.
32. Knipp and Thomas, *History,* p. 10.
33. *Ibid.,* pp. 10-11, italics added.
34. *Ibid.*
35. WEA circular to pastors, March 20, 1884, GP.
36. WEA circular to secretaries, March 20, 1884, GP.
37. Knipp and Thomas, *History,* pp. 12-13.
38. Not all churches followed this lead. See First M. E. Church circular, May 13, 1884, GP.
39. Knipp and Thomas, *History,* pp. 15, 557.
40. *Baltimore Sun,* March 6, 1885, in Knipp and Thomas, *History,* p. 17.
41. Florence Hooper, "Women in the Baltimore Conference, 1815–1965," in Baker, *Incredible Methodists,* p. 382; Knipp and Thomas, *History,* pp. 31-32; WEA flyer, May 1888, GP.
42. Knipp and Thomas, *History,* p. 26.
43. Francis A. Crook and John M. Dashiell to John Goucher, May 30, 1890, GP.
44. Earl Cranston, "John Franklin Goucher—Modern Apostle and Civilized Saint," *Methodist Review* 106/1 (January 1923): 14.
45. Buckley, "Master Calling," p. 6.

CHAPTER 8. The Pacific Northwest

1. For secular historians, the Pacific Northwest also includes Oregon, the rest of Idaho, and parts of Montana, Wyoming, and British Columbia, but here we will use the term in its Methodist sense. What is now the Pacific Northwest Annual Conference (hereafter cited as PNWAC) originally was part of the Oregon Annual Conference of the Methodist Episcopal Church. It obtained its present boundaries through divisions of that conference in 1874 and 1884 and a conference merger in 1929. Most sources

for this article are in the M. E. tradition. The records of the Evangelical United Brethren, the Methodist Episcopal Church, South, and the ethnic conferences were not reviewed, nor were accounts in other languages or records in local churches. Available sources are voluminous.

2. Washington became a state in 1889, and Idaho, in 1890. In 1848 the region belonged to the Oregon Territory, and from 1853, to the smaller Washington Territory carved from it. See the recent bicentennial histories *Washington* and *Idaho*, by Norman H. Clark and Ross Peterson, respectively, The States and the Nation Series (New York: W. W. Norton & Co., 1976); Dorothy O. Johanson and Charles M. Gates, *Empire of the Columbia*, 2nd ed. (New York: Harper & Row, 1967); H. H. Bancroft, *History of Washington, Idaho, and Montana* (San Francisco: History Company, 1890).

3. The library of the University of Puget Sound, Tacoma, Washington, houses the archives of the PNWAC. The discovery there of the minute books of the organizations of clergy wives sparked this study. Three provide an unbroken record from 1897 to the present, beginning in the old Puget Sound Conference. Another chronicles the meetings of the wives from 1922 in the Columbia River Conference, through merger in 1930 with the Puget Sound Conference, out of which grew the Ministers' Wives Association of the Pacific Northwest Conference. See also in the conference archives, transcripts of memoirs for deceased clergy and their wives compiled by Richard A. Seiber, and an inventory of records in the possession of local churches compiled by PNWAC United Methodist Women.

4. For quotation, see PNWAC *Journal*, 1975, p. 100.

5. Thomas D. Yarnes, *A History of Oregon Methodism*, ed. Harvey E. Tobie (Nashville: Oregon Methodist Conference Historical Society, [after 1957]), p. 37.

6. Erle Howell settled a long dispute as to whether Mrs. Richmond's Christian name was *America* or *Amelia* when he located an original marriage record for John P. Richmond and America Walker Talley, subsequent to the publication of his *Methodism in the Northwest* (Nashville: Pacific Northwest Conference Historical Society, 1966). He uses *Amelia* in the text of that work (p. 36) and cites authorities for the use of both names (p. 380, ch. 1, n. 7). The marriage record is cited in his "John P. Richmond, M.D.: First Methodist Minister Assigned to the Present State of Washington," *Methodist History* 9/1 (October 1970): 27, n. 3. In noting that Jason Lee "appointed Dr. J. P. Richmond *and his wife*" (italics added) to the Nisqually Mission, Bishop Bashford in a sense gave Mrs. Richmond missionary status, see James W. Bashford, *The Oregon Missions: The Story of How the Line Was Run Between Canada and the United States* (New York: Abingdon Press, 1918), 193-94.

7. American Lake is located a few miles from the old Nisqually Mission site, about halfway between the present town of Nisqually and the center of Tacoma. For this celebration, see A. Atwood, *Glimpses in Pioneer Life on Puget Sound* (Seattle: Denny-Corvell Co., 1903), pp. 41-43; Edmond S. Meany, *History of the State of Washington* (New York: Macmillan Co., 1943), pp. 71-72.

8. Howell, *Methodism in the Northwest*, p. 42.

9. Richard A. Seiber, ed., *Memoirs of Puget Sound: Early Seattle, 1853-1856. The Letters of David & Catherine Blaine* (Fairfield, Wash.: Ye Galleon Press, 1978), p. 86.

10. Puget Sound Conference *Journal* (hereafter cited as PS *Journal*), 1915, p. 76.
11. "Record of Chehalis (Grays Harbor) Circuit, MEC, 1856–1887," PNWAC archives. This source was rediscovered in May 1980, when Ray L. Whitlow removed shelving and partitions in The United Methodist Church at Montesano, Washington, to enlarge a study. See also sketch of Montesano church, Howell, *Methodism in the Northwest,* p. 36.
12. Columbia River Conference *Journal* (hereafter cited as CR *Journal*), 1910, p. 7.
13. Cora McDermoth, "Early Days Recalled," scrapbook in public library, Aberdeen, Wash. (n.d.), pp. 20-27.
14. Wallace J. Miller, *Southwestern Washington* (Olympia: Pacific Publishing Co., 1890), p. 48.
15. PS *Journal*, 1911, p. 78. *Wealthy* is Mrs. Hopkins' name, not her financial status. Julie Roy Jeffrey discusses mate selection in clerical marriage on the American frontier in "Ministry Through Marriage: Methodist Clergy Wives on the Trans-Mississippi Frontier," in *Women in New Worlds,* vol. 1, ed. Hilah F. Thomas and Rosemary Skinner Keller (Nashville: Abingdon, 1981).
16. For quotation, see Sutton, "The Preacher's Wife—A Leader," *The Pacific Christian Advocate* (October 2, 1907): 9, 19.
17. For detailed accounts of daily life in the Pacific Northwest in pioneer days, see Seiber, *Memoirs,* and McDermoth, "Early Days Recalled."
18. Seiber, *Memoirs,* p. 39.
19. For quotation, see Edwin Van Syckle, *They Tried to Cut It All: Grays Harbor, Turbulent Years of Greed and Greatness* (Seattle: Friends of the Aberdeen Public Library, 1980), p. 1.
20. PS *Journal*, 1908, p. 67.
21. CR *Journal*, 1888, p. 46; cf. PNWAC *Journal*, 1942, pp. 423-29.
22. PS *Journal*, 1908, p. 71.
23. Seiber, *Memoirs,* pp. 21, 69.
24. PS *Journal*, 1913, p. 89.
25. PNWAC *Journal*, 1946, p. 382.
26. PS *Journal*, 1891, p. 56.
27. Flora E. Wartman-Arland, "The Story of Montesano," *Montesano* (Washington) *Vidette,* Golden Anniversary Ed. (October 12, 1933), facsimile repro. (Seattle: Shorey Book Store, 1968), p. 8.
28. PS *Journal*, 1896, p. 39.
29. CR *Journal*, 1925, p. 122.
30. PS *Journal*, 1915, p. 77.
31. PNWAC *Journal*, 1936, p. 75.
32. Daniel D. Walker, "Composite Report of District Superintendents," PNWAC *Journal*, 1978, p. 137.
33. Minute Book, PNWAC Ministers' Wives Association, 1929–1972 (hereafter cited as PNWAC Wives No. 1), pp. 49-105, PNWAC archives; see also PNWAC *Journal*, 1955, p. 613; 1956, pp. 41, 42, 94.
34. PNWAC *Journal*, 1947, p. 530.
35. PNWAC *Journal*, 1977, p. 279.
36. Suzanne Martinson, "Letitia Bergstresser: She Faced Hardship But Didn't Forsake Humor," Longview, Wash., *Daily News,* [1970s]. See also Dale A. Johnson, *Oh, I've Seen It All,* life story of Letitia Bergstresser (Portland, Ore.: Privately Published, 1981).
37. PNWAC *Journal*, 1938, p. 385.

38. Georgia Harkness, *Women in Church and Society* (Nashville: Abingdon Press, 1972), pp. 126-37.
39. CR *Journal,* 1904, p. 52; PNWAC *Journal,* 1952, p. 113.
40. PNWAC *Journal,* 1975, p. 103, italics added.
41. Cora McDermoth, "Historical Sketch," Minute Book, Pastors' Wives Association, Puget Sound Conference, 1897–1928 (hereafter cited as PS Wives), pp. 1-5.
    The "bar" of the annual conference is that part of an auditorium within which business is transacted by members. The wives probably were asked to leave when the expulsion of a minister was being considered—a matter dealt with only by clergy. There were no women on the 1897 clergy roster. Several laymen were present, and they too would have been asked to leave (see PS *Journal,* 1897, pp. 28-32, 38).
42. Cora Chamberlin, a McDermoth granddaughter residing near Aberdeen, Wash., provided this information.
43. PS Wives, p. 3.
44. *Ibid.,* pp. 6-35.
45. *Ibid.,* pp. 10-11.
46. *Ibid.,* pp. 20-21; Sutton, "The Preacher's Wife," p. 9.
47. PS Wives, pp. 32-33.
48. Secretary's Book, Ministers' Wives Association, Columbia River Conference, 1922–1930 (hereafter cited as CR Wives), pp. 19-22.
49. PNWAC Wives No. 1, unpaged insert.
50. *Ibid.,* pp. 3-4.
51. *Ibid.,* pp. 49-115.
52. PNWAC *Journal,* 1978, p. 267. Used with Bishop Choy's permission.
53. On divorce, see Patricia Evans Coots, "Queens Without Kingdoms: Women Divorced from United Methodist Ministers," *Occasional Papers* published by The United Methodist Board of Higher Education and Ministry, 1/17 (February 14, 1978); see also David and Vera Mace, *What's Happening to Clergy Marriages* (Nashville: Abingdon, 1980).
54. "What's My Line? My, What Lines!" newsletter prepared for annual meeting of PNWAC clergy wives (June 12, 1965), Minute Book, Ministers' Wives Association, 1973 to date (hereafter cited as PNWAC Wives No. 2), in possession of current officers.
55. PNWAC *Journal,* 1978, p. 137.
56. *Ibid.,* 1975, p. 97; 1978; p. 220; 1979, p. 223.
57. *Ibid.,* 1978, pp. 136-37.
58. PNWAC Wives No. 2, 1978.
59. Marian L. Muench to Rosa Peffly Motes, June 22, 1979.
60. PNWAC Wives No. 2, 1979.
61. See Frederick A. Norwood, *The Story of American Methodism* (Nashville: Abingdon Press, 1974), p. 10, for reference to the male bias of church historians.

CHAPTER 9. The Countess of Huntingdon

1. For a description of "enthusiasm," see Charles Chauncy, *Enthusiasm Described and Caution'd Against* (Boston: S. Eliot, 1742). The Countess also was known as Pope Joan by those who wished to deride her. Those like Whitefield who were indebted to her spoke of her in awe and used such titles as Mother in Israel and Good Lady Huntingdon. Horace Walpole

called her Patriarchess, and a recent writer termed her Queen (David Mitchell, "Queen of the Methodists: Selina, Countess of Huntingdon," *History Today* 15 [December 1965]: 846-53). I am grateful to Hilah F. Thomas for calling my attention to the article by Mitchell, and for other references. For general information, see [Aaron Crossley Hobart Seymour], *The Life and Times of Selina, Countess of Huntingdon*, 2 vols. (London: William Edward Painter, 1844); Leslie Stephen and Sidney Lee, eds., *Dictionary of National Biography* (cited hereafter as *DNB*), 22 vols. (London: Oxford University Press, 1921-22), vol. 9, pp. 133-35; Sarah Tytler [Henrietta Keddie], *The Countess of Huntingdon and Her Circle* (London: Sir I. Pitman & Sons, 1907); Helen G. Knight, *Lady Huntingdon and Her Friends* (New York: American Tract Society, 1853); Abel Stevens, *Women of Methodism* (New York: Carlton & Porter, 1866); Lucia Myers, *Lady Huntingdon, Friend of the Wesleys* (Montgomery, Ala.: Huntingdon College Alumnae Association, 1956).

2. See Mollie C. Davis, "The Countess of Huntingdon and Whitefield's Bethesda," *Georgia Historical Quarterly* 56 (Spring 1972): 72-82.

3. For a perceptive analysis of female religious leadership, see Rosemary Ruether and Eleanor McLaughlin, "Women's Leadership in the Jewish and Christian Traditions: Continuity and Change," in *Women of Spirit, Female Leadership in the Jewish and Christian Traditions*, ed. Ruether and McLaughlin (New York: Simon & Schuster, 1979), pp. 16-28.

4. *Ibid.;* see also Nancy F. Cott, *The Bonds of Womanhood* (New Haven: Yale University Press, 1977); cf. Mary Beth Norton, *Liberty's Daughters: The Revolutionary Experience of American Women, 1750–1800* (Boston/ Toronto: Little, Brown & Co., 1980), p. 125.

5. For dependency, see Phyllis Stock, *Better than Rubies: A History of Women's Education* (New York: G. P. Putnam's Sons, 1978), p. 118.

6. Ruether and McLaughlin, "Women's Leadership," p. 22.

7. Stock, *Better than Rubies*, p. 471.

8. See Davis, "Countess of Huntingdon," p. 7. For background, see also [Seymour], *Life and Times*, vol. 1, pp. 1-10, 22-23; Myers, *Lady Huntingdon*, pp. 4-8; Mitchell, "Queen of Methodists," p. 847.

9. *Unitas Fratum* was the correct name of the group. The Church of the United Brethren in Christ is an entirely different ecclesiastical body, not to be confused with the Moravians.

10. For a survey of Ingham's role in Georgia, see E. Merton Coulter, *Georgia: A Short History* (Chapel Hill: University of North Carolina Press, 1960), pp. 70-73; see also Knight, *Lady Huntingdon*, pp. 109-10; [Seymour], *Life and Times*, vol. 1, pp. 242-69.

11. The date is an estimate. See [Seymour], *Life and Times*, vol. 1, p. 10; Myers, *Lady Huntingdon*, p. 9.

12. For lay ministry, see Stevens, *Women of Methodism*, p. 148; [Seymour], *Life and Times*, vol. 1, pp. 32-33. For general information, see Myers, *Lady Huntingdon*, p. 10.

13. Stevens, *Women of Methodism*, pp. 154-55.

14. Davis, "Countess of Huntingdon," pp. 74, 81. Lady Huntingdon probably heard Whitefield preach in London or Bristol before 1744; they were in communication in 1745 and 1746 through the Welsh minister Howel Harris; see also Mollie C. Davis, "Whitefield's Attempt to Establish a College in Georgia," *Georgia Historical Quarterly* 55 (Winter 1971): 460, based on colonial primary records, including George Whitefield, *The Works of The Reverend George Whitefield, M.A. Late of Pembroke-*

College, Oxford, And Chaplain to the Rt. Hon. the Countess of Huntingdon, 6 vols. (London: Edward & Charles Dilly . . . Kincaid & Bell, 1771).

15. By *conversion* I mean to imply sympathy with the Countess in her efforts to reform the established church from within. Technically, Whitefield remained within the church, though his procedures frequently were challenged and his impassioned style of revivalism incited the wrath of the orthodox clergy. After Whitefield's death the Countess was forced to register her chapels as Dissenting places of worship. For complaints of Whitefield's itinerants, see, e.g., Alexander Garden, Commissary at Charleston, February 1, 1750, The Fulham Palace Papers, Lambeth Palace Library, microfilm, University of Georgia, 10: 67-68, 86-89, 106-107, 134-35; Edward Wigglesworth, Jr., to Ezra Stiles, December 23, 1754, in *Extracts from the Itineraries and Other Miscellanies of Ezra Stiles,* ed. Franklin Bowditch Dexter (New Haven: Yale University Press, 1916), pp. 594-95.

16. Davis, "Whitefield's Attempt," p. 467.

17. *Ibid.,* pp. 459-68.

18. Using her status as a peeress, the Countess appointed chaplains of her choice and thus protected those suspected of Methodism. The connection she founded grew gradually during this decade; see *DNB,* vol. 9, pp. 133-34.

19. Stevens, *Women of Methodism,* pp. 150-53.

20. Mitchell, "Queen of Methodists," pp. 851-52. This entire article is entertaining, despite its ridicule of the Countess.

21. *Ibid.,* p. 850. During the early period of her marriage the Countess had indicated a political sympathy with Sir Robert Walpole ([Seymour], *Life and Times,* vol. 1, p. 23). Shortly after he married in 1755, Lord Dartmouth, a friend of Lady Fanny Shirley, met the Countess, who introduced him to Whitefield, Wesley, and others (vol. 2, p. 33).

22. Mitchell, "Queen of Methodists," p. 850.

23. See James Habersham to William Knox, Georgia Historical Society, *Collections,* vol. 6, p. 54; George Whitefield, *A Letter to His Excellency Governor Wright, Giving an Account of the Steps taken relative to the converting the Georgia Orphan-House into a College* (London: J. Millan & C. Dilly & M. Felingsley, 1768), pp. 1-10, 16-17.

24. See *DNB,* vol. 9, p. 134; *Some Account of the Proceedings . . . at the College of . . . the Countess of Huntingdon* (London: Privately printed, 1772).

25. Davis, "Countess of Huntingdon," p. 72.

26. For complaints, see James Seymour to Secretary of the Society for the Propagation of the Gospel in Foreign Parts, February 24, 1774, S. P. G. Miscellaneous Manuscripts, microfilm, University of Georgia Library; for an account of the mission, see *Some Account.*

27. [Seymour], *Life and Times,* vol. 2, pp. 266-72; Davis, "Countess of Huntingdon," pp. 77-78.

28. [Seymour], *Life and Times,* vol. 2, pp. 266-72.

29. Hastings to Laurens, June 30, 1783, Papers of Selina, Countess of Huntingdon [copies], Cheshunt College, Cambridge, England, microfilm, University of South Carolina (hereafter cited as Papers of Selina).

30. Papers of Selina; correspondence between the Countess and Laurens reveals that both were in ill health.

31. *Ibid.,* Laurens to Hastings, January 31, 1784.

32. *Ibid.,* Laurens to Hastings, March 26, 1785.

33. *Ibid.*, John Cosson to Hastings, March 25, 1785.
34. *Ibid.*, Hastings to Edward Bridgen, September 10, 1785.
35. *Ibid.*, Habersham to Hastings, June 25, 1786.
36. *Ibid.*, Hastings to Trustees of the University of Georgia, January 15, 1787; see also Davis, "Countess of Huntingdon," pp. 78-79.
37. Lilla Mills Hawes, "Notes on Bethesda in Jackson's Hand," *Georgia Historical Quarterly* 37 (December 1953): 147.
38. Davis, "Countess of Huntingdon," p. 80.
39. For example, the Countess received a very low profile in the article on Whitefield, *DNB*, vol. 21, pp. 85-92, in which their intimate friendship is suspect and the failure of his plans for Bethesda are made to seem her responsibility: "He might probably have obtained for it a charter had he placed it under the direction of the state authorities, but he bequeathed the whole institution to Lady Huntingdon" (p. 91). In another article, Whitefield's impact on the aristocracy is laid entirely to his "remarkable preaching," while not a word is spoken of Selina Hastings' personal efforts to bring the nobility to hear her chaplain (Walter B. T. Douglas, "George Whitefield: The Man and His Mission," *Methodist History* 16/1 [October 1977]: 48).
40. There is no indication that Selina Hastings spoke to conferences of Methodists, but she did address friends and prayed with guests in her home, see Tytler, *Countess of Huntingdon*, pp. 56-57; Myers, *Lady Huntingdon*, p. 16.
41. For Lady Montagu, see Stock, *Better than Rubies*, p. 101.
42. Writing in 1866, Abel Stevens, that Victorian champion of Methodist women, intended a compliment when he apologized for the behavior of the Countess. Stevens went to great trouble to insist that the Countess kept her proper place and that she "adorned" the "doctrine" by living a holy life. Further, she kept her "womanly decorum" by planning and counseling in private, not in public (*Women in Methodism*, pp. 151, 154).

CHAPTER 10. American Indian Women

1. *Woman's Home Missions* (hereafter cited as *WHM*) 55/9 (September 1938): 5. This was the first of 11 articles on the history of northern home missions, which ran until July 1939.
2. *Ibid.* 6/1 (January 1889): 2-3.
3. *Ibid.* 3/2 (February 1886): 24, 184; 4/9 (September 1887): 132.
4. Woman's Home Missionary Society (hereafter cited as WHMS) *Annual Report*, 1887-88, p. 55; *WHM* 5/4 (April 1888): 50, 163; 6/6 (June 1889): 19-20, 82.
5. *WHM* 55/4 (April 1938): 4.
6. WHMS *Annual Report*, 1887-88, p. 52.
7. *WHM* 56/10 (November 1939): 14-15; Ruth Esther Meeker, *Six Decades of Service, 1880–1940* (n.p.: WHMS, 1969), pp. 147-49.
8. *WHM* 16/7 (July 1899): 123-25.
9. *Ibid.* 16/10 (October 1899): 183-84.
10. Betty Epps Arnett, "Helping Troubled Children in Alaska," *Response* 13 (January 1981): 4-6, 37.
11. Sidney H. Babcock and John Y. Bryce, *History of Methodism in Oklahoma* (n.p., 1937), pp. 274-76; Walter N. Vernon, "Indian Methodists in South Central States," in *One in the Lord*, ed. Walter N. Vernon (Oklahoma

City: South Central Jurisdiction Commission on Archives and History, 1977), pp. 9-10.

12. *Our Brother in Red,* 7 (April 6, 1889): 6.

13. Walter N. Vernon, "Methodist Beginnings Among Southwest Oklahoma Indians," *Chronicles of Oklahoma* 50/4 (Winter 1980/81): 392; Woman's Missionary Society *Annual Report,* 1888, pp. 63-64; Butler, *History of WFMS,* pp. 131-32.

14. *Woman's Missionary Advocate* (hereafter cited as *WMA*) (February 1893): 235.

15. *WMA* (June 1893): 363.

16. *Ibid.* (January 1894): 211; cf. (December 1891): 176; (January 1895): 207-208; (May 1895): 336.

17. Vernon, "Methodist Beginnings," p. 18; *WMA* (January 1895): 207. For Fort Sill, see *WMA* (March 1893): 269.

18. Noreen Dunn Tatum, *A Crown of Service: A Story of Woman's Work in the Methodist Episcopal Church, South, from 1878–1940* (Nashville: Board of Missions, Woman's Division of Christian Service, 1960), p. 298.

19. WHMS *Annual Report,* 1884-85, p. 88.

20. *WMA* (August 1903): 52-53.

21. *Ibid.* (September 1898): 80.

22. *Ibid.* (May 1895): 335.

23. *Christian Advocate and Journal* 2/16 (December 21, 1827): 61.

24. *Christian Advocate and Journal and Zion's Herald* 4/24 (February 12, 1830): 94.

25. *Ibid.*

26. *The Methodist Magazine* 3 (1820): 435.

27. *WHM* 8/11 (November 1891): 168.

28. *14th Annual Session, Indian Mission of Oklahoma, The Methodist Church,* 1952, p. 47.

29. *The Methodist Review of Missions* 14/4 (October 1893): 208.

30. Quoted in Gary E. Moulton, *John Ross, Cherokee Chief* (Athens: University of Georgia Press, 1978), p. 181.

31. See *WMA* (November 1895): 140-41; (July 1896): 18-19.

32. Upon Nannie's death, Guy wrote a moving tribute, published many years later by the Southwest Oklahoma Historical Society in *Prairie Lore* (January 1965): 86-87.

33. Most of the data on Carrie comes from a nomination form of American Mothers Committee, New York, provided by Walter Vernon. For Virginia, see Indian Mission Conference *Advocate* (June 27, 1980).

34. This information was furnished by Walter N. Vernon, from interview with Hazel Botone.

CHAPTER 11. Sisterhoods of Service

1. Sallie Southall Cotten, "Second Speech to Winterville Mother's Club" (n.d.), Cotten Family Papers, Southern Historical Collection, University of North Carolina at Chapel Hill.

2. For a succinct description of the antebellum feminine ideal, see Barbara Welter, "The Cult of True Womanhood: 1820–1860," in Welter, *Dimity Convictions: The American Woman in the Nineteenth Century* (Athens: Ohio University Press, 1976), pp. 21-41. Anne Firor Scott, describing the southern adaptation of this model in *The Southern Lady: From Pedestal to*

Politics, 1830–1930 (Chicago: University of Chicago Press, 1970), demonstrated the survival of the ideal into the twentieth century, as did Peter Gabriel Filene, *Him/Her/Self: Sex Roles in Modern America* (New York/London: Harcourt, Brace, Jovanovich, 1975), pp. 12-16. In *The Ideas of the Woman Suffrage Movement 1890–1920* (Garden City: Anchor Books, Doubleday & Co., 1971), Aileen S. Kraditor showed how American suffragists used the cult of domesticity as an argument for female enfranchisement (pp. 45-57 *et passim*).

3. William Stevens Powell, *North Carolina: A Bicentennial History*, The States and The Nation Series (New York: W. W. Norton & Co., 1977), pp. 180, 196.

4. For the origins of the woman's home mission movement in the Methodist Episcopal Church, South, see Mary E. Frederickson, "Shaping a New Society: Methodist Women and Industrial Reform in the South, 1880–1940," in *Women in New Worlds*, vol. 1, ed. Hilah F. Thomas and Rosemary Skinner Keller (Nashville: Abingdon, 1981); Virginia Shadron, "Out of Our Homes: The Woman's Rights Movement in the Methodist Episcopal Church, South, 1890–1918" (M.A. thesis, Emory University, 1976); Noreen Dunn Tatum, *A Crown of Service: A Story of Woman's Work in the Methodist Episcopal Church, South, from 1878–1940* (Nashville: Board of Missions, Woman's Division of Christian Service, 1960). Women's home mission work was conducted under several names, beginning in 1886 as the Woman's Department of Church Extension. In 1890 the name was changed to Woman's Parsonage and Home Mission Society, and eight years later it became the Woman's Home Mission Society. In 1910 this merged with the Woman's Foreign Missionary Society to form the Woman's Missionary Society. Its governing board, composed of officers of the whole society as well as the presidents and secretaries of the conference societies, was called the Woman's Missionary Council.

5. Mrs. C. P. Dey, "The Woman's Issue"; Mrs. H. B. Anderson, "The Open Door," *North Carolina Christian Advocate* (April 14, 1897): 1, 3.

6. Lillie Moore Everett, *Seven Times Seven: A History of the Seven Sabbaths of Years in the North Carolina Conference Woman's Missionary Society* (Greensboro, N.C.: Piedmont Press, 1929), p. 216.

7. Nettie Scott to Mrs. J. LeGrand Everett, June 11, 1927, Mrs. J. LeGrand Everett Correspondence, Woman's Missionary Society Papers, Methodist Episcopal Church, South, Manuscripts Dept., Perkins Library, Duke University, Durham, N.C. (hereafter cited as Everett Corres.).

8. *Ibid.*

9. "From Mrs. Lee Johnson, Weldon, N.C.," Everett Corres., typescript (c. 1927).

10. This work was similar to the work of female benevolent societies in the North before the Civil War. See Keith Melder, "Ladies Bountiful: Organized Woman's Benevolence in Early Nineteenth Century America," *New York History* 48 (July 1967): 231-54.

11. Carrie Dosher to Everett, June 23, 1927, Everett Corres.; *Report of the Thirty-fifth Annual Meeting of the Woman's Foreign Missionary Society and the Twenty-second Annual Meeting of the Woman's Home Mission Society, North Carolina Conference, M. E. Church, South* (hereafter cited as *Report of WMS NCC*, with date), 1913, p. 75; 1919, p. 35; 1922, pp. 35-36; 1924, p. 33; 1926, pp. 33-34; *North Carolina Christian Advocate* (March 4, 1915): 8; *Fourteenth Annual Meeting of the Woman's Missionary Society,*

Western North Carolina Conference, M. E. Church, South (hereafter cited as *Report of WMS WNCC*, with date), 1926, p. 36; 1930, p. 61.

12. Ninth Annual Report of the Woman's Home Mission Society of the Western North Carolina Conference (hereafter cited as *Report of WHMS WNCC*, with date), 1910, pp. 61-63; 1911, pp. 49-52; *Report of WMS NCC*, 1913, pp. 61-63.

13. Discussion of the activities of North Carolina Methodist women concerns the conference societies, for the most part. Because of the scarcity of records for individual local auxiliaries, it is difficult to determine the degree to which the rank and file supported the programs implemented by their leaders. The sources used do not reveal policymaking procedures within the organization. Did leaders initiate policies in response to what they perceived to be pressing social needs? Or did they act in response to the ideas of members about what the role of the society should be? Unfortunately these questions must remain unanswered pending further research.

14. See Scott, *Southern Lady*, pp. 52-56.

15. *North Carolina Christian Advocate* (April 14, 1897): 7; *Report of WMS WNCC*, 1913, p. 36.

16. *North Carolina Christian Advocate* (January 20, 1910): 11.

17. *Report of WMS NCC*, 1915, p. 42.

18. *Report of WMS NCC*, 1916, p. 40; similar resolutions were adopted in 1917 and 1918. For 1919, see *North Carolina Christian Advocate* (April 3, 1919): 8.

19. *Report of WMS WNCC*, 1913, p. 67; *Report of WMS NCC*, 1923, p. 44.

20. Donald Jay Whitener, *Prohibition in North Carolina 1715-1945* (Chapel Hill: University of North Carolina Press, 1945), p. 104; Emily Newby Correll, "Woman's Work for Woman: The Methodist and Baptist Woman's Missionary Societies in North Carolina, 1878-1930" (M.A. thesis, University of North Carolina, 1977), p. 24; Forrest Dearborn Hedden, "The Attitude of the North Carolina Conference of the Methodist Episcopal Church, South, Toward the Liquor Traffic in North Carolina 1872-1935" (B.D. thesis, Duke University, 1936), p. 89.

21. For quotation, see *Report of WMS NCC*, 1916, p. 41. See also *Report of WMS NCC*, 1915, p. 42; 1919, pp. 40-41; 1921, p. 47; 1923, p. 44; 1925, p. 41; *Report of WNCC*, 1926, p. 60; 1928, pp. 16-17; 1930, p. 35; 1931, p. 61.

22. Sallie Southall Cotten, "A National Training School for Women," *North Carolina Christian Advocate* (April 14, 1897): 2; see also *Report of WMS NCC*, 1927, in which the conference society vice-president called motherhood "the crowning honor of womanhood"; Anne L. Kuhn, *The Mother's Role in Childhood Education: New England Concepts, 1830-1860* (New Haven: Yale University Press, 1947), *passim;* Ruth H. Bloch, "American Feminine Ideals in Transition: The Rise of the Moral Mother, 1785-1815," *Feminist Studies* 4 (1978): 101-26.

23. *Report of WMS WNCC*, 1913, p. 40; 1927, pp. 37, 71; 1928, pp. 37-38; 1929, pp. 40-41; 1930, p. 61; 1931, pp. 60-61; *Report of WMS NCC*, 1913, p. 76; 1918, p. 46; 1923, p. 44; 1924, p. 33; 1926, pp. 33-34; 1927, pp. 37-38; 1928, p. 38; 1930, pp. 54, 62; 1931, p. 62. *North Carolina Christian Advocate* (March 11, 1915): 8.

24. *Report of WMS NCC*, 1913, p. 76; 1916, pp. 20, 40; 1917, p. 33; 1918, p. 46; 1924, p. 33; 1927, pp. 37, 71; 1929, p. 70; 1930, pp. 54, 73-74; 1931, p. 61; *Report of WMS WNCC*, 1913, p. 40; 1928, p. 72; 1929, p. 41; 1930, p. 31; *North Carolina Christian Advocate* (April 3, 1919): 8; (June 7, 1917): 8-9.

25. For quotations, see *Report of WMS WNCC*, 1926, p. 35; *Report of WMS*

NCC, 1926, p. 34. See also *Report of WMS WNCC,* 1929, p. 41; 1931, p. 61; *Report of WMS NCC,* 1913, p. 76; 1917, p. 33; 1918, p. 46; 1924, p. 33; 1925, pp. 40-41; 1930, p. 73; *North Carolina Christian Advocate* (March 11, 1915): 8; (April 3, 1919): 8.

26. *Report of WMS WNCC,* 1926, p. 35; 1927, p. 38; *Report of WMS NCC,* 1926, p. 34.

27. *Report of WMS WNCC,* 1913, p. 36.

28. *Report of WMS NCC,* 1916, p. 30; 1917, p. 33; 1918, p. 38; 1923, p. 44; 1924, p. 39; 1927, p. 37; 1928, p. 38; 1929, p. 70; 1931, p. 78; *Report of WMS WNCC,* 1926, p. 60; 1927, p. 71; 1929, p. 40; 1930, pp. 30-31, 60; 1931, p. 62; *North Carolina Christian Advocate* (May 20, 1915): 8.

29. *Report of WMS NCC,* 1923, pp. 35-36; *Report of WMS WNCC,* 1927, p. 38. Most North Carolina blacks lived in the eastern part of the state, within the jurisdiction of the North Carolina Conference.

30. *Report of WMS NCC,* 1924, p. 29.

31. For membership, see Sallie Southall Cotten, *History of the North Carolina Federation of Women's Clubs, 1901–1925* (Raleigh, N.C.: Edwards & Broughton, 1925), p. 196. That same year the woman's missionary societies of both North Carolina conferences reported a total of 15,290 members, see *Fifteenth Annual Report of the Woman's Missionary Council of the Methodist Episcopal Church, South,* 1924-1925, p. 129.

32. Cotten, *History of Women's Clubs,* pp. 1-8.

33. Unfortunately, as with Methodist records, NCFWC materials do not reveal policymaking procedures. It is impossible to determine to what extent NCFWC programs were developed in response to grass-roots pressure or reflected the views of federation officers.

34. Cotten, *History of Women's Clubs,* p. 39; North Carolina Federation of Women's Clubs, *Yearbook,* 1906, p. 18; 1909-1910, pp. 23-24; 1913-1914, p. 35; 1914-1915, pp. 31-32, 35; 1915-1916, p. 69; 1921-1922, p. 58; 1922-1923, p. 70; 1923-1924, p. 75; 1925-1926, p. 61; 1927-1928, p. 72.

35. Cotten, *History of Women's Clubs,* p. 43; *Yearbook,* 1909-1910, p. 28; 1911-1912, p. 44.

36. *Yearbook,* 1918-1919, p. 84; 1919-1920, pp. 63-64.

37. *Ibid.,* 1913-1914, p. 56; 1917-1918, p. 37; 1919-1920, p. 63; Cotten, *History of Women's Clubs,* pp. 156-57.

38. *Yearbook,* 1903, p. 7; 1906, p. 11; 1913-1914, p. 48; 1915-1916, p. 69; 1922-1923, p. 107; 1923-1924, pp. 75, 131; 1925-1926, p. 77; 1927-1928, p. 99; clippings and pamphlets, Nell Battle Lewis Papers, box 30, North Carolina Division of Archives and History, Raleigh, N. C.

39. *Yearbook,* 1929-1930, p. 91.

40. *Ibid.,* 1902, p. 9; 1905, p. 17; 1906, pp. 11, 28.

41. Cotten, *History of Women's Clubs,* pp. 22, 26. Clubwomen hoped their scholarship to Oxford University would offer American women opportunities similar to those afforded men by the Cecil Rhodes scholarship. Unlike the Rhodes scholarship, however, the clubwomen's program was open only to U.S. citizens.

42. *Yearbook,* 1911-1912, pp. 47-48; 1913-1914, pp. 46-47; 1923-1924, p. 74; 1925-1926, p. 75; Cotten, *History of Women's Clubs,* p. 62.

43. *Yearbook,* 1903, pp. 13-14; 1905, pp. 12, 14, 17; 1913-1914, p. 39; 1914-1915, p. 31; 1920-1921, p. 60; 1921-1922, p. 60; 1922-1923, p. 73; 1927-1928, pp. 73-74.

44. *Ibid.,* 1912-1913, p. 42; 1918-1919, pp. 44-45; 1920-1921, p. 50; Cotten, *History of Women's Clubs,* p. 72.

45. Fairbrother, "About the Women's Clubs of North Carolina," clipping [1910], Sallie Southall Cotten Papers (hereafter cited as Cotten Papers), vol. 3, Southern Historical Collection, University of North Carolina, Chapel Hill.

46. Diary of Sallie Southall Cotten, May 5, 1912, North Carolina Collection, University of North Carolina, Chapel Hill.

47. Clipping, *Wilmington Morning Star*, May 14, 1911, Cotten Papers, vol. 3. Cotten, *History of Women's Clubs,* pp. 50, 58, 61-62, 64, 72. NCFWC *Yearbook*, 1918-1919, pp. 37, 44-45.

48. Virginia Shadron, "The Laity Rights Movement, 1906–1918: Woman's Suffrage in the Methodist Episcopal Church, South," in *Women in New Worlds*, vol. 1, ed. Thomas and Keller (Nashville: Abingdon, 1981).

49. "Aycock Memorial as Women's Clubs Would Arrange It," clipping (n.d.), Cotten Papers, vol. 3.

50. "Mrs. Daniels Says City Opens Gates and Hearts to Visitors," clipping, May 7, 1924, Cotten Papers, vol. 10.

51. *North Carolina Christian Advocate* (October 24, 1918): 8.

CHAPTER 12. Civil Rights, 1920–1970

1. Lovick Winter, "The Rev. W. A. Parks," *Year Book and Minutes . . . of the North Georgia Conference, M. E. Church, South*, 1910, pp. 73-76; Atlanta *Journal*, December 3, 1929, p. 2; Atlanta *Constitution*, December 3, 1929, p. 28; death certificate of Mrs. Johnson (copy in author's possession).

2. Atlanta *Constitution*, June 1, 1924, p. 2-E; Carolyn Burgess to Arnold Shankman, October 9, 1980 (Mrs. Burgess is alumni director at LaGrange College).

3. Mrs. Wallace Rogers, "A Tribute to Mrs. Johnson," *Missionary Voice* 20 (February 1930): 64; *Missionary Yearbook of the Methodist Episcopal Church, South*, 1930, ed. Elmer T. Clark (Nashville: Board of Missions, 1930), p. 177.

4. "Memorial on Mrs. Johnson," in *20th Annual Report of the Woman's Missionary Council of the Methodist Episcopal Church, South*, 1929-30, ed. Mrs. Fitzgerald Parker (Nashville: Methodist Publishing Company, 1931), p. 203.

5. Mrs. Elijah Brown, "Mrs. Johnson—An Appreciation," Atlanta *Constitution*, June 1, 1924; *Annual Report of the Woman's Home Missionary Society, North Georgia Conference*, 1899, p. 2; 1901, p. 3; 1903, p. 2; Mabel K. Howell, *Women and the Kingdom* (Nashville: Cokesbury Press, 1928), pp. 58, 80, 82, 84, 230-31.

6. Alva Maxwell, "Mrs. Luke Johnson," (Macon and Atlanta) *Wesleyan Christian Advocate* (December 20, 1929); W. A. Shelton, "Mrs. Luke Johnson," *Missionary Voice* 20 (February 1930): 63.

7. Robert Sledge, *Hands on the Ark: The Struggle for Change in the Methodist Episcopal Church, South, 1914-1939* (Lake Junaluska, N.C.: The United Methodist Church, Commission on Archives and History, 1975), pp. 44-45; Alfred Pierce, *A History of Methodism in Georgia* (Atlanta: North Georgia Conference, 1956), p. 184; Noreen Dunn Tatum, *A Crown of Service* (Nashville: Board of Missions, Woman's Division of Christian Service, 1960), p. 40.

8. Wilma Dykeman and James Stokeley, *Seeds of Southern Change* (Chicago:

The University of Chicago Press, 1962), p. 96; Jacquelyn Dowd Hall, *Revolt Against Chivalry: Jessie Daniel Ames and the Women's Campaign Against Lynching* (New York: Columbia University Press, 1979), pp. 62, 87; Ann Ellis, "The Commission on Interracial Cooperation" (Ph.D. diss., Georgia State University, 1975), p. 24; "The Background," essay, 1931, Commission on Interracial Cooperation (hereafter cited as CIC) Papers, box 89, Trevor Arnett Library, Atlanta University. Citations to this collection will indicate either box number or series, whichever makes the documents easier to locate.

9. Origins of CIC, memorandum, undated, Neighborhood Union Papers (hereafter cited as NU Papers), box 6, Atlanta University; Hall, *Revolt,* pp. 86-87; Edward F. Burrows, "The Commission on Interracial Cooperation" (Ph.D. diss., University of Wisconsin, 1954), p. 58.

10. Carrie Johnson, "Report of the Commission on Race Relations, 1921," NU Papers, box 6; Minutes, CIC, November 17, 1920, CIC Papers, box 89.

11. "Background"; se also Hall, *Revolt,* p. 89; Ellis, "CIC," pp. 25-26.

12. Burrows, "CIC," p. 60; Ellis, "CIC," p. 26; report, Mrs. Johnson, in *Eleventh Annual Report of the Woman's Missionary Council,* 1920-21, pp. 152-55.

13. "Background"; Hall, *Revolt,* p. 89; Johnson to Mrs. Z. I. Fitzpatrick, September 1, 1920, CIC Papers, box 76.

14. Haskin to Lugenia Hope, June 18, 1920, and July 3, 1920, NU Papers, box 6; see also corres., CIC Papers, boxes 73, 76, and 89.

15. Dykeman and Stokeley, *Seeds,* p. 93; Memphis Conference, memorandum, undated, CIC Papers, box 76; Hall, *Revolt,* pp. 90-94.

16. Brown, "Address at Memphis," *The Christian Work* 10 (August 5, 1922): 165-66; report, Mrs. J. W. Perry, July 21, 1922, CIC Papers, box 76; Haskin to Jessie Daniel Ames, July 28, 1930, CIC Papers, box 76.

17. Robert Eleazar, *Southern Women and the South's Race Problem* (Atlanta: CIC, 1929), p. 2.

18. Hall, *Revolt,* p. 98; CIC Minutes, November 17, 1920; Washington to Lugenia Hope, November 15, 1920, NU Papers, box 6.

19. Minutes, Continuation Committee, November 16, 1920, CIC Papers, box 76; report, Mrs. Johnson, April 29, 1925, NU Papers, box 6.

20. Mrs. C. S. Wilcox to Johnson, November 11, 1920, CIC Papers, box 76.

21. Ellis, "CIC," pp. 29-32; Hall, *Revolt,* pp. 95-96. Johnson to Beverly Munford, August 11, 1920; Johnson to Will Alexander, December 11, 1920, CIC Papers, box 76.

22. Hope to Charlotte Brown, February 12, 1921; Hope to Mrs. Archibald Davis, March 1, 1921; Johnson to Hope, May 11, 1921; Hope to Johnson, June 24, 1921, NU Papers, box 6. *Southern Negro Women and Race Cooperation* ([Atlanta]: Southeastern Federation of Negro Women's Clubs, 1921), pamphlet, *passim.*

23. Henry Warnock, "Moderate Racial Thought and Attitudes of Southern Baptists and Methodists" (Ph.D. diss., Northwestern University, 1963), p. 48.

24. Minutes, CIC, July 19-21, 1922, CIC Papers, box 99; Johnson to Hope, September 16, 1921, NU Papers, box 6; news releases, CIC Papers, box 96; Ruth Powell, "History of the Southern Commission on Interracial Cooperation" (M.A. thesis, University of South Carolina, 1935), pp. 109-10; R. B. Eleazar, *An Adventure in Good Will* (Atlanta: CIC, 1925); Virginia Shadron, "Out of Our Homes" (M.A. thesis, Emory University, 1976), p. 42; Elizabeth McGregor, "A Study of the Press Service of the

Commission on Interracial Cooperation" (M.A. thesis, Scarritt College, 1930), p. 14; *Bulletin of Missionary News of WMC*, July 20, 1923; Ellis, "CIC," pp. 96-98.

25. Mrs. Luke Johnson, "The Race Problem" (Address to the international convention of the Disciples of Christ, Winona Lake, Indiana, August 30, 1922), CIC Papers.

26. For Scarritt, see Virginia Lieson Brereton, "Preparing Women for the Lord's Work: The Story of Three Methodist Training Schools, 1880-1940," in *Women in New Worlds,* vol. 1, ed. Hilah F. Thomas and Rosemary Skinner Keller (Nashville: Abingdon, 1981).

27. See Alandus C. Johnson, "The Growth of Paine College: A Successful Interracial Venture, 1903–46" (Ph.D. diss., University of Georgia, 1970).

28. Howell, *Women,* p. 59; Tatum, *Crown,* p. 24; Atlanta *Constitution,* April 19, 1925; Report, Mrs. Johnson, August 1, 1923, CIC Papers, box 89; Hall, *Revolt,* p. 102; Clark, *1930 Yearbook,* pp. 178-79.

29. Minutes, CIC, March 29, 1921, CIC Papers, box 89; Washington to Lugenia Hope, February 13, 1924, NU Papers, box 6; "Report on the Informal Conference of State Leaders," February 18-20, 1924, NU Papers, box 6; Hall, *Revolt,* p. 109.

30. Ames, then a CIC fieldworker for the Southwest, alleged that Mrs. Johnson resigned because of jealousy at a meeting in 1927 (sic) at which she (Ames) had given a stirring speech. "Mrs. Johnson was very indignant because I had been the star for a minute or two. So she went down to the office and resigned" (Ames, "Reminiscences of Jessie Daniel Ames," ed. Jacquelyn Hall, *New South* 27 [Spring 1972]: 34-35). The writer can find no verification that this incident ever took place.

31. Johnson to Will Alexander, April 24, 1925; Alexander to Johnson, April 27, 1925; M. Ashby Jones to Johnson, April 29, 1925; Jones to Lugenia Hope, May 2, 1925; Jones to Johnson, May 7, 1925, NU Papers, box 6.

32. Thelma Stevens, *Legacy for the Future: The History of Christian Social Relations in the Woman's Division of Christian Service, 1940–1968* (New York: Women's Division, Board of Global Ministries, The United Methodist Church, 1978) offers corroboration. In noting the problem of funding the fledgling Department of Christian Social Relations and Local Church Activities of the newly merged Woman's Division of the Board of Missions (created as part of church reunification in 1939), Stevens wrote:
   "To develop a budget for a department not fully recognized as part of *'missions'* took time and tension and tough negotiations. . . . For the first ten years . . . and to a degree even in the decade of the Fifties . . . programs of any experimental . . . type could never be budgeted in appropriations lest 'missions' be cut. The 'program' money came from some special fund. For example, in 1943 the former Woman's Missionary Council in its transfer of funds to the Woman's Division designated to the department . . . $5,000 plus interest from the Carrie Parks Johnson Endowment Fund . . . for work with rural Negro women in leadership development" (pp. 21-22).

33. M. Ashby Jones, memorandum, undated, CIC Papers, box 76. McCrorey to Hope, July 6, 1931; Merritt to Hope, March 4, 1930, NU Papers, box 6; Jennie Moton, "Mrs. Luke Johnson," *Missionary Voice* 20 (February 1930): 64, 79, 84.

34. Minutes, CIC, November 20-28, 1928, CIC Papers, series 17-B-1.

35. Jacquelyn Hall, "Jessie Daniel Ames," in *Notable American Women: The*

Modern Period, ed. Barbara Sicherman and Carol Hurd Green (Cambridge: Harvard University Press, 1980), pp. 16-18.

36. Hall, *Revolt,* pp. 1-14.
37. Ames to Una Roberts, August 27, 1940, CIC Papers, series 17-A-3; Hall, *Revolt,* p. 27.
38. Ellis, "CIC," p. 60; Hall, *Revolt,* pp. 50-54, 104, 110, 114, 116; Ames, "Reminiscences," pp. 32-35; Dallas *Morning News,* March 21-22, 1922.
39. Report given at Tuskegee, April 7-8, 1926, CIC Papers, box 36; for quotation, see R. B. Eleazar, "Report of the 1925 CIC Annual Meeting," CIC Papers, box 96. Ames to Johnson, quoted in Morton Sosna, *In Search of the Silent South* (New York: Columbia University Press, 1977), p. 30.
40. Dykeman and Stokeley, *Seeds,* pp. 115-17; Hall, *Revolt,* p. 24, 124; Ames, "Reminiscences," pp. 35-37.
41. Marion Wright, interviewed by author March 11, 1976. For quotation, Alice Spearman Wright, interviewed April 1, 1977.
42. Hall, *Revolt,* p. 29; Ames to Una Lawrence, August 27, 1940.
43. Ellis, "CIC," pp. 69, 83; *Southern Leaders Impeach Judge Lynch* (Atlanta: CIC, 1932), pp. 2-4.
44. Hall, *Revolt,* pp. 130, 161-62; Ames, "Reminiscences," p. 35.
45. Julius Dudley, "A History of the Association of Southern Women for the Prevention of Lynching," (Ph.D. diss., University of Cincinnati, 1979) (hereafter cited as "History of ASWPL"), pp. 34-35; Hall, *Revolt,* p. 127.
46. Jessie Daniel Ames, *Beginning of the Movement* (Atlanta: CIC, 1932); Dykeman and Stokeley, *Seeds,* p. 143; Ames to Dear Friend, October 1, 1930, NU Papers, box 6; Burrows, "CIC," pp. 225-26.
47. Jacquelyn Dowd Hall, "A Truly Subversive Affair," in *Women of America, A History,* ed. Carol Ruth Berkin and Mary Beth Norton (Boston: Houghton Mifflin, 1979), p. 364.
48. Ellis, "CIC," p. 83; Henry Barber, "The Association of Southern Women for the Prevention of Lynching" (M.A. thesis, University of Georgia, 1967), *passim;* Kathleen Miller, "The Ladies and the Lynchers," *Southern Studies* 17 (Fall 1978): 225-27.
49. Atlanta *Constitution,* January 15, 1931; Hall, *Revolt,* pp. 171-72; Ames to Monroe Work, July 21, 1936, Association of Southern Women for the Prevention of Lynching Papers (hereafter cited as ASWPL Papers), box 13, Atlanta University; Ames to Mildred Hewes, September 21, 1936, CIC Papers, series 17-B-3.
50. Hall, *Revolt,* p. 162; Dudley, "History of ASWPL," pp. 65-66.
51. *The Interracial Front* (Atlanta: CIC, 1933), pamphlet, pp. 10-11.
52. Burrows, "CIC," pp. 229-30; Hall, *Revolt,* p. 179; Ellis, "CIC," p. 84; Dudley, "History of ASWPL," pp. 47-48, 67-68.
53. Hall, *Revolt,* pp. 176, 182-85, 241-42. See also Ellis, "CIC," p. 84; Dudley, "History of ASWPL," pp. 64, 175-78, 185-90.
54. Hall, *Revolt,* pp. 173, 219-20, 227; Ames, "Report on Women's Work for 1933," CIC Papers, series 17-B-1; Burrows, "CIC," pp. 230-32; Ames, *Free Schools for All Alike* (Atlanta: CIC, [1936]); Ellis, "CIC," p. 84; Robert Zangrando, *The NAACP Crusade Against Lynching* (Philadelphia: Temple University Press, 1980), p. 103.
55. Ellis, "CIC," p. 84; Hall, *Revolt,* pp. 219-20, 225, 236.
56. Ames, *Free Schools, passim;* Sosna, *Silent South,* p. 34n; Dykeman and Stokeley, *Seeds,* p. 115; Ames, *Towards Lynchless America* (Atlanta: Association of Southern Women for the Prevention of Lynching, 1940); Burrows, "CIC," p. 223.

57. Dudley, "History of ASWPL," p. 190; Ellis, "CIC," pp. 85, 89-91.
58. Dudley, "History of ASWPL," p. 236; Dykeman and Stokeley, *Seeds,* p. 149.
59. Hall, *Revolt,* pp. 182, 197, 250; Miller, "Ladies," pp. 232, 237.
60. Walter White to Julian Harris, January 12, 1934; Harris to White, January 20, 1934, Harris Papers, box 16, Emory University; Dudley, "History of ASWPL," pp. 3, 93-96; Zangrando, *NAACP Crusade,* p. 149; Virginius Dabney, *Below the Potomac* (New York: Appleton Century, 1942), p. 188; Atlanta *Constitution,* November 6, 1934; Ames, "Reminiscences," p. 39.
61. Dudley, "History of ASWPL," pp. 127-28.
62. Ames to Porter, May 9, 1935, CIC Papers, series 7-B-7a; Dudley, "History of ASWPL," pp. 128-32.
63. Ellis, "CIC," p. 90; Dudley, "History of ASWPL," p. 353; Hall, *Revolt,* pp. 238-47; Mrs. Atwood Martin to Katherine Gardner, February 12, 1940, ASWPL Papers, box 14.
64. In 1935, the ASWPL came close to endorsing the Costigan-Wagner Bill, and Mrs. Ames was forced to admit that debate over the bill did some good since it called public attention to the crime of lynching. Zangrando, *NAACP Crusade,* pp. 105, 126; Hall, *Revolt,* pp. 239-45; Dudley, "History of ASWPL," p. 124.
65. Zangrando, *NAACP Crusade,* pp. 105, 157; Dudley, "History of ASWPL," pp. 134-41.
66. Ames to Mary Waring, August 23, 1940, CIC Papers, series 17-B-3. On Ames and blacks, see Ames to Mrs. Frederick Paist, December 20, 1933, January 24, 1934; Ames to Rackham Holt, July 13, 1943, CIC Papers, box 14.
67. Barber, "ASWPL," *passim;* Dykeman and Stokeley, *Seeds,* p. 152; Sosna, *Silent South,* p. 30.
68. Ames, "Reminiscences," p. 40; Sosna, *Silent South,* pp. 116-19; Ellis, "CIC," pp. 53-58, 342-43, 354-56; Burrows, "CIC," p. 278.
69. Ellis, "CIC," p. 356; Hall, *Revolt,* pp. 259-60; Ames to Mrs. R. Moton, March 18, 1935, CIC Papers, series 17-B-7a.
70. Ames to Mrs. Atwood Martin, Ames to Thelma Stevens, February 11, 1944, CIC Papers, series 17-B-3; Atlanta *Constitution,* February 23, 1972; Hall, *Revolt,* pp. 255-61.
71. Arnold Shankman, "Dorothy Tilly" (hereafter cited as "Tilly"), in *Notable American Women,* ed. Sicherman and Green, p. 691.
72. Arnold Shankman, "Dorothy Tilly, Civil Rights and the Methodist Church" (hereafter cited as "Methodist"), *Methodist History* 18 (January 1980): 96-97.
73. Shankman, "Tilly," pp. 691-92.
74. Shankman, "Methodist," p. 98.
75. *Ibid.;* Dudley, "History of ASWPL," pp. 56-57, 101; Hall, *Revolt,* pp. 217, 321.
76. Marion Wright and Alice Wright, interviewed by author, see note 38; Ruth Howard, interviewed by author August 15, 1975; Ames to Mrs. J. E. Phillips, July 17, 1935, CIC Papers, series 17-B-3; Lynching in Decatur, memorandum, January 16, 1942, ASWPL Papers, box 14.
77. Shankman, "Tilly," p. 692; Dudley, "History of ASWPL," pp. 69-70.
78. Shankman, "Tilly," p. 692.
79. Shankman, "Methodist," p. 103.
80. *Ibid.,* p. 104.
81. Shankman, "Tilly," p. 692.

NOTES FOR PAGES 230-235

82. Tilly, *Christan Conscience and the Supreme Court Decision on Segregated Schools* (Atlanta: Southern Regional Council, [1954]), *passim;* William Allred, "The Southern Regional Council" (M.A. thesis, Emory University, 1966), p. 121; Southern Regional Council Minutes, January 26, 1959, Josephine Wilkins Papers, box 2, Emory University.
83. Shankman, "Methodist," pp. 105-107.
84. Tilly to Dorothy Thompson, July 24, 1959; Tilly to Bill Cleghorn, December 5, 1958; Tilly to Charles Turck, September 11, 1958; Tilly to Dear Friends in Alabama, December 17, 1958, Southern Regional Council Papers (not catalogued at this time), Atlanta University.
85. Margaret Long, "Mrs. Dorothy Tilly, a Memoir," *New South* 25 (Spring 1970): 46-48; Shankman, "Tilly," p. 692.

Note cards for the research represented in this paper are deposited in the Winthrop College Archives, Rock Hill, South Carolina, and are available for use.

CHAPTER 13. The Case of Ann Hasseltine Judson

1. Hannah Chaplin Conant, *The Earnest Man, or the Character and Labors of Adoniram Judson* (Boston: Phillips, Sampson & Co., 1856), p. 470.
2. Information on this series was supplied to me by Hilah F. Thomas, then project coordinator of the Women's History Project of the General Commission on Archives and History, The United Methodist Church. Several numbers from this series are in the library of the General Commission at Madison, N. J., but not that on Adoniram Judson.
3. Traditionally, the term *evangelical* is used to signify specific groups of Protestants, especially Methodists and Baptists, who made proselytizing, conversion, and the revival basic procedural tenets. I use the uncapitalized designation *evangelical* here in a larger context, to include those Congregationalist-Presbyterians, and even Episcopalians, who, although repudiating the "excesses" of the revival, adopted the notion of a "mission for life." Here the term denotes those values and forms associated with those Protestant denominations that laid special stress on the gospel as a basis for their belief and social practice. The religious and social imperative to create a Protestant "empire" under the cultural jurisdiction of the evangelical churches has been described by Martin Marty in *The Righteous Empire* (New York: Dial Press, 1970). My assumptions in this essay are that despite the fact that 50 percent of the antebellum population was simply "unchurched," evangelicals were the largest and most influential group within American Protestantism, and they articulated a set of values that they were able to transmit to successive generations.
4. Pamela S. Vining, *Christian Herald,* clipping (n.d.), Maria Mansfield Papers; no. 601, dept. of Manuscripts and University Archives, Olin Library, Cornell University.
5. Knowles, *Memoir of Mrs. Ann H. Judson, Late Missionary to Burmah; with an account of the American Baptist mission to that empire. . . .,* rev. (Philadelphia: American Sunday School Union, 1830). Data on editions are from *The National Union Catalog, Pre-1956 Imprints* (London: Mansell Information/Publishing Limited, 1973) (hereafter cited as Mansell), vol. 300, pp. 583-84; Edward Caryl Starr, ed., *A Baptist Bibliography, being a*

394

register of printed material by and about Baptists . . ., 25 vols. (Philadelphia: Judson Press, 1947-76) (hereafter cited as Starr), vol. 12, pp. 203-205.

6. Lydia Maria Child, *Good Wives* (Boston: Carter, Hendee & Co., 1833), p. 246.

7. Maternal Association of Jericho, Vermont (First Congregational Church), records, Congregational Library, Boston.

8. Child, *Good Wives;* later editions appeared under the titles *Biographies of Good Wives; Celebrated Women, or Biographies of Good Wives; Married Women: Biographies of Good Wives.* Hale, *Woman's Record, or Sketches of All Distinguished Women, from "the beginning" till A.D. 1850,* 2nd ed. rev. (New York: Harper & Brothers, 1853; 1855), p. 369.

9. Samuel Lorenzo Knapp, *Female Biography, Containing Notices of Distinguished Women, in different nations and ages* (New York: J. Carpenter, 1834), p. 279.

10. Arabella M. (Stuart) Willson, *The Lives of Mrs. Ann H. Judson and Mrs. Sarah B. Judson, with a biographical sketch of Mrs. Emily C. Judson, Missionaries to Burmah* (Auburn, N.Y.: Miller, Orton & Mulligan, 1854 [c. 1851]), p. iv. Information on reprinting and sales are from Mansell, vol. 666 (1980), pp. 202-203; Starr, vol. 12, pp. 206-207.

11. Eddy, *Heroines of the Missionary Enterprise, or Sketches of Prominent Female Missionaries* (Boston: Ticknor, Reed & Fields, 1850); *Daughters of the Cross: or, Woman's Mission* (New York: Dayton & Wentworth, 1855); *The Three Mrs. Judsons, and Other Daughters of the Cross* (Boston: n.p., 1859).

12. For the origins of the American foreign mission movement, see John A. Andrew, III, *Rebuilding the Christian Commonwealth: New England Congregationalists and Foreign Missions, 1800–1830* (Lexington: University Press of Kentucky, 1976); Joan Jacobs Brumberg, *Mission for Life: The Story of the Family of Adoniram Judson* (New York: Free Press, Macmillan Co., 1980); Clifton Jackson Phillips, *Protestant America and the Pagan World: The First Half Century of the American Board of Commissioners for Foreign Missions, 1810–60* (Cambridge, Mass.: East Asian Research Center, Harvard University Press, 1969); Oliver Wendell Elsbree, *The Rise of the Missionary Spirit in America, 1790–1815* (Williamsport, Pa.: O. W. Elsbree, 1928).

13. R. Pierce Beaver analyzed Protestant women's early involvement in the foreign mission movement in *American Protestant Women in World Mission: A History of the First Feminist Movement in North America,* 2nd ed. rev. of *All Loves Excelling* (Grand Rapids, Mich.: William B. Eerdmans Publishing Co., 1968, 1980), chs. 1-3. See also Mrs. L. H. Daggett, ed., *Historical Sketches of Woman's Missionary Societies in America and England* (Boston: Mrs. L. H. Daggett, 1879, 1883). Beaver saw early missionary wives as the keys to antebellum churchwomen's commitment to foreign missions: "Missionary wives exercised a role of ministry such as no laywoman or pastor's wife in America might dare to undertake. The women in the homeland identified themselves with the wives, who were vicariously serving for them" (pp. 47-48). See Joan Jacobs Brumberg, "Zenanas and Girlless Villages," *Journal of American History* 69/2 (September 1982): 347-71.

14. For the development of all Methodist missions and the original retardation of American Methodist work overseas, see Wade Crawford Barclay, *History of Methodist Missions,* 3 vols. (New York: Board of Missions & Church Extension of The Methodist Church, 1949-57), esp. vols. 1, 3.

15. Autonomous women's foreign mission groups began to emerge in 1868

with the Congregationalists' New England Woman's Foreign Missionary Society. In 1869, Methodist women created the Woman's Foreign Missionary Society of the Methodist Episcopal Church; a year later the Ladies Board of Missions was formed in the Presbyterian Church. In 1871, the Woman's Baptist Missionary Society was organized. The Episcopal group, Woman's Auxiliary to the Board of Missions, Protestant Episcopal Church, formed in 1872, was not autonomous.

16. *Heathen Woman's Friend* 20/1 (1890): 223.

17. *Massachusetts Baptist Missionary Magazine* (hereafter cited as *MBMM*) 3 (May 1813): 244-46.

18. Denominational publishing was not a new phenomenon. In the late eighteenth century, Methodists, Catholics, and Mennonites operated presses in the United States. See John William Tebbel, *A History of Book Publishing in the United States*, 3 vols. (New York: R. R. Bowker Co., 1972), vol. 1. By 1850 each of the major Protestant denominations had a charitable publication society: American Baptist Publication Society, Presbyterian Publication Society, and Methodist Book Concern. In the antebellum period, American Baptists could subscribe to the following periodicals, which generally included news of the Judsons: *London Baptist Magazine, American Baptist Magazine, The Latter Day Luminary, Christian Watchman, Columbian Star, The Christian Secretary, Religious Intelligencer, Western New York Baptist Missionary Magazine.*

19. *The Methodist Magazine* began publication in January 1818 at New York and appeared monthly until 1828; it was a quarterly from 1830 to 1884 and experienced changes of title, including *Methodist Review.* Between 1818 and 1830, it published nothing on the Judsons. *The Christian Advocate* (New York) began publication in 1826 but printed no word of the Judson mission until after 1830. The events at Ava and the news of Ann's death were reported elsewhere. *The Ladies Repository* started publication in 1841 and made no mention of the Judsons through 1852, when memorials began to pour forth at the time of Adoniram's death.

    The year 1845 is generally taken as the departure point for a new era of outreach, see Barclay, *Methodist Missions,* vol. 3, p. vi. It was put dramatically by W. Richey Hogg: "In 1844, except for a handful in Liberia, there were virtually no Methodists outside the continental United States who had sprung from American Methodist missions. Seventy-five years later, in 1919, there were approximately 800,000 who . . . had received the gospel through Methodism's agency" (Emory Stevens Bucke, ed., *The History of American Methodism,* 3 vols. [Nashville/New York: Abingdon Press, 1964], vol. 3, p. 128).

20. Barclay, *Methodist Missions,* notes Adoniram Judson among those Americans already in the foreign mission field who possibly were an inspiration to Nathan Bangs and the other Methodists who founded this society (vol. 1, p. 206, n.*).

21. Bucke, *American Methodism,* vol. 3, pp. 64-65.

22. Report of May 25, 1820, to the General Conference, cited in Barclay, *Methodist Missions,* vol. 1, p. 210.

23. An abortive overseas mission in South America was begun in 1835-36 but abandoned for lack of funds. The same financial crisis contributed to the recall of Jason Lee from his Oregon Indian Mission in 1843 (Bucke, *American Methodism,* vol. 3, p. 65).

24. Perhaps because "good" women's actions were supposedly tied to an admirable quality called *disinterest,* or perhaps because antebellum women

had almost no personal stake in ecclesiastical structures, women often were less sectarian than churchmen. This may explain why so many non-Baptists wrote more about the Judson women than about Adoniram. The patriarch still had power to evoke sectarian feelings; the women were simply outside or above denominational politics. For societies, see Beaver, *Protestant Women,* pp. 39-40; Barclay, *Methodist Missions,* vol. 1, pp. 41-42, 317-18.

25. "The Late Mrs. Judson" 2/3 (June 1846): 23; "Missionary Speech of the Rev. Dr. Judson" 2/7 (October 1846): 55; "Dr. Judson's Farewell" 2/9 (December 1846): 71. In his farewell, Adoniram Judson compared this departure to that of 1812, inevitably evoking echoes of Ann Hasseltine Judson. About Emily C. Judson, see 3/7 (October 1847): 48. By Mrs. Judson, see 3/12 (March 1848): 89; 4/2 (May 1848): 16. For Adoniram leaving Rangoon, 4/3 (June 1848): 24. From *Malcom's Travels,* 5/12 (March 1850): 89-90.

26. *MBMM* 4 (December 1814): 11.

27. Knowles, *Memoirs* (1830), pp. 91, 96.

28. *Ibid.,* p. 150.

29. Beaver, *Protestant Women,* contrasts the visibility of early American missionary wives with the relative obscurity of the British wives and mentions Ann as an influence, pp. 55-56.

30. Knowles, *Memoirs* (1830), p. 96.

31. *Ibid.,* p. 58.

32. August 23, 1812, from Calcutta, in Knowles, *Memoir . . . Including a history of the American Baptist mission in the Burman empire* (Boston: Lincoln & Edmands, 1829), p. 60.

33. A zenana is a living space in which women and young girls are segregated. A seraglio is the equivalent of a harem, a place in a Muslim household where wives and concubines are secluded. The degraded position of women abroad was a major concern of women's foreign missionary activities well into the twentieth century. A 1910 pamphlet by Mrs. Moses Smith, a Congregationalist, *Woman Under the Ethnic Religions* (Chicago: Women's Board of Missions of The Interior) reiterated the themes raised by Ann Judson. Smith's analysis mentioned child marriage, infanticide, suttee, consecrated prostitution, nautch and dancing girls, polygamy, divorce, female seclusion, purdah, and bound feet. Smith attributed "the cruel brutal degradation of women . . . not to race or environment or accident, but to a lack of Christianity" (p. 5).

34. John Alonzo Clark, ed., *The Christian Keepsake and Missionary Annual* (Philadelphia: W. Marshall & Co., 1838), p. 9.

35. Child, *History of Condition of Women; In Various Ages and Nations* (Boston: J. Allen & Co., 1835), p. 111.

36. Quoted in Isaac F. Shepard, ed., *The Christian Souvenir: An Offering for Christmas and the New Year* (Boston: H. B. Williams, 1843), pp. 81-83.

37. Ann Judson's visit may have been noticed by Methodist women at Boston, New York City, and Baltimore, since all these witnessed early Methodist women's auxiliaries, as did Philadelphia and numerous towns in New York state. But by 1822, only the Female Missionary Society of New York can be established to have existed, Barclay, *Methodist Missions,* vol. 1, p. 317; Beaver, *Protestant Women,* pp. 40-41.

38. See Barbara Welter's pioneering essay, "The Cult of True Womanhood, 1820–60," *American Quarterly* 18 (Summer 1966): 151-74; reprinted in

Welter, *Dimity Convictions: The American Woman in the Nineteenth Century* (Athens: Ohio University Press, 1976).

39. Religious feminism is further elaborated in Brumberg, *Mission for Life,* ch. 4.
40. Knowles, *Memoirs* (1830), p. 273.
41. *American Baptist Magazine* (hereafter cited as *ABM*) 5 (February 1825): 50; 5 (November 1825): 338.
42. *ABM* 6 (October 1826): 315.
43. Knowles, *Memoirs* (1830), p. 282.
44. *ABM* 7 (March 1827): 74.
45. Samuel Colgate to Mary Colgate, January 30, 1846, Colgate University Archives.
46. Beaver, *Protestant Women,* pp. 56-57.
47. Edward Porter, *Address at Bradford Academy, March 26, 1884* (Haverhill, Mass.: Mitchell & Hoyt, 1884), pp. 24-25.
48. William Hague, *The Life and Character of Adoniram Judson, Late Missionary to Burmah: A Commemorative Discourse delivered before the American Baptist Missionary Union, in Boston, May 15, 1851* (Boston: Gould & Lincoln, 1851), pp. 10-11.
49. Brumberg, *Mission for Life,* pp. 109-110.
50. Asahel Clark Kendrick, *The Life and Letters of Mrs. Emily C. Judson* (New York: Sheldon & Co., 1861), pp. 38-39.
51. See John W. Cawelti, *Adventure, Mystery and Romance: Formula Stories as Popular Culture* (Chicago: University of Chicago Press, 1976). Cawelti's "impact theory" posits a direct relationship between art and human behavior. He argues, I think reasonably, that all major story formulas of a particular culture require definition. The analysis need not be restricted to fiction but can include evangelical biography as well.

CHAPTER 14. Doing More Than They Intended

1. E.g., see Mary Claubaugh Wright, ed., *China in Revolution: The First Phase, 1900–1913* (New Haven: Yale University Press, 1968); Marilyn B. Young, ed., *Women in China Studies in Social Change and Feminism* (Ann Arbor: The University of Michigan Press, 1973); Margery Wolf and Roxane Witke, eds., *Women in Chinese Society* (Stanford, Calif.: Stanford University Press, 1975); Elisabeth Croll, *Feminism and Socialism in China* (New York: Schocken Books, 1978).
2. Wright, *China in Revolution,* pp. 33-34; Charlotte L. Beahan, "Mothers of Citizens: Feminism and Nationalism in the Late Ch'ing" (Paper delivered at 29th Annual Meeting of the Midwest Conference on Asian Affairs, University of Iowa, Iowa City, October 1980).
3. Anne Firor Scott, *The Southern Lady: From Pedestal to Politics, 1830–1930* (Chicago: University of Chicago Press, 1970), pp. 135-36.
4. *Fourth Annual Report of the Woman's Missionary Society of the Methodist Episcopal Church, South,* 1882 (hereafter cited as *Report of WMS MECS,* with date), p. 26.
5. Allen to Mrs. Cobb, March 21, 1881, *Woman's Missionary Advocate* (hereafter cited as *WMA*), 2/1 (July, 1881): 5.
6. For a discussion of imperialism as a force for change, see Arthur Schlesinger, Jr., "The Missionary Enterprise and Imperialism," in *The Missionary Enterprise in China and America,* ed. John K. Fairbank

(Cambridge: Harvard University Press, 1974), pp. 337-38. For comments on the intellectual/psychological impact of the West, see Marianne Bastid-Bruguiere, "Currents of Social Change," p. 590, in *The Cambridge History of China*, ed. John K. Fairbank and Kwang-Ching Liu, (New York: The University of Cambridge Press, 1980), vol. 2, pt. 2; also p. xviii.

7. Allen to Mrs. D. H. McGavock, January 21, 1882, Young J. Allen Memorabilia (hereafter cited as Allen Memorabilia), Woodruff Library for Advanced Studies, Emory University. At the same time, within the missionary community itself, there was disagreement over which approach to take—a strictly evangelical, with street-corner and chapel preaching coupled with home visits; or a more secular, through schools, translating, medical work, and journalism, in combination with preaching.

8. James Cannon, III, *The History of Southern Methodist Missions* (Nashville: Cokesbury Press, 1926), p. 101; Noreen Dunn Tatum, *A Crown of Service: A Story of Woman's Work in the Methodist Episcopal Church, South, from 1878–1940* (Nashville: Board of Missions, Woman's Division of Christian Service, 1960), p. 22.

9. *Report of WMS MECS*, 1879, pp. 47-48. Helen Barrett Montgomery, *Western Women in Eastern Lands* (New York: Macmillan Co., 1910), pp. 21-31. Since missionaries first arrived, they had seen the need for "unmarried females to reach and teach the women and children. Men were shut off from this ministry by the iron-bound bars of custom," claimed Dr. David Abeel in 1834. The missionaries also pointed out the request of Chinese women: "Are there no female men who can come to teach us?" Mabel K. Howell, *Women and the Kingdom* (Nashville: Cokesbury Press, 1928), pp. 21-22; Scott, *Southern Lady*, p. 137.

10. *Organization of the WMS MECS*, 1879, pamphlet, p. 5.

11. *Report of the WMS MECS*, 1886, pp. 16-17.

12. The society proposed that their newly arrived missionaries take a two- to three-year course of study, which, if followed, would have made them productive members in their fourth year in the field. Apparently few completed the course, see *Report of WMS MECS*, 1889, p. 3. In 1890 the annual report noted that "newly arrived missionaries spend time studying the language only to become ill and have to give up language study." Upon recovering, the missionaries began to teach "without facility in the language," *Report of WMS MECS*, 1890, pp. 17-18. It was required that those selected to be missionaries should possess the following qualities: good health, thorough intellectual training, financial and executive ability, power of adaptation to circumstances, experience in teaching, facility in acquiring languages, and an unusual ability for Christian work. They must also have been divinely called and be between the ages of 21 and 30. If accepted, they were to devote five years of service while unmarried, and should they withdraw for any reason other than health, they were to refund the "sum expended for . . . outfit and travel [ca. $630]" *Report of WMS MECS*, 1879.

13. *Report of WMS MECS*, 1896, p. 24.

14. Mrs. James W. Lambuth, in China since 1854; Mrs. Young J. Allen, since 1860 (but not active in "woman's work"); Mrs. Alice S. Parker, since 1877; and Mrs. Walter R. Lambuth, since 1877, *Report of WMS MECS*, 1879, p. 29.

15. *Journal of the General Conference of the Methodist Episcopal Church, South*, 1882, p. 149, italics added.

16. *Report of WMS MECS*, 1879, pp. 20, 23, 24, 29; Mrs. F. A. Butler, *History*

of the Woman's Foreign Missionary Society, Methodist Episcopal Church, South (Nashville: Publishing House of the Methodist Episcopal Church, South, 1904), p. 69; Tatum, *Crown of Service*, pp. 88, 95-96; *Report of WMS MECS*, 1893, pp. 25-26; 1894, p. 13.

17. *Report of WMS MECS*, 1879, p. 29; 1884, p. 14; 1885, p. 17.
18. *Report of WMS MECS*, 1890, p. 9; 1895, pp. 27, 28; 1896, p. 28.
19. *Report of WMS MECS*, 1890, p. 9; 1893, pp. 10, 25-26; 1894, p. 13; *Golden Jubilee Commemoration Volume of the Fiftieth Anniversary of the China Annual Conference of the Methodist Episcopal Church, South* (Shanghai: Methodist Episcopal Church, South, 1935), p. 49; Tatum, *Crown of Service*, p. 88; Howell, *Women and Kingdom*, p. 133.
20. *Report of WMS MECS*, 1883, p. 23.
21. Allen to McGavock, March 27, 1883; April 9, 1883, Allen Memorabilia; *WMA* 2/9 (March 1882): 3. *Report of WMS MECS*, 1891, p. 17; 1894, p. 14; 1895, p. 16; 1897, p. 17; Oswald Brown and Anna Muse Brown, *Life and Letters of Laura Askew Haygood* (Nashville/Dallas: Publishing House of the Methodist Episcopal Church, South, 1904), pp. 151-52, 155, 175, 411.
22. Tatum, *Crown of Service*, p. 93.
23. Mrs. Alice S. Parker, in *Report of WMS MECS*, 1885, pp. 17-18.
24. Brown, *Laura Haygood*, p. 411.
25. *Report of WMS MECS*, 1887, p. 8.
26. *WMA* 10/3 (September 1889): 2.
27. See *Reports of WMS MECS*, 1890s.
28. Evelyn Sakakida Rawski, *Education and Popular Literacy in Ch'ing China* (Ann Arbor: University of Michigan Press, 1979), pp. 24-53. See also Brown, *Laura Haygood*, pp. 151-52. For texts, see *Report of WMS MECS*, 1885, p. 12.
29. *Report of WMS MECS*, 1889, p. 14.
30. *Report of WMS MECS*, 1892, p. 9.
31. For quotation, see Mrs. Alice S. Parker to Mrs. D. H. McGavock, *WMA* 2/9 (March 1882): 5. See also *Report of WMS MECS*, 1888, p. 159; 1891, p. 22.
32. Mrs. James W. Lambuth to Mrs. D. H. McGavock, *WMA* 2/9 (March 1882): 4.
33. *Report of WMS MECS*, 1888, p. 34. See also *WMA* 11/3 (September 1890): 80; 11/4 (October 1890): 107; 11/6 (December 1890): 172; 18/10 (April 1898): 103; 19/3 (September 1898): 73, 76.
34. Allen to McGavock, *WMA* 1/5 (November 1881): 2; for Laura, see 9/1 (June 1888): 14.
35. *Report of WMS MECS*, 1894, p. 112.
36. *Report of WMS MECS*, 1879, pp. 23-24.
37. *Report of WMS MECS*, 1881, p. 17. For quotation, see *WMA* 10/4 (September 1890): 75.
38. For quotation, see Howell, *Women and Kingdom*, p. 198. *Golden Jubilee Volume*, p. 24.
39. Brown, *Laura Haygood*, p. 288. See also *WMA* 10/1 (July 1890): 3; 11/10 (April 1891): 300; 15/4 (October 1894): 105; 15/7 (January 1895): 205; 17/10 (April 1897): 301; *Report of WMS MECS*, 1891, p. 16.
40. *Report of WMS MECS*, 1895, p. 15; 1896, p. 13.
41. *Report of WMS MECS*, 1882, p. 5. See also *Report of WMS MECS*, 1880, p. 16; *WMA* 2/10 (April 1882): 2.
42. Sue Blake Crozier, letter of 1892, as cited in Mrs. I. G. John, *Missionary*

Cameos (Nashville: Publishing House of the Methodist Episcopal Church, South, 1899), p. 64.

43. For quotation, see *Report of WMS MECS,* 1890, p. 23. See also *Report of WMS MECS,* 1894, p. 22.

44. *Report of WMS MECS,* 1895, p. 32.

45. *Report of WMS MECS,* 1881, p. 21; *Report of WMS MECS,* 1888, p. 36.

46. *Report of WMS MECS,* 1890, p. 22. See also *Reports of WMS,* 1890s; *WMA,* 1890s.

47. *Report of WMS MECS,* 1891, p. 21, and John, *Missionary Cameos,* p. 70. The WMS was aware of the language issue and the 1891 report noted that the training program must provide "medical training to Chinese in Chinese" in order to "give a large increase to the working force of China." But as far as can be ascertained, a Chinese language curriculum never developed (*Report of WMS MECS,* 1891, p. 28). For data on the quality of the nurse training program, see *Report of WMS MECS,* 1894, p. 23. Dr. Mildred Philips served as WMS doctor 1888–1889 and 1890–1891; Dr. Anne Walter, 1893–1896; Dr. Margaret Polk, 1896–1910; Dr. Ethel Polk, 1910–1913; Dr. Hattie Love, 1913–1919, when the hospital closed (Tatum, *Crown of Service,* pp. 102-103). In the period 1915–1917 the Rockefeller Foundation sponsored the Chinese Medical Association in assessing the quality of hospitals in China. Because the foundation drew its criteria from the Johns Hopkins Medical School, which was research-oriented and also funded by the foundation, most hospitals in China could not meet the high standards and were forced to close. It is true that by this time the society's hospital suffered from poor outdated equipment and physical limitations; nevertheless, it did provide basic medical care. For accounts of the Rockefeller Foundation's impact, essentially negative because it was so elitist, see Mary Brown Bullock, *The American Transplant: The Rockefeller Foundation and Peking Union Medical College* (Berkeley: University of California Press, 1980); Peter Buck, *American Science and Modern China* (New York: Cambridge University Press, 1980), esp. pp. 48-64.

48. Tatum, *Crown of Service,* p. 103.

49. *Report of WMS MECS,* 1896, p. 31.

50. *WMA* 10/3 (September 1889): 2.

51. Schlesinger, "Missionary Enterprise," pp. 360-73, esp. 372.

52. *WMA* (September 1890): 78-79.

53. Cannon, *A History of Southern Methodist Missions,* p. 109; Howard L. Boorman, ed., *Biographical Dictionary of Republican China* (New York: Columbia University Press, 1971), vol. 3, pp. 137-53.

CHAPTER 15. Three Afro-American Women

1. This comment was made by L. G. Jordan, "The Responsibility of the American Negro for the Evangelization of Africa," in *The United Negro: His Problems and Progress,* ed. I. Garland Penn and J. W. E. Bowen (Atlanta: D. E. Luther Publishing Co., 1902), p. 310.

2. Wade Crawford Barclay, *History of Methodist Missions,* 3 vols. (New York: Board of Missions & Church Extension of The Methodist Church, 1949-1957), vol. 1, pp. 329, 332; I. G. John, *Handbook of Methodist Missions* (Nashville: Publishing House of the M. E. Church, South, 1893), pp. 96-97, 453; Privately Published, *The Negro in the History of Methodism* (Nashville: Privately published, 1954), p. 221; Emory Ross, *Out of Africa*

(New York: Friendship Press, 1936), p. 124; Willard E. Wight, ed., "Two Letters from Liberia," *Journal of Negro History* 44 (October 1959): 379.

3. Daniel A. Payne, *History of the A.M.E. Church* (Nashville: Publishing House of the A.M.E. Sunday School Union, 1891), p. 484; Charles Spencer Smith, *A History of the African Methodist Episcopal Church* (Philadelphia: A.M.E. Book Concern, 1922), p. 174; Lewellyn L. Berry, *A Century of Missions of the African Methodist Episcopal Church 1840-1940* (New York: Gutenberg Press, 1942), pp. 41, 44; Artishia Wilkerson Jordan, *The African Methodist Episcopal Church in Africa* (n.p., n.d.), pp. 13, 46; George A. Singleton, *The Romance of African Methodism, Study of the African Methodist Episcopal Church* (New York: Exposition Press, 1952), p. 68; Emory Stevens Bucke, ed., *The History of American Methodism*, 3 vols. (Nashville/New York: Abingdon Press, 1964), vol. 2, p. 553.

4. Berry, *Century of Missions*, pp. 91, 101, 103-104; Jordan, *AME Church in Africa*, pp. 147-49.

5. Singleton, *Romance of African Methodism*, p. 70; Bucke, *American Methodism*, vol. 2, p. 553.

6. Payne, *History of AME Church*, p. 485; Smith, *History of African ME Church*, p. 175; Jordan, *AME Church in Africa*, p. 47; Bucke, *American Methodism*, vol. 2, pp. 553-54; John, *Handbook*, p. 603.

7. Smith, *History of African ME Church*, p. 175; Berry, *Century of Missions*, pp. 71, 73; Jordan, *AME Church in Africa*, p. 34.

8. Smith, *History of African ME Church*, pp. 181-83; Berry, *Century of Missions*, pp. 73, 75-76; Jordan, *AME Church in Africa*, pp. 59-60; Bucke, *American Methodism*, vol. 2, p. 554.

9. Berry, *Century of Missions*, p. 88.

10. For quotation, see Amanda Berry Smith, *The Story of the Lord's Dealings with Mrs. Amanda Smith . . . An Autobiography* (Chicago: Meyer & Brothers, 1893), p. 96; also see pp. 17-25, 42, 57, 90; Marshall W. Taylor, *The Life, Travels and Helpers of Mrs. Amanda Smith, the Famous Negro Missionary Evangelist* (Cincinnati: Cranston & Stowe, 1887), pp. 13, 16-21, 23; Sylvia G. L. Dannett, *Profiles of Negro Womanhood* (Yonkers, N.Y.: Educational Heritage, 1964), vol. 1, pp. 146-47.

11. Smith, *Autobiography*, p. 217.

12. *Ibid.*, pp. 215-17, 219, 285, 300; Taylor, *Amanda Smith*, pp. 26-29, 35, 40; Dannett, *Profiles*, p. 147.

13. M. H. Cadbury, *The Life of Amanda Smith* (Birmingham, Ala.: Cornish Brothers, 1916), p. 71; Smith, *Autobiography*, pp. 331, 335, 338-39; Taylor, *Amanda Smith*, pp. 42-44, 46-48; Dannett, *Profiles*, p. 149.

14. Smith, *Autobiography*, pp. 378, 384, 389, 393, 437.

15. *Ibid.*, pp. 342, 453; Cadbury, *Amanda Smith*, p. 72.

16. Smith, *Autobiography*, p. 487.

17. *Ibid.*, pp. 486-87, 498, 502; Dannett, *Profiles*, p. 149; Cadbury, *Amanda Smith*, preface, pp. 77, 82; "Amanda Berry Smith," in *Notable American Women, 1607-1950*, ed. Edward T. James (Cambridge: Belknap Press, Harvard University Press, 1971), vol. 3, pp. 304-305.

18. Berry, *Century of Missions*, pp. 70-71; J. R. Frederick, "In Memoriam," *Voice of Missions* (October 1894): 4.

19. Frederick, "In Memoriam," p. 4; H. B. Parks, *Africa, The Problem of the New Century* (New York: n.p., 1899), pp. 56-57.

20. Emily Christmas Kinch, *West Africa, An Open Door* (Philadelphia: A.M.E. Book Concern, 1917), pp. 19, 30. I would like to thank Dr. Randall K. Burkett for a copy of this book.

21. *Ibid.;* Smith, *History of African ME Church,* pp. 171-72; Berry, *Century of Missions,* p. 139; Jordan, *AME Church in Africa,* p. 48; Frederick, "In Memoriam," p. 4.
22. Kinch, *West Africa,* pp. 19, 30; *Journal of the Twentieth Quadrennial Session of the General Conference Proceedings of the African Methodist Episcopal Church,* 1896, pp. 85, 154.
23. Fanny Jackson Coppin, "A Plea for Industrial Opportunity," in *Masterpieces of Negro Eloquence,* ed. Alice Moore Dunbar (New York: Bookery Publishing Co., 1914), p. 251. See also "A Noble Woman," *Crisis* (March 1913): 225.
24. Fanny Jackson Coppin, *Reminiscences of School Life and Hints on Teaching* (Philadelphia: A.M.E. Book Concern, 1913), pp. 122-23; Martin Kilson and Adelaide Hill, *Apropos of Africa, Afro-American Leaders and the Romance of Africa* (Garden City, N.Y.: Doubleday & Co., 1971), pp. 281-82; Margaret E. Burton, *Comrades in Service* (New York: Missionary Education Movement of the United States & Canada, 1915), p. 160; "Noble Woman," p. 225; Josephus R. Coan, "The Expansion of Missions of the African Methodist Episcopal Church in South Africa, 1896–1908" (Ph.D. diss., Hartford Seminary Foundation, 1961), pp. 293-94, 327-28.
25. Fanny Coppin, *Reminiscences,* pp. 123-25.
26. For quotation, see *Ibid.;* also see Levi J. Coppin, *Observation of Persons and Things in South Africa, 1900–1904* (Philadelphia: A.M.E. Book Concern, 1904), pp. 200, 203.
27. Fanny Coppin, *Reminiscences,* pp. 125, 129-30; Burton, *Comrades,* p. 160.
28. Levi Coppin, *Observations,* p. 42; Burton, *Comrades,* pp. 161-62.
29. Fanny Coppin, *Reminiscences,* p. 126.
30. *Ibid.,* pp. 124-28.
31. Levi Coppin, *Observations,* p. 200.
32. Burton, *Comrades,* p. 163; Coan, "Expansion of Missions," p. 293; "Mrs. F. J. Coppin's Great Missionary Appeal," letter, *Voice of Missions* (December 1908): 14.
33. Fanny Coppin, *Reminiscences,* pp. 126, 133.

CHAPTER 16. Charlotte Manye Maxeke

1. T. D. Mweli Skota, *The African Yearly Register* (Johannesburg: R. L. Esson & Co., 1932).
2. J. B. Hertzog's election as Prime Minister in 1924 marked the ascendency of national capital in South Africa. Hertzog was determined that South Africa would no longer remain a satellite of foreign capital but would generate its own development. Toward this end, labor, both European and African, but most particularly African, was kept in check, regulated, and controlled by a series of segregationist laws and legislation which maintained the flow of cheap labor to South Africa's centers of production. While the post-World War I economy increasingly drew blacks and whites together in the urban areas, Hertzog's segregationist policy drove them physically apart. The basis of his policy was a quartet of bills enacted in 1936 which legally excluded Africans from the "white man's world"—the cities. Africans were effectively reduced to transients who shuffled back and forth between the "white" cities and the black reserves.
3. Alfred B. Xuma, *What an Educated African Girl Can Do* (Nashville: The Women's Parent Mite Missionary Society of the AME Church, 1930), p. 10.

4. *The Cape Mercury,* November 15, 1890.
5. Artishia W. Jordan, *The African Methodist Episcopal Church in Africa* (n.p., [1960]), p. 59; *Voice of Missions* (May 1896).
6. *Voice of Missions* (April 1898); (July 1899); (August 1900).
7. J. M. Mokone, *The Early Life of Our Founder* (Johannesburg: A. S. Hunt, 1935), pp. 17-18. Mokone organized his Ethiopian Church as a protest against the racism he encountered in the Wesleyan Church of South Africa.
8. Xuma, *African Girl,* foreword by W. E. B. DuBois, p. 13; *South African News Weekly Edition,* September 18, 1901.
9. Xuma, *African Girl,* p. 13; *Voice of Missions* (November 1903).
10. Xuma, *African Girl,* p. 14. By all accounts, theirs was a solid union. Until Maxeke's death in 1928, they combined two successful and complementary careers. In addition to the educational work, Maxeke was a prominent member of the African National Congress and for a time was editor of a Johannesburg weekly, *Umteleli wa Bantu.*
11. *The Star of Zion,* November 9, 1899.
12. Carol A. Page, "Black America in White South Africa: Church and State Reaction to the A.M.E. Church in Cape Colony and Transvaal, 1896–1910" (Ph.d. diss., University of Edinburgh, 1978), ch. 4.
13. The black African elite took particular offense at their inclusion in pass laws; they viewed the pass as a badge of inferiority. All black men (and later women) were required to carry a pass unless specifically exempted, and to obtain an exemption involved a long, protracted process. The pass bore the carrier's name, place of employment, ethnic group, place of domicile, and so on. This pass underpinned the migrant labor system and was the key to low labor costs. Moreover, the sale of passes was a source of state revenue.
14. *South African News Weekly Edition,* September 18, 1901.
15. B. W. Arnett, ed., *Episcopal Handbook for 1900* (n.p., n.d.), p. 56.
16. *Voice of Missions* (July 1899).
17. According to Peter Walshe, when the ANC was organized in 1912, there were no female members, and the Bantu Women's League was an outgrowth of that situation (*The Rise of African Nationalism in South Africa* [Berkeley: University of California Press, 1971], p. 80).
18. Sol. T. Plaatje, *Native Life in South Africa* (London: P. S. King & Son, 1916), pp. 94-97.
19. Xuma, *African Girl,* p. 18.
20. Charlotte Manye Maxeke, "Social Conditions Among Bantu Women and Girls" (Address at Conference of European and Bantu Christian Student Associations, Fort Hare, June 27–July 3, 1930).
21. Charlotte M. Maxeke, "The Progress of Native Womanhood in South Africa," in *Christianity and the Natives of South Africa,* ed. J. Dexter Taylor (Lovedale, S. Africa: Lovedale Institution Press, n.d.), p. 178.
22. Thomas Karis and Gwendolen M. Carter, eds., *From Protest to Challenge: A Documentary History of African Politics in South Africa, 1822-1964,* 4 vols. (Stanford, Calif.: Hoover Institution Press, 1979), vol. 4, p. 82.
23. Xuma, *African Girl,* p. 20.
24. *Ibid.,* p. 27.

CHAPTER 17. Ordination of Women

1. See, e.g., Donald K. Gorrell, "Ecclesiastical Equality for Women," Case 9-378-890 (Boston: Intercollegiate Case Clearing House, 1978). Also see

Frederick A. Norwood, *The Story of American Methodism* (Nashville: Abingdon Press, 1974), pp. 350-53; Anna Oliver, *Test Case on the Ordination of Women* (New York: William N. Jennings, 1880). The Congregational Church was the first to ordain a woman: Antoinette Brown (1825-1921), on September 15, 1853, see Luther Lee, "Woman's Right to Preach the Gospel," in *Five Sermons and a Tract by Luther Lee*, ed. Donald W. Dayton (Chicago: Holdred House, 1975), pp. 77-100; Alice S. Rossi, ed., *The Feminist Papers: From Adams to Beauvoir* (New York: Columbia University Press, 1973), p. 342.

2. See E. L. Shuey, *A Handbook of the United Brethren in Christ* (Dayton, Ohio: United Brethren Publishing House, 1901), p. 63; A. W. Drury, *History of the Church of the United Brethren in Christ* (Dayton, Ohio: United Brethren Publishing House, 1931), p. 424.

3. A. W. Drury, ed., *Disciplines of the United Brethren in Christ 1818-1841* (Dayton, Ohio: United Brethren Publishing House, 1895), pp. 168-85, 205-218.

4. *Minutes of the Scioto Conference 1829-1899* (Cleveland: Microfilm Corp. n.d.), 1841; see also Drury, *History of U.B.*, p. 425. The intent of the motion, at least in part, was to respond to Courtland's request for counseling on the matter of her impressions. Thus the conference action could be understood as dealing with the issue of one's call to ministry, rather than whether the call was to a man or a woman.

5. *Minutes of Scioto Conference*, 1843, 1844.

6. Drury, *History of U.B.*, p. 423.

7. "Proceedings of the General Conference," (Dayton, Ohio) *Religious Telescope* (May 21, 1845): 172; (June 4, 1845): 180. The minutes incorrectly record the name as Luisa C. Clemence.

8. *Minutes of the White River Conference 1846-1891*, microfilm. Also in Walter F. Roush, "Annual Conference Minutes of the White River Conference of the Church of the United Brethren in Christ 1847-1865," (transcript, 1948, United Theological Seminary), p. 4. The edition of the minutes printed in the *Religious Telescope* (February 10, 1847) apparently provided the text of the note itself, recognizing Opheral as "an acceptable laborer in the Gospel." See also Drury, *History of the U.B.*, p. 425.

9. "Proceedings of the General Conference," *Religious Telescope* (May 20, 1857): 150-51; (May 27, 1857): 154-55.

10. Lydia Sexton, *Autobiography of Lydia Sexton* (Dayton, Ohio: United Brethren Publishing House, 1882), p. 240.

11. *Ibid.*, pp. 401-403.

12. *Ibid.*, p. 403. The Upper Wabash Conference came into existence in 1857 when the Wabash Conference was split. Lydia Sexton had become a member of the latter conference due to a boundary shift between Wabash and the neighboring Illinois Conference.

13. A brief but well-written account of the women's movement in America in the period before the Civil War may be found in Eleanor Flexner, *Century of Struggle* (Cambridge: Belknap Press, Harvard University Press, 1975).

14. Of the nine conferences represented, all but one were located in the Midwest (Virginia was the only exception). Most were large conferences, representing over 40 percent of the total church membership, see Shuey, *Handbook*, p. 41 (Shuey differs from other sources in recording only eight conferences); also see D. K. Flickinger, *Our Missionary Work* (Dayton, Ohio: United Brethren Publishing House, 1889), p. 208. For membership figures, see *United Brethren in Christ Almanac-Yearbook-Annual 1876* (Dayton, Ohio: United Brethren Publishing House, 1876).

405

15. The seminary's name was changed to Bonebrake Theological Seminary in 1909 and was renamed United Theological Seminary in 1954.
16. See John L. Ferris and Donald K. Gorrell, "Educating Women for Ministry at the United Brethren Seminary," in *Woman's Rightful Place*, ed. Donald K. Gorrell (Dayton, Ohio: United Theological Seminary, 1980), pp. 41-53.
17. Adam Byron Condo, *History of the Indiana Conference* (n.p. [c. 1927]), p. 178; "Rev. Maggie Elliott" (obituary), *Religious Telescope* (April 26, 1924): 19. At present this period of Thompson's career cannot be precisely dated. Condo indicates that she served as an evangelist early in her career but gives no clue as to dates or length of service. However, the chronology outlined in her obituary clearly states that she served as evangelist for fourteen years and suggests that this period preceded her transfer to the Central Illinois Conference in 1889.
18. *Minutes of the Indiana Conference 1830-1892*, microfilm, p. 59. The Committee on Applicants dealt with matters of licensing to preach.
19. *Ibid.*, p. 77. See also D. Best, "Indiana Conference Minutes," *Religious Telescope* (September 13, 1876): 403; Condo, *History of Indiana Conference*, p. 74. There is some disagreement as to whether this letter of commendation constituted a license to preach. Condo's statistical table lists the licensing as 1876 (pp. 391-403). Similarly Maggie (Thompson) Elliott's obituary states that "at Hartsville, Indiana, on August 25, 1876, she received annual conference license from Bishop J. Dickson." But earlier documents are less definitive. The language of the Indiana Conference Minutes resembles very closely that used in the case of Lydia Sexton, suggesting that legally, this was not a license to preach. And the *Minutes of the Central Illinois Conference 1885-1898*, microfilm, 1889, imply that she was licensed in 1889 by that conference.
20. An analysis of the voting pattern by conference blocks indicates that the average church membership of those conferences voting for the amendment was 4,582, while the average membership of those voting against was 2,472, see *Proceedings of the Sixteenth General Conference* (Dayton, Ohio: United Brethren Printing Establishment, 1873), pp. 105-106, 144-52, 168-71, 193-200. For statistical data, see *U.B. Almanac-Yearbook*, 1874.
21. *Proceedings of the Twentieth General Conference of the United Brethren in Christ* (Dayton, Ohio: United Brethren Publishing House, 1889), pp. 236-41. On the discussions in the Methodist Episcopal Church, see "The Methodist General Conference," *Religious Telescope* (May 9, 1888): 296; "Editorial Notes" (May 16, 1888): 313. On the position of the United Brethren Church, see W. M. Givens, "Shall Women Be Licensed to Preach?" (May 16, 1888): 314; J. Weaver, "Shall Women Be Licensed to Preach?" (December 25, 1888): 820-21. That the general attitude toward women was improving is also noted in an article entitled "Missionary Women" (March 7, 1888): 145.
22. *Twentieth General Conference*, p. 236. Also see *Discipline of the United Brethren in Christ 1889* (Dayton, Ohio: United Brethren Publishing House, 1889), pp. 52-53.
23. See *Minutes of the Central Illinois Conference*, 1889, pp. 124, 125, 141, 142.
24. The Central Illinois Conference at this time counted 26 charges and apparently was in need of "a greater number of efficient young itinerants." In addition, the Streator Mission Station was said to be a significant one, and thus her assignment there probably was a reflection of her ministerial

ability; or it may be that her ability contributed to Streator's reputation, see William McKee, "Central Illinois Conference," *Religious Telescope* (September 26, 1888): 609.

25. G. M. Mathews et al., *Souvenir: Twenty-third Session Centennial General Conference of the Church of the United Brethren in Christ* (Dayton, Ohio: United Brethren Publishing House, 1901), p. 66.

26. Not all those women were ordained, or at least they were not ordained in the year they were first listed. After 1894, any data is at best approximate. In many cases relevant data is unavailable simply because it has not yet been tabulated. No annual records were kept of women ordained, except for a few tallies maintained by individual United Brethren historians. Therefore as a rule, each name must be traced separately to determine the date of ordination, if any. In addition, names occasionally become confused in the record and must be checked carefully to avoid duplication or other error.

27. *Proceedings of the Thirty-third General Conference* (Dayton, Ohio: United Brethren Publishing House, 1941), p. 383.

28. "Actions of the Boards of Bishops in Joint Sessions in Matters Pertaining to Church Union," in *The General Conference of The Evangelical United Brethren Church Convening in the First United Brethren Church, 430 Vine Street, Johnstown, Pa., November 16, 1946*, p. 54.

29. For the United Brethren Church, see *Minutes of the Board of Bishops 1870–1884 and 1917–1946* (Chicago: Dept. of Photoduplication, University of Chicago Library, 1964). For the Evangelical Church, see *Minutes of the Board of Bishops 1922–1946* (Chicago: Dept. of Photoduplication, University of Chicago Library, 1964). For Joint Commissions, see William C. Beal, Jr., Archivist, General Commission on Archives and History of The United Methodist Church, to Donald K. Gorrell, August 7, 1978.

30. Yearbooks list *Ellen Runkle* through 1892, *Ellen R. King* after 1892; *Minutes of the East Ohio Conference,* 1892-93 follow the same pattern. Evidently Ellen Runkle married in late 1892 or early 1893.

31. Some yearbooks show *Maggie M. Elliott,* probably an error; *Maggie T. Elliott* is the usual listing, see *Minutes of the Indiana Conference,* 1876; also see Condo, *History of Indiana Conference.*

32. Ill during 1892, see *Minutes of the Arkansas Valley Conference,* 1892, p. 13.

33. Conflicting reports on licensure—either 1889 or 1890; unassigned in 1894, see *Minutes of the White River Conference,* 1890s; A. C. Wilmore, *History of the White River Conference* (Dayton, Ohio: United Brethren Publishing House, 1899), p. 523.

34. Died 1892.

35. According to the *Minutes of the Ohio East Conference,* 1955 (EUB), Metsker often served small struggling churches. Her obituary may be found in *Telescope Messenger* (July 30, 1955): 15.

36. Prior to 1895, yearbooks list *Nettie Moore.*

37. The 1892 yearbook lists Allie Sipe with the Virginia Conference. However, this conflicts with data in Wilmore's *History of White River Conference* and the White River Conference minutes, which are assumed to be accurate.

38. Several editions of the yearbook show *Mrs. C. R. Stevenson,* probably an error.

39. Withdrew from the conference (and the church?) in 1899, see *Minutes of the White River Conference,* 1899, p. 481.

40. Yearbook lists *Carrie McDougal* for 1893; *Minutes of White River Conference,* 1893, indicate she was received in 1892. After 1893, yearbooks

list *Carrie Boose*. The minutes of 1894 and 1893 agree as to year of reception into conference; there is no *Carrie M. Boose* entry, but an 1893 or 1894 marriage is assumed.

41. Early editions of the yearbook show *Emma H. Weller*. Later editions are assumed to be correct.

42. Married 1898.

CHAPTER 18. Maggie Newton Van Cott

1. The later edition does not bear Foster's name, but differs from *Life and Labors* only in the concluding chapter, which contains newspaper clippings about Van Cott's work.

2. [John O. Foster], *Life and Labors of Maggie Newton Van Cott* (Cincinnati: Hitchcock & Walden, 1872), p. 15.

3. *Ibid.*, pp. 54-55.

4. *Ibid.*, p. 67. It is unclear whether Van Cott and Palmer ever met, or whether Van Cott had read Palmer's landmark work *Promise of the Father*, which provides a biblical defense of women's right to preach the gospel.

5. A. C. Morehouse, in *Autobiography* (New York: Tibbals Book Co., 1895) recounts another ecstatic experience which he identifies as Van Cott's call to preach. During the ordination service of the 1867 New York Conference, "She was overwhelmed with a desire to be a man so she could be ordained, and prayed that God would ordain her to the Christian ministry" (pp. 120-21). Since Van Cott did not narrate this experience to her biographer, its importance to her ministry is unclear. She did tell of a dream in which she heard a voice commanding her to preach; after her sermon, John Wesley arose from the congregation and greeted her: "Do not be alarmed, my child, you will speak before greater than I" [Foster], (*Life and Labors*, p. 153).

6. [Foster], *Life and Labors*, pp. 69-70.

7. *Ibid.*, pp. 71, 87.

8. *Ibid.*, p. 185.

9. *Ibid.*, p. 206.

10. Morehouse, *Autobiography*, p. 125.

11. [Foster], *Life and Labors*, p. 221.

12. *Minutes of the New York Conference of the Methodist Episcopal Church*, 1869, p. 18. Morris D'C. Crawford was a trustee of the conference and was appointed to Yonkers in 1869.

13. *New York Times*, April 25, 1869, p. 5.

14. *The Methodist* (April 9, 1870): 113.

15. *The Christian Advocate* (hereafter cited as *CA*) (April 7, 1870): 108. *Zion's Herald* (April 7, 1870) notes that the resolution was tabled by a "small majority" (p. 157).

16. *Pittsburgh CA* (April 16, 1870): 5; (May 7, 1870): 5. A. B. Hyde, in his *History of Methodism* (Springfield, Mass.: Wiley & Co., 1888), reports that Van Cott obtained a local preacher's license in 1868 from the Springfield District. I can find no documentation for this, and her biography indicates that she was not in New England during 1868. Therefore I have concluded that Hyde's reference is to the 1870 renewal of Van Cott's license in Springfield (p. 428).

17. *Minutes of the New York Conference*, 1870, p. 16. A. C. Morehouse, *Autobiography*, notes that before the 1870 conference, "Mrs. Van Cott

had been instrumental in the conversion of many thousand souls in the cities from the Atlantic to the Pacific, and the opponents weakened and no report was ever made to the conference" (p. 126).

18. (New York) *CA* (September 18, 1873): 300.
19. *Zion's Herald* (April 14, 1870): 169.
20. Haven, in [Foster], *Life and Labors*, p. xxiii.
21. *Southwestern Advocate* (March 26, 1874): 2.
22. *Journal of the General Conference, Methodist Episcopal Church*, 1872, p. 392.
23. *Pittsburgh CA* (July 23, 1874): 4.
24. *Northwestern CA,* quoted in *Pittsburgh Advocate* (July 30, 1874): 5.
25. *Minutes of the California Annual Conference,* 1874, p. 21.
26. (New York) *CA* (September 18, 1873): 300.
27. *Northwestern CA* (December 9, 1874): 6.
28. *Southwestern Advocate* (June 3, 1875): 2.
29. *Journal of the General Conference,* 1876, pp. 96-97.
30. Interestingly, despite the lack of change in disciplinary language, the issue apparently received sufficient publicity at the 1876 General Conference to deter some presiding elders from renewing women's licenses. Mary Lathrop and Mary McAllister, both of the Albion District, Michigan Conference, had their licenses "held in abeyance" (*Pittsburgh CA* [August 14, 1876]: 5). Jennie Fowler Willing's license, granted in 1873 from the Joliet District of the Rock River Conference and renewed in 1874 and 1875, was not renewed in 1876.
31. *Northwestern CA* (August 6, 1873): 254. The documentation for Richardson's license is secondary, appearing nine years after the fact in a periodical.
32. *Journal of the General Conference,* 1880, p. 354; 1884, p. 314.
33. Ann Douglas, *The Feminization of American Culture,* reprint (New York: Avon Books, 1978), p. 131.
34. *CA* (March 3, 1870): 65.
35. [Foster], *Life and Labors,* p. 221.
36. Haven, in *ibid.,* p. xvii-xviii.
37. [Foster], *Life and Labors,* overleaf; p. 221.
38. Nancy Hardesty, Lucille Sider Dayton, and Donald W. Dayton, "Women in the Holiness Movement," in *Women of Spirit: Female Leadership in the Jewish and Christian Traditions,* ed. Rosemary Ruether and Eleanor McLaughlin (New York: Simon & Schuster, 1979), pp. 241, 244, 245; see also Phoebe Palmer, *Promise of the Father* (Boston: H. V. Degen, 1859).
39. Hardesty, Dayton, and Dayton, "Women in Holiness Movement," p. 245.
40. Van Cott, *The Harvest and the Reaper* (New York: N. Tibbles & Sons, 1876), p. 15.
41. *CA* (September 18, 1873): 300.
42. Sherman, "Woman's Place in the Gospel," in [Foster], *Life and Labors,* p. xxx.
43. Haven, in [Foster], *Life and Labors,* pp. xvii-xviii.
44. *Northwestern CA* (September 16, 1874): 1.
45. "The Woman at Work," *Southwestern CA* (January 15, 1885): 4.
46. *Minutes of the California Conference,* 1874, pp. 13-14.
47. *Zion's Herald* (March 7, 1872): 116. This excerpt from Van Cott's journal suggests that she did keep a fairly close written record of her activities, at least during this period of her life. The location of the journal, if it still exists, is unknown to this author.
48. *The Methodist* (April 9, 1870): 113.

CHAPTER 19. The Function of Female Bonding

1. This is the inscription on his tombstone as well as the title of the book by his son Georg Fliedner, *Theodor Fliedner, Durch Gottes Gnade Erneurer des apostolischen Diakonissenamtes in der evangelischen Kirche: Sein Leben und Wirken,* 3 vols. (Kaiserswerth: Buchhandlung der Diakonissenanstalt, 1933-37).

2. Meyer, *Deaconesses: Biblical, Early Church, European, American,* 2nd. ed. (Chicago/Cincinnati: Cranston & Stowe; New York: Hunt & Eaton, 1889).

3. Martin von Gerhardt, *Theodor Fliedner, Ein Lebensbild,* 2 vols. (Dusseldorf-Kaiserswerth: Buchhandlung der Diakonissenanstalt, 1933-37), vol. 1, p. 146.

4. Anna Sticker, *Friedericke Fliedner und die Anfänge der Frauendiakonie: Ein Quellenbuch,* 2nd ed. (Neukirchen-Vluyn: Neukirchener Verlag, 1963), p. 15.

5. *Das erste Jahr-Zehnt der Diakonissen-Anstalt . . . in einem Abdrucke der zehn ersten Jahresberichte* (Kaiserswerth: Verlag der Diakonissenanstalt, 1847), pp. 14, 81, 148.

6. Fliedner Archiv, Briefe der Schwestern, Pfarrer usw. betr. Aufnahme in die Diakonissenanstalt . . . Christine Klett.

7. *Ibid.,* Luise Mann.

8. "Bilder aus den Diakonissen-Leben: Gertrud Reichardt, die erste Diakonissin der Neuzeit," *Kaiserswerther christlicher Volkskalender* 99 Jahrgang (1940); 35-37.

9. Fliedner Archiv, Sophie Eberle an ihre Eltern, no. 1.

10. Quoted in Sticker, *Friedericke Fliedner,* p. 353.

11. *Ibid.,* p. 140.

12. Quoted in G. Fliedner *Theodor Fliedner, Kurzer Abriss seines Lebens und Wirkens* (Dusseldorf-Kaiserswerth: Buchhandlung der Diakonissenanstalt, 1936), p. 76.

13. Quoted in Sticker, *Friedericke Fliedner,* p. 342.

14. Fliedner Archiv, Sophie Eberle an ihre Eltern, no. 1.

15. Friedericke Bremer, "Kaiserswerth am Rhein 1846," in *Deutsches Lesebuch für die oberen Klassen der höheren Töchterschulen,* ed. Ferdinand Seinecke (Hannover: Ehlermann, 1850), p. 389.

16. Gerhard Uhlhorn, *Die christliche Liebestätigkeit* (Neukirchen, Kreis Moers: Neukirchener Verlag, 1959), p. 735; Gerhardt, *Theodor Fliedner,* vol. 2, p. 91.

17. George Henry Gerberding, *Life and Letters of W. A. Passavant, D.D.,* 3rd ed. (Greenville, Pa.: Young Lutheran Co., 1906), p. 146.

18. *The Missionary* 3 (1850): 52.

19. The story of the Chicago Training School, its Deaconess Society, and the life of Lucy Rider Meyer are found in Meyer, *Deaconesses;* Isabelle Horton, *The Builders* (Chicago: n.p., 1910), *The Burden of the City* (New York: Fleming H. Revell Co., 1904), *High Adventure: Life of Lucy Rider Meyer* (New York: Methodist Book Concern, 1928); Robert Coats Miller, "Lucy Rider Meyer," in *Notable American Women,* ed. Edward T. James et al. (Cambridge: Harvard University Press, 1971), vol. 2, pp. 534-36.

20. Horton, *Burden of the City,* p. 61; *The Message and Deaconess Advocate* 11/12 (December 1895): 15; 11/3 (March 1895): 2-3.

21. Horton, *Burden of the City,* pp. 145-46.

22. *Ibid.,* pp. 77, 172.

23. *The Message and Deaconess Advocate* 11/12 (December 1895): 3.

24. *Ibid.*, 11/9 (September 1895): 1; 11/7 (July 1895): 1; *Deaconess Advocate* 29/5 (May 1914): 10.
25. *Deaconess Advocate* 29/1 (January 1914): 3, 4; 29/2 (February 1914): 6; 29/3 (March 1914): 5; 29/6 (June 1914): 8; 29/5 (May 1914): 5-6; *The Message and Deaconess Advocate* 11/6 (June 1895): 12; 11/12 (December 1895): 1, 2.
26. *The Message and Deaconess Advocate* 11/6 (June 1895): 12.
27. *Ibid.*, 11/11 (November 1895): 1, 2; *Deaconess Advocate* 29/5 (May 1914): 1.
28. *Deaconess Advocate* 29/1 (January 1914): 1.
29. Horton, *Burden of the City,* p. 13.
30. Meyer, *Deaconesses,* pp. 106-108.
31. *Ibid.*, pp. 168-73.
32. *Deaconess Advocate* 29/5 (May 1914): 7.
33. *The Message and Deaconess Advocate* 11/11 (November 1895): 16.
34. For Bristol address, see *The Message and Deaconess Advocate* 11/11 (November 1895): 11. For Brodbeck, see 11/4 (April 1895): 5-6.
35. *Ibid.*, 11/7 (July 1895): 2.
36. Meyer, *Deaconesses,* pp. 210-11.
37. *Ibid.*, pp. 211-12.
38. *Deaconess Advocate* 29/1 (January 1914): 7.
39. *The Message and Deaconess Advocate* 11/3 (March 1895): 7.
40. *Deaconess Advocate* 29/5 (May 1914): 9, 12.
41. *The Message and Deaconess Advocate* 11/12 (December 1895): 8.
42. *The Deaconess Advocate* 29/4 (April 1914): 8.
43. *Deaconess Advocate* 29/2 (February 1914): 8.

CHAPTER 20. The Legacy of Georgia Harkness

1. Dorothy Bass, "Georgia Harkness," in *Notable American Women: The Modern Period,* ed. Barbara Sicherman and Carol Hurd Green (Cambridge: Belknap Press, Harvard University Press, 1980), pp. 312-13.
2. Harkness, *Conflicts in Religious Thought* (New York: H. Holt & Co., 1929), p. xi.
3. Bass, "Georgia Harkness."
4. Harkness, *The Modern Rival of Christian Faith* (New York/Nashville: Abingdon-Cokesbury Press, 1952), pp. 203-204.
5. Harkness, *Women in Church and Society: A Historical and Theological Inquiry* (Nashville: Abingdon Press, 1972), pp. 92, 90.
6. Henry Warren Bowden, ed., *Dictionary of American Religious Biography* (Westport, Conn.: Greenwood Press, 1977), pp. 191-92.
7. *Journal of the General Conference of The Methodist Church,* 1948, 1952, 1956, 1964, 1968, 1970, 1972. The 1970 meeting was a special session.
8. Harkness, *Christian Ethics* (New York: Abingdon Press, 1957), p. 123.
9. Harkness, *Mysticism, Its Meaning and Message* (Nashville: Abingdon Press, 1973), acknowledgments.
10. Harkness, *Foundations of Christian Knowledge* (Nashville/New York: Abingdon Press, 1955), foreword.
11. (Nashville: Abingdon Press, 1968).
12. *Mysticism,* pp. 17, 74-75, 15.
13. *Modern Rival,* pp. 210-11.
14. *Conflicts in Religious Thought,* pp. 84-85.
15. *Women in Church and Society,* p. 148.
16. *Christian Ethics,* p. 202.

17. *Women in Church and Society,* p. 166.
18. *Conflicts in Religious Thought,* p. 242.
19. *Women in Church and Society,* p. 166.
20. *Conflicts in Religious Thought,* p. 206.
21. *Ibid.,* p. 147.
22. *Ibid.,* pp. 166-67.
23. Harkness, *Does God Care?* (Waco, Tex.: Word Books, 1960), pp. 63-64.
24. Harkness, *Understanding the Christian Faith* (Nashville: Abingdon Press, 1974), pp. 74-75.
25. *Christian Ethics,* p. 31.
26. *Understanding the Christian Faith,* p. 67.
27. *Mysticism,* p. 121.
28. *Conflicts in Religious Thought,* p. 239.
29. *Ibid.,* p. 131.
30. *Christian Ethics,* p. 225.
31. *Understanding the Christian Faith,* p. 171.
32. *Conflicts in Religious Thought,* p. 291.
33. For self-love, see *Understanding the Christian Faith,* p. 102; for quotation, see *Conflicts in Religious Thought,* p. 227.
34. *Christian Ethics,* p. 110.
35. Harkness, *The Dark Night of the Soul* (New York/Nashville: Abingdon Press, 1945), p. 147 ff.
36. *Conflicts in Religious Thought,* p. 257.
37. *Mysticism,* p. 28.
38. *Ibid.,* p. 112.
39. *Modern Rival,* pp. 28, 52, 214.
40. *Christian Ethics,* pp. 79-80.
41. Harkness, *The Methodist Church in Social Thought and Action* (New York/Nashville: Abingdon Press, 1964), p. 13.
42. *Devotional Treasury,* p. 13.
43. *Christian Ethics,* p. 122 ff.
44. *Ibid.,* p. 130.
45. *Conflicts in Religious Thought,* pp. 12-13, 9.
46. *Ibid.,* pp. 46, 39.
47. *Foundations of Christian Knowledge,* p. 98.
48. *Ibid.,* p. 100.
49. Helen Johnson, "Georgia Harkness: She Made Theology Understandable," *United Methodists Today* 1/10 (October 1974): 57.
50. Linda Clark, "We Are Also Sarah's Children," *The Drew Gateway* 48/3 (Spring 1978): 27.
51. For theistic revolution, see William McLoughlin, *Revival, Awakenings, and Reform: An Essay on Religion and Social Change in America, 1607–1977* (Chicago: University of Chicago Press, 1978), p. 152.
52. *Understanding the Christian Faith,* p. 171.
53. *Devotional Treasury,* p. 13.
54. *Women in Church and Society,* p. 27.
55. See Ann Douglas, *The Feminization of American Culture* (New York: Knopf, 1977); Janet Fishburn, *The Fatherhood of God and the Victorian Family* (Philadelphia: Fortress Press, 1981).
56. For God's love, see *Conflicts in Religious Thought,* p. 261.
57. *Women in Church and Society,* p. 30.
58. Carolyn G. Heilbrun, *Reinventing Womanhood* (New York: W. W. Norton & Co., 1979), p. 29 ff.

CONTRIBUTORS

FRANK BAKER was professor of English church history at the Divinity School, Duke University, until his retirement in 1980. For more than thirty years he has collected books, pamphlets, and manuscripts related to early British Methodism. Most of these writings now comprise the Frank Baker Collection at Duke University Library. Dr. Baker has published more than three hundred articles and many books, including *John Wesley and the Church of England* and *Representative Verse of Charles Wesley*. He is editor-in-chief of the Oxford Edition of *Wesley's Works,* forthcoming, a thirty-four volume work to contain the original prose works of John Wesley.

ANNE LLEWELLYN BARSTOW is associate professor of medieval history at SUNY/College at Old Westbury, where she also offers courses in women's religious history. She holds a Ph.D. in Medieval History from Columbia University. Dr. Barstow is working on a study of early religious influences on Joan of Arc and will soon publish two books on the struggle over priests' right to marry—in the eleventh century and today.

ADRIAN A. BENNETT, III, is professor of history at Iowa State University. He received the B.A. from Antioch College and the M.A. and Ph.D. in Chinese History from the University of California at Davis. He is the author of *John Fryer and the Introduction of Western Science and Technology into Nineteenth Century China,* East Asian Monograph Series (Cambridge: Harvard University Press, 1967), two research guides to Chinese-language newspapers, and *Missionary Journalist in China: Young J. Allen and His Magazines, 1868–1874,* forthcoming from the University of Georgia Press.

EMORA T. BRANNAN is pastor of Lovely Lane United Methodist Church in Baltimore. He holds the B.A. degree from The Johns Hopkins University, B.D. from The Theological School, Drew University, and the Ph.D. from Duke University, where his dissertation was titled "The Presiding Elder Question: Its Critical Importance in American Methodism, 1820–1824, and Its Impact upon Ecclesiastical Institutions." Dr. Brannan is a member of the General Commission on Archives and History of The United Methodist Church and has published in *Methodist History.*

413

WOMEN IN NEW WORLDS

JOAN JACOBS BRUMBERG is assistant professor in the Women's Studies Program, Cornell University. Her Ph.D. in American Intellectual and Social History was earned at the University of Virginia. Dr. Brumberg's book, *Mission for Life: The Story of the Family of Adoniram Judson,* was published in New York by The Free Press in 1980.

MOLLIE C. DAVIS, associate professor of history at Queens College, Charlotte, North Carolina, is on leave as program officer of the Division of Fellowships and Seminars, National Endowment for the Humanities in Washington, D.C. Her Ph.D. in History was earned at the University of Georgia. Her numerous professional involvements include co-founding and co-chairing the Southern Association of Women Historians. She has written and lectured on aspects of women's history and United States social history.

JOAN CHAMBERLAIN ENGELSMAN received her Ph.D. in Historical Theology from Drew University. Her writing and lecturing have focused on theology and Christian feminism. In 1979 The Westminster Press published her book *The Feminine Dimension of the Divine.*

JANET S. EVERHART is associate pastor at First United Methodist Church, Sunnyvale, California. She holds the B.A. in American History from the University of California at Davis, and the M.Div. from Drew University Theological School, where she graduated summa cum laude in 1981. Her undergraduate Honors Thesis, which explored the movement to legalize birth control in the United States, has been published as a Working Paper at the Women's Resource and Research Center, University of California at Davis.

JOANNA BOWEN GILLESPIE, former associate professor of sociology at Drew University, is currently an affiliated scholar at Stanford University's Center for Research on Women. Her research focuses on the relationship between Methodism and the developing "common-school" movement in early nineteenth-century America, as presented in the medium of Methodist Sunday School Union publications.

ALAN L. HAYES received his Ph.D. in Religious Studies from McGill University, Montreal. Since 1975 he has taught at Wycliffe College, Toronto, and at the Toronto School of Theology, where he is now associate professor of church history and chairperson of the department.

SYLVIA M. JACOBS is a professor at North Carolina Central University. She earned the Ph.D. from Howard University with a dissertation on "Black American Perspectives on European Imperialism in Africa, 1870–1920." She has participated in recent sessions of the Association for the Study of Afro-American Life and History, and the American Academy of Religion. In October 1980 she was elected to a two-year term as southern regional director of the Association of Black Women Historians. Her book *The African Nexus: Black American Perspectives on the European Partitioning of Africa, 1880–1920* was published by Greenwood Press in 1981.

ROSEMARY S. KELLER, co-editor of this volume, is associate professor of religion and American culture at Garrett-Evangelical Theological Seminary. She holds a Ph.D. from the University of Illinois at Chicago Circle in American History and the History of Women, with a dissertation on Abigail Adams, which was published by Arno in 1981. She is currently working with Rosemary Ruether on a three-volume documentary history, *Women and Religion in America,* forthcoming from Harper & Row, the first volume having appeared in 1981. Dr. Keller is a member of the United Methodist General Commission on Archives and History and currently chairs that agency's committee on Women's History and Status. A clergy wife and diaconal minister, she has long been active in the church.

JAMES L. LELOUDIS, II, is a Ph.D. candidate in American History at the University of North Carolina at Chapel Hill and holds the M.A. in History from Northwestern University, where he had a university fellowship. He presently holds a university research assistantship in the Department of History at Chapel Hill. He is active in researching the social history of the South and has published in the *Journal of American History.*

ROSA PEFFLY MOTES currently serves as historian of her local church, as a member of the Commission on Archives and History of the Pacific Northwest Annual Conference, and as historian of United Methodist Women in her conference. Mrs. Motes has conducted workshops relating to churchwomen's history at district and annual conference meetings of United Methodist Women.

FREDERICK A. NORWOOD was professor of history of Christianity at Garrett-Evangelical Theological Seminary until his retirement in 1978. He is well known as a church historian, particularly in the field of American Methodist history. Dr. Norwood served as co-editor of *Church History* for six years and was a member of the editorial board and a contributor to both *The Encyclopedia of World Methodism* and the three-volume *History of American Methodism.* His books include *The Development of Modern Christianity Since 1500,* a two-volume history of religious refugees; *Strangers and Exiles;* and *The Story of American Methodism.*

SARANNE PRICE O'DONNELL is pastor of First United Methodist Church in Lorain, Ohio, and an ordained elder in the East Ohio Annual Conference. She holds the M.Div. from United Theological Seminary, where she is also a member of the President's Advisory

Council and the Board of Associates. She is active in United Methodist conference and district organizations in East Ohio and is presently secretary of the conference Board of Ordained Ministry and a member of the board of trustees of the Elyria Home. She has written for *Woman's Rightful Place,* and is currently writing curriculum material for The United Methodist Church.

CAROL A. PAGE is a member of the history faculty of Howard University. She received her M.A. in African History from Roosevelt University in Chicago and her Ph.D. in History from the University of Edinburgh, Scotland, with an emphasis on Southern Africa and a dissertation titled, "Black America in White South Africa: Church and State Reaction to the A.M.E. Church in Cape Colony and Transvaal, 1896–1910." She has delivered papers and published articles on aspects of the A.M.E. Church mission effort in South Africa.

CATHERINE M. PRELINGER is on leave from her position as assistant editor of The Papers of Benjamin Franklin at Yale University. She received her Ph.D. from Yale University and has been a visiting lecturer at Yale College. She presently (1982-83) holds a research associateship and lectureship in Women's Studies at Harvard University Divinity School. Dr. Prelinger has been engaged in studying the connection between religion and feminism in Germany and has just completed a manuscript titled "In a Charitable Context," which is being considered for publication. She is active in various professional organizations for women historians.

LOUISE L. QUEEN, co-editor of this volume, is assistant general secretary of the General Commission on Archives and History, The United Methodist Church, where she has been a staff member since 1951. She is currently editor of the quarterly journal *Methodist History.*

ARNOLD M. SHANKMAN is associate professor of history at Winthrop College in South Carolina. He holds a Ph.D. from Emory University, where he was a Woodrow Wilson Fellow. His book *The Pennsylvania Anti-War Movement* was published by Fairleigh Dickinson University Press in 1980, and he has published numerous articles in professional journals, particularly in the areas of state and ethnic history. His sketch of Dorothy Tilly appeared in *Notable American Women: The Modern Period,* and his article about Tilly was published in *Methodist History.*

ANASTATIA SIMS is a visiting instructor at North Carolina State University and a candidate for the Ph.D. in American History from the University of North Carolina at Chapel Hill. Her dissertation analyzes women's organizations in North Carolina from 1890 to 1930. She holds the B.A. from the University of Texas and the M.A.

CONTRIBUTORS

from the University of North Carolina. She has served as a teaching
assistant, as graduate assistant in the Southern Historical Collection
and in the Southern Oral History Program, and as researcher for
Historic Hope Foundation, Inc.

HILAH F. THOMAS, co-editor of this volume, was project
coordinator of the Women's History Project of the General
Commission on Archives and History, The United Methodist
Church, from 1978 through 1980, and was instrumental in
organizing the Women in New Worlds Conference. She holds the
M.A. and M.Phil. degrees in Modern European History from
Columbia University and has done archival and oral research
toward her Ph.D. dissertation from Columbia on the founding of the
twentieth-century French review, *Annales d'histoire economique et
sociale*. She has taught in the History Department of Brooklyn
College, City University of New York, and in 1975 and 1976 she was
instrumental in founding The Institute for Research in History, New
York City, whose board she has chaired. Currently she is consultant
for the oral history project of the Women's Division, United
Methodist General Board of Global Ministries.

JAMES E. WILL is enrolled in the Ph.D. program of Philosophy of
Religion and Theology at Claremont Graduate School. He holds the
B.A. in Religion from Wright State University and the M.Div.
from United Theological Seminary.

INDEX

Brown, Charlotte Hawkins, II:215

Brown, Earl Kent, I:69, 437

Brown, John Mifflin, I:284

Brown, Maggie, II:152

Brown, Martha McClellan, I:307

Brumberg, Joan Jacobs, I:443; II:19, 234, 414

Bryan, Henrietta W., I:10

Bryce, Mr., I:78

Buckley, Abby Lonsdale Monroe, II:77

Buckley, James Monroe, I:444; II:13, 76-93, 135, 136, 140, 145

Bucyrus, Ohio, I:305

Bulgaria, I:259

Bureau of Indians, II:188

Burma, II:19, 237, 240, 241, 244, 245

Burroughs, Nannie H., II:220

Butler, Charles, II:269

C

Caddo Indians, II:186

Caldwell, Ella, II:299

California, state of, I:145, 160, 173, 366

California Conference, II:182, 183

Calvinistic Methodists, II:162, 167, 174

Calvinists, I:38; II:126

Campbell, Barbara E., I:10

Campbell, Mrs. J. P., II:264

Campbell, S. J., II:273

Camp meetings, I:284

Canadian Methodist Episcopal Church, II:309

Canales, Rebecca, I:175

Candler, John S., I:273

Cape Colony Conference (AME), II:270

Capitalism, I:125

Cardenas, Benigno, I:164

Carpenter, W. J., I:271

Carr, John H., II:184

Carthage, Mo., I:304

Case, W. C., II:190

Causton, Martha, II:31, 32, 33, 36, 38

Causton, Thomas. *See* Causton, Martha

Cave, William, II:40

Centenary Biblical Institute of Baltimore, II:139, 140

Centennial education emphasis, II:140; and medal for children, II:144

Central Illinois Conference (UB), II:294, 295

Central Jurisdiction, I:110, 127

Central Methodist Advocate, I:269

Chadwick, T. W., II:303

Chafe, William H., I:34

Chai, Alice, I:24, 328, 437

Chapman, Patty, I:83

Chapone, John, II:129

Chappell, Ellis Samuel, I:363

Chappell, Winifred L., I:25, 362-78

Charity Organization Society, I:326

Chautauqua Circuit, II:152

Checote, Mrs. Samuel, II:193

Cherokee Indians, II:193

Chesnut, James, II:72

Chesterfield, Lady, II:167

Chiang Kai-shek, II:267

Chicago Deaconess Home, I:183, 376

Chicago Social Action Conference, I:372

Chicago Training School, I:13, 25, 178-99, 202, 208, 251, 364, 377; II:23, 318, 319, 325-26, 327, 330, 333, 334, 336

Chickasaw Indians, II:184

Child, Lydia Maria, II:235, 243

Child development, II:52

I

Ibarra, Enriqueta, I:171
Illinois, state of, I:210, 295
Illinois Conference (UB), II:292
Illinois Sunday School Association, I:202
Illinois Wesleyan University, I:307
Immigrant women, in Hawaii, I:333
Inclusiveness, in U.M. tradition, I:15, 16
Independence movement, in Korea, I:335
India, I:250, 252, 253, 259, 348; II:138
Indiana, state of, I:295
Indiana Conference (MP), I:226
Indiana Conference (UB), II:293, 294
Indian Bureau (ME), II:17
Indian mission, II:172
Indian Mission Conference, II:185, 187, 193, 194
Industrial reform, I:24, 125, 345, 358, 361
Industrial schools, I:20
Infant baptism, II:238
Ingham, Benjamin, II:164, 165
Ingram, Jane, I:144
Inman, Godfrey, II:123, 124
Institute for Colored Youth (AME), II:276
Integration, promotion of, II:211
International Red Cross, I:341
International relations, I:372
International University, Chengtu, China, II:137
International Workers of the World, I:366
Interracial work, II:220
Iowa Conference (MP), I:226
Itinerants, I:18, 70, 77-82

J

Jackson, Sheldon, II:183, 184
Jacksonville, Fla., I:110
Jacobs, Sylvia M., I:444; II:20, 268, 414
Jail gospel services, I:355
James, Janet Wilson, I:56
Japan, I:136, 222, 223, 224, 226, 234
Japanese Americans, I:126, 127
Jarvis, John, II:115
Jay, James, II:172
Jay, John, II:172
Jefferson, Thomas, I:34
Jeffersonville, Ind., I:305
Jeffrey, Julie Roy, I:19, 143, 439
Jerman, Cornelia, II:209
Jesse Lee Home, II:183, 184
Jewish women, I:58
Jicarilla Apache Indians, II:179, 181
John Rylands Library, I:83
Johnson, Carrie Parks, I:444; II:18, 211-19, 231, 232, 233
Johnson, Emma V., I:287
Johnson, James Weldon, I:34
Johnson, John, II:173
Johnson, Luke G., II:211-12
Johnson, S., II:184
John Street Church, II:115-16, 301
Jones, Catherine, I:11
Jones, Elizabeth Ann, II:154
Jones, George Heber, I:330
Jones, Hattie, II:186
Jones, Joseph, II:71
Jones, Rufus, II:341
Jones, Sam, I:187
Jones, Wesley, I:288
Josselin, Jane, II:110, 111
Josselin, Ralph, II:110, 111
Judson, Adoniram, II:19, 234-48
Judson, Ann Hasseltine, I:443; II:19, 234-48
Judson, Emily, II:239. *See also* Chubbuck, Emily